ARCHEOLOGIES OF CO

CH00761326

SPEKTRUM: Publications of the German Studies Association

Series Editor: David M. Luebke, University of Oregon

Published under the auspices of the German Studies Association, *Spektrum* offers current perspectives on culture, society, and political life in the German-speaking lands of central Europe—Austria, Switzerland, and the Federal Republic—from the late Middle Ages to the present day. Its titles and themes reflect the composition of the GSA and the work of its members within and across the disciplines to which they belong—literary criticism, history, cultural studies, political science, and anthropology.

Archeologies of Confession

Writing the German Reformation, 1517–2017

EDITED BY CARINA L. JOHNSON, DAVID M. LUEBKE,
MARJORIE ELIZABETH PLUMMER, AND JESSE SPOHNHOLZ

berghahn
NEW YORK · OXFORD
www.berghahnbooks.com

First published in 2017 by
Berghahn Books
www.berghahnbooks.com

© 2017, 2019 Carina L. Johnson, David M. Luebke, Marjorie Elizabeth Plummer, and
Jesse Spohnholz
First paperback edition published in 2019

All rights reserved. Except for the quotation of short passages
for the purposes of criticism and review, no part of this book
may be reproduced in any form or by any means, electronic or
mechanical, including photocopying, recording, or any information
storage and retrieval system now known or to be invented,
without written permission of the publisher.

Library of Congress Cataloging-in-Publication Data

Names: Johnson, Carina L., 1967– editor of compilation. | Luebke, David Martin, 1960– editor
of compilation. | Plummer, Marjorie Elizabeth, editor of compilation. | Spohnholz, Jesse, 1974–
editor of compilation.
Title: Archaeologies of confession : writing the German Reformation, 1517–2017 / edited by
Carina L. Johnson, David M. Luebke, Marjorie E. Plummer, and Jesse Spohnholz.
Description: New York : Berghahn Books, 2017. | Series: Spektrum : publications of the
German Studies Association ; volume 16 | Includes bibliographical references and index.
Identifiers: LCCN 2017010901 (print) | LCCN 2017015774 (ebook) | ISBN 9781785335419
(eBook) | ISBN 9781785335402 (hardback : alk. paper)
Subjects: LCSH: Reformation—Germany—Historiography. | Identification (Religion)—
Social aspects—Germany—Historiography. | Religious pluralism—Germany—Historiography.
| Collective memory—Germany. | Germany—Church history—Historiography. | Church
historians—Germany. | Germany—Religious life and customs—Historiography.
Classification: LCC BR307 (ebook) | LCC BR307 .A83 2017 (print) | DDC 274.3/06—dc23
LC record available at https://lccn.loc.gov/2017010901

British Library Cataloguing in Publication Data

A catalogue record for this book is available from the British Library

ISBN 978-1-78533-540-2 hardback
ISBN 978-1-78920-496-4 paperback
ISBN 978-1-78533-541-9 ebook

~: CONTENTS :~

III. Excavating Histories of Religion

IV. Remembering and Forgetting

Reformations Lost and Found

CARINA L. JOHNSON

When Johannes Sleidanus became the official historian of the Schmal-kaldic League in 1545–46, he was charged with describing "the whole matter of religion as it had started in our times, how far it has proceeded, and the events that have happened concerning this." To advance the project, Elector John Frederick of Saxony and Landgrave Philip of Hesse agreed to supply Sleidanus with documentary source materials as needed. The princes also stipulated that they should have final approval over the resulting history. After the League was defeated and the princes imprisoned, Sleidanus perse-vered in his research, seeking documentary sources elsewhere. His history of the initial decades of religious reform was published in 1555 during the Diet of Augsburg. Sleidanus and his printer expected a controversial reception of the *Commentaries on the Condition of Religion and the State under Charles V* by Catholics and the Habsburg court, and sought to limit its social disruptiveness by printing it only in Latin. Protestant objections to the *Commentaries* were less anticipated, yet Philipp Melanchthon criticized it for containing "much which should be buried in eternal silence." Sleidanus defended his history by emphasizing its dependence on the documentary evidence. Despite such cri-tiques, the *Commentaries* became extremely popular, and the book was soon translated into German, French, and other vernaculars. The history was con-sidered an indispensable account of politics and religion in the Holy Roman Empire during the first half of the sixteenth century. Its success led Sleidanus to be heralded as the first historian of the Reformation.[1]

Sleidanus's experiences highlight the complexities of writing and reading histories of the Reformation. As Protestant (later Lutheran and Calvinist) and Catholic confessions developed and became linked with state interests, confessional identities were promoted by political, religious, and cultural institutions and structures. The production and propagation of historical narratives figured prominently among these confessionalizing processes. As the self-titled "historiographus protestantium," Sleidanus engaged with the writing of history on multiple levels. He composed official documents on the Schmalkaldic League's behalf (thus authoring sources for future historians). He gained access to archives and used their contents to shape his twenty-five-part narrative.[2] Melanchthon's wish that historical oblivion would subsume some events and actions was a contemporary acknowledgment of historical narratives' power to influence decisions or outcomes and to establish the legacies of the Reformation's participants. The inseparable connection between the writing of history and the silences of history is this volume's problematic and theme.

Michel-Rolph Trouillot theorizes the interconnection between writing and silence in *Silencing the Past: Power and the Production of History*. For Trouillot, silences or omissions in historical writing are not simply consequences of power relations, they are also a method of historical research. The shapes and forms of absence and erasure are a type of historical evidence that expresses the contours of power in a given historical moment. "History is the fruit of power, but power itself is never so transparent that its analysis becomes superfluous. The ultimate mark of power may be its invisibility; the ultimate challenge, the exposition of its roots." This expression of power is "constitutive of the story." Making power visible requires uncovering and identifying the silencing stratagems of historical production. As Trouillot points out, silences occur at many points and scales in the crafting of history; they occur in the making of sources, the making of archives, the making of narratives, and the making of historical significance. "[A]ny historical narrative is a particular bundle of silences, the result of a unique process, and the operation required to deconstruct these silences will vary accordingly."[3]

Trouillot's understanding of history goes much further than an elegant statement of a truism about who writes and controls history. The careful and aware historian must consider not only who exercises power, but how they do so. Exposing the silences and gaps of history to scrutiny, as well as possible research or narratological redress, is one part of the process that interests Trouillot. Considering the historicity of those occlusions is the other. Narratives and sources occlude power in historically specific ways; they ignore people as members of structural groups, as actors, and as subjects with their own voices. Ultimately, in Trouillot's project of giving voice to the disempowered, both positivist unveilings of hidden facts and constructivist historical retellings are needed to expose the elisions of the past in each step and process of history-making.[4]

In the decentralized Holy Roman Empire, the processes of history writing were also the processes of erasing the historical evidence of religious plurality. The fourteen essays assembled in this volume not only examine the formation of confessional identities through the construction of historical knowledge, they also pay close attention to the strategies employed to silence alternate narratives of religious identity. Each essay is a case study of sources, archives, or narratives that reveals acts of willful excision and unintentional exclusion in the shaping of confessional identity or knowledges. These processes were integral to polarizing and streamlining confessional identities over time. Some of these essays expand our understanding of the roles played by key actors in the history of the Reformation, such as Martin Luther, Johann Lorenz von Mosheim, and Heinrich von Treitschke. Others point to the enduring influences of less-visible historians and other authors, whose stamp on historical sources and narratives has sometimes been greater than that of the dominant actors and annalists themselves. Multiple essays concern themselves with confessional identity projects of the two (Catholic and Protestant), then three (Catholic, Lutheran, and Reformed) legally accepted Christian confessions in post-Reformation eras; others examine projects of dialogic religious identity formation beyond the confessions strictly speaking (Jewish and Christian, orthodox Lutheran and Pietist). Each history under scrutiny here defended or promoted confessional identities and boundaries and stood opposed to the continuation of religious or confessional plurality in the German lands.

The volume's chronological range, spanning the sixteenth through the nineteenth centuries and in several essays continuing to the present, alerts us to the longevity and particularities of these polemical silences. Tactics of silence are inescapably present in these histories of Reformation and confessional identity formation. In each period, historical elision took specific forms for specific aims. In this volume's archeological metaphor, the essays taken together reveal strata of historical methods and concerns. During the sixteenth century, projects of historical writing sought to create myths of origin and narratives of shared identity for emerging confessions. In the eighteenth century, historical methods were crucial tools utilized to clarify divisions and boundaries between confessions or religious communities. By the nineteenth century, histories and scholars were enmeshed in questions of nationalism and the place of confessional identities within the increasingly Protestant German nation-state. By highlighting these acts of historical production, stemming from either amnesia or careful craftsmanship, and by tracing their ramifications through the centuries, our authors uncover and recover some of the histories of plurality lost, obscured, or distorted during the past five hundred years.[5]

Historiography

This volume appears at a historiographical juncture caused by the waning dominance of confessionalization as a research paradigm. Confessionalization as a historiographical concept emerged in the late 1970s to describe the evolving societal and political dimensions of confessional formation and institutionalization. Its questions shaped much historical inquiry during the 1990s and 2000s. Recently, scholars have moved from exploring the strength and efficacy of political and religious institutions' capacities for promoting confessional churches and identities to addressing the limits, oversights, and cultural ramifications of confessionalization.[6] Chief among the examined cultural consequences of confessionalization has been its role in the writing of history. Confessionally informed histories have served as key entry points into early modern understandings of the Reformation as either continuation or radical break with the past, probing how Protestant and Catholic reformers (and their supporters) perceived and presented their actions and ideas in the flow of time.[7] Previously dismissed as polemical, these historical texts stand in productive tension with the practices of humanism, which offered models for characterological histories of individuals and methods of source presentation.[8] The formation and expression of Protestant confessional identities through life histories and narratives has received the lion's share of attention, as historians have sought to explicate links between historical method and the principle of *sola scriptura* as well as evidence of an awareness of the Protestant rupture with Rome.[9]

Another form of confessionalized historical writing, sacred history, has also received recent productive attention. Through these sacred or ecclesiastical histories, the confessions advanced their competing claims to embody the true legacy of Christianity, seeking to demonstrate the integrity of their confessions through their ties to the early church. These histories were segregated from other historical writing for much of the twentieth century as "church history" and their authors charged with a limited commitment to humanist practices of evidence and argumentation.[10] The titanic projects of early church history produced in the later sixteenth century, the Protestant *Magdeburg Centuries* led by Matthias Flacius Illyricus and the conscious Catholic response by Cesare Baronio, have been recently recuperated. Flacius, Baronio, and their fellows are now appreciated for their contributions to evolving practices of history writing and for their careful standards of evidence, proof, and argumentation.[11]

As Anthony Grafton has noted, these Protestant and Catholic histories of the early church were fundamentally involved in the formation of the great research libraries and scholarly teams. Such institutions have often been considered the fruit of modern, post-Rankean historical practice. Thus, their existence before the nineteenth century disrupts a teleological notion of history as a discipline.[12] The resulting voluminous compendia are only one of the forms of knowledge produced in the era of early modern mega-data. This early modern information era was roughly contemporaneous with that of confessionalization, and it bears confessionalization's stamp. Along with projects of ecclesiastical history and libraries, the period witnessed the reformation of the archive and archival classification. Archives served as instruments of early modern governance by confessionalized states and churches, and their silences and scrutinies were confessionally informed. And, of course, knowledge about a newly expanded world was often collected and organized by individuals and institutions with strong confessional affiliations.[13]

This volume's essays, particularly as they focus on the themes and omissions of history writing in the long nineteenth century, are also informed by the historiographical debate about history's use and misuse in societal memory and memorialization. Early in the twentieth century, sociologist of knowledge Maurice Halbwachs described "collective memory" as distinctively separate from history. Post-World War II, the search to write meaningful history after the Holocaust has inspired much reflection on the relationship between history, memory, and society. The stakes are high: events of the first half of the twentieth century caution historians about the dangerous consequences of history placed at the service of the nation-state as well as the challenges of remembering and commemorating traumatic histories. In the late 1980s, Pierre Nora's *lieux de mémoire*, or sites of memory, gained broad currency as a method to explicate the relationship between social memory, history writing, and nation formation in France, applying critical methods of history to public symbols with powerful cultural currency. Such sites function as symbols of memorialization by a common social group (akin to Benedict Anderson's imagined community), yet Nora's characterization of these sites as sacred rests uneasily for the reader or writer of German history.[14]

Breaking away from nation-statist studies of memory, Aleida Assmann proposes defining history and memory as interwoven and complementary, as storage memory and functional memory. Her definition of a deracialized "cultural memory" interrelated with history offers an alternative to late-nineteenth- and twentieth-century exclusionary oppositions of history and memory. In this processual model, some records of the past are transformed into cultural memories deployed by publics, while others are shelved in dusty archives. Assmann's focus on cultural memory delineates its often political tasks as distinction (the work of the *lieux de mémoire*), legitimation, and delegitimation in society.[15] While the theory of cultural memory has not been developed exclusively for the German nation, its tasks were prominent in historical writing within the former Holy Roman Empire during the nineteenth and early twentieth centuries. Some histories were silenced or remained shelved; those that contributed to a usable past were intentionally brought into prominence by authors.

Overview

Archeologies of Confession begins in the stratum of the long nineteenth century with "Silencing Plurality." This first section explores a distinctive layer of history writing, during which histories were made "usable" through erasures of religious plurality. These confessionally inspired exclusions were produced amid the professionalization of history in the emergent German nation. In the post-Napoleonic era, the confessions sought to establish their positions in the new political and cultural orders. Influenced by the imperatives of political nationalism, the growing ideology of Germany as a Protestant state, and the casting of Luther as its national hero, histories of the Reformation and of the era of confessionalization took new shapes that excluded religious plurality.[16] The narratives, source editions, and scripted commemorative or ceremonial performances generated by these projects were intended for broad audiences as well as professional historians.[17] The confessional affiliations and national loyalties of one or more publics were to be galvanized or stabilized through the authority of these histories.

David M. Luebke (chapter 1) demonstrates that in the lower Saxon village of Goldenstedt, the conceptual space for religious plurality continued long after the Peace of Westphalia and only faltered under nineteenth-century pressure. Luebke identifies two silences: first, he establishes that Goldenstedt's institutionalized *simultaneum mixtum* emerged during the late sixteenth century and continued despite occasional resistance by incumbent priests. Second, in tracing the accounts of Goldenstedt's religious practices from the early eighteenth through the nineteenth centuries, he reveals how authors in these centuries grappled with the undeniable reality of religious plurality within a community. The discomfiture of eighteenth-century observers, including supporters of legal religious tolerance who preferred the confessions to be pure and segregated, was eventually replaced by open hostility in the nineteenth. By the close of the nineteenth century (and after the Kulturkampf), Catholic Karl Willoh's history could and did effectively deny Goldenstedt's long history of a functioning hybrid rite.

Stan M. Landry (chapter 2) examines the cultural memorialization of Martin Luther in the early nineteenth century and more generally the range of inclusive and divisive consequences resulting from such reworkings of historical significance. As Germans marked the tercentennial of the Reformation in 1817, the strongly Lutheran character of previous centenaries was replaced by broad calls for interconfessional irenicism and for valorizing Luther as a role model for every German. Impetus for this new Luther and new Reformation came from the Prussian state, which inaugurated its union of the Lutheran and Reformed Churches on the date inscribed in cultural memory as the anniversary of the posting of the Ninety-Five Theses. Lutheran and Catholic churchmen beyond Prussia also heralded the tercentenary as an opportunity for cross-confessional tolerance and dialogue among Christians and between Christians and Jews. Such interpretations of an irenic Luther as a pan-German advocate of religious tolerance did not go unchallenged. Orthodox Lutheran pastors and theologians resisted the anniversary's appropriation by the supporters of the Prussian Union, decrying its erasure of doctrinal distinctions that had been irreducible since the early Reformation.

Anthony J. Steinhoff (chapter 3) offers a counterpoint with his study of orthodox Lutherans' struggle to maintain their confessional distinctiveness against Prussian "Unionist-Pietism" in late nineteenth-century Strasbourg. During Strasbourg's reunification with the German Empire in the decades after the Franco-Prussian War, Strasbourg's Protestants faced new challenges and opportunities. Pastor Wilhelm Horning sought to bolster the identification of Strasbourg Protestants with Lutheranism through a series of historical texts that valorized the sixteenth- and seventeenth-century work of Lutheran reformers and their post-1598 Ecclesiastical Ordinance. These texts gave little space to the work of preceding reformers, influenced more by Martin Bucer than Martin Luther. The figure of Martin Luther and the celebration of anniversary commemorations were important tools for Horning's efforts, which took published form in historical narratives and editions of sources. Together, Landry and Steinhoff point to the polarizing importance not only of the Kulturkampf, but also of intra-Protestant struggles, in the writing of confessionalized histories during the nineteenth century.

Merry Wiesner-Hanks (chapter 4) directs our attention to a nineteenth-century silencing project shared by historians regardless of confession, the erasure of women from the histories of Reformation as well as their exclusion from the emerging professional discipline. This erasure contrasts starkly with their visibility in eighteenth-century histories. Pietist Gottfried Arnold's history of religious plurality, the *Impartial History of the Church and Heretics*, presented women as prominent recipients of God's word or spirit, and women's historical prominence continued in the confessionally polemical biographies of Katharina von Bora. With university professors sternly excluding women from historical narratives and from the profession, the public appetite for Reformation histories of women as protagonists was met by "amateur" histories. These histories, many written by women, celebrated Protestant plurality from their authors' locations in Britain or the United States and found broad popular reception. Women's return to subjecthood in professional history occurred, at the end of the twentieth century, through a confessional lens. Confessionally framed studies of women's agency within and outside of marriage in the Reformation era were coeval with women's entrance into the profession of history in larger numbers. In the twenty-first century, gender studies have begun regularly crossing confessional boundaries, yet the older legacy of amateur historians has not survived this trend. Women and gender remain largely absent in recent general histories that shape public understanding and cultural memory of the Reformation.

Like Luebke and Wiesner-Hanks, Ralf-Peter Fuchs (chapter 5) compares shifts in histories of religious plurality from the eighteenth to the nineteenth centuries. Fuchs traces the confessional agendas of eighteenth- and nineteenth-century historians of the county of Mark, concluding with works published in the decades leading to the three hundredth anniversary of the 1609 Treaty of Dortmund. That treaty established joint control over the county by two princes, the count of Palatinate-Neuburg and the elector of Brandenburg. Confessional amity between the rulers soon dissolved, as the count converted to Catholicism and the elector to Calvinism, resulting over time in a tri-confessional land populated by Lutherans, Catholics, and Calvinists. This rich example allows Fuchs to examine Lutheran approaches, methods, and strategies to exclude rival Reformed and Catholic churches from their territory's history. A mid-eighteenth-century history acknowledged that all three confessions were present in the county. In subsequent Lutheran histories, Calvinists disappear. Tactics ranged from silence about the ruling dynasty's Calvinism, ignoring strong number of adherents in the population at large, and designating the Reformed Church a tardy latecomer to the region. Catholics suffered a different, more nuanced fate in historical writing. Catholicism was branded foreign, a faith brought to the county by Spaniards, Italians, Silesians, and Poles. Nineteenth-century historians judged Catholic rulers intolerant and vengeful, publishing archival documents organized to emphasize the relative weakness of Catholic positions and the strength of Lutheran ones. A narrative of Lutheran enlightened tolerance, stretching back to the sixteenth century, was firmly in place by the tercentenary of the Treaty of Dortmund.

Nineteenth-century histories often sought to erase evidence of religious plurality, but the objects of these attempts did not passively accept oblivion. Several of this volume's authors offer examples of resistance to effacement in historical writing: Landry's orthodox Lutherans rejected Prussian Unionist interpretations, and Wiesner-Hanks's amateur historians insisted on the value of women's contributions to the Protestant Reformation. Essays in part I reveal that a history's nineteenth-century value often depended on its capacity to memorialize events as precursors to Protestant German nationhood. Essays in part II "Recovering Plurality," move deeper into the past, examining projects of eighteenth- and early nineteenth-century authors to reinforce their confessional churches by other methods. These efforts resulted, paradoxically, in evidentiary recuperations of religious plurality. Richard Schaefer (chapter 6) highlights Catholic critiques of Protestant epistemology in the 1820s, just after the 1817 Reformation tercentenary. Schaefer's Catholic authors did not identify common, pan-Christian philosophical ground with Protestants. Rather, they sought to regain intellectual legitimacy for contemporary Catholic concepts of the religious spirit that they felt had been dismissed by Protestant philosophical rationalism. Their efforts to reestablish space for a Catholic epistemology were grounded in their understanding of the Protestant Reformation's historical contribution to philosophical rationalism. Protestant rationalism and notions of the modern individual were, they argued, derived from confessional errors, evidence of which could be found in Protestant sacred histories as well as Luther's misunderstandings of grace. These early nineteenth-century genealogical deployments of sacred history and Reformation-era source material depended on the preceding centuries' extensive reliance on the use of sacred history in confessional identity formation.

From the late sixteenth through the eighteenth centuries, historians charted the truth of the confessions with the help of vigorously collected and copiously cited historical sources. Documents and archives were marshaled in the service of confessional suasion, and history writing was grounded in humanist and Enlightenment-era practices of knowledge formation. In this era of confessionalization, a history's function was to be instructive and polemical, inspiring readers to reject rival confessions. Over time, the focus on the early church—the Magdeburg Centuriators' histories, for example, only reached the twelfth century—expanded to include more recent periods. By the eighteenth century, historical sources and narratives of the Reformation also became important components of confessionalized history. Gottfried Arnold's Pietist *Impartial History of the Church and Heretics* utilized such evidence to condemn the Lutheran institutional church to a wide vernacular audience. Authors countering the influential Arnold followed these evidentiary methods.

Early in the eighteenth century, orthodox Lutheran Ernst Salomon Cyprian was galvanized by the provocations of Arnold's history. Alexander Schunka's profile in chapter 7 of the theologian and librarian Cyprian, who worked for the Ernestine branch of Saxony's ruling dynasty during much of his career, offers insights into the complexities of polemical history writing in the early eighteenth century. Cyprian's emphasis on the value of material evidence was thoroughgoing and visible in his dissertation, his amassing of Reformation-era documents for the Gotha library, his publication of manuscripts, and his preservation of over eleven thousand pages of his own voluminous contributions to the expanding republic of letters. Both his correspondence and his scholarship demonstrate the artificiality of separating the confessionalized state's projects into categories of religion and politics. The two were intertwined in Ernestine Gotha. Cyprian's writing included many elements later associated with Prussian nationalism: his histories defined the Reformation as German, and his writings identified its opponents as enemies both abroad (erroneous Swiss, Italians, and Netherlanders) and internally (atheists, Pietists, and other misguided Protestants). His adherence to rigorous historical methods of source collection, publication, and citation led to the preservation of a religious plurality he decried.[18] The demands of historical method required the documentation of confessional plurality, however objectionable.

By the mid-eighteenth century, deism was equally if not more threatening than Pietism, and Michael Printy (chapter 8) highlights Lutheran historians' move beyond voluminous evidentiary rebuttals to reshaping broad historical narratives. Johann Lorenz von Mosheim's study of exemplary heresies sought to demonstrate that Lutheranism was the truly tolerant and rational confession. His *History of Michael Servetus* reinterpreted an infamous act of the Genevan Reformation led by John Calvin, the execution of Michael Servetus for heresy. Servetus's anti-Trinitarianism and his resistance to institutional authority required judicious treatment, as both positions were easily interpretable as precursors of deism or Pietism. Mosheim reconstructed Servetus's life, writings, and trial with careful source evaluation but a strongly confessionalized narrative. Both Servetus and Calvin were guilty of intolerant and hotheaded willfulness, in contrast to the moderate Protestant rationalism that Mosheim advocated. Overzealous pursuit of exclusionary truths, an all too human failing, led to Servetus's execution. Despite this evaluation, Mosheim recuperated both sixteenth-century actors by emphasizing their final acts of forgiveness as devout Christians. For Mosheim, the shaping of historical narrative rather than the silencing of facts provided a route to confessional validation.

These forms of Enlightenment-era historical production, while allied with the interests of states and confessions, did not result in the erasures so evident in the nineteenth century. Rather, in this final century of the Holy Roman Empire, we see the acknowledgment, albeit without endorsement, of religious diversity. In the early Enlightenment, recording religious diversity extended beyond the Christian confessions to chroniclers of Jewish peoples and religious identities. Dean Phillip Bell's exploration of religious plurality in Frankfurt am Main (chapter 9) reveals a functioning Jewish-Christian coexistence in the face of a terrible disaster, the great fire of 1711. This example stands in contrast to the dominant histories of Jewish-Christian dynamics in the empire from the sixteenth through nineteenth centuries, which have largely focused on hostile oppositions, when they have been written at all.[19] In Frankfurt, accounts of the fire itself, imperial and local legislative prescriptions, and rebuilding projects in the following decade delineate a civic community that planned for the continuing presence of a Jewish topography under much the same terms as Christian neighborhoods. The cooperative aspects of interreligious relationships in the wake of disaster also figured prominently in Jewish accounts such as that of David ben Simon Souger. Christians in Frankfurt opened their houses and charitable spaces to the Jewish population, even as Jewish and Christian religious identities remained distinct. Commentary on the continuation of a Jewish presence in the city was not without Christian confessional bias; the archbishop of Mainz and some burgers deployed anti-Jewish rhetoric to lobby for their interests. Christian Hebraist Johann Jacob Schudt offered judgmental translations of Jewish prayers and Jewish religious practices. Yet during the intermural period, before a more distanced coexistence was reestablished, Schudt also authored a detailed multivolume account of Jewish life that documented religious plurality.

Bell's study strips away cultural memories and historiographical preoccupations of the nineteenth and twentieth centuries, revealing dynamics and experiences of interreligious relationships. This methodological approach depends on the close examination of multiple sources for their multivalent and sometimes competing evidence. Deploying similar methods, the essays of part III, "Excavating Histories of Religion," expose sixteenth- and seventeenth-century histories forgotten or buried soon after their occurrences. Natalie Krentz, Robert Christman, and Marjorie Elizabeth Plummer examine the rewriting of the formative first decade of Reformation history by early reformers and their opponents while participants and eyewitnesses still lived, breathed, and wrote. In those decades, revisions often excluded the plurality of actors or motives. Mid-sixteenth-century confessionalizing historians accepted those early erasures of multiple actors and ambiguous events, perhaps finding the history of the early Reformation better served by definitive agents and definitive events.

Krentz's essay (chapter 10) exposes Martin Luther's role as mythomancer in what would become known, by the nineteenth century, as Luther's burning of the papal bull. In 1520, Johann Agricola and Philipp Melanchthon planned a bonfire of canon law, with a procession of students ensuring its visibility. Luther played only a subsidiary role. The day after the bonfire, Luther's morning lecture actively re-narrated the event, heightening his prominence in the event's significance. Spreading quickly, his account was readily accepted by his contemporaries and, after his death, by Johannes Sleidanus. In the nineteenth century, Luther's version was embraced by scholars for whom Luther symbolized the spirit of German nationalism. The enthusiasm for Luther as German hero would converge with late nineteenth-century historical method to produce the Weimar edition of Luther's writings, a critical edition that began the recuperation of the 1520 bonfire's forgotten plurality of actors. Delineating the swift development of this hegemonic narrative, and its subsequent deployments by mid-sixteenth-, nineteenth-, and twentieth-century scholars, Krentz offers a nuanced reinterpretation of authorial responsibility for Luther's transformation into saintly hero.

Through the histories of the 1523 executions of Augustinians Henrik Voes and Johann van den Esschen as unrepentant heretics, Christman (chapter 11) unpacks another case of conflicting, manifold accounts and interpretations. Immediately after the event in Brussels, reform-minded eyewitnesses memorialized the two men as martyrs, and Luther composed his first printed song to explain the cosmic significance of their deaths. In contrast, jurist and inquisitor Frans van der Hulst and others publicized claims that the men recanted at the moment of death, while still other commentators including Desiderius Erasmus rejected miraculous interpretations and rather focused on the executions' human consequences as triggers for widespread defiance of the unreformed church in the Low Countries. Unlike the case of the 1520 bonfire, all of these interpretations of the executions appeared in subsequent histories and chronicles; even among Protestant historians some events did not so easily lend themselves to a univalent interpretation. With this study, Christman reevaluates the historiography of martyrdom. Christman's evidence argues that while typologies of sixteenth-century martyrdom can stand much as Brad Gregory proposed, Gregory's reading of martyrdom accounts as the experiential truth does not.[20] Accounts of Voes and van den Esschen's martyrdom depend on conflicting eyewitnesses, rather than the truths as experienced by the martyrs themselves. Christman demonstrates these authors' engagements with contradictory narratives of the events they had witnessed. Arguably this multivalency of interpretation was a crucial process of the early Reformation itself, as theologians and uneducated alike debated the source and location of true religiosity.

Plummer's essay (chapter 12) on the events and multiple histories of early reformer Stephen Castenbauer's life illustrates the malleability of early Reformation history. Through the careful recovery of broadly scattered archival material, Plummer probes the forging of Protestant identity during a forty-year span in the sixteenth century. Archival evidence of Castenbauer's likely prison recantation highlights his conspicuous silence on this point in his own writings. By the 1560s, the template for Protestant martyrdom had been established, as had the need for historical evidence to bolster the new confessional histories; Castenbauer's harrowing experience was recast. Citing the authority of Castenbauer's oral account, Cyriacus Spangenberg described him as a steadfast near-martyr rescued by divine intervention. Even as Plummer's essay calls for a chronologically nuanced understanding of early Protestant biographical histories, her archival evidence reveals another level of sixteenth-century silencing. In their efforts to shape the account of a Reformation hero, Castenbauer and Spangenberg both failed to acknowledge the social communities and collectivities whose protests influenced the course of Castenbauer's fate in the 1520s. Instead, they allowed these protesting commoners to fade from historical memory as the Reformation became the work of heroic men, not social movements. This narrowed focus dovetailed with nineteenth-century imperatives. Nineteenth-century historical methodologies did not fully recuperate these erased historical agents; while historians on both Catholic and Lutheran sides of the confessional divide rejected the possibility of Castenbauer's miraculous escape, they saw no need to look beyond the individual reformer to the complex social and political pressures that contributed to Castenbauer's, and other recanting priests', survival.

Plummer's excavation of the layers of historical evidence requires careful parsing of archival evidence to recuperate forgotten diversity in the early Reformation. Using similar methods, Jesse Spohnholz (chapter 13) exposes the role of the archive in the production of confessionalized knowledge through a study of the archival and historiographical fate of the so-called Convent of Wesel of 1568. The document's archival classification, naming, eventual renaming, and publication in a nineteenth-century critical edition of Dutch Reformed sources all highlight the importance of confessional origin-stories for scholars of Reformation history.[21] Even with the application of increasingly rigorous analysis to the document, opportunities to discredit this fabulous document were sidestepped in favor of the seductive power of the archive. The consequences of acceding to seventeenth-century Simeon Ruytinck's confessionally informed interpretation of the 1568 manuscript lasted until the close of twentieth century. Seventeenth-, eighteenth-, nineteenth-, and twentieth-century historians on this emerging border between the Netherlands and the German lands redeployed the idea of the Convent of Wesel in the service of different confessional or nationalist projects. The Convent of Wesel serves as a cautionary tale of archival mislabeling and willful or accidental misinterpretation by historians, as well as the contingency of history writing.

Archeologies of Confession concludes with Thomas A. Brady, Jr.'s long view of the enduring importance of religious plurality in the German lands from the sixteenth century to the present (chapter 14). This plurality, in the form of the legal confessions, was rarely understood as positive after the Peace of Westphalia's resolutions. Eighteenth-century thinkers condemned the messy religious disunities of the Holy Roman Empire as monstrous, and nineteenth-century philosophers mourned the confessions as barriers to rationality, whether the rationality of Prussia or of Marxist revolution. Cultural memory, rather than exhaustive consultation of the archivally-stored evidence, animated these nineteenth-century authors' ideas. As philosophers were replaced by professors of history, a nationalist Luther only became more robust, culminating in his 1883 lionization, on the occasion of his four hundredth birthday during the Kulturkampf, as the surgeon who lanced Germany's wound of Catholicism. The rejection of religious plurality in favor of nationalism proved disastrous. The cultural memories promoted by philosophers, historians, and politicians in support of an increasingly racialized nationalism led to devastating consequences in the twentieth century. Brady's analysis ends with a denationalized Luther on the eve of the Ninety-Five Theses' quincentenary in 2017. Reminding us that historians in the twenty-first century are still embroiled in the strictures of confessionally channeled frames, he leaves open the fate of religious plurality's history in the twenty-first century but offers no doubt that the history of confessionalization must be coupled with the study of religious plurality.

Conclusion

To interrogate the historicization of the Reformation, and of its early actors, agents and subjects, is to open rather than close the door on the proposition that the Reformation, or rather the Reformations, mark a radical break that is the beginning of modernity.[22] By focusing on the uses of power in history-making and telling and on the layers and practices of silencing, this volume draws attention to the ways that the Reformation attained and then maintained that status. Only by further examining the uses of silence and erasure in the history of the Reformation and by delimiting historical memory freed from confessional concerns can we meaningfully evaluate the role of the Reformation in the history of modernity.

Our authors warn against accepting patterns of thought and uses of historical production too complacently. Writing at the beginning of the twenty-first century, they remind us that the historical legacies of the Reformations and of confessionalizing projects perdure. The essays in this volume characterize the shape of silencing and occlusion in sixteenth-, eighteenth-, nineteenth-, and twentieth-century histories of the confessional era. The following essays suggest that it is time to go back to the archives, to the repositories of personal papers, to the critical editions and ask what has been left out and why.[23] Trouillot's theory of silence and historical writing emerged out of the school of Caribbean archipelagic history, which values historical divergence, distinctiveness, and diversity. In common with archipelagic history, the history of the Reformations within the Holy Roman Empire occurs across a landscape that demands attention to religious and other forms of diversity. The interrogation of silence need not stop with the boundaries of the German-speaking lands. The production of history has served as a tool for and against the processes of confessionalization, for and against religious plurality and confessional coexistence throughout post-Reformation Europe.[24] Our intention is to reveal, through the fruits of power, actors busy in the making of sources, in the making of archives, and in the making of narratives about confessional history. To the extent that this approach allows our authors to engage with familiar or neglected historical explanations and stories in eye-opening or disruptive ways, this volume has succeeded in answering Trouillot's call to expose silence and power in the writing of history.

Carina L. Johnson is a professor of history at Pitzer College and extended faculty at Claremont Graduate University. She specializes in the cultural history of the sixteenth-century Habsburg Empire, particularly in relation to the extra-European world. She is the author of *Cultural Hierarchy in Sixteenth-Century Europe: The Ottomans and Mexicans* (New York, 2011) and many articles, including "Aztec Regalia and the Reformation of Display" in *Collecting Across Cultures* (Philadelphia, 2011) and "Imperial Succession and Mirrors of Tyranny in the Houses of Habsburg and Osman" in *Rivalry and Rhetoric in the Mediterranean* (Toronto, 2015).

Notes

1. Alexandra Kess, *Johann Sleidan and the Protestant Vision of History* (Aldershot, 2008), 45, 72–77; and Donald R. Kelley, *Faces of History: Historical Inquiry from Herodotus to Herder* (New Haven, 1998), 162–87.
2. Hermann Baumgartner, ed., *Sleidans Briefwechsel* (Strasbourg, 1881), 90; and Kess, *Johann Sleiden*, 44–45.
3. Michel-Rolph Trouillot, *Silencing the Past: Power and the Production of History* (Boston, 1995), xix, 28. His concept of power revealed in historical action has affinities with Michel Foucault's networks of power; see *History of Sexuality*, vol. 1 (New York, 1978). Foucault calls attention to the importance of the "distribution of gaps, voids, absences, limits, divisions" in *The Archaeology of Knowledge and the Discourse on Language* (New York, 1972), 119.
4. Trouillot, *Silencing the Past*, 28.
5. "[Archaeology's] problem is to define discourses in their specificity; to show in what way the set of rules that they put into operation is irreducible to any other; to follow them the whole length of their exterior ridges, in order to underline them the better." Foucault, *Archaeology*, 139.
6. Thomas A. Brady, "Confessionalization—The Career of a Concept," in *Confessionalization in Europe, 1555–1700: Essays in Honor and Memory of Bodo Nischan*, ed. John M. Headley, Hans J. Hillerbrand, and Anthony J. Papalas (Burlington, 2004), 1–20, surveys the paradigm's origins and expansion; see also Ute Lotz-Heumann, "Confessionalization," in *Reformation and Early Modern Europe: A Guide to Research*, ed. David M. Whitford (Kirksville, 2008), 136–57, for critical responses.
7. Susanne Rau's analysis crosses confessional boundaries. Her findings in *Geschichte und Konfession: Städtische Geschichtsschreibung und Erinnerungskultur im Zeitalter von Reformation und Konfessionalisierung in Bremen, Breslau, Hamburg, und Köln* (Munich, 2002) are summarized in "Reformation, Time, and History: The Construction of (Dis)Continuities in the Historiography of the Reformation in the Early Modern Period," in *Cultural Memory and Historical Consciousness in the German-Speaking World Since 1500*, ed. Christian Emden and David Midgley (Bern, 2004), 115–38.
8. For sixteenth-century histories as Renaissance humanist projects, see Eric Cochrane, *Historians and Historiography in the Italian Renaissance* (Chicago, 1981); and T. C. Price Zimmerman, *Paolo Giovio: The Historian and the Crisis of Sixteenth-Century Italy* (Princeton, 1995).

9. For Protestant identity formation in the German lands through historical writing, see Bruce Gordon, ed., *Protestant History and Identity in Sixteenth-Century Europe*, 2 vols. (Aldershot, 1996), especially "The Changing Face of Protestant History and Identity in the Sixteenth Century," vol. 1, 1–22; Irena Backus, *Life Writing in Reformation Europe: Lives of Reformers by Friends, Disciplines, and Foes* (Aldershot, 2008); Matthias Pohlig, *Zwischen Gelehrsamkeit und konfessionellen Identitätsstiftung* (Tübingen, 2007); and Kess, *Johann Sleiden*. For Catholic authors in the Germanies, see Stefan Benz, *Zwischen Tradition und Kritik* (Husum, 2003); and in Italy, Simon Ditchfield, *Liturgy, Sanctity, and History in Tridentine Italy: Pietro Maria Campi and the Preservation of the Particular* (Cambridge, 1995).

10. The recent revival of sacred history as a field of study was galvanized by Irena Backus's *Historical Method and Confessional Identity in the Era of the Reformation (1378–1615)* (Leiden, 2003), an expository response to Pontien Polman's *L'élément historique dans la controverse religieuse du 16e siècle* (Gembloux, 1932). The essays in Katherine Van Liere, Simon Ditchfield, and Howard Louthan, ed., *Sacred History: Uses of the Christian Past in the Renaissance World* (Oxford, 2012), especially those by Anthony Grafton, Euan Cameron, and Simon Ditchfield, grapple with this historiographical legacy. Late twentieth-century attention to narratological pressures in nonreligious histories such as Natalie Z. Davis's *Fiction in the Archives: Pardon Tales and Their Tellers in Sixteenth-Century France* (Stanford, 1987) has also reduced rigid barriers between categories of polemic and history.

11. For Flacius Illyricus, useful starting points are Martina Hartmann, *Humanismus und Kirchenkritik: Matthias Flacius Illyricus als Erforscher des Mittelalters* (Stuttgart, 2001); Gregory B. Lyon, "Baudouin, Flacius, and the Plan for the Magdeburg Centuries," *Journal of the History of Ideas* 64 (2003): 253–72; and for Cesare Baronio, Giuseppe Antonio Guazzelli, "Cesare Baronio and the Roman Catholic Vision of the Early Church," in Van Liere, Ditchfield, and Louthan, *Sacred History*, 52–71; and Stefania Tutino, "'For the Sake of the Truth of History and of the Catholic Doctrines': History, Documents, and Dogma in Cesare Baronio's *Annales Ecclesiastici*," *Journal of Early Modern History* 17 (2013): 125–59.

12. Anthony Grafton, "Church History in Early Modern Europe: Tradition and Innovation," in Van Liere, Ditchfield, and Louthan, *Sacred History*, 3–26. See also Ann Blair, *Too Much to Know: Managing Scholarly Information Before the Modern Age* (New Haven, 2010).

13. Randolph Head, "Knowing Like a State: The Transformation of Political Knowledge in Swiss Archives, 1450–1770," *Journal of Modern History* 75 (2003): 745–82; and Markus Friedrich, *Die Geburt des Archivs: Eine Wissensgeschichte* (Munich, 2013). For Jesuits, see Luke Clossey, *Salvation and Globalization in the Early Jesuit Missions* (Cambridge, 2008); and Markus Friedrich, "Government and Information-Management in Early Modern Europe: The Case of the Society of Jesus (1540–1773)," *Journal of Early Modern History* 12 (2008): 539–63.

14. Pierre Nora, ed., *Les lieux de mémoire*, 7 vols. (Paris, 1984–92). The German response to Nora was formulated by Etienne François and Hagen Schulze, ed., *Deutsche Erinnerungsorte*, 3 vols. (Munich, 2001–2), with subsequent contributions including *Eüropaische Erinnerungsorte*, ed. Pim den Boer, Heinz Duchhardt, Georg Kreis, and Wolfgang Schmale, 3 vols. (Munich, 2012).

15. The English edition *Cultural Memory and Western Civilization: Functions, Media, Archives* (New York, 2011) was a revised version of the German original *Erinne-*

rungsräume: Formen und Wandlungen des kulturellen Gedächtnisses (Munich, 1999), cf. 128–29. Jan Assmann, who developed elements of cultural memory with Aleida Assmann, notes that the concept's predecessor, collective memory, sought to exclude perilous racializing possibilities in "Collective Memory and Cultural Identity," *New German Critique* 65 (1995): 125–33.

16. Wilhelm Ribhegge correlates the decline and rise of Erasmus's reputation with an opposite effect for Luther in "German or European Identity? Luther and Erasmus in Nineteenth- and Twentieth-Century German Cultural History and Historiography," in Emden and Midgley, *Cultural Memory,* 139–63. For a broad contemporaneous critique of these nineteenth-century projects, see Michel Foucault's discussion of Friedrich Nietzsche in "Nietzsche, Genealogy, History," in *Language, Counter-memory, Practice: Selected Essays and Interviews,* ed. Donald F. Bouchard (Ithaca, 1977), 139–64.

17. Some of those scripted events, including the Wartburg Festival of 1817, were further reworked after the fact for greater impact. Steven Michael Press, "False Fire: The Wartburg Book-Burning of 1817," *Central European History* 42 (2009): 621–46.

18. C. Scott Dixon explores an early seventeenth-century example of a similar divergence between intention and historical method in "The Sense of the Past in Reformation Germany," *German History* 30 (2012): 1–21, 175–98.

19. Helmut Walser Smith and Christopher Clark, "The Fate of Nathan," in *Protestants, Catholics, and Jews in Germany, 1800–1914,* ed. Helmut Walser Smith (New York, 2001), 3–29, problematize historians' neglect of Jewish communities in studies of nineteenth-century religious polarization.

20. Brad S. Gregory, *Salvation at Stake: Christian Martyrdom in Early Modern Europe* (Cambridge, MA, 1999), dismisses what he calls a "relativized" approach to sources and descriptions of sixteenth-century martyrs and their motives.

21. Daniela Saxer, "Archival Objects in Motion: Historians' Appropriation of Sources in Nineteenth-Century Austria and Switzerland," *Archival Science* 10 (2010): 315–31. Some nineteenth-century critical editions are more reliable than others. For the problems of the nineteenth-century edition of John Foxe, see John King, "Fiction and Fact in Foxe's *Book of Martyrs,*" in *John Foxe and the English Reformation,* ed. David Loades (Aldershot, 1997), 12–35, esp. 13–14.

22. Constantin Fasolt offers a critique of this idea in "Hegel's Ghost: Europe, the Reformation, and the Middle Ages," *Viator* 39 (2008): 345–86. For another view on the necessity of grappling with the legacy of the Reformation, see Alexandra Walsham, "History, Memory, and the English Reformation," *Historical Journal* 55 (2012): 899–938.

23. Even so, we recognize that some historical questions necessarily remain unresolved. For the ongoing historical debate over the story of the church-door nailing of the Ninety-Five Theses, see Joachim Ott and Martin Treu, ed., *Luthers Thesenanschlag— Faktum oder Fiktion* (Leipzig, 2008).

24. Natalia Nowakowska examines the malleability of Reformation history in the service of Polish nationalism in "Forgetting Lutheranism: Historians and the Early Reformation in Poland (1517–1548)," *Church History and Religious Culture* 92 (2012): 281–303. The emerging scholarship on religious plurality and confessionalizing responses outside of the Holy Roman Empire suggests a much wider geographic scope for such inquiries. Influential studies in English include Keith Luria, *Sacred Boundaries: Religious Coexistence and Conflict in Early-Modern France* (Washington, DC, 2005); and Alexandra Walsham, *Charitable Hatred: Tolerance and Intolerance in England, 1500–1700* (Manchester, 2006).

Bibliography

Assmann, Aleida. *Cultural Memory and Western Civilization: Functions, Media, Archives.* New York, 2011.

———. *Erinnerungsräume: Formen und Wandlungen des kulturellen Gedächtnisses.* Munich, 1999.

Assmann, Jan. "Collective Memory and Cultural Identity." *New German Critique* 65 (1995): 125–33.

Backus, Irena. *Historical Method and Confessional Identity in the Era of the Reformation (1378–1615).* Leiden, 2003.

———. *Life Writing in Reformation Europe: Lives of Reformers by Friends, Disciplines, and Foes.* Aldershot, 2008.

Baumgartner, Hermann, ed. *Sleidans Briefwechsel.* Strasbourg, 1881.

Benz, Stefan. *Zwischen Tradition und Kritik.* Husum, 2003.

Blair, Ann. *Too Much to Know: Managing Scholarly Information Before the Modern Age.* New Haven, 2010.

Brady, Thomas A. "Confessionalization—The Career of a Concept." In *Confessionalization in Europe, 1555–1700: Essays in Honor and Memory of Bodo Nischan,* edited by John M. Headley, Hans J. Hillerbrand, and Anthony J. Papalas, 1–20. Burlington, 2004.

Clossey, Luke. *Salvation and Globalization in the Early Jesuit Missions.* Cambridge, 2008.

Cochrane, Eric. *Historians and Historiography in the Italian Renaissance.* Chicago, 1981.

Davis, Natalie Z. *Fiction in the Archives: Pardon Tales and Their Tellers in Sixteenth-Century France.* Stanford, 1987.

den Boer, Pim, Heinz Duchhardt, Georg Kreis, and Wolfgang Schmale, ed. *Eüropaische Erinnerungsorte.* 3 vols. Munich, 2012.

Ditchfield, Simon. *Liturgy, Sanctity, and History in Tridentine Italy: Pietro Maria Campi and the Preservation of the Particular.* Cambridge, 1995.

Dixon, C. Scott. "The Sense of the Past in Reformation Germany." *German History* 30 (2012): 1–21, 175–98.

Fasolt, Constantin. "Hegel's Ghost: Europe, The Reformation, and the Middle Ages." *Viator* 39 (2008): 345–86.

Foucault, Michel. *The Archaeology of Knowledge and the Discourse on Language.* New York, 1972.

———. *History of Sexuality.* Vol. 1. New York, 1978.

———. "Nietzsche, Genealogy, History." In *Language, Counter-memory, Practice: Selected Essays and Interviews,* edited by Donald F. Bouchard, 139–64. Ithaca, 1977.

François, Etienne, and Hagen Schulze, ed. *Deutsche Erinnerungsorte.* 3 vols. Munich, 2001–2.

Friedrich, Markus. *Die Geburt des Archivs: Eine Wissensgeschichte.* Munich 2013.

———. "Government and Information-Management in Early Modern Europe: The Case of the Society of Jesus (1540–1773)." *Journal of Early Modern History* 12 (2008): 539–63.

Gordon, Bruce, ed. *Protestant History and Identity in Sixteenth-Century Europe.* 2 vols. Aldershot, 1996.

Grafton, Anthony. "Church History in Early Modern Europe: Tradition and Innovation." In *Sacred History: Uses of the Christian Past in the Renaissance World*, edited by Katherine Van Liere, Simon Ditchfield, and Howard Louthan, 3–26. Oxford, 2012.

Gregory, Brad S. *Salvation at Stake: Christian Martyrdom in Early Modern Europe.* Cambridge, MA, 1999.

Guazzelli, Giuseppe Antonio. "Cesare Baronio and the Roman Catholic Vision of the Early Church." In *Sacred History: Uses of the Christian Past in the Renaissance World*, edited by Katherine Van Liere, Simon Ditchfield, and Howard Louthan, 52–71. Oxford, 2012.

Hartmann, Martina. *Humanismus und Kirchenkritik: Matthias Flacius Illyricus als Erforscher des Mittelalters.* Stuttgart, 2001.

Head, Randolph. "Knowing like a State: The Transformation of Political Knowledge in Swiss Archives, 1450–1770." *Journal of Modern History* 75 (2003): 745–82.

Kelley, Donald R. *Faces of History: Historical Inquiry from Herodotus to Herder.* New Haven, 1998.

Kess, Alexandra. *Johann Sleidan and the Protestant Vision of History.* Aldershot, 2008.

King, John. "Fiction and Fact in Foxe's *Book of Martyrs*." In *John Foxe and the English Reformation*, edited by David Loades, 12–35. Aldershot, 1997.

Lotz-Heumann, Ute. "Confessionalization." In *Reformation and Early Modern Europe: A Guide to Research*, edited by David M. Whitford, 136–57. Kirksville, 2008.

Luria, Keith. *Sacred Boundaries: Religious Coexistence and Conflict in Early-Modern France.* Washington, DC, 2005.

Lyon, Gregory B. "Baudouin, Flacius, and the Plan for the Magdeburg Centuries." *Journal of the History of Ideas* 64 (2003): 253–72.

Nora, Pierre, ed. *Les lieux de mémoire.* 7 vols. Paris, 1984–92.

Nowakowska, Natalia. "Forgetting Lutheranism: Historians and the Early Reformation in Poland (1517–1548)." *Church History and Religious Culture* 92 (2012): 281–303.

Ott, Joachim, and Martin Treu, ed. *Luthers Thesenanschlag—Faktum oder Fiktion.* Leipzig, 2008.

Pohlig, Matthias. *Zwischen Gelehrsamkeit und konfessioneller Identitätsstiftung: Lutherische Kirchen- und Universalgeschichtsschreibung 1546–1617.* Tübingen, 2007.

Polman, Pontien. *L'élément historique dans la controverse religieuse du 16e siècle.* Gembloux, 1932.

Press, Steven Michael. "False Fire: The Wartburg Book-Burning of 1817." *Central European History* 42 (2009): 621–46.

Rau, Susanne. *Geschichte und Konfession: Städtische Geschichtsschreibung und Erinnerungskultur im Zeitalter von Reformation und Konfessionalisierung in Bremen, Breslau, Hamburg, und Köln.* Munich, 2002.

———. "Reformation, Time, and History." In *Cultural Memory and Historical Consciousness in the German-Speaking World Since 1500*, edited by Christian Emden and David Midgley, 115–38. Bern, 2004.

Ribhegge, Wilhelm. "German or European Identity? Luther and Erasmus in Nineteenth- and Twentieth-Century German Cultural History and Historiography." In *Cultural Memory and Historical Consciousness in the German-Speaking World Since 1500*, edited by Christian Emden and David Midgley, 139–63. Bern, 2004.

Saxer, Daniela. "Archival Objects in Motion: Historians' Appropriation of Sources in Nineteenth-Century Austria and Switzerland." *Archival Science* 10 (2010): 315–31.

Smith, Helmut Walser, and Christopher Clark. "The Fate of Nathan." In *Protestants, Catholics, and Jews in Germany, 1800–1914*, edited by Helmut Walser Smith, 3–29. New York, 2001.

Trouillot, Michel-Rolph. *Silencing the Past: Power and the Production of History*. Boston, 1995.

Tutino, Stefania. "'For the Sake of the Truth of History and of the Catholic Doctrines': History, Documents, and Dogma in Cesare Baronio's *Annales Ecclesiastici*." *Journal of Early Modern History* 17 (2013): 125–59.

Van Liere, Katherine, Simon Ditchfield, and Howard Louthan, ed. *Sacred History: Uses of the Christian Past in the Renaissance World*. Oxford, 2012.

Walsham, Alexandra. *Charitable Hatred: Tolerance and Intolerance in England, 1500–1700*. Manchester, 2006.

———. "History, Memory, and the English Reformation." *Historical Journal* 55 (2012): 899–938.

Zimmerman, T. C. Price. *Paolo Giovio: The Historian and the Crisis of Sixteenth-Century Italy*. Princeton, 1995.

I

Silencing Plurality

CHAPTER ONE

Misremembering Hybridity
The Myth of Goldenstedt

DAVID M. LUEBKE

"Noteworthy . . . maybe one of a kind."[1] "Possibly the only one [of its kind] in the German fatherland."[2] "Probably the only place [like it] in the world."[3] "The only known [instance] in the history of the church."[4] "Unique in the entire world."[5] Over the years, antiquarians, jurists, musicologists, historians, and theologians have deployed these phrases to characterize a set of liturgical practices that took shape during the middle decades of the seventeenth century in Goldenstedt, a village in lower Saxony. In one form or another, these behaviors endured two hundred years—through the height of the Thirty Years' War, the Enlightenment, the wars of the French Revolution, the collapse of the Holy Roman Empire, foreign occupation, and the restoration of post-Napoleonic order after 1814—until the middle of the nineteenth century. The verdict pronouncing their radical distinctiveness also enjoyed a strikingly long continuity: the judgments quoted above were rendered in 1790, 1842, 1898, 1946, and 2011, respectively.

Why all the superlatives? Goldenstedt was a biconfessional (or "simultaneous") parish, furnished with a single sanctuary, the church of St. Gorgonius, which was shared by two religious communities, Catholic and Lutheran. But Goldenstedt's *simultaneum* is not what made it unique. Simultaneous parishes were not uncommon in the Holy Roman Empire and in Goldenstedt's immediate vicinity were plenty: Neuenkirchen, Vörden, Badbergen, and Damme all lay within fifty kilometers' radius. In these parishes, each congregation sustained its own clergy and used the same sanctuary at different times of the day or the week, hence the term *simultaneum subsequens* or *simultaneum successivum* used to describe them. In Goldenstedt the resident clergy of *both* confessions participated, actively and as a matter of routine, *in one and the same rite*. This, according to one historian, was what distinguished Goldenstedt from all the rest: the rite was a fully integrated and institutionalized *simultaneum mixtum.* This liturgical blending set it apart from the norm of rigidly segregated religious observances that obtained even in "simultaneous" parishes.[6] Even the most recent judgments on this state of affairs underscore its departure from that standard.[7]

This perception is an amnesiac effect brought on, in large measure, by the conservative alliance between secular and ecclesiastical authority that historians have come to call "confessionalization." As Ernst Walter Zeeden reminded us long ago, the first and overriding effect of sixteenth-century evangelical reform was less the division of Christianity than a pluralization of religious doctrines that provoked countless liturgical experiments in response.[8] Some were autochthonous efforts to work out the ritual implications of theological innovation; others seized upon the collapse of ecclesiastical authority to fulfill long-standing liturgical needs among the population at large; still others strove to hold together parishes that were divided, increasingly, by rival doctrines. These hybrid forms persisted at least until authoritative standards of doctrinal orthodoxy and liturgical purity were established and enforced—in some cases far longer where state formation remained weak. The early modern confessions imagined hybridity as pollution—liturgical matter and gestures out of place—and strove to suppress its manifestations. Inevitably, the separation of confessions into isolated landscapes of credal homogeneity also entailed the forgetting of local experiments with liturgical accommodation.[9]

Goldenstedt's hybrid rite, because it formed relatively late and in a borderland between competing spheres of power, entered into the European consciousness as an utterly unique specimen. By the time Goldenstedt's blended rite became widely known, in the early nineteenth century, almost all memory of similarities between it and others like it had gone missing. Part of the explanation for this seems clear enough: even among the *simultanea* that still dotted the German ecclesiastical landscape, Goldenstedt's blended rite had indeed become an anomalous exception to the rule of confessionally segregated spaces. Examined against the sixteenth-century backdrop of religious hybridity, however, the rite appears *characteristic* of a set of strategies, widespread in the northwest of the empire, for coping with religious pluralization. To see how and why misperceptions of Goldenstedt's distinctiveness took shape requires a shift of perspective, away from consistories and seminaries, away from concepts of purity or normativity, and toward the standpoint of parishioners, their spiritual needs and local, social imperatives. Told from the parishioners' vantage, the story of Goldenstedt reveals not simply a failure of state building (as one recent analysis has it), but also the largely peaceable reorganization of religious affiliations and their relation to hierarchical subordinations, kinship ties, communal identities, and civic institutions.[10] This involved bending the rules of confessional orthopraxy to accommodate increasingly divergent systems of belief among parishioners, resulting in a locally idiosyncratic, hybrid liturgy. In this connection, too, Goldenstedt if anything typified broader trends.

It would be misleading, however, to present the evolution of Goldenstedt's putative uniqueness as nothing more than the by-product of state power on its victory march toward confessional homogeneity. The myth of Goldenstedt's uniqueness also has a history, each phase of which was shaped by intellectual tides and political engagements related to the secularization of relations between church and state.[11] Eighteenth-century *Aufklärer* discovered in Goldenstedt a model for the enlightened promotion of both piety and religious toleration. Then, in the nineteenth century, German Catholics drew a different set of conclusions. In an environment defined by the establishment of legal religious toleration, the collapse of confessional segregation along territorial lines, and the reorganization of religion around concepts of authenticity and belief, Catholics discovered in Goldenstedt a boundary-violating repudiation of the denominational self-segregation that these new realities seemed to encourage. The record of Goldenstedt's *simultaneum* contained plenty of evidence to suggest it was largely homegrown and more or less amicable through most of its existence. But its significance was overlooked, for to recognize the possibility of peaceable *convivium*, let alone the sources of disturbance, would have meant denying the very attributes that gave Goldenstedt its social meaning as an object lesson in the danger and futility of mixing religion. For nineteenth-century Catholics, Goldenstedt was unique *because it had to be*.

Simultaneum in Goldenstedt

When the mythomancers of Goldenstedt proclaimed its singularity, most of them had in mind a set of liturgical practices that emerged, in fits and starts, between 1616 and 1674. The structure of these practices reproduced a balance of ecclesiopolitical power between the two confessions and their corresponding benefactors in the village, the duke of Braunschweig-Lüneburg and the prince-bishop of Münster. The former exerted power in the village by virtue of the seigneurial authority (*Grundherrschaft*) he held over a segment of Goldenstedt and its inhabitants. The Guelph dukes had inherited these prerogatives in 1585 from the counts of Diepholz, who before their extinction used them to introduce evangelical reforms in Goldenstedt. Ecclesiastical jurisdiction, however, lay with the bishop of Osnabrück, while the bishops of Münster exercised territorial overlordship (*Landesherrschaft*). No one lord dominated in Goldenstedt or its administrative district, consequently, with the result that Protestant beliefs and practices had spread with little hindrance. In 1613, however, Prince-Bishop Ferdinand of Münster reasserted his territorial lordship and also acquired ecclesiastical patronage rights over the village itself. But he was unable to extinguish Lüneburg's influence entirely. The result was a tense but roughly even balance of power between them. The composition of Goldenstedt's ecclesiastical staff reproduced these competing claims. From 1616 on, every pastor was an ordained Roman Catholic priest.[12] The basic form of Sunday observance, likewise, was Catholic. The liturgical personification of the dukes' rights was a Lutheran sexton, or *Küster*, who played an active but subordinate part in Goldenstedt's rite.[13] Thus the assignment of liturgical functions mirrored a delicate balance of ecclesiopolitical power at the outer margins of two domains.

Goldenstedt's hybrid rite also reproduced these segmented hierarchies. The earliest report we have of it comes from Johann Wessel, the Lutheran sexton from 1678 to 1721.[14] At the beginning of each service, he relates, the Catholic curate would process down the nave to the altar, accompanied by two Catholic altar boys, then pray quietly as the Lutheran sexton led the Protestant congregants in singing the "Kyrie fons bonitatis." From then on, the service alternated between the Catholic priest's Latin chants and the Lutherans' vernacular singing. After the prayer, for example, the priest sang the "Gloria in excelsis Deo," which the Lutherans followed with a round of "Allein Gott in der Höh'." After the epistle and gospel readings, similarly, the priest chanted "Credo in unum Deum," followed by the Lutherans' rendition of "Wir glauben all' an einem Gott." The Lutherans fell silent at the *elevatio*; after the priest performed the Eucharistic rite in the Roman manner, *sub una specie*, for the Catholic parishioners, the Lutherans sang another hymn. Lutheran parishioners were not compelled to receive the Eucharistic host in the Catholic manner; for communion, they traveled to the nearby Lutheran parishes of Colnrade and Barnstorf, six and twelve kilometers distant, respectively.[15] At the conclusion of the rite, the priest delivered his homily for any parishioners who had not already departed. Finally, Catholic parishioners recessed to the vernacular singing of Lutheran schoolchildren and congregants. Later accounts added a few details—that, for example, the priest sprayed the entire congregation with holy water as he processed toward the altar.[16] But the general picture is one of overriding liturgical continuity.

Only gradually did the wider world become aware of this unusual rite. One of the first books to mention it was the 1696 *Compendium Genealogico-Geographicum*, a sprawling collection of useful facts about the "reigning High Persons" of Europe and the lands they ruled. But this text mentioned only that "the pastor is Roman Catholic / but the sexton a Lutheran."[17] The first to describe the *simultaneum* in any detail was Anton Friedrich Büsching, author of a widely read "Global Geography" (*Erdbeschreibung*), published in five massive tomes between 1754 and 1782.[18] Büsching merely conveyed its basic characteristics, although that was enough to attract the attention of Johann Jakob Moser, the hyper-prolific Swabian jurist, who mentioned

Goldenstedt in a discussion of *simultanea* in an addendum to his massive *Neues Teutsches Staatsrecht*.[19] Like Büsching, however, Moser conveyed only its basic characteristics.

Considerably more expansive was the description offered by Göttingen professor Carl Friedrich Stäudlin in his monumental *Kirchliche Geographie und Statistik* (*Ecclesiastical Geography and Statistics*), published in 1804.[20] Thanks in large measure to Stäudlin, the fame of Goldenstedt began to shine beyond German horizons. In 1819, for example, the *Literary Panorama and National Register* editorialized on the basis of Stäudlin's account that "there is, certainly, something extremely pleasing in the benevolence of the [Catholic and Lutheran] parties toward each other, though differing in opinion on certain subjects." Lest zeal for togetherness overcome liturgical propriety, however, the editors cautioned "whether our countrymen, especially certain jealous sects among us, would *quite* approve of an indiscriminate sprinkling with Holy Water. . . . [This] we must be allowed to think, very questionable."[21]

The first to assert its uniqueness were late eighteenth-century Saxon commentators, whose reactions to the *simultaneum* ranged from supercilious unease to guarded praise. "A sorry state of affairs, in which no devotion can well survive," wrote the Protestant jurist J. C. A. Müller in 1790. Müller's concern was that Goldenstedt's rite would get Lutherans involved, willynilly, in distinctively Catholic forms of worship. Among other "discomforts" (*Unbequemlichkeiten*), Müller noted that the Lutheran sexton was obligated to participate in Ash Wednesday and Corpus Christi services.[22] Even to observers who embraced the principle of religious toleration, all this mixing seemed dubious. The Protestant jurist Johann Karl Fürchtegott Schlegel (1758–1831)—the Romantic poet's older brother—fretted that this "peculiar relationship" might generate "indifference toward religion," with "disadvantageous effects on morality," even as it handed Catholics a venue for proselytizing Lutherans (*Proselytenmacherey*).[23] A century later, Catholic observers shared qualms about interconfessional mixing. The most thorough historian of Goldenstedt's *simultaneum*, a priest in Oldenburg's prison system named Karl Willoh (1846–1915), had only contempt for those who saw in its hybrid rite "an attractive possibility for reconciliation between the two confessions."[24] Catholics and Protestants could live in peace, but only if they worshiped separately. Inside his own sanctuary, any Catholic priest was entirely within his rights to proselytize.[25]

Liturgies of Accommodation

Whatever their verdict, most of these eighteenth- and nineteenth-century observers agreed that Goldenstedt's liturgy was unprecedented and that it had resulted from confessional competition between Catholic Münster and Protestant Braunschweig-Lüneburg. Most also assumed that among the population at large, beliefs flowed smoothly from obedience—that is, that Hannover's dependents were reflexively Lutheran and Münster's Catholic—and that parishioners generally accepted the two faiths' totalizing and mutually negating claims, enforced by the arm of worldly authority, to the status of true religion. Because power and belief mapped onto one another closely, they assumed, tension and antagonism were inevitable and steady-state—the "story of two centuries, more or less," as Willoh put it.[26] Their narrative, in other words, was one of confessionalization, as we have been calling it since the 1980s, albeit an "incomplete" or "ambivalent" one in institutional terms.[27]

This verdict is tautological anachronism, a narrative of competing purities that is dependent historically on the suppression of alternatives to the thing it proclaims as normative. Viewed from the standpoint of the sixteenth century, as opposed to the nineteenth, Goldenstedt's blended rite appears less "unique" than simply *tardy*. As a growing number of studies show, the liturgical accommodation of credal differences was a widespread response to religious pluralization. Already in 1939, Hermann Hoberg showed that in the prince-bishopric of Osnabrück, large numbers of Protestant parishioners regularly attended Catholic services in their native parishes—not out of theological persuasion, obviously, but for social and civic reasons, to hear the latest official decrees read from the pulpit, or to assert their presence as members of the political community to which the parish church was attached.[28] For the most part, these parishes did not incorporate Protestant elements into the Mass—although in several parishes, Protestant churchwardens helped carry the baldachin in Catholic processions.

In northwestern Germany, such efforts to preserve civic community at the price of liturgical purity were widespread. In the late 1550s, for example, Lutheran magistrates in the city of Wesel adopted a public liturgy that emphasized harmony and obedience over theological precision. While recognizably Lutheran, Wesel's rite retained many trappings of the old faith—devotional candles on the high altar, clerical vestments, images of saints and the Virgin Mary—in order to appeal to those who were more inclined to Catholic liturgical practices. The magistrates' aim, as Jesse Spohnholz explains, was to preserve civic unity against the tides of religious disorder. Consequently citizens of all creeds—Catholic, Lutheran, and Reformed—were required to attend.[29] A slightly different pattern took shape during the 1550s and 1560s in Duisburg, Goch, Gennep, and elsewhere in the duchies of Kleve and Berg, and the county of Mark. There, wrote the Osnabrück reformer Johannes Pollius, a "mixed manner of divine service" was practiced, in which "the entire [Catholic] Mass is held in such a way that . . . the [evangelical] servant of the Word delivers the purer teaching and administers the sacraments, but is constrained to do this in the middle of the Mass." This solution achieved confessional segregation within a single and continuous liturgical framework. After the offertory, Pollius explained, Catholics would exit the church as the Protestants entered to hear their minister's sermon. His sermon concluded, Catholics reentered; Protestants departed at the elevation of the Eucharistic host, "in order to show that they did not want anything to do with that rite."[30] Although it is likely that no one parishioner participated in it from start to finish, the rite remained one for both confessions and as such retained a vestige of communal unity in religious observance.

In parishes throughout the prince-bishopric of Münster, too, priests and sextons strove to maintain the liturgical unity of their flocks by a variety of means, such as allowing evangelically inclined parishioners to take communion in both kinds, *sub utraque specie*. How this was done and by whom varied considerably from place to place. Until the 1570s, priests in the medium-sized town of Warendorf, for example, distributed the Eucharistic host in one or both kinds, however the parishioner wished to have it, a practice that had been initiated sometime in the 1540s and likely persisted into the 1580s.[31] Similar patterns of liturgical hybridity and accommodation obtained in some eighteen villages and towns throughout the diocese.

Even the finer details of Goldenstedt's rite had antecedents and parallels elsewhere in the region. Its confessional division of liturgical labor, for example, turned up in 1625 at St. Matthew's parish in Melle, a town in the prince-bishopric of Osnabrück, where the Catholic priest, Georg Coeverden, was assisted by a Lutheran vicar (Gerhard Hossel) and a Lutheran sexton (Johann Schuirmann).[32] This division of ceremonial tasks may well have been pioneered in the city of Münster, soon after the defeat of Jan van Leyden's millennial Anabaptist Kingdom. For many years during the 1540s and 1550s a "moderately fluent student of true [evangelical] doctrine," Rudolf Köster, served as chaplain in the parish of St. Ludgeri, at the side of its Catholic priest. Köster distributed the sacraments in both kinds to the evangelically inclined parishioners, even though the parish itself—a collegiate church—remained predominantly Catholic.[33] Protestant parishioners entered and departed St. Ludgeri through the south portal, adorned with the inscription "V.D.M.I.E."— *verbum Domini manet in eternum* (the word of the Lord endures forever), the first motto of Protestantism.[34]

One could pile on many more examples, but the central point would remain: Goldenstedt's adaptations to confessional plurality were not *sui generis*, but reproduced a widespread, regional manner of preserving parochial and communal cohesion by adapting liturgy to accommodate theological differences among the congregation. Arguably, the informal *simultanea* that took shape in the prince-bishopric of Münster integrated Protestant clergy and parishioners even *more* actively than Goldenstedt's. Most of these accommodations originated in the mid-sixteenth century and persisted until they succumbed under the pressure of Tridentine reforms, typically during the first decades of the seventeenth century. Where little pressure was exerted, as in the prince-bishopric of Osnabrück, hybrid liturgies persisted and eventually generated a patchwork of monoconfessional and biconfessional parishes. Goldenstedt's uniqueness in the eyes of eighteenth- and nineteenth-century observers was an illusion, a by-product of the fact that, compared with the biconfessional parishes in Münster and Osnabrück, its liturgical adaptations emerged so *late* and that they lasted so *long*.

Obedient Parishioners?

It would be misleading to suggest that Goldenstedt's *convivium* was always tranquil and orderly. Historians commenting on simultaneous parishes, whether in Goldenstedt or anywhere else, have rarely ignored the tensions they generated. On the contrary, historical accounts of confessional relations during the post-Westphalian era tend to assume that strife was constant. This is hardly surprising, given that most of what we know about their inner workings comes from the paper trail that conflicts generated.[35] The assumption, however, begs two heuristic questions—first, whether in the study of pluriconfessional communities, conflict should or should not be taken as the paradigmatic mode of interaction; and second, whether conflicts of the sort that generated a paper trail necessarily reflected generally conflictual relations among the community at large. These questions have no generic answers.

In Goldenstedt, the nature of evidence-generating conflicts, as well as the long silences between them, suggest that conflict was *not* the typical state of affairs but interrupted an otherwise peaceable status quo. Sparks flew when ecclesiastical authorities on one side or the other tried to shift the balance in their favor. In 1660, for example, the Lutheran superintendent from Diepholz tried to inspect the church and parish school in Goldenstedt but was thwarted, resulting in the first of many interstate conferences on the parish's status and observance.[36] More often, disruption occurred when an overzealous priest attempted to make Goldenstedt's rite more Catholic or injected confessional polemics into the common, biconfessional observance. Controversy enveloped the pastorate of Hermann Wernsing (1674–87), for example, who sought to catholicize the parish by, among other things, introducing communal Corpus Christi processions, "with the assistance of [Catholic] officials in Vechta" and "against the wishes of the Lüneburgers." These efforts broke with custom—until Wernsing, Goldenstedt's priests eschewed processions that obligated parishioners to signify their adhesion to Catholic Eucharistic theology.[37] Wernsing also wanted to purchase an organ "in order to drown out the songs of the Lutherans' sexton" (*ad turbandum canticum custodis lutherani*).[38] Another round of confrontations ensued when the combative Philipp Friedrich Voigt (1774–1801) took it upon himself to preach a series of sermons on the depravity of Lutheran beliefs.[39] In order to combat the Lutherans in his flock, Voigt compiled a long litany of outrages that the sexton and his minions had perpetrated against a succession of Catholic priests.[40]

Taking his cues from Voigt's list, Karl Willoh concluded that tension was the normal state of affairs in Goldenstedt, that parishioners dutifully followed the theological and liturgical lead of their clergymen and their respective overlords in Münster and Hannover.[41] Needless to add, this perspective cast as abnormal the long phases of parochial calm between the outbreaks of conflict. Most importantly, Willoh's verdict left out any consideration of the parishioners' attitudes and behaviors on their own terms. Why would Catholic parishioners have indulged the presence of their Lutheran neighbors in the divine service, let alone their singing? Why would Protestants have insisted on attending church in Goldenstedt if doing so meant exposing themselves to contaminating "popish" ceremonies or defying orders to stay away? Such orders appear to have been issued from time to time. In 1652, for example, the Lutheran parishioners were forbidden to attend services in Goldenstedt, but according to the Catholic priest, they attended anyway.[42] Convenience, certainly, was one reason for Protestants to attend services in the church of St. Gorgonius: the nearest available Lutheran parishes, Colnrade and Barnstorf, were for many "too far away." Others confessed that they were "simply accustomed to the Goldenstedt liturgy" (*wir sind an den Goldenstedtischen Gottesdienst einmal gewöhnt*) and had no desire to change their ways if that meant attending an all-Catholic or all-Lutheran rite.[43]

But there was more to their motivations than convenience and familiarity— as Willoh's own account reveals. In 1682, for example, the priest Hermann Wernsing wrote that "because of cohabitation with Protestants, collections of evangelical sermons [*Postillen*] and other Lutheran books are found in many Catholic households; when I go to visit them, they hide these [books]."[44] After Wernsing departed in 1687, his attempts to catholicize the parish were reversed or modified, to the satisfaction of Lutheran parishioners. By 1696, for example, Corpus Christi processions *through the village* had been replaced with Corpus Christi processions *around the parish churchyard*.[45] This arrangement enabled the Lutheran choir to accompany the procession with song, but from within the adjacent church, so that the Lutheran singers would not be obligated to join the procession in person and, in so doing, signify adhesion to Catholic doctrine on the transubstantiation of the sacramental host.[46] An organ was eventually installed in 1698, but to *augment* the Lutherans' singing, not to drown it out.[47] The doctrinal commitments of Goldenstedters' parishioners, evidently, were not so rigid as to rule out a little interfaith accommodation. To the contemporary partisans of Münster and Lüneburg, all of this was baffling. "It is astonishing," remarked J. C. A. Müller, "that [Goldenstedt's] blended observance has persisted for many years, quite calmly and without brawling."[48]

Astonishing indeed—but only if one rules out non-confessional motivations for keeping the status quo in place. A more compelling explanation emerges when we regard participation in the rituals of Christian observance not solely as an expression of theological adhesion, but as a sign of civic honor and an emblem of communal belonging. Lutherans *insisted* on attending services in Goldenstedt as a privilege of membership in the parish, and the commune to which it corresponded. Under the terms of Goldenstedt's condominium, Lutheran parishioners paid fees and dues to uphold their portion of the church's upkeep; Goldenstedt therefore had two churchwardens, one for each group, who were assigned to collect dues and maintain those parts of the church building for which each group was responsible.[49] In the sanctuary itself, the arrangement of churchgoers was a confessional mishmash: parishioners of both faiths "owned" seats in pews under leasehold, which they could buy or sell or bequeath to the next generation. These terms of ownership encouraged a confessionally blended seating arrangement. To hold *and to use* a church pew meant to assert one's claim to the prerogatives of communal belonging or to affirm one's rightful place in a privileged status category.

In Goldenstedt, Lutheran as well as Catholic families reserved pews or portions of them against an annual lease payment. The leases were heritable and remained in the same family for generations. Consequently, according to a register from around 1687, over two-thirds of Goldenstedt's sixty-nine benches were "biconfessional," seating Catholics beside Lutherans.[50] Status, in other words, weighed as heavily as confession in the choice of a Sunday service. As Schlegel observed, "The evangelical inhabitants of Goldenstedt parish [assert] . . . their status in the church, which attaches by inheritance to their farmsteads [*Höfen*]"—even to the extent of participating in Catholic festivals.[51] The same logic played out with the indiscriminate burial of Lutherans and Catholics in Goldenstedt's churchyard, in which every resident in good standing had a right to be interred, regardless of confession, and heedless, it seems, of the contamination that according to canon law resulted from interring "heretics" among the bones of true believers.[52]

A categorical distinction underlay this behavior, one that separated rites of passage—marriage, baptism, and burial, which most parishioners did not regard as demonstrations of confessionally specific theological stances—from communion, the rite that more than any other crystallized doctrinal distinctions between Catholics and Protestants. Thus Lutheran Goldenstedters presented their infants for baptism to the Catholic priest, the only available officiant in their parish, who was obligated to use the rite contained in the Catholic diocesan agenda of 1592.[53] Evidently, the taint of "popish" ceremony was no hindrance. Even the Lutheran sexton, Heinrich Wessel, allowed his children to be baptized *more catholico*.[54] Similarly the choice of a marriage rite depended not on confession but on jurisdictional subordination: Lutheran and Catholic subjects of the prince-bishop were married before the Catholic priest in Goldenstedt, while the dependents of Braunschweig-Lüneburg presented themselves to Lutheran ministers elsewhere.[55]

Goldenstedters treated communion differently: Catholics communicated *sub una specie* in the church of St. Gorgonius, while Lutherans took the sacraments in Barnstorf and Colnrade or not at all. By the mid-seventeenth century, the Goldenstedters' confessional commitments were sufficiently well formed to render the manner of communion significant in ways that rites of passage were not. Nothing demonstrated theological adhesion as visibly as participating in communion, and all the available evidence suggests that on this point, the Goldenstedters behaved consistently throughout the two hundred years of their cohabitation. This fact brings us closer to the proper place of doctrine in Goldenstedt's *simultaneum* and how parishioners managed to blunt the edge of confessional division. As the tempests surrounding Hermann Wernsing and Philipp Friedrich Voigt suggest, the parish might remain at peace as long as priests and sextons did not attempt to seek advantage for one confession over the other. Thus Gerhard Meier, Wernsing's predecessor as priest in Goldenstedt, had avoided doctrinal controversy by confining his sermons to general moral instruction.[56] Voigt violated this principle by criticizing the Lutherans' belief system openly.

Transformation from Below

So far, I have been describing the Goldenstedt's rite as if the narrators of its singularity had been uniformly hostile to its basic structures. That is not entirely accurate. Some observers found it worthy of cautious praise. The eighteenth-century patriot of Osnabrück Justus Möser (1720–94), for example, saw in Goldenstedt a model for overcoming the barriers of "theological patriotism" that still inhibited allegiance to the secular state on its own terms.[57] Möser hoped to elevate secular authority to the status of a guarantor of moral order and an arbiter of interconfessional peace.[58] He perceived the main threats to peaceable cohabitation not in credal difference, but in the insistence of ecclesiastical staff, external or internal, on exclusive and totalizing claims to theological truth. If only church authorities would instruct clergy to refrain from theological controversy, untroubled confessional *convivium* would ensue naturally.

Perhaps these predilections attuned Möser more acutely to the cultural logic of confessional cohabitation. But he could perceive a subtle transformation among Goldenstedt's parishioners, one that also characterized relations between the confessions everywhere they mingled. Slowly but steadily, the two communities were organizing into confessionally self-contained spheres, whose members sequestered themselves for the purposes of doctrinal upbringing, who married across the confessional divide only under strict rules of status inheritance, and who rarely converted. Consider schooling: from 1676 on, a Catholic was hired to educate the children of the prince-bishop's subjects, separately from the Lüneburger children, who were taught by the Lutheran sexton. But the prince-bishop's subjects included not a few Lutherans, just as Catholics were among the duke's subjects. Within this framework, Catholics and Lutheran worked out a kind of informal confessional exchange, whereby Catholic subjects of Braunschweig-Lüneburg sent their children to Münster's school, in return for Lutheran students who lived within the prince-bishop's domain. This self-segregation was accomplished during the late seventeenth or early eighteenth century, without direction or the mandate of law from Münster or Lüneburg. Only after 1800 did parents acquire the formal right to send their children to the school of their own confession.[59] This solution did not undermine confessional cohabitation, but *served* it: by locating religious indoctrination well away from the site of common worship, Goldenstedters tried to neutralize the church of St. Gorgonius as a site of doctrinal conflict.

The reach of such self-segregation extended into childbed. By 1700, Goldenstedt's four midwives were segregated by confession, two each, so that no Lutheran hands would touch the body of an unbaptized Catholic newborn.[60] A similar sort of folk segregation also governed the religion of offspring from mixed marriages. Mixed marriages continued to occur throughout the period of Goldenstedt's *simultaneum* but typically did not disrupt the confessional equilibrium as long as girls were raised in the religion of their mother and boys in the faith of their father. This customary manner of dealing with confessional intermarriage, as Dagmar Freist has shown, was widespread throughout northwestern Germany.[61]

Conversion threatened to undo this balance. In 1766, for example, the status quo was disrupted when the Lutheran son of a mixed marriage, Johann Heinrich Bredemeyer, converted to his mother's religion and eventually became a Catholic priest. Bredemeyer's defection and the harsh response it elicited from Goldenstedt's Lutheran sexton nearly wrecked Goldenstedt's biconfessional regime.[62] So did the attempt of Johann Dietrich Kieselhorst to convert in 1822. The priest at the time, Johann Heinrich Südholz (1802–43), had abetted the switch with secret catechization, earning himself the enmity of Kieselhorst's kinfolk, who tried to prevent the conversion by confining Johann Dietrich and who registered their displeasure with Südholz by firing bullets through the parsonage window.[63]

As spectacular as this incident was, the point remains that conflict, not confessional cohabitation, was exceptional. Kieselhorst's conversion grabbed attention because it violated the rules of confessional status inheritance and taboos against switching sides; his conversion was significant not simply because it exposed the difficulty of confessional cohabitation, but also because it revealed a change in the nature of confessional boundaries. Divisions that had once been porous were becoming ever more rigid, so much so that by the mid-eighteenth century, peaceable cohabitation depended vitally on the perpetuation of inherited social identities. In this, too, Goldenstedters were entirely conventional.[64]

Confession and Forgetting

The *simultaneum* of Goldenstedt and its antecedents alert us to possibilities for confessional accommodation in the Holy Roman Empire, with its elaborately segmented hierarchies and complex religious settlements, even after the Peace of Westphalia sealed the alliance between secular and ecclesiastical authority in the empire's constituent states. But we must not be too harsh on the mythomancers for missing the subtler dynamics of biconfessional cohabitation. Partly as a result of the Peace of Westphalia, amnesia settled over the hybrid forms of worship that religious pluralization had generated a century earlier. Specifically, the treaty's solution to the question of official religion—namely, to revert to the status quo of 1 January 1624—assumed that confessional distinctions had been as cut-and-dried *before* the Thirty Years' War as they became during and after. As a result, principalities that had been internally diverse in 1624, such as the prince-bishopric of Münster, became monoconfessional after 1648 simply because Roman Catholicism had been the only publicly acknowledged form of worship. A special provision allowed the prince-bishopric of Osnabrück to remain biconfessional, which meant that the "normative year" would be applied not to the territory as a whole, but to its constituent parishes. Even in Osnabrück, though, implementing this solution meant reducing the intractably gray ambiguities of sixteenth-century religious practices to the binary, seventeenth-century alternatives of black or white. In the end, Osnabrück's parishes were apportioned on the basis of a rough equality in goods and souls: twenty-eight parishes became exclusively Catholic, seventeen exclusively Lutheran, and in the remaining eight a regime of biconfessional sharing was put in place. Even in the bishopric's "simultaneous" parishes, little trace of hybridity remained.[65] Small wonder that a century after the Peace of Westphalia, Goldenstedt's *simultaneum* seemed "unique."

At the turn of the nineteenth century, Johann Karl Fürchtegott Schlegel looked back on Goldenstedt's history from a time when confessional boundaries were already fully formed and so was barely able to discern how they had acquired their rigidity. He also wrote in a time when the confessional foundations of the early modern state were crumbling rapidly—though not, from his point of view, quickly enough. Schlegel's predispositions were establishmentarian, within the parameters set by imperial law or territorial precedent; therefore the regent, in Schlegel's view, possessed every right to determine the public form of religious observance. But his predispositions also led him to embrace religious toleration and pluralism as a positive good. Although he worried about the blurring of confessional boundaries in Goldenstedt, this was not because he opposed religious toleration. On the contrary, the regent's duty to promote the welfare of the state, Schlegel argued, stopped at any violation of freedom of conscience, "humanity's most noble possession," and imposed a duty to ensure that "the tolerated religious parties . . . enjoy the rights conferred on them without hindrance."[66] Because the "unity of concepts concerning matters of religion were not absolutely necessary to the welfare of the state," he concluded, a plurality of independent and autonomous "religious associations" (Religions-Gesellschaften) was not only inevitable but deserved the protection of secular authority.[67]

One generation later, the circumstances of Karl Willoh's upbringing led him to very different conclusions. The renewed piety and ultramontanism of early nineteenth-century German Catholicism only attenuated the sociocultural apartheid inherited from the seventeenth and eighteenth centuries. For about three million North German Catholics, this alienation was exacerbated by the disorienting experience of a new and unfamiliar status. As the Holy Roman Empire collapsed, German princes acquired the right to tolerate religions that had been forbidden under the old regime, confirming in law what had already become established practice in several "enlightened" German monarchies.[68] Then the founding act of the German Confederation established full equality among all the "Christian religious parties."[69] Catholics in the Rhineland and in northwestern Germany were now the adherents of a compartmentalized and "tolerated" church, subject to the supremacy of secular monarchs who, however much they identified themselves and their states with Protestant religion, did not depend on any particular confession for their own legitimation.[70] Thrown back onto their own resources in confessionally mixed environments, Catholics developed an even keener sense of all-encompassing confessional differences, an "internal radar," as Margaret Anderson puts it, that "registered confessional inflections" in every detail of daily life.[71]

These trends did not bode well for the survival of Germany's simultaneous churches. Not all of them disappeared; indeed, sixty-four simultaneous churches exist to this day, some of which were founded after 1806.[72] But the empire's political and judicial system no longer impeded their dissolution either, and a great many were disbanded in the decades after the empire had collapsed. Loosed from the empire's institutional moorings, Catholic bishops were at liberty to make good on the canonical ban against sharing churches with "heretics."[73] At their first general conference in 1848, they accepted the rights of existing simultaneous churches but expressed their opposition to the creation of any new ones, reiterated the canonical ban against *communio cum haereticis*, and stipulated that if Catholics must share space with Protestants, then the latter must never perform their communion rite at the high altar.[74] Johann Joseph Hirschel, a Catholic jurist and cathedral canon in Mainz, captured the prevailing view—that "it contradicts the very nature of the thing, that one and the same building should be used for the divine services of several religious associations."[75]

These trends also shaped Karl Willoh's perception of Goldenstedt's *simultaneum*, its putative uniqueness and its inner workings during the seventeenth and eighteenth centuries. By the time he was born in 1848, the process of dissolving Goldenstedt's *simultaneum* was almost complete. Negotiations to that end had begun in 1818, soon after a treaty was signed that assigned Goldenstedt to the duchy of Oldenburg. They finally bore fruit on 5 June 1850, with the consecration of a Lutheran parish church. At long last, Goldenstedt's "one-of-a-kind" *simultaneum* came to an end.[76]

Only then did the myth of Goldenstedt acquire its greatest exponent. When Willoh was in his late twenties, Germany united under a Protestant Prussian monarch, and Chancellor Otto von Bismarck launched an "internal preventive war," as Ronald J. Ross has called it, against the perceived threat that Roman Catholicism posed to the consolidation of his newly unified state.[77] Like Bismarck's Socialist Laws of the 1880s, however, his Kulturkampf generated only the perverse effect of deepening internal social and cultural solidarity among North German Catholics, even as it catapulted the party of political Catholicism—the Zentrumspartei—onto a newly built, national stage.

These were the circumstances under which Willoh researched and wrote his multivolume history of the Catholic parishes in the duchy of Oldenburg, among them Goldenstedt, and it would be surprising indeed if these struggles had *not* shaped his perception of relations among the confessions. By his own account, Willoh hoped that his book would help his fellow subjects to remain steadfast in their beliefs, like their ancient Saxon ancestors, a people that had "championed its political and religious convictions fearlessly," even as it "extended willingly its hand to *true* progress."[78] As a piece of "patriotic history" (*Vaterlandsgeschichte*), moreover, Willoh implied a contrast between his own, relatively tolerant duchy of Oldenburg—the object of his patriotism—and the oppressive German Empire, the source of discriminatory legislation against Catholics.[79] In Willoh's telling, the story of Oldenburg's Catholic parishes proved that his coreligionists could live peaceably as the loyal subjects of a Protestant lord, but only if they were allowed to worship in quiet separation.

As his scorn for Goldenstedt's blended rite suggests, the political lessons of the Kulturkampf offered little hope that good could come from such confessional cohabitation, let alone interconfessional worship; as a priest, its blended rite must have offended him. Catholics could no more easily worship together with Protestants than they could expect a warm reception in Bismarck's unified, Protestant-dominated state.

David M. Luebke is professor of history at the University of Oregon and author of *His Majesty's Rebels: Factions, Communities and Rural Revolt in the Black Forest* (Ithaca, 1997), *Hometown Religion: Regimes of Coexistence in Early Modern Westphalia* (Charlottesville, 2016), and many articles, including "Confessions of the Dead: Interpreting Burial Practice in the Late Reformation," *Archive of Reformation History/Archiv für Reformationsgeschichte* 101 (2010). He is also coeditor of *Conversions and the Politics of Religion in Early Modern Germany* (New York, 2012) and *Mixed Matches: Transgressive Unions in Germany from the Reformation to the Enlightenment* (New York, 2014); series editor of *Spektrum: Publications of the German Studies Association*; and series coeditor of *Studies in Central European Histories*.

Notes

1. J. C. A. Müller, "Versuch einer topographisch-statistischen und historischen Beschreibung des Amtes Diepholz, in der Grafschaft Diepholz," *Annalen der Braunschweigisch-Lüneburgischen Churlande* 4 (1790): 249–68, here 255.
2. Ernst Gottfried Adolf Böckel, "Beiträge zur Oldenburgischen Reformations-Geschichte," in *Almanach für evangelische Prediger auf das Jahr 1842* (Leipzig, 1842), 64–74, here 72.
3. Karl Willoh, *Geschichte der katholischen Pfarreien im Herzogtum Oldenburg*, 5 vols. (Cologne, 1898), vol. 1, 295.
4. Heinrich Börsting and Alois Schröer, *Handbuch des Bistums Münster*, 2 vols. (Münster, 1946), vol. 1, 403.
5. Bernhard Brockmann, *Das weltweit einzigartige Simultaneum mixtum in Goldenstedt: Evangelisch und katholisch gemeinsam von 1650 bis 1850* (Vechta, 2011), 11.
6. Brockmann, *Das weltweit einzigartige Simultaneum*, 12.
7. See most recently Joachim Whaley, *Germany and the Holy Roman Empire*, 2 vols. (Oxford, 2012), vol. 2, 237.
8. Ernst Walter Zeeden, *Die Entstehung der Konfessionen: Grundlagen und Formen der Konfessionsbildung im Zeitalter der Glaubenskämpfe* (Munich, 1965), 68–80.
9. On the concept of hybridity in Reformation studies, see above all Susan R. Boettcher, "Post-Colonial Reformation? Hybridity in Sixteenth-Century Christianity," *Social Compass* 52 (2005): 443–52; and Hillard von Thiessen, "Konfessionelle Identitäten—hybride Praktiken: Katholische Konfessionalisierung im Konfliktraum des Fürstentums Hildesheim (1650–1750)," in *Europäische Wahrnehmungen 1650–1850: Interkulturelle Kommunikation und Medienereignisse*, ed. Joachim Eibach and Horst Carl (Hannover, 2008), 102–29.

10. Tim Unger, "Ein Gottestdienst—zwei Konfessionen: Die Bikonfessionalität des Kirchspiels Goldenstedt als Resultat einer gescheiterten Territorialisierung," *Jahrbuch für niedersächsische Kirchengeschichte* 101 (2003): 101–16.

11. Martin Heckel, "Das Säkularisierungsproblem in der Entwicklung des deutschen Staatskirchenrechts," in *Christentum und modernes Recht*, ed. Gerhard Dilcher and Ilse Staff (Frankfurt am Main, 1984), 35–95.

12. Heinrich August Julius Mutzenbecher, "Das Kirchspiel Goldenstedt vor der Vereinigung mit Oldenburg," *Zeitschrift für Verwaltung und Rechtspflege im Großherzogthum Oldenburg* 12, no. 1 (1845): 19–45; and Unger, "Ein Gottesdienst—zwei Konfessionen," 103–4.

13. On the appointment of Goldenstedt's priests and sextons, see Johann Karl Fürchtegott Schlegel, *Churhannöversches Kirchenrecht*, 2 vols. (Hannover, 1801–4), vol. 2, 87; and Mutzenbecher, "Das Kirchspiel Goldenstedt," 30–31.

14. "Spezifikation wie allhier zu Goldenstedt der Gottesdienst in der Kirche aufgefangen und geendigt wird," reprinted in Unger, "Ein Gottesdienst—zwei Konfessionen," 108; and Brockmann, *Das weltweit einzigartige Simultaneum*, 87.

15. Or, as the visitation of 1682 indicated, the pastors in Barnstorf and Colnrade came to Goldenstedt, where presumably they distributed the sacraments in private ceremonies; see Willoh, *Geschichte*, vol. 1, 374.

16. Böckel, "Beiträge," 72; and Carl Friedrich Stäudlin, *Kirchliche Geographie und Statistik*, 2 vols. (Tübingen, 1804), vol. 2, 370–71.

17. *Compendium Genealogico-Geographicum, Das ist: Beschreibung der heutigen in Europa, regierenden Hohen Personen . . .* (Leipzig, 1696), 163–64.

18. Anton Friedrich Büsching, *Neue Erdbeschreibung*, 5 vols. (Hamburg, 1754–82), vol. 3, 972–73.

19. Johann Jakob Moser, *Zusätze zu seinem neuen Teutschen Staatsrecht; darinn, nebst vilen ungedruckten, zum Theil sehr wichtigen, Urkunden und Nachrichten*, 2 vols. (Frankfurt am Main, 1781), vol. 1, 534.

20. Stäudlin, *Kirchliche Geographie*, vol. 2, 370–71.

21. "Catholics in Foreign States," *Literary Panorama and National Register* 9 (1819): 477–93, 637–52, 805–17.

22. "An sich eine traurige Sache, wobey keine Andacht gut bestehen kann!" Müller, "Versuch," 255. See also Schlegel, *Churhannöversches Kirchenrecht*, vol. 2, 80–82.

23. Schlegel, *Churhannöversches Kirchenrecht*, vol. 2, 87–88. On Johann Karl Fürchtegott Schlegel, see *Allgemeine Deutsche Biographie* 31 (1890): 388–89; and *Neue Deutsche Biographie* 23 (2007): 36.

24. Willoh, *Geschichte*, vol. 1, 381.

25. See in this connection his treatment of the proselytizing priest, Philipp Friedrich Voigt (1774–1801); Willoh, *Geschichte*, vol. 1, 382–90.

26. Willoh, *Geschichte*, vol. 1, 390.

27. See Unger, "Ein Gottesdienst—zwei Konfessionen," 107.

28. Hermann Hoberg, *Die Gemeinschaft der Bekenntnisse in kirchlichen Dingen: Rechtszustände im Fürstentum Osnabrück vom Westfälischen Frieden bis zum Anfang des 19. Jahrhunderts* (Osnabrück, 1939), here 35.

29. See Jesse Spohnholz, "Multiconfessional Celebration of the Eucharist in Sixteenth-Century Wesel," *Sixteenth Century Journal* 39 (2008): 705–29.

30. Johannes Pollius to Rudolph Gualther [1562], in *Communio clandestina: Archivalien der Konsistorien der heimlichen niederländischen reformierten Flüchtlingsgeminden in*

Goch und Gennep im Herzogtum Kleve 1570–circa 1610, ed. Jan G. J. van Booma, 2 vols. (Bonn, 2011), vol. 1, 58–60.

31. "Pastores veteris et novae confessi, quod communicantes tam accedentes altare quam infirmos pro eorum petitione sub una vel utraque juxta institutum Christi participare soleant, quam consuetudinem a priore pastore praedfuncto habeant." Wilhelm Eberhard Schwarz, *Die Akten der Visitation des Bistums Münster aus der Zeit Johanns von Hoya (1571–1573)* (Münster, 1913), 154.

32. Max Bär, ed., "Das Protokoll des Albert Lucenius über die Kirchenvisitation von 1624/25," *Osnabrücker Mitteilungen* 25 (1907): 230–82, here 251–52. The manner of distributing the sacrament in Melle, however, was "double." The Catholic priest participated in this rite, he claimed, because it was the will of the parish and the custom of the region.

33. The characterization of Köster as "moderately fluent" comes from the contemporary Lutheran historiographer Hermann Hamelmann (1526–95), *Opera Genealogico-Historica de Westphalia & Saxonia inferiori* (Lemgo, 1711), 1298.

34. Johannes Bauermann, "Die neue Lehre in St. Ludgeri in Münster: Eine evangelische Inschrift über der südlichen Pforte der Kirche aus dem Jahre 1537," in *Sieben Aufsätze, Jugenderinnerungen und Schriftenverzeichnis von Johannes Bauermann*, ed. Wilhelm Kohl (Münster, 1987), 33–40. On the motto itself, see F. J. Stopp, "*Verbum Domini manet in aeternum*: The Dissemination of a Reformation Slogan," in *Essays in German Language, Culture and Society*, ed. Siegbert Prawer et al. (London, 1969), 123–35.

35. See, for example, Jürgen Luh, *Unheiliges Römisches Reich: Der konfessionellen Gegensatz, 1648 bis 1806* (Potsdam, 1995).

36. Brockmann, *Das weltweit einzigartige Simultaneum*, 162–63; and Willoh, *Geschichte*, vol. 1, 354–57. Subsequent conferences followed in 1681, 1734, 1764, and 1778.

37. Willoh, *Geschichte*, vol. 1, 361.

38. Willoh, *Geschichte*, vol. 1, 370.

39. Willoh, *Geschichte*, vol. 1, 382–90; and Unger, "Ein Gottesdienst—zwei Konfessionen," 113.

40. Tim Unger, "Die Kontroverse um die Predigten des Goldenstedter Pfarrers Philipp Voigt im Jahre 1789," *Jahrbuch für das Oldenburger Münsterland* 56 (2007): 147–69.

41. Willoh, *Geschichte*, vol. 1, 390. Even the otherwise balanced Tim Unger, an evangelical pastor in Wiefelstede, invokes Goldenstedt four times to expose the violent intensity of confessional identity among the rural population. But he cites only a single incident, the stoning of a Catholic priest, who arrived, inebriated and unwanted, in Goldenstedt in 1616, only three years after the bishop of Münster had reasserted his authority; see his *Das Niederstift Münster im Zeitalter der Reformation: Der Reformationsversuch von 1543 und seine Folgen bis 1620* (Vechta, 1997), 69, 149, 166, and 179.

42. Willoh, *Geschichte*, vol. 1, 356n1.

43. Mutzenbecher, "Das Kirchspiel Goldenstedt," 34. Mutzenbrecher repeats the observations of one Superintendent Schorcht, compiled in October 1805, from seventeenth- and eighteenth-century reports on Goldstedt's internal state.

44. Willoh, *Geschichte*, vol. 1, 374.

45. Willoh, *Geschichte*, vol. 1, 371–72.

46. Willoh, *Geschichte*, vol. 1, 372n1. Willoh records the observations of the suffragan bishop in Münster, to the effect that this compromise allowed the Lutherans to continue participating in the rite without marching in it. On Corpus Christi proces-

sions as demonstrations of doctrinal adhesion, see Miri Rubin, *Corpus Christi: The Eucharist in Late Medieval Culture* (Cambridge, 1991), 243–71.

47. Winfried Schlepphorst, *Der Orgelbau im westlichen Niedersachsen*, 2 vols. (Kassel, 1975), vol. 1, 104–5.

48. Müller, "Versuch," 256.

49. Willoh, *Geschichte*, vol. 1, 375.

50. Data compiled from Brockmann, *Das weltweit einzigartige Simultaneum*, 57–70.

51. Schlegel, *Churhannöversches Kirchenrecht*, vol. 2, 81.

52. Willoh, *Gechichte*, vol. 1, 378, and Brockmann, *Das weltweit einzigartige Simultaneum*, 130–33.

53. *Agenda ecclesiastica sive legitimata ac solennis sacramentorum Ecclesie administratio . . . Iussu & auctoritate Reverend. et Seren. Principis ac Dñi. D. Ernesti Archiepiscopi Colonien. . . . Pastoribus & animarum curatoribus per Dioecesin Monasteriensem ad ritè Ecclesiasticam functionem obeundam vtilis necessaria* (Münster, 1592).

54. Brockmann, *Das weltweit einzigartige Simultaneum*, 118–21. This was the first diocesan agenda published in Münster after, and in conformity with, the canons and decrees of the Council of Trent.

55. Mutzenbecher, "Das Kirchspiel Goldenstedt," 35; Unger, "Ein Gottesdienst—zwei Konfessionen," 108; and Brockmann, *Das weltweit einzigartige Simultaneum*, 122–24.

56. Willoh, *Geschichte*, vol. 1, 356n1.

57. The characterization comes from Karl Welker, *Rechtsgeschichte als Rechtspolitik: Justus Möser als Jurist und Staatsmann*, 2 vols. (Osnabrück, 1996), vol. 1, 250.

58. Justus Möser, review of Johan Christian Majer's *Teutsches geistliches Staatsrecht*, in *Auserlesene Bibliothek der neuesten deutschen Litteratur* 4 (1773): 575–92, here 579; reprinted in *Justus Mösers Sämtliche Werke*, ed. Werner Kohlschmidt et al., 14 vols. (Osnabrück, 1943–90), vol. 3, 256–67, here 258–59.

59. Willoh, *Geschichte*, vol. 1, 458–59; and Brockmann, *Das weltweit einzigartige Simultaneum*, 157–58.

60. Willoh, *Geschichte*, vol. 1, 380.

61. See Dagmar Freist, "Zwischen Glaubensfreiheit und Gewissenzwang: Das Reichsrecht und der Umgang mit Mischehen nach 1648," in *Frieden und Krieg in der Frühen Neuzeit: Die europäische Staatenordnung und die außereuropäische Welt*, ed. Ronald G. Asch et al. (Munich, 2007), 293–322.

62. Brockmann, *Das weltweit einzigartige Simultaneum*, 170–72.

63. Willoh, *Geschichte*, vol. 1, 392.

64. Etienne François, *Die unsichtbare Grenze: Protestanten und Katholiken in Augsburg 1648–1806* (Sigmaringen, 1991).

65. See Ralf-Peter Fuchs, *Ein Medium zum Frieden: Die Normaljahrsregel und die Beendigung des Dreissigjährigen Krieges* (Munich, 2010), 218–19.

66. Schlegel, *Churhannöversches Kirchenrecht*, vol. 1, 73–78.

67. Schlegel, *Churhannöversches Kirchenrecht*, vol. 2, 2–3.

68. Hauptschluß der außerordentlichen Reichstdeputation, 25 February 1803, §63, in *Quellensammlung zur Geschichte der Deutschen Reichsverfassung in Mittelalter und Neuzeit*, ed. Karl Zeumer, 2nd ed., 2 vols. (Tübingen, 1913), vol. 2, 509–28, here 524–25.

69. Deutsche Bundesakte, 8 June 1815, Art, XVI, in Zeumer, *Quellensammlung*, vol. 2, 540–45, here 544.

70. See James Brophy, *Popular Culture and the Public Sphere in the Rhineland, 1800–1850* (Cambridge, 2007), 254–59.

71. Margaret Lavinia Anderson, "Afterword," in *Protestants, Catholics, and Jews in Germany, 1800–1914*, ed. Helmut Walser Smith (Oxford, 2001), 319–32, here 320.
72. Heinz Henke, *Wohngemeinschaften unter deutschen Kirchendächern: Eine Bestandaufnahme* (Leipzig, 2008).
73. Johann Joseph Hirschel, "Die rechtlichen Verhältnisse bezüglich der Simultankirchen," *Archiv für katholisches Kirchenrecht* 46 (1881): 329–84.
74. "Verhandlungen der deutschen Erzbischöfe und Bischöfe zu Würzburg," *Archiv für katholisches Kirchenrecht* 22 (1869): 214–303, here 264–65. See also Otto Kramer, *Kirchliche Simultanverhältnisse: Rechtsgeschichtliche Untersuchung mit besonderer Berücksichtigung der württembergischen Simultaneen* (Munich, 1968), 58.
75. Hirschel, "Die rechtlichen Verhältnisse," 329.
76. Brockmann, *Das weltweit einzigartige Simultaneum*, 187–97.
77. Ronald J. Ross, *The Failure of Bismarck's Kulturkampf: Catholicism and State Power in Imperial Germany, 1871–1887* (Washington, DC, 1998), 5.
78. Willoh, *Geschichte*, vol. 1, iv–v (emphasis added).
79. Willoh, *Geschichte*, vol. 1, v.

Bibliography

Agenda ecclesiastica sive legitimata ac solennis sacramentorum Ecclesie administratio . . . Iussu & auctoritate Reverend. et Seren. Principis ac Dñi. D. Ernesti Archiepiscopi Colonien. . . . Pastoribus & animarum curatoribus per Dioecesin Monasteriensem ad ritè Ecclesiasticam functionem obeundam vtilis necessaria. Münster, 1592.

Anderson, Margaret Lavinia. "Afterword: Living Apart and Together in Germany." In *Protestants, Catholics, and Jews in Germany, 1800–1914*, edited by Helmut Walser Smith, 319–32. Oxford, 2001.

Bär, Max, ed. "Das Protokoll des Albert Lucenius über die Kirchenvisitation von 1624/25." *Osnabrücker Mitteilungen* 25 (1907): 230–82.

Bauermann, Johannes. "Die neue Lehre in St. Ludgeri in Münster: Eine evangelische Inschrift über der südlichen Pforte der Kirche aus dem Jahre 1537." In *Sieben Aufsätze, Jugenderinnerungen und Schriftenverzeichnis von Johannes Bauermann*, edited by Wilhelm Kohl, 33–40. Münster, 1987.

Böckel, Ernst Gottfried Adolf. *Almanach für evangelische Prediger auf das Jahr 1842*. Leipzig, 1842.

Boettcher, Susan R. "Post-Colonial Reformation? Hybridity in 16th-Century Christianity." *Social Compass* 52 (2005): 443–52.

Booma, Jan G. J. van, ed. *Communio clandestina: Archivalien der Konsistorien der heimlichen niederländischen reformierten Flüchtlingsgeminden in Goch und Gennep im Herzogtum Kleve 1570–circa 1610*. 2 vols. Bonn, 2011.

Börsting, Heinrich, and Alois Schröer. *Handbuch des Bistums Münster*. 2 vols. Münster, 1946.

Brockmann, Bernhard. *Das weltweit einzigartige Simultaneum mixtum in Goldenstedt: Evangelisch und katholisch gemeinsam von 1650 bis 1850*. Vechta, 2011.

Brophy, James. *Popular Culture and the Public Sphere in the Rhineland, 1800–1850*. Cambridge, 2007.

Büsching, Anton Friedrich. *Neue Erdbeschreibung*. 5 vols. Hamburg, 1754–82.

"Catholics in Foreign States." *The Literary Panorama and National Register* 9 (1819): 477–93, 637–52, 805–17.

Compendium Genealogico-Geographicum, Das ist: Beschreibung der heutigen in Europa, regierenden Hohen Personen [. . .]. Leipzig, 1696.

François, Etienne. *Die unsichtbare Grenze: Protestanten und Katholiken in Augsburg 1648–1806*. Sigmaringen, 1991.

Freist, Dagmar. "Zwischen Glaubensfreiheit und Gewissenzwang: Das Reichsrecht und der Umgang mit Mischehen nach 1648." In *Frieden und Krieg in der Frühen Neuzeit: Die europäische Staatenordnung und die außereuropäische Welt*, edited by Ronald G. Asch et al., 293–322. Munich: 2007.

Fuchs, Ralf-Peter. *Ein Medium zum Frieden: Die Normaljahrsregel und die Beendigung des Dreissigjährigen Krieges*. Munich, 2010.

Hamelmann, Hermann. *Opera Genealogico-Historica de Westphalia & Saxonia inferiori*. Lemgo, 1711.

Heckel, Martin. "Das Säkularisierungsproblem in der Entwicklung des deutschen Staatskirchenrechts." In *Christentum und modernes Recht*, edited by Gerhard Dilcher and Ilse Staff, 35–95. Frankfurt am Main, 1984.

Henke, Heinz. *Wohngemeinschaften unter deutschen Kirchendächern: Eine Bestandaufnahme*. Leipzig, 2008.

Hirschel, Johann Joseph. "Die rechtlichen Verhältnisse bezüglich der Simultankirchen." *Archiv für katholisches Kirchenrecht* 46 (1881): 329–84.

Hoberg, Hermann. *Die Gemeinschaft der Bekenntnisse in kirchlichen Dingen: Rechtszustände im Fürstentum Osnabrück vom Westfälischen Frieden bis zum Anfang des 19. Jahrhunderts*. Osnabrück, 1939.

Kramer, Otto. *Kirchliche Simultanverhältnisse: Rechtsgeschichtliche Untersuchung mit besonderer Berücksichtigung der württembergischen Simultaneen*. Munich, 1968.

Luh, Jürgen. *Unheiliges Römisches Reich: Der konfessionellen Gegensatz, 1648 bis 1806*. Potsdam, 1995.

Moser, Johann Jakob. *Zusätze zu seinem neuen Teutschen Staatsrecht; darinn, nebst vilen ungedruckten, zum Theil sehr wichtigen, Urkunden und Nachrichten*. 2 vols. Frankfurt am Main, 1781.

Möser, Justus. *Justus Mösers Sämtliche Werke*. Edited by Werner Kohlschmidt et al. 14 vols. Osnabrück, 1943–90.

Müller, J. C. A. "Versuch einer topographisch-statistischen und historischen Beschreibung des Amtes Diepholz, in der Grafschaft Diepholz." *Annalen der Braunschweigisch-Lüneburgischen Churlande* 4 (1790): 249–68.

Mutzenbecher, Heinrich August Julius. "Das Kirchspiel Goldenstedt vor der Vereinigung mit Oldenburg." *Zeitschrift für Verwaltung und Rechtspflege im Großherzogthum Oldenburg* 12, no. 1 (1845): 19–45.

Ross, Ronald J. *The Failure of Bismarck's Kulturkampf: Catholicism and State Power in Imperial Germany, 1871–1887*. Washington, DC, 1998.

Rubin, Miri. *Corpus Christi: The Eucharist in Late Medieval Culture*. Cambridge, 1991.

Schlegel, Johann Karl Fürchtegott. *Churhannöversches Kirchenrecht*. 2 vols. Hannover, 1801–4.

Schlepphorst, Winfried. *Der Orgelbau im westlichen Niedersachsen*. 2 vols. Kassel, 1975.

Schwarz, Wilhelm Eberhard. *Die Akten der Visitation des Bistums Münster aus der Zeit Johanns von Hoya (1571–1573)*. Münster, 1913.

Spohnholz, Jesse. "Multiconfessional Celebration of the Eucharist in Sixteenth-Century Wesel." *Sixteenth Century Journal* 39 (2008): 705–29.

Stäudlin, Carl Friedrich. *Kirchliche Geographie und Statistik*. 2 vols. Tübingen, 1804.

Stopp, F. J. "*Verbum Domini manet in aeternum*: The Dissemination of a Reformation Slogan." In *Essays in German Language, Culture and Society*, edited by Siegbert Prawer et al., 123–35. London, 1969.

Thiessen, Hillard von. "Konfessionelle Identitäten—hybride Praktiken: Katholische Konfessionalisierung im Konfliktraum des Fürstentums Hildesheim (1650–1750)." In *Europäische Wahrnehmungen 1650–1850: Interkulturelle Kommunikation und Medienereignisse*, edited by Joachim Eibach and Horst Carl, 102–29. Hannover, 2008.

Unger, Tim. "Ein Gottestdienst—zwei Konfessionen: Die Bikonfessionalität des Kirchspiels Goldenstedt als Resultat einer gescheiterten Territorialisierung." *Jahrbuch für niedersächsische Kirchengeschichte* 101 (2003): 101–16.

———. "Die Kontroverse um die Predigten des Goldenstedter Pfarrers Philipp Voigt im Jahre 1789." *Jahrbuch für das Oldenburger Münsterland* 56 (2007): 147–69.

———. *Das Niederstift Münster im Zeitalter der Reformation: Der Reformationsversuch von 1543 und seine Folgen bis 1620*. Vechta, 1997.

"Verhandlungen der deutschen Erzbischöfe und Bischöfe zu Würzburg." *Archiv für katholisches Kirchenrecht* 22 (1869): 214–303.

Welker, Karl. *Rechtsgeschichte als Rechtspolitik: Justus Möser als Jurist und Staatsmann*, 2 vols. Osnabrück, 1996.

Whaley, Joachim. *Germany and the Holy Roman Empire*. 2 vols. Oxford, 2012.

Willoh, Karl. *Geschichte der katholischen Pfarreien im Herzogtum Oldenburg*. 5 vols. Cologne, 1898.

Zeeden, Ernst Walter. *Die Entstehung der Konfessionen: Grundlagen und Formen der Konfessionsbildung im Zeitalter der Glaubenskämpfe*. Munich, 1965.

Zeumer, Karl, ed. *Quellensammlung zur Geschichte der Deutschen Reichsverfassung in Mittelalter und Neuzeit*. 2nd ed. 2 vols. Tübingen, 1913.

CHAPTER TWO

A Luther for Everyone
Irenicism and Memory at the German Reformation Anniversaries of 1817

STAN M. LANDRY

Anniversaries are moments at which memories are recollected, contested, and remade. Anniversaries focus the mind on the objects of their commemoration. But memory is also historically conditioned. That is, memories of the past evoked by anniversaries are remembered in relation to contemporary concerns. The meaning of the memories and the anniversaries that commemorate them are thus remade in the process.[1] The 1817 anniversaries of the Reformation in Germany were sites of memory at which German Protestants and Catholics revisited and rewrote the sectarian histories and confessionally exclusive narratives of the Reformation in order to render Martin Luther and the Reformation accessible to all Germans. Unlike previous anniversaries of the Reformation in 1617 and 1717, which were solemnly observed holy days within the Lutheran Church, the 1817 anniversary festivals were secular events attended by German Protestants, Catholics, and even Jews.

The predominant theme of the 1817 anniversaries was the person of Martin Luther. As Gérald Chaix has noted, in nineteenth-century Germany both Luther and the Reformation functioned as "foundational events, multifaceted usable historical realities and conflict-afflicted sites of memory."[2] Celebrated in the wake of German liberation from Napoleonic France, in the midst of the Awakening Movement, and increasing sectarianism within German Protestantism, the tercentennial anniversaries of the Reformation allowed celebrants to invoke Luther as a touchstone to rewrite conventional narratives of the Reformation. The main impetus for the reevaluation of the memory of Luther at the 1817 anniversaries was the Prussian Union of the Lutheran and Reformed Churches. Imposed by Prussian King Frederick William III on the occasion of the 1817 Reformation anniversary, this union merged the

Lutheran and Reformed Churches in Prussia into a single Evangelical Church. Frederick William proclaimed the Prussian Union on the occasion of the Reformation anniversary festival to legitimize the union by associating it with the memory of Luther and the Ninety-Five Theses and to underline the new Evangelical Church's continuity with the Reformation. In this way, the Reformation anniversary of 1817 recalled a foundational Protestant event but could also function as a mnemonic tool utilized by the king in support of Prussian ecclesiastical policy.

In their anniversary sermons and speeches, pamphlets and plays, histories and hagiographies, irenical and orthodox Lutherans would use and abuse memories of Luther and the Reformation to position themselves vis-à-vis the Prussian Union. Memories of Luther and the Reformation were not always populated by specific references to Luther's works, teachings, or episodes from his life. They were also informed by popular traditions, folk memories, and contemporary accounts of Luther and the Reformation, all of which were mediated by presentist concerns. As such, supporters of the union recalled an irenical Luther who had eschewed Protestant sectarianism. Opponents remembered a dogmatist who had established a new confession. Skeptics of the union invoked memories of the Thirty Years' War, wondering if a compulsory union might rekindle confessional strife. Still others asked how theological and liturgical differences between Reformed Christians and Lutherans would be accommodated in a contemporary Evangelical Church when the sixteenth-century reformers themselves had not resolved such disagreements.

While the anniversary celebrations were still primarily Protestant sites of memory, some German Catholics and in limited cases even Jews participated in them, as the secular and public character of the 1817 festivals rendered memories of Luther and the Reformation accessible to ever more Germans. Moreover, the boundaries of German confessional identity and difference were increasingly internalized—though not erased—during the early nineteenth century. This process, which was smartly recounted by Etienne François, may have allowed contemporaries to individualize their memories of the confessional past outside of the confessional narratives of the Reformation.[3]

But as these memories of Luther and the Reformation became more accessible, they were increasingly claimed by competing groups within German Protestantism who hoped to appropriate the reformer in support of their own causes. Pro-union German Protestants claimed Luther for themselves, as did orthodox Lutherans in opposition to the union. German students and proto-nationalists co-opted the memory of Luther and the Reformation on behalf of their own causes. Even Catholics and Jews, who were conspicuous attendees of the anniversary festivals throughout the German lands, appropriated the memory of the Reformation to call for interconfessional peace. The proliferation of competing memories of Luther—a veritable "Luther for everyone"—marked the most significant development of the historiography of the Reformation in early nineteenth-century Germany. This proliferation of cultural memory, and the myriad appropriations of Luther and his legacy, led to increasing sectarianism within German Protestantism and a fragmentation of the narratives of the Reformation between pro-union Evangelicals and orthodox Lutherans and Reformed. This is a process that Olaf Blaschke has identified as the nineteenth-century reconfessionalization of German Christianity.[4] But the irenical and interconfessional celebrations of the 1817 Reformation festivals trumped their confessionalism. The irenical character of the anniversaries is all the more remarkable because prior Reformation anniversaries had been confessionally exclusive affairs that evoked painful memories of the German confessional divide.

The German Reformation Anniversaries of 1617 and 1717

The memory of Luther and the Reformation had been commemorated at anniversary festivals in Germany every year since 1617. Individual states also celebrated anniversaries to commemorate their state or ancestral rulers' adoption of Lutheranism or Calvinism. Each Reformation anniversary reflected changes in how Luther was remembered. The 1617 Reformation anniversary was an orthodox Lutheran affair. Celebrated like holy days such as Christmas and Easter, the centennial of the Reformation reflected the contemporary concern with Lutheran confession-building and the establishment of Lutheran orthodoxy. Indeed, from 1550 to 1700 Luther was the subject of dogmatic theology and confessional polemics, and contemporary representations of the reformer concentrated on his doctrine rather than his person.[5]

In contrast, the 1717 Reformation anniversary was celebrated in the spirit of German Pietism. Pietism was associated with a renewal of individual spirituality, and Luther's eighteenth-century biographers, who were increasingly laymen rather than clerics, emphasized the reformer's pious zeal and individual personality.[6] Despite the different inflections of their commemoration, both the 1617 and 1717 Reformation anniversary celebrations were strictly Lutheran affairs. No German Calvinists, Roman Catholics, or Jews participated in these anniversaries.[7] The 1817 Reformation anniversaries, on the other hand, were celebrated in an irenical fashion, with German Catholics, Reformed Christians, and Jews attending and participating in the festivities. But two weeks before the 1817 festivities celebrating the memory of the Ninety-Five Theses, a different very anniversary was held that invoked Luther and the Reformation nonetheless.

The Wartburg Festival of 1817

On 18 October 1817 a group of German university students with liberal and nationalist tendencies, many of whom were veterans of the Wars of Liberation, assembled at the Wartburg Castle in Eisenach. United under the mantra of "Honor, Freedom, Fatherland," the students agitated for a reform of German colleges, demanded a liberal constitution for Prussia, and envisaged a unification of the German states. The occasion for the Wartburg Festival itself was heavy with nationalist sentiments. The date 18 October was in fact the fourth anniversary of the Battle of Leipzig, a decisive Prussian victory over Napoleon. The year 1817 was also the tercentennial of the Protestant Reformation, and the students' political demands and the Wartburg Castle itself were steeped in memories of Martin Luther and the Reformation. Indeed, the Wartburg Castle was the place where Saxon duke Frederick the Wise (1463–1525) had given refuge to Martin Luther after the latter's excommunication from the Roman Church and where Luther translated the New Testament into German.

Luther's memory was manifest among the students, who celebrated the reformer as a German citizen and patriot who had embodied the liberal characteristics of reason, virtue, and freedom. The celebrants of the festival sang the Lutheran hymn "A Mighty Fortress Is Our God" along with other patriotic songs, and in a ritual that recalled Luther's burning of the papal bull that excommunicated him, they burned books written by conservative and anti-democratic authors.[8] As such, the celebrants of the Wartburg Festival identified the Reformation as the first salvo of a long process of German national liberation and unification. Indeed, claimed the students, just as Luther had freed the German people from the spiritual bondage of the Roman Catholic Church, the Wartburger would advocate for the political liberation of the German states from the conservative princes.[9]

Like the Wartburger, celebrants of the Reformation anniversaries appealed to a distinct memory of Luther and the Reformation that gave credence to their visions of German confessional unity. But rather than the enlightened and nationalist Luther invoked by the students at Wartburg, other celebrants of the 1817 anniversaries recalled a Luther who eschewed sectarianism and one that could function as a religious symbol accessible to all Germans. This irenical memory of Luther would ultimately be realized in the 1817 union of the Reformed and Lutheran Churches in Prussia.

Prelude to the Prussian Union of 1817

Changing ecclesiastical and political conditions in the late eighteenth and early nineteenth centuries contributed to increasing confessional integration and pointed to the viability of both intra-Protestant (i.e., Lutheran and Reformed) and interconfessional unity. By the early nineteenth century confessional relations had improved in Germany and Austria. Dogmatic differences between denominations were blunted by enlightened opposition to the religious enthusiasm of the previous century and by 150 years of respite from religious war.[10] Confessional tensions decreased as Roman Catholicism became less of a threat to Protestantism and it became clear that for the time being no great power was dedicated to abolishing any particular confession.[11] During the Wars of Liberation, German Catholics and Protestants united in opposition to Napoleon.[12] Napoleon's dissolution of the German ecclesiastical states—sovereign territories within the German lands that were ruled by prince-bishops—contributed to increasing confessional integration even after the Wars of Liberation. These developments were consistent with the irenical character of the contemporaneous German Awakening Movement. Leaders of the Awakening Movement, including the cleric Nikolaus von Zinzendorf (1700–60), the Jesuit Johann M. Sailer (1751–1832), and the Lutheran theologian Gottfried Thomasius (1802–75), de-emphasized confessional difference for the possibility of a pan-Christian spiritual renewal.

Historians have also noted the existence of a post-revolutionary renewal of piety among Catholic intellectuals in the figures of the German theologian and mystic Franz von Baader (1765–1841), for example, who proposed a "holy alliance" of Christian states and a reunion of the Roman and Orthodox Churches, and Ignaz Lindl (1774–1846), a south German priest who preached an apocalyptic and ecumenical message to Catholics and Protestants in Bavaria.[13] The figures of Baader and Lindl reflected the desire among at least some Romantic intellectuals for the renewal of a unified, pre-Reformation catholic church.

Some early nineteenth-century German Protestant clerics also expressed a desire for church unity. In 1803, the Lutheran Church historian Jacob Gottlieb Planck (1751–1833) advocated an unhurried, voluntary, and formal union of the Reformed and Lutheran Churches that would reconcile what he saw as their minor external differences.[14] In an 1812 pamphlet, Reformed theologian Friedrich Samuel Gottfried Sack (1738–1817), presiding cleric at young Frederick William III's confirmation, noted improving confessional relations as a sign that now was the appropriate time to attempt a reunion of the Reformed and Lutheran Churches.[15]

Moreover, the Prussian annexation of Catholic Silesia in 1742 and the Bavarian acquisition of the heavily Protestant Palatinate in 1816 made Prussia and Bavaria confessionally heterogeneous. The annexation of regions heavily populated by religious minorities provided states a stake in the maintenance and encouragement of confessional peace. This religious heterogeneity, coupled with the post-Napoleonic revival of Christian piety, led to increasing confessional tensions later in the century. Nevertheless, state officials in confessionally mixed regions encouraged confessional integration for the purpose of de-emphasizing confessional difference and the social discord that sometimes resulted.[16]

To be sure, multiple confessional divides existed within the German lands. These included the Catholic-Protestant divide, as well as divisions between Lutherans and Reformed and between Christians and Jews. Multiple religious divides entailed different conceptions of church unity and different strategies for utilizing memories of Luther and the Reformation in an effort to bridge those divides. In each instance of irenicism, memories of Luther and the Reformation provided a usable past for Germans that were used and abused in order to shape the present. But memories of Luther and the Reformation were rarely neutral, nor were they uncontested. German Catholics and Protestants, confessional Lutherans and Evangelical ecumenists all claimed to best represent the memories and legacies of Luther and the Reformation. As with so many cultural and national heroes, the invocation of Luther could divide as well as unite communities as some memories were celebrated and others were silenced.

The German Reformation Anniversaries of 1817 and the Prussian Union

It was within this context of increasing confessional integration and popular demands for interconfessional peace that King Frederick William III called for a unification of the Reformed and Lutheran Churches in Prussia. The Prussian Union would be inaugurated on 31 October 1817 and celebrated at the Reformation anniversary festivals of the same weekend. But in order to establish a union of the Reformed and Lutheran Churches on the occasion of an anniversary traditionally identified with Luther, Frederick William III and other pro-union figures would have to remake the memory of Luther from one that evoked confessional Lutheranism to one that suggested intra-Protestant unity.

Frederick William himself was among the most outspoken supporters of a union of the Reformed and Lutheran Churches. The king was a devoted Calvinist whose spirituality was influenced by Pietism. He desired to be known as a righteous ruler of a strong Christian state and believed that a strong and unified church was essential to the well-being of state and society. The king's

interfaith marriages might also have informed his ecclesiastical policies—
Frederick William's first wife, the immensely popular Queen Louise (d. 1810),
was devoutly Lutheran. His second wife, Princess Auguste von Harrach, was
Catholic. But in fact, Frederick had desired a union of the Prussian Reformed
and Lutheran Churches as early the 1790s. The king had envisioned that such
a union might serve as the kernel for a German national church that would
welcome other Protestant state churches and even Catholic congregations.[17]
As the 1817 anniversary approached, the king's ministers advised him to
pursue a union of Reformed and Lutheran Churches, assuring him that it
would broaden and strengthen the Prussian state church, that it would represent an enlightened form of religious tolerance, and that it might address the
growing problems of confessionally mixed marriages and confessional discord
within his confessionally heterogeneous kingdom.[18]

On 27 September 1817 the king issued an order summoning representatives
of the Lutheran and Reformed Churches to attendance at an intra-Protestant
service and celebration of the Eucharist on 30 October in Berlin. This service
had two purposes: to celebrate the memory of the Reformation and to inaugurate the Prussian Union of the Reformed and Lutheran Churches into a unified Evangelical Church.[19] Frederick William III proposed a shared celebration
of the Eucharist between Reformed and Lutheran churchgoers at the services
to inaugurate the Prussian Union. Sidestepping the potentially thorny issue of
the Real Presence, communicants would be allowed to interpret the meaning
of the Eucharist for themselves. Frederick believed this shared celebration
of communion could have a unifying effect on his Reformed and Lutheran
subjects. He identified the shared celebration of communion as evidence of
adoption of the Prussian Union—a performative act that would denote a congregation's membership into the new Evangelical Church.

Orthodox Lutheran Opposition to the Prussian Union

Despite Frederick's best efforts to accommodate the religious sensibilities of
his subjects, a vocal minority of orthodox Lutherans protested the compulsory
union of their church with the Reformed Church. In anniversary sermons and
speeches opposing the Prussian Union, orthodox Lutherans invoked memories of a dogmatic Luther to use as a foil against pro-union invocations of an
irenical Luther. They were outraged that the 1817 Reformation anniversary
would be used to inaugurate a union that they felt would only weaken the
Lutheran Church. Opposition to union was most widespread and vociferous in northern and eastern Germany, where a strong tradition of orthodox
Lutheranism persisted. This opposition lasted well into the 1840s, primarily
in Holstein, Saxony, and Silesia.[20]

The Lutheran pastor in Kiel, Claus Harms (1778–1855) was the most prominent critic of union. Harms, whose admirers compared him to Luther for the passion of his evangelism, embodied orthodox Lutheran opposition to the Prussian Union.[21] Harms argued that the proposed Evangelical Church neglected confessional dogmas and differences that the reformers themselves had defined. Refusing to forget the confessional Lutheran past, he invoked Reformation-era councils and confessional documents that had established these dogmas and differences to reclaim the memory of Luther from proponents of intra-Protestant unity. On 31 October 1817 Harms published his own Ninety-Five Theses alongside Luther's originals to protest the Prussian Union. He claimed that his theses were as necessary to the contemporary church as Luther's had been to the sixteenth-century church and viewed his new theses within a three-hundred-year tradition of rousing and reforming Lutheran polemicists.[22]

Harms was especially concerned with how the Evangelical Church would resolve the theological differences between Reformed and Lutherans on the Lord's Supper. He noted that if Luther at the Marburg Colloquy of 1529 had determined that Christ's body and blood were present in the bread and wine, then they must remain so in 1817. Nineteenth-century Lutherans could not whimsically rewrite or abandon an essential doctrine that Luther himself had defined and defended. Indeed, the dispute over the Real Presence was the doctrine that had caused the most disagreement between Luther and Zwingli. The common celebration of communion between Reformed and Lutherans proposed by Frederick William III was impossible. It entailed turning one's back on the legacy of Luther and on the wise judgment of those Reformation-era councils at which Reformed and Lutherans had separated over the matter of the Real Presence.[23] Harms concluded his theses with a strong condemnation of this "forced marriage" of the Reformed and Lutheran Churches and implied that the ghost of Luther would haunt the Evangelical Church because it had forgotten its origins with the reformer.[24]

Ecclesiastical and Popular Support for the Prussian Union

The noisy protestations of orthodox Lutherans such as Harms notwithstanding, the king found overwhelming support for the union from the Berlin Synod, the governing body of the Prussian Lutheran Church. Friedrich Schleiermacher (1768–1834), presiding officer of the Synod of Berlin and supporter of the Evangelical Union, published an official declaration on behalf of the synod that expressed support for the king's order of 27 September. The synod's declaration noted that throughout the early nineteenth century, Reformed had attended Lutheran services and sermons, Lutherans had their children baptized and catechized by Reformed pastors, and Reformed and Lutheran clergy and laity had blessed interconfessional marriages. Schleiermacher and the synod envisioned the common celebration of communion proposed by the king as a progression of these irenical practices and the consummating act of unification of the separated confessions.[25]

The Berlin Synod's official endorsement of the union was affirmed by Schleiermacher's own fond memories of the Reformation and a shared Protestant heritage. This memory acknowledged both Luther and Zwingli's contributions to German Protestantism. In his 1817 Reformation anniversary address to the University of Berlin, Schleiermacher noted that at the anniversary festivals, Protestants celebrated the memory of that event that was common to both Luther and Zwingli: the restoration of the authority of Scripture, the recognition that faith alone could atone for man's sins, the defeat of superstition and ritualism, and the abolition of intermediaries between God and man.[26] This memory rendered Luther and the early Protestant reformers as pre-dogmatic and pre-confessional figures that had never intended the sectarian divide. Thus Schleiermacher invoked a Reformation history of shared traditions and trajectories rather than one of separation between the two Protestant confessions. He sought to remake the confessional memory of the 1817 anniversary into one that evoked intra-Protestant unity in order to reconcile Reformed and Lutherans within the new Evangelical Church.

Based on Frederick's 27 September order, Reformed and Lutheran ministers met at the Church of St. Nicholas in Berlin and celebrated the anniversary of the Reformation on Saturday 30 October 1817 by taking communion in common. The king attended the service but did not accept communion, preferring to wait until the Sunday service to accept the sacrament. On the morning of Sunday 31 October 1817 the king introduced the first unified Evangelical Christian congregation at the royal chapel in Potsdam by announcing a union of the chapel's Reformed and Lutheran congregations. The royal court was in attendance, along with sixty prominent Reformed and Lutheran ministers. The king hoped that the unification of the Potsdam chapel would serve as an irenical model for all Protestant communities in Prussia. On the evening of Sunday 31 October Frederick traveled from Potsdam to Wittenberg, where he attended the festival service at the Wittenberg Schloßkirche, and then the king attended the groundbreaking ceremonies of the city's new Luther memorial.[27]

Immediately following the event in Potsdam, Frederick began a public campaign to support the union. In order to legitimize the new church, the king had identified himself and the proposed union not only with Luther and the Reformation, but with a long-standing Hohenzollern policy of religious toleration and with a line of Prussian rulers who had persistently tried to unify the separated confessions. He wrote in his 27 September proclamation:

> My enlightened ancestors, the elector Johann Sigismund, the elector Georg Wilhelm, the great elector Friedrich Wilhelm, King Friedrich I, and King Friedrich Wilhelm I, as the history of their reign and their lives prove, had already attempted with pious solemnity, to unite both separated Protestant churches, the Reformed and the Lutheran into an Evangelical-Christian Church in their lands.[28]

Following this tradition, Frederick William III argued that the Reformed and Lutheran Churches were "two slightly divergent confessions" separated only by external differences and thus should be united.[29] Moreover, the Prussian Union was in accordance with the ultimate purposes of Christian unity and corresponded with the original intentions of the reformers, whom the king claimed had not desired a separation of Protestantism into Lutheran and Reformed confessions. The king finally noted that his Reformed and Lutheran subjects had enthusiastically demanded the union and that it would revitalize German Protestantism, contribute to the renewal of domestic piety, and alleviate the social discord that accompanied the intra-Protestant confessional divide. Anticipating reservations, Frederick argued that the union would not constitute a conversion of Reformed to Lutheranism or Lutherans to the Reformed Church, but a revitalized Evangelical Church in the spirit of the Reformation and the reformers.[30] But in order to effect such a union, histories of the sectarianism and confessionalism of the Reformation era would have to be parried and then rewritten to include irenical memories of Luther and the reformers. The king was of course the most vociferous proponent of the Prussian Union, but it also enjoyed significant clerical and popular support. Entry into the union was optional for each congregation, but by May 1825 almost 70 percent of Prussian congregations had adopted it.

Advocates of union in regions outside Prussia used the occasion of the Reformation anniversary to call for a reunion of local Reformed and Lutheran congregations in their own communities. Supporters of union in Nassau did not wish to be known as Lutherans or Calvinists because they claimed that reformers themselves had eschewed such sectarianism and did not want Protestant Christians to establish separate denominations. Instead, advocates of union in Nassau desired the name of Evangelical Christian Church to underline their unity.[31] In fact, the use of the word "evangelical" to describe the newly unified congregations evoked memories of the early Reformation. Irenical Protestants appropriated this designation, which the first generation of reformers had used to refer to themselves, in order to underline the continuity of the contemporary unions with the Reformation.

Reflecting its widespread popular support, the Nassau Union proposal was composed by a local synod and voted on by Protestant heads of household.[32] The duke of Nassau officially proclaimed the union of the Reformed and Lutheran Churches in his duchy on 31 October 1817. Further south, in

Frankfurt, Reformed pastors preached in Lutheran churches, while Lutheran pastors administered communion in Reformed churches in support of a union.[33] Indeed, a local union effected in the Palatinate town of Bad Berg-zabern claimed the new Evangelical Church recalled the congregations of the apostolic age and early Reformation, before confessional distinctions and denominational differences were established.[34] For this congregation, the union evoked memories of a pre-confessional period of Christianity and the early Reformation that were representative of the new intra-Protestant unity realized in the Evangelical Church.

Indeed, with royal, ecclesiastical, and popular support, unions were ulti-mately recognized by Fulda (1818), the Rhineland-Palatinate (1818), Anhalt (1820), Baden (1821), Rhenish Hesse (1822), Hesse (1823), and Württemberg (1827). Unions were not effected in Bavaria, Saxony, Mecklenburg, or Han-nover due to the negligible numbers of Reformed Christians in those states, although individual Reformed and Lutheran congregations were free to unite themselves.

The Interconfessional Celebration of the 1817 Anniversaries

Evangelical Protestants were not the only ones celebrating the Reformation anniversaries in a spirit of German confessional unity. Across Germany, inspired by the Prussian king's ecumenical efforts and by their own desire to bridge the German confessional divide, irenical Catholics and Protestants, and in limited cases even Jews, enthusiastically participated in the Reformation anniversary festivals, calling for a cessation of religious antagonism, plead-ing for interconfessional coexistence and cooperation, and advocating church unity. German collective memories of Luther and the Reformation had been linked to memories of separation, religious war, and the confessional divide for over two centuries. But the interconfessional participation in these festivals and their invocation of irenical memories of Luther marked a shift in German collective memories of the Reformation. By proposing solutions for overcom-ing this separation in anniversary sermons, speeches, and pamphlets and by celebrating the anniversaries in common with Catholics, Reformed, Luther-ans, and Jews, irenical participants in the 1817 Reformation anniversaries refashioned the hitherto confessionally exclusive character of the anniversary festivals into celebrations of Christian interconfessional unity and religious pluralism.

Many of the sermons and speeches delivered at the 1817 anniversaries invoked memories of Luther and the Reformation to call for interconfessional peace and to explore the possibilities of a reunion of German Catholics and Protestants. In his Reformation sermon, Valentin Karl Veillodter (1769–

1828), a Lutheran pastor in Nuremberg, preached that the anniversary was no occasion for bitter feelings between Lutherans, Reformed, or their Catholic brothers.[35] Instead, Veillodter suggested that his congregation act in the "spirit of brotherly concord" toward Catholics and Reformed during the Reformation anniversary.[36] Indeed, he reminded his congregation that during the Napoleonic Wars, members of the Catholic, Lutheran, and Reformed Churches had united in their shared love of the fatherland to oppose external threats to German freedom. Once again, at the 1817 Reformation anniversaries, they were united in their desire for interconfessional peace.[37]

The Bamberg Lutheran pastor Ernst Anton Clarus (1776–1848) began his Reformation sermon by explicitly stating that the Reformation anniversary should not be a celebration of the confessional divide between German Catholics and Protestants.[38] Clarus called on his congregation to give thanks to everyone who was united in attendance at the service and anniversary festival, without distinction of confession.[39] He then asked his congregation to recall the centuries of religious bigotry and violence that had plagued Germany and contrasted these painful memories to the union of the Reformed and Lutheran Churches in Prussia, which he believed represented a final nullification of the animosities between the Protestant denominations.[40] Clarus concluded his sermon by reminding the congregation that the gospel bound them and German Catholics together as brothers. He enumerated the similarities between the Evangelical and Catholic Churches, including shared histories and traditions that might serve as a basis for rapprochement between, and an ultimate reunion of, the separated confessions. Clarus hoped that a reunion of the separated confessions could strengthen the German churches.[41]

In nearby Erlangen, the Lutheran theologian Gottlieb Philipp Christian Kaiser (1781–1848) told his congregation that the Reformation was still in progress, that it must remain in progress, and that it would only be completed through a reunification of all of the Christian confessions.[42] Kaiser contrasted the expressions of tolerance and cooperation between Catholics, Reformed, and Lutherans at the 1817 anniversary with the Lutheran exclusivity of the 1617 and 1717 anniversaries. According to Kaiser, the irenical celebration of the 1817 anniversary pointed to the hopeful prospects of a final reunion of the separated Christian confessions.[43] The ecumenical sermons of Veillodter, Clarus, and Kaiser were representative of the general Lutheran pro-union position. Based on reports describing the irenical celebrations of the Reformation anniversary in Bamberg and other neighboring towns, the reception of the ecumenical sentiments of Veillodter, Clarus, and Kaiser's sermons was positive. Esteemed members of the Bamberg Catholic church attended Reformation Sunday services at the local Evangelical church and participated in the festivities that followed. Catholic notables shared a common meal with local Evangelical clerics at the city museum.[44]

Irenical celebrations of the Reformation anniversary were repeated further afield from those in Bamberg. Lutheran, Reformed, and Catholic children attended catechism classes together in Gleusen.[45] Catholics and Jews attended the anniversary festivities in Mühlhausen and Trabelsdorf.[46] Also in Trabelsdorf, short books on Reformation history were donated to the poor, and money was raised for German translations of the New Testament for Christian children and the Old Testament for Jewish children.[47] Confessionally mixed families in Küps celebrated together. The Küps city pastor expressed hope that these celebrations, by their "concord, decency, and fraternal spirit," would leave an unforgettable joyful memory within his congregation of the interconfessional participation at the anniversary.[48]

Some German Catholics noted the ecumenical possibilities of the 1817 Reformation anniversary as well. In their campaigns for confessional unity, irenical Catholics recalled a pre-Reformation past that evoked a shared German Christian culture and history. But in invoking this idealized past, German Catholics sidestepped painful memories of religious separation, violence, and religious war. Or at the least, these painful memories were recognized as an obstacle that had to be overcome in order to achieve their irenical goals. For example, Maximilian Prechtl (1757–1832), a Benedictine priest from Bavaria who had written several ecumenical treatises and histories, noted that the Reformation anniversary had aroused the piety of German Protestants, whom he called Catholics' "separated brothers."[49] Prechtl encouraged Catholics to use the occasion of the anniversary to review those tendencies that had contributed to the persistence of the confessional divide and to try to overcome them. The key to interconfessional peace was a confrontation with those painful memories of separation.[50] To this end, many German Catholics took a sympathetic view of the Reformation anniversary and became better acquainted with Luther, the Reformation, and their Protestant neighbors through the festival, according to an Evangelical historian of the 1817 anniversaries who had read widely among the festival reports, sermons, and speeches.[51] But, Prechtl argued, the celebrants must take care that the anniversary does not reawaken or strengthen old sectarian animosities.[52] Instead, he recommended that Catholics and Protestants celebrate the festival in the spirit of love. Through their irenical celebration, an anniversary that had for two centuries evoked the German confessional divide might become an anniversary of confessional reunion.[53]

The ecumenical hopes expressed by Veillodter, Clarus, Kaiser, and Prechtl were evident at anniversary festivals in Thuringia, where Reformed, Catholics, and a handful of Jews marched together in the festival processions. One chronicler of the anniversaries noted the participation of an unnamed Thuringian Jew who had marched in the procession and contributed to the festival's poor collection. The man claimed he had done so because Luther's work had benefited the Jews and the Reformation had blessed every religion.[54] Jewish participation in the Reformation anniversary festivals, although atypical, was all the more noteworthy given the anti-Semitic inflection of the Wartburg Festival and the violent anti-Semitic Hep-Hep Riots that would sweep through Germany in 1819. The German students and liberals assembled at the Wartburg Festival burned Jewish books that they deemed "anti-German" and used anti-Semitic rhetoric in their speeches. But contemporary enlightened and Reform Jews regarded Luther as a reformer who had embodied religious toleration and emancipation.[55] In fact, Luther's anti-Jewish writings were completely unknown in early nineteenth-century Germany.[56] This fact made memories of Luther and the Reformation usable to contemporary German Jews. None of the primary sources from 1817 that I have examined suggest that Jewish participants in the Reformation anniversary festivals were objects of proselytization. Instead, they were willing celebrants in those irenical commemorations of Luther and the Reformation that seemed to suggest at least a temporary dissolution of the German confessional and religious divide. By participating in these public anniversaries of the Reformation, German Jews were in fact inserting themselves squarely within the social and civic life of the German towns and cities in which they lived.

Conclusion

It is not entirely surprising that some German Catholics, Protestants, and Jews came together at the Reformation anniversaries in 1817 to participate in what Johannes Burkhardt described as a German national *Volksfest*.[57] What is truly significant is that these German Catholics, Protestants, and Jews came together to participate in a German national *Volksfest* that celebrated the memory of Martin Luther and the Reformation during an era in which the confessional divide was still ostensibly strong. Burkhardt has identified the expressions of intra-Protestant unity and examples of interconfessional participation at these festivals as instances of "enlightened urbanity," a secular, communal, and political rather than confessional celebration of the German collective memory of religion.[58] This explanation cannot be wholly discounted. The historians Lutz Winckler, Rainer Fuhrman, Max L. Baeumer, and Burkhardt himself have recognized these anniversaries and festivals as enlightened expressions of nascent German liberalism, of bourgeois class formation, as susceptible to cynical political manipulation and early forms of German civil society and secular sociability.[59] That is, the celebrants of these anniversaries secularized and politicized their memories of Luther and the Reformation.

But that is to omit as afterthought the sacred meaning these festivals and what they celebrated held for so many orthodox Lutherans and Evangelical

Christians, clergy and laity. Indeed, none of the anniversary celebrations of the Reformation were held without an accompanying religious service.[60] We should view these anniversaries and the ecclesiastical debates that accompanied them not only within narratives of secularization, politicization, or class formation. Instead they may also be understood within a narrative of revived nineteenth-century piety—a revived piety Olaf Blaschke recognized as a sign of a second confessional era. Collective memories of Luther and the Reformation were important components of this revival, as contemporaries appealed to Reformation-era symbols and memories both to strengthen orthodoxy and to encourage irenicism. Blaschke argues that this nineteenth-century revival occurred in a confessional manner: Frederick William III's compulsory union of the Reformed and Lutheran Churches in Prussia touched off fiercely confessional polemics among pro-union Evangelicals, orthodox Lutherans, and Reformed Christians.

But my evidence suggests that strands of this revival of nineteenth-century piety took on an irenical perspective. The 1817 Reformation anniversaries were sites of both intra-Protestant and interconfessional ecumenism. Motivated by popular piety rather than politics, we should not blithely dismiss these bona fide calls for Christian fraternity as mere epiphenomena of other social and cultural processes. Instead, they are corroborating evidence of the strength of nineteenth-century piety and the enduring importance of memories of Luther and the Reformation.

Gottfried Maron has argued that Luther's place in church history belongs between the confessions and between the Middles Ages and modernity.[61] Confessionalization occurred shortly after Luther's death—but not during his lifetime. Thus we may recognize Luther as a pre-confessional figure who saw his church as a unity—not a Roman, nor Nuremberger, nor Wittenberger Church, but a Christian Church to which all belonged, albeit deeply split.[62] Perhaps this accounts for why German Catholics, Reformed, and Lutherans could all participate in a festival that celebrated the memory of Martin Luther and the Reformation. But an irenical memory of the reformer could only be invoked if memories that evoked sectarianism and confessional strife were overcome. Never strictly suppressed nor forgotten, the painful memories of a violent, sectarian confessional history were shadows cast by the idealized pasts that irenical Christians used to imagine a unified Christian community in the nineteenth-century present.

To be sure, Franz Schnabel argued that every era has had a dispute over the "authentic" Luther. And in fact, no era has known a unified, coherent image of Luther.[63] E. W. Zeeden has deftly noted the varying interpretations of Luther by lay and clerical factions since the Reformation.[64] But it may be more appropriate to say that every group in every era has its own Luther. This was surely true of the irenical and orthodox Lutherans, Reformed Christians,

Evangelicals, and irenical Catholics who invoked wildly divergent memories of Luther and the Reformation to remake the meaning of the 1817 Reformation anniversaries and to negotiate the possibilities and peril of intra-Protestant and interconfessional German unity.

Stan M. Landry earned a PhD in European cultural history at the University of Arizona in May 2010. His primary research explores how the religious divide between Catholics, Protestants, and Jews inflected the histories of the German-speaking lands, with a special focus on those sites at which religion, theology, and political culture intersected. In particular, he is interested in the "presence" of the Reformation in the modern world through memory, historical consciousness, and commemoration. He has published in *Church History*, the *Journal of Religion and Society*, and the *Lutheran Quarterly*. His book, *Ecumenism, Memory, and German Nationalism, 1817–1917*, was published in 2013. He currently serves as a lecturer in history at Arizona State University.

Notes

Portions of this chapter previously appeared in Stan M. Landry, *Ecumenism, Memory, and German Nationalism, 1817–1917* (Syracuse University Press, 2013). Used with permission.

1. For historical and theoretical examinations of anniversaries, holidays, and festivals in a specifically German context, see Dieter Düding, Peter Friedemann, and Paul Münch, ed., *Öffentliche Festkultur: Politische Feste in Deutschland von der Aufklärung bis zum Ersten Weltkrieg* (Hamburg, 1988); and Emil Brix and Hannes Stekl, ed., *Der Kampf um das Gedächtnis: Öffentliche Gedenktage in Mitteleuropa* (Vienna, 1997). My use of the terms cultural and collective memory is informed by Jan Assmann, "Collective Memory and Cultural Identity," trans. John Czaplicka, *New German Critique* 65 (1995): 125–33.

2. Gérald Chaix, "Die Reformation," trans. Reinhard Tiffert, in *Deutsche Erinnerungsorte*, ed. Etienne François and Hagen Schluze, 3 vols. (Munich, 2001–2), vol. 2, 9–27.

3. Etienne François, *Die unsichtbare Grenze: Protestanten und Katholiken in Augsburg, 1648–1806*, trans. Angelika Steiner-Wendt (Sigmaringen, 1991).

4. See Olaf Blaschke, "Das 19. Jahrhundert: Ein Zweites Konfessionelles Zeitalter?," *Geschichte und Gesellschaft* 26 (2000): 38–75; and Olaf Blaschke, ed., *Konfessionen im Konflikt. Deutschland zwischen 1800 und 1970: Ein zweites konfessionelles Zeitalter* (Göttingen, 2002). For a critique of Blaschke's thesis, see Anthony J. Steinhoff, "Ein zweites konfessionelles Zeitalter? Nachdenken über die Religion im langen 19. Jahrhundert," *Geschichte und Gesellschaft* 30 (2004): 549–70.

5. Ernst Walter Zeeden, *The Legacy of Luther: Martin Luther and the Reformation in the Estimation of the German Lutherans from Luther's Death to the Beginning of the Age of Goethe*, trans. Ruth Mary Bethell (London, 1954), 36.

6. Friedrich Loofs, "Die Jahrhundertfeier der Reformation an den Universitäten Wittenberg und Halle, 1617, 1717, und 1817," *Zeitschrift des Vereins für Kirchengeschichte in der Provinz Sachsen* 14 (1917): 66–67.

7. Loof, "Die Jahrhundertfeier," 55–56. Despite the confessional nature of these particular anniversaries, David M. Luebke has identified "pockets" of multiconfessionalism in the early modern German lands. See David M. Luebke, "A Multiconfessional Empire," in *A Companion to Multiconfessionalism in the Early Modern World*, ed. Thomas Max Safley (Leiden, 2011), 129–54.

8. For a discussion of Luther's own reconstruction of memories surrounding this event already in 1520, see chapter 10 in this volume.

9. For the "political Protestantism" of the Wartburg Festival, see D. G. Kieser, *Das Wartburgfest am 18. October 1817: In seiner Entstehung, Ausführung und Folgen* (Jena, 1818); and Lutz Winckler, *Martin Luther als Bürger und Patriot: Das Reformationsjubiläum von 1817 und der politische Protestantismus des Wartburgfestes* (Lübeck, 1969).

10. Nigel Aston, *Christianity and Revolutionary Europe, c. 1750–1830* (Cambridge, 2002), 11–12, 18–20; and Rudolf Vierhaus, *Germany in the Age of Absolutism*, trans. Jonathan B. Knudsen (Cambridge, 1988), 63–64.

11. Aston, *Christianity and Revolutionary Europe*, 12, 19.

12. Aston, *Christianity and Revolutionary Europe*, 198, 207.

13. Susan Crane, "Holy Alliances: Creating Religious Communities after the Napoleonic Wars," in *Die Gegenwart Gottes in der modernen Gesellschaft: Transzendenz und Religiöse Vergemeinschaftung in Deutschland*, ed. Michael Geyer and Lucian Hölscher (Göttingen, 2006), 37–59. On von Baader's parallel but not necessarily contradictory anti-Protestantism, see Richard Schaefer's contribution in this volume.

14. Jacob Gottlieb Planck, *Über die Trennung und Wiedervereinigung der getrennten christlichen Haupt-Partheyen* (Tübingen, 1803).

15. Friedrich Samuel Gottfried Sack, *Ueber die Vereinigung der beiden protestantischen Kirchenparteien in der Preußischen Monarchie* (Berlin, 1812).

16. Lucian Hölscher, "The Religious Divide: Piety in Nineteenth-Century Germany," in *Protestants, Catholics, and Jews in Germany, 1800–1914*, ed. Helmut Walser Smith (Oxford, 2001), 42.

17. Lucian Hölscher, *Geschichte der protestantischen Frömmigkeit in Deutschland* (Munich, 2005), 211.

18. Walter H. Conser, Jr., *Church and Confession: Conservative Theologians in Germany, England, and America, 1815–1866* (Macon, GA, 1984), 16–17.

19. "Kabinettsordre Friedrich Wilhelm III. vom 27 September 1817," in *Urkundenbuch der Evangelischen Union mit Erläuterungen*, ed. Carl Immanuel Nitzsch (Bonn, 1853), 125.

20. Nicholas Hope, *German and Scandinavian Protestantism 1700 to 1918* (Oxford, 1995), 442.

21. K. R. Hagenbach, *History of the Church in the Eighteenth and Nineteenth Centuries*, trans. John F. Hurst (New York, 1869), 347.

22. Claus Harms, *Briefe zu einer nähern Verstandigung über verschiedene meine Theses betreffende Puncte. Nebst Einem namhaften Briefe, an den Herrn Dr. Schleiermacher* (Kiel, 1818), 8.

23. Harms, *Briefe*, 32.

24. Harms, *Briefe*, 31.

25. "Official Declaration of the Synod of Berlin Concerning the Celebration of Holy Communion Which It Will Hold on 30 October 1817," in *Friedrich Schleiermacher on Creeds, Confessions, and Church Union: That They May Be One*, ed. Iain G. Nicol (Lewiston, NY, 2004), 20.

26. Friedrich Schleiermacher, "Address Celebrating the Third Centennial of the Reformation of the Church by Luther at the University of Berlin held on 3 November 1817," in *Reformed but Ever Reforming: Sermons in Relation to the Celebration of the Handing over of the Augsburg Confession (1830)*, ed. Iain G. Nicol (Lewiston, NY, 1997), 45.

27. Klaus Wappler, "Reformationsjubiläum und Kirchenunion (1817)," in *Die Geschichte der Evangelischen Kirche der Union*, ed. J. F. Gerhard Goeters and Rudolf Mau, 3 vols. (Leipzig, 1992), vol. 1, 112–13.

28. "Kabinettsordre Friedrich Wilhelm III. vom 27 September 1817," in Nitzsch, *Urkundenbuch*, 125.

29. Hagenbach, *History of the Church*, 350.

30. "Kabinettsordre Friedrich Wilhelm III. vom 27 September 1817," in Nitzsch, *Urkundenbuch*, 125–26.

31. Christian Schreiber, Valentin Karl Veillodter, and William Hennings, ed., *Allgemeine Chronik der dritten Jubel-Feier der deutschen evangelischen Kirche. Im Jahre 1817*, 2 vols. (Erfurt, 1819), vol. 1, 35.

32. Christopher Clark, "Confessional Policy and the Limits of State Action: Frederick William III and the Prussian Church Union 1817–1840," *Historical Journal* 39 (1996): 986.

33. Gerhard Friederich, ed., *Chronik der dritten Jubelfeier der Reformation in Frankfurt am Main* (Frankfurt am Main, 1817), 5.

34. "Die Lokalunion in Bergzabern, 2 Dezember 1817," in *Kirchenunionen im 19. Jahrhundert*, ed. Gerhard Ruhbach (Guterslöh, 1967), 45.

35. Valentin Karl Veillodter, *Zwei Predigten am dritten Säkularfeste der Reformation im Jahre 1817* (Nuremberg, 1817), 8.

36. Veillodter, *Zwei Predigten*, 24.

37. Veillodter, *Zwei Predigten*, 7–8.

38. E. A. Clarus, *Erinnerung an die dritte Säcularfeier des Reformationsfestes in der evangelischen Stadtkirche zu Bamberg* (Bamberg, 1817), 11.

39. Clarus, *Erinnerung*, 15.

40. Clarus, *Erinnerung*, 27.

41. Clarus, *Erinnerung*, 26–28.

42. Gottlieb Philipp Christian Kaiser, "Zwei Predigten am Reformations-Jubelfeste 1817 in der Stadtkirche der evangelisch, lutherischen Neustadt zu Erlangen," in Schreiber et al., *Allgemeine Chronik*, vol. 2, 108, 112.

43. Kaiser, "Zwei Predigten," 109.

44. Clarus, *Erinnerung*, 5–6.

45. Clarus, *Erinnerung*, 36.

46. Clarus, *Erinnerung*, 51, 60–66.

47. Clarus, *Erinnerung*, 66.

48. Clarus, *Erinnerung*, 84.

49. Maximilian Prechtl, *Seitenstück zur Weisheit Dr. Martin Luthers zum Jubeljahre der Lutherischen Reformation* (Sulzbach, 1817), iii. See also Maximilian Prechtl, *Friedens-Benehmen zwischen Boussuet, Leibniz und Molanus* (Sulzbach, 1815); and *Friedensworte an die katholische und protestantische Kirche für ihre Wiedervereinigung* (Sulzbach, 1820).

50. Prechtl, *Seitenstück*, vii–viii.

51. Georg Arndt, *Das Reformationsjubelfest in vergangenen Jahrhunderten* (Berlin, 1917), 28–29.

52. Prechtl, *Seitenstück*, x.

53. Prechtl, *Seitenstück*, xvi.
54. Arndt, *Das Reformationsjubelfest*, 29.
55. Christian Wiese, "Überwinder des Mittelalters? Ahnherr des Nationasozialismus? Zur Vielstimmigkeit und Tragik der jüdischen Lutherrezeption im wilhelmischen Deutschland und in der Weimarer Republik," in *Lutherinszenierung und Reformationserinnerung*, ed. Stefan Laube and Karl-Heinz Fix (Leipzig, 2002), 169–71.
56. Johannes Wallmann, "The Reception of Luther's Writings on the Jews from the Reformation to the End of the 19th Century," *Lutheran Quarterly* 1 (1987): 86–87.
57. Johannes Burkhardt, "Reformations- und Lutherfeiern: Die Verbürgerlichung der reformatorischen Jubiläumskultur," in *Öffentliche Festkultur: Politische Feste in Deutschland von der Aufklärung bis zum Ersten Weltkrieg*, ed. Dieter Düding, Peter Friedemann, and Paul Münch (Hamburg, 1988), 222.
58. Ibid.
59. See Winckler, *Martin Luther als Bürger und Patriot*; Rainer Fuhrman, "Das Reformationsjubiläum 1817: Martin Luther und die Reformation im Urteil der protestantischen Festpredigt des Jahres 1817" (PhD diss., Eberhard Karls University of Tübingen, 1973); and Max L. Baeumer, "Lutherfeiern und ihre politische Manipulation," in *Deutsche Feiern*, ed. Reinhold Grimm and Jost Hermand (Wiesbaden, 1977), 46–61.
60. Michael Mitterauer, "Anniversarium und Jubiläum: Zur Entstehung und Entwicklung öffentlicher Gedenktage," in Brix and Stekl, *Der Kampf um das Gedächtnis*, 82.
61. Gottfried Maron, "Luther zwischen den Konfessionen: Die ökumenische Bedeutung Martin Luthers," in *Luthers bleibende Bedeutung*, ed. Jürgen Becker (Husum, 1983), 121.
62. Maron, "Luther zwischen den Konfessionen," 122.
63. Franz Schnabel, *Deutschlands geschichtliche Quellen und Darstellungen in der Neuzeit: Das Zeitalter der Reformation 1500–1550* (Leipzig, 1931), 285.
64. Zeeden, *The Legacy of Luther*.

Bibliography

Arndt, Georg. *Das Reformationsjubelfest in vergangenen Jahrhunderten*. Berlin, 1917.
Assmann, Jan. "Collective Memory and Cultural Identity." *New German Critique* 65 (1995): 124–33.
Aston, Nigel. *Christianity and Revolutionary Europe c. 1750–1830*. Cambridge, 2002.
Baeumer, Max L. "Lutherfeiern und ihre politische Manipulation." In *Deutsche Feiern*, edited by Reinhold Grimm and Jost Hermand, 46–61. Wiesbaden, 1977.
Blaschke, Olaf. *Katholizismus und Antisemitismus im Deutschen Kaiserreich*. Göttingen, 1997.
———. "Das 19. Jahrhundert: Ein Zweites Konfessionelles Zeitalter?" *Geschichte und Gesellschaft* 26 (2000): 38–75.
Brix, Emil, and Hannes Stekl, ed. *Der Kampf um das Gedächtnis: Öffentliche Gedenktage in Mitteleuropa*. Vienna, 1997.
Burkhardt, Johannes. "Reformations- und Lutherfeiern: Die Verbürgerlichung der reformatorischen Jubiläumskultur." In *Öffentliche Festkultur: Politische Feste in Deutschland von der Aufklärung bis zum Ersten Weltkrieg*, edited by Dieter Düding, Peter Friedemann, and Paul Münch, 212–36. Hamburg: 1988.

Chaix, Gérald. "Die Reformation." In *Deutsche Erinnerungsorte*, edited by Etienne François and Hagen Schluze, vol. 2, 9–27. Munich, 2001.

Clark, Christopher. "Confessional Policy and the Limits of State Action: Frederick William III and the Prussian Church Union 1817–1840." *Historical Journal* 39 (1996): 985–1004.

Clarus, E. A. *Erinnerung an die dritte Säcularfeier des Reformationsfestes in der evangelischen Stadtkirche zu Bamberg*. Bamberg, 1817.

Conser, Walter H., Jr. *Church and Confession: Conservative Theologians in Germany, England, and America, 1815–1866*. Macon, GA, 1984.

Crane, Susan. "Holy Alliances: Creating Religious Communities after the Napoleonic Wars." In *Die Gegenwart Gottes in der modernen Gesellschaft: Transzendenz und Religiöse Vergemeinschaftung in Deutschland*, edited by Michael Geyer and Lucian Hölscher, 37–59. Göttingen: 2006.

Düding, Dieter, Peter Friedemann, and Paul Münch, ed. *Öffentliche Festkultur: Politische Feste in Deutschland von der Aufklärung bis zum Ersten Weltkrieg*. Hamburg, 1988.

François, Etienne. *Die unsichtbare Grenze: Protestanten und Katholiken in Augsburg 1648–1806*. Sigmaringen, 1991.

François, Etienne, and Hagen Schulze, ed. *Deutsche Erinnerungsorte*. 3 vols. Munich, 2001–2.

Friederich, Gerhard, ed. *Chronik der dritten Jubelfeier der Reformation in Frankfurt am Main*. Frankfurt am Main, 1817.

Fuhrman, Rainer. "Das Reformationsjubiläum 1817: Martin Luther und die Reformation im Urteil der protestantischen Festpredigt des Jahres 1817." PhD diss., Eberhard Karls University of Tübingen, 1973.

Hagenbach, K. R. *History of the Church in the Eighteenth and Nineteenth Centuries*. Translated by John F. Hurst. New York, 1869.

Harms, Claus. *Briefe zu einer nähern Verstandigung über verschiedene meine Theses betreffende Puncte. Nebst Einem namhaften Briefe, an den Herrn Dr. Schleiermacher*. Kiel, 1818.

Hölscher, Lucian. *Geschichte der protestantischen Frömmigkeit in Deutschland*. Munich, 2005.

———. "The Religious Divide: Piety in Nineteenth-Century Germany." In *Protestants, Catholics, and Jews in Germany, 1800–1914*, edited by Helmut Walser Smith, 33–47. Oxford, 2001.

Hope, Nicholas. *German and Scandinavian Protestantism 1700 to 1918*. Oxford, 1995.

Kieser, Georg D., ed. *Das Warburgfest am 18. October 1817: In seiner Entstehung, Ausführung und Folgen. Nach Actenstücken und Augenzeugnissen*. Jena, 1818.

Loofs, Friedrich. "Die Jahrhundertfeier der Reformation an den Universitäten Wittenberg und Halle, 1617, 1717, und 1817." *Zeitschrift des Vereins für Kirchengeschichte in der Provinz Sachsen* 14 (1917): 1–68.

Luebke, David M. "A Multiconfessional Empire." In *A Companion to Multiconfessionalism in the Early Modern World*, edited by Thomas Max Safley, 129–54. Leiden, 2011.

Maron, Gottfried. "Luther zwischen den Konfessionen: Die ökumenische Bedeutung Martin Luthers." In *Luthers bleibende Bedeutung*, edited by Jürgen Becker, 117–26. Husum, 1983.

Nitzsch, Carl Immanuel, ed. *Urkundenbuch der Evangelischen Union mit Erläuterungen.* Bonn, 1853.

Planck, Jacob Gottlieb. *Über die Trennung und Wiedervereinigung der getrennten christlichen Haupt-Partheyen.* Tübingen, 1803.

Prechtl, Maximilian. *Friedens-Benehmen zwischen Boussuet, Leibniz und Molanus.* Sulzbach, 1815.

———. *Friedensworte an die katholische und protestantische Kirche für ihre Wiedervereinigung.* Sulzbach, 1820.

———. *Seitenstück zur Weisheit Dr. Martin Luthers zum Jubeljahre der Lutherischen Reformation.* Sulzbach, 1817.

Ruhbach, Gerhard, ed. *Kirchenunionen im 19. Jahrhundert.* Guterslöh, 1967.

Sack, Friedrich Samuel Gottfried. *Ueber die Vereinigung der beiden protestantischen Kirchenparteien in der Preußischen Monarchie.* Berlin, 1812.

Scheliermacher, Friedrich. *Friedrich Schleiermacher on Creeds, Confessions, and Church Union: That They May be One.* Edited by Iain G. Nicol. Lewiston, NY, 2004.

———. *Reformed but Ever Reforming: Sermons in Relation to the Celebration of the Handing over of the Augsburg Confession (1830).* Edited by Iain G. Nicol. Lewiston, NY, 1997.

Schnabel, Franz. *Deutschlands geschichtliche Quellen und Darstellungen in der Neuzeit: Das Zeitalter der Reformation 1500–1550.* Leipzig, 1931.

Schreiber, Christian, Valentin Karl Veillodter, and William Hennings, ed. *Allgemeine Chronik der dritten Jubel-Feier der deutschen evangelischen Kirche. Im Jahre 1817.* 2 vols. Erfurt, 1819.

Steinhoff, Anthony J. "Ein zweites konfessionelles Zeitalter? Nachdenken über die Religion im langen 19. Jahrhundert." *Geschichte und Gesellschaft* 30 (2004): 549–70.

Veillodter, Valentin Karl. *Zwei Predigten am dritten Säkularfeste der Reformation im Jahre 1817.* Nuremberg, 1817.

Vierhaus, Rudolf. *Germany in the Age of Absolutism.* Translated by Jonathan B. Knudsen. Cambridge, 1988.

Wallmann, Johannes. "The Reception of Luther's Writings on the Jews from the Reformation to the End of the 19th Century." *Lutheran Quarterly* 1 (1987): 72–97.

Wappler, Klaus. "Reformationsjubiläum und Kirchenunion (1817)." In *Die Geschichte der Evangelischen Kirche der Union*, edited by J. F. G. Goeters and Rudolf Mau, vol. 3, 112–13. Leipzig, 1992.

Wiese, Christian. "Überwinder des Mittelalters? Ahnherr des Nationasozialismus? Zur Vielstimmigkeit und Tragik der jüdischen Lutherrezeption im wilhelmischen Deutschland und in der Weimarer Republik." In *Lutherinszenierung und Reformationserinnerung*, edited by Stefan Laube and Karl-Heinz Fix, 169–71. Leipzig, 2002.

Winckler, Lutz. *Martin Luther als Bürger und Patriot: Das Reformationsjubiläum von 1817 und der politische Protestantismus des Wartburgfestes.* Lübeck, 1969.

Zeeden, Ernst Walter. *The Legacy of Luther: Martin Luther and the Reformation in the Estimation of the German Lutherans from Luther's Death to the Beginning of the Age of Goethe.* Translated by Ruth Mary Bethell. London, 1954.

CHAPTER THREE

Challenging Plurality
Wilhelm Horning and the Histories
of Alsatian Lutheranism

ANTHONY J. STEINHOFF

In the mid-1890s, the Lutheran minister at Strasbourg's Young St. Peter's Church, Wilhelm Horning, published a parish guidebook destined for the members of his personal congregation. This brief publication was quite typical of the times. It provided practical information about the congregation—worship times, policies for sacraments and church rites, names of parish organizations, and so on—that new parishioners, most to Strasbourg itself, would need. As such, it was a direct response to the challenges that late nineteenth-century urbanization posed to urban religious practice and ecclesiastical organization.[1] The guidebook's opening section, "The Confessional Character of the Congregation: A Short History of the Augsburg Confession in Alsace-Lorraine, to Which This Congregation Belongs," was rather atypical. It briefly sketches the accomplishments of the men who established and promoted Lutheran orthodoxy in early modern Strasbourg, a tradition that Horning's father, Friedrich, promoted in the nineteenth century as the sole legitimate version of Lutheranism in Strasbourg and Alsace. This congregation, Wilhelm Horning observed, was the fruit of his father's labors, and he felt privileged to lead it "along the same lines of fidelity to biblical and Lutheran ecclesiastical principles."[2]

Wilhelm Horning's recourse to the history of the Reformation and immediate post-Reformation periods was far from unusual. Throughout the nineteenth century, the events of what Wolfgang Reinhard and Heinz Schilling have described as the "confessional age" figured prominently in efforts to define and shape public identities in German-speaking Europe.[3] Although Leopold von Ranke's *History of Germany in the Reformation Era* tended to promote a neutral reading of that past, the prevailing tendency was to view it from a partisan, confessional perspective.[4] Whereas the 1817 Wartburg Festival famously stressed Martin Luther's and the Protestant Reformation's fundamental contributions to the German national cause, the Catholic jurist Carl Ludwig von Haller decried the Reformation as the "harbinger of the period's baleful political revolutions."[5] Later in the century, liberal, middle-class German nationalists parsed the wars of unification as a "second" Thirty Years' War pitting Protestant Prussia against Catholic Austria and then Catholic France, which culminated with the successful creation of a new "Protestant" German Empire (*Kaiserreich*).[6] German Catholics, to be certain, resisted this confessionalization of national identities, particularly the attacks on political Catholicism during the 1870s that came to be known as the Kulturkampf (culture war). Groups on the political right, from the Protestant League to the Pan-German League, tirelessly defended their vision of a fundamentally Protestant nature of the *Kaiserreich*, so that Catholics were at best Germans second class.[7]

The recourse to memories of the confessional past featured prominently in faith communities' own efforts to reestablish themselves after the French Revolution and the Napoleonic Wars and then maintain cultural and social relevance for themselves in the face of the challenges posed by European modernity. In part it is precisely this reinvigoration of inter- and intra-confessional religious and ecclesiastical rivalries to which Olaf Blaschke called attention in proposing that the post-Napoleonic decades ushered in a "second confessional age."[8] Nineteenth-century confessionalization differed in one key respect from its early modern antecedents among Protestants. After 1815, the sixteenth and seventeenth centuries became a point of contestation, as nineteenth-century Protestants disagreed over what to remember, what to forget, and how to do both.

This essay explores the role that confessional history writing played in these struggles to remember and forget the first confessional age. It focuses on the historical turn within orthodox ("confessional") Lutheranism in late nineteenth-century Alsace, a turn closely tied to the literary activities of Wilhelm Horning. His engagement with the Lutheran past, especially that of early modern Strasbourg, responded to a particular church-political imperative: his need to defend the "true" Lutheran tradition from its present-day detractors—liberal Protestantism and "Unionist-Pietism." Uncovering and writing about the confessional Lutheran past both helped to validate his theological positions and legitimate his polemical tactics. Horning's efforts to promote a pluralistic history of the Reformation by recovering the forgotten orthodox past was decidedly non-pluralist in intent, for the grand objective was returning the Alsatian Lutheran church to a rigidly orthodox orientation.

Confessional Memories and Protestantism
in Post-Napoleonic Alsace

Napoleon Bonaparte's efforts to end the chaos and dissent of the French Revolution's controversial religious and ecclesiastical policies ushered in a new era for Alsatian Protestants. In 1802, he restored the right of public worship to Catholics, Reformed Protestants, and Lutherans (the *cultes reconnus*).[9] The legislation through which this was accomplished—the Concordat and a set of laws called the "Organic Articles," both promulgated on 8 April 1802— confirmed the revolutionary heritage by granting these three communities' members full equality under the law.[10] With respect to Alsace, this effectively replaced the early modern system of limited tolerance of Protestantism (owing to clauses in the Peace of Westphalia and Strasbourg's 1681 capitulation agreement) with an arrangement that had much in common with the *paritätische* arrangements (principle of confessional parity) that emerged after 1815 in the German Confederation's pluriconfessional states.[11] While Alsatian Protestants lauded these new terms of confessional coexistence, the majority Catholics (on both sides of the Vosges mountains) resisted. Their efforts to challenge Protestants' civil and religious rights, first during the Bourbon Restoration (1814–30) and then during the Second Empire (1852–70), helped animate and sustain interconfessional rivalries in Alsace deep into the nineteenth century.[12]

The Organic Articles did not just recognize the three French churches and place them under similar regimes of state control and surveillance. They also instituted new ecclesiastical structures for the two Protestant churches. For the Reformed community, a decentralized system of local consistories was established, thereby preventing a potentially dangerous concentration of Huguenot influence in Paris.[13] West of the Vosges, this departure from Huguenot tradition was roundly decried.[14] Alsatians welcomed this new system because it allowed the historically distinct (and relatively small) Reformed communities in Bischweiler, Markirch, Mulhouse, and Strasbourg to maintain their autonomy.[15] By contrast, the Organic Articles established a centralized, hierarchical Lutheran Church structure, largely because the Lutheran population was smaller and concentrated in eastern France. In effect, the Organic Articles transformed the multitude of former territorial Lutheran churches into a single organization, with the official seat in Strasbourg. Located there were both the new organs of church government (president, executive Directory, and General Consistory) and the state-sponsored Faculty of Protestant Theology.[16]

In certain respects, France's new Lutheran Church found itself in a position similar to that of its German counterparts after 1814. On the one hand, it had to create and implement policies to promote the integration of previously distinct communities into the new, ecclesiastical whole.[17] On the other hand, it faced the challenge of rebuilding religious communities and encouraging piety following the disruptions caused by the French Revolution and war. Political and theological factors pushed Alsatian Lutheranism in a distinct direction after the Congress of Vienna. First, there were no efforts in France to create united Protestant churches as occurred in Prussia, the Bavarian Palatinate, and Baden.[18] This reflected the lack of significant overlap in the geographic concentrations of the two religious communities in France. As in Hannover and Bavarian Franconia, such church union offered few practical benefits. More importantly, the staunchly pro-Catholic Bourbon monarchs had no interest in intervening in the Protestant churches' internal affairs, much less encouraging structural changes that might strengthen the Protestant position within France.

This hands-off approach to Protestantism in France helps to explain the other major peculiarity of French Lutheranism's evolution in the nineteenth century: the ongoing vitality of religious rationalism and the delayed appearance of revivalist tendencies. Briefly put, the individuals primarily responsible for restoring Lutheranism in Alsace after 1802, notably the pastors Isaak Haffner and Johann Lorenz Blessig of Strasbourg and the jurists Christoph Wilhelm Koch and Philipp Frederick Kern, were all committed rationalists. They held influential positions in the new church government, in local parish life (especially in Strasbourg), and in the case of Bessig and Haffner, at Strasbourg's theological faculty.[19] Consistent with their rationalist perspective, they decided against creating a new church ordinance (*Kirchenordnung*) for the new "Church of the Confession of Augsburg" (as the Organic Articles designated it). This meant that not only were the pastors and theology professors not required to subscribe to the Augustana, but also no official church liturgy or hymnbook was designated for the church. Pastors were thus free to organize their liturgies according to their own theological proclivities and conscience. This tack made any subsequent efforts to establish an official creed, liturgy, or hymnal difficult, for the Organic Articles made that contingent on state approval. Once more, the French government's outlook on Protestantism effectively precluded that such approval ever be granted.[20]

The French policy of benign neglect of Lutheran affairs also played a major role in rationalism's survival in Alsace during the age of political reaction. Whereas Protestant rulers east of the Rhine (notably King Frederick William III of Prussia) and jurists used ecclesiastical privileges to promote more conservative political and theological positions in the Protestant churches, in Alsace local figures wielded considerable influence over major appointments in the Lutheran church hierarchy and the theological faculty.[21] Liberal-rationalist tendencies thus permeated Lutheran institutional structures and cultures, substantially impeding significant theological or doctrinal realignments. Rationalism also continued on in Alsace because of a weakening of traditional theological links between Alsace and German Europe. Whereas Friedrich Schleiermacher's teaching progressively annihilated the "shallow rationalism which preceded it" throughout German Europe during the nineteenth century's early decade, the Berlin professor exerted little influence west of the Rhine.[22] After 1815, the Alsatian Charles Théodore Gérold observed, Alsatian theologians took only minor interest in German academic developments. Consequently, although a new generation of scholars at Strasbourg's theological seminar were aware of "Schleiermacher's mysticism," they remained cool to it.[23]

Challenges to Lutheran rationalism, though, did emerge. The first came from Franz Haerter, a Lutheran minister at Strasbourg's New Church. Appointed to the parish in 1829, he stunned his bourgeois congregation in 1831 by announcing that he had been converted to Christ. He devoted the rest of his life to furthering the cause of the Pietist awakening, urging the faithful to repent and to devote their hearts to the crucified Christ. Haerter's movement attracted a considerable following in rural and urban Alsace, but Lutheran Church officials remained critical. They were displeased by Pietism's embrace of the symbolic confessions, even if Haerter himself remained largely indifferent to doctrinal matters. Church authorities were bothered by Pietism's disregard of extant ecclesiastical structures. In addition to organizing his charitable activities and missionary associations outside of parish units, Haerter reached out to Lutheran and Reformed Protestants, causing some clerics to accuse him of haboring "unionist" tendencies.[24]

Then came Friedrich Theodor Horning, who emerged as a militant advocate of orthodox Lutheranism after his installation at Strasbourg's Young St. Peter's Church in 1846. Inspired, ironically, by the Calvinist revival he had encountered previously in Geneva, Horning became persuaded that the French Lutheran Church needed to return to its roots. In his ministry, he followed the Strasbourg Church Ordinance of 1598's liturgical and ritual prescriptions. He contended that only the orthodox Lutheran line was valid for the Church of the Augsburg Confession, a position that proved disruptive. When Haerter and his followers refused to endorse this exclusivist stance, Horning parted ways with them and encouraged his own supporters to found a series of properly "Evangelical-Lutheran" associations and, in time, publications.[25] Horning likewise snubbed his liberal peers. He refused to collaborate with his Strasbourg colleagues and withdrew from the Alsatian Pastoral Conference. He admonished the Directory and the French government to grant the Augustana authoritative status within the church and appoint only orthodox

Lutheran professors to the seminary and the theological faculty. During the 1860s, he even encouraged orthodox Lutherans in rural parishes to boycott the appointment of liberal pastors to their parishes by seeking ministerial care from an orthodox pastor at another parish.[26]

Precisely at this moment of renewed intraconfessional tension did the first new histories of the Reformation and post-Reformation periods in Alsace begin to appear. It is tempting to view this as pure coincidence, since Timotheus Wilhelm Roehrich's pioneering two-volume study was published just as Haerter was committing himself to the Pietist awakening.[27] Nonetheless, given its tone and approach we can still regard Roehrich's monograph as the rationalist-liberal opening move in its use of history to reinforce the theological-ecclesiastical status quo.[28] In part, Roehrich identifies the "Bucerian moment" as the Strasbourg Reformation's high point. That is, he idealized its relatively tolerant, cosmopolitan phase, when matters of doctrine and ritual positions were still fairly fluid. Accordingly, he casts the subsequent period of orthodox Lutheran ascendency as a move away from the "true" Strasbourg Reformation. Moreover, later works by liberals, notably those written during the 1850s and 1860s, when intra-Protestant squabbling in Alsace reached fever pitch, largely filled in and developed the picture Roehrich had drawn. This is particularly evident in Charles Schmidt's study of Jean Sturm, the first director of Strasbourg's *Gymnasium*, and in Johann Wilhelm Baum's monograph on Bucer and his comrade in Reformation, Wolfgang Capito.[29]

Prior to 1870, rationalist and liberal theologians enjoyed an effective monopoly on the Reformation period's narrative, largely because the revivalists privileged practical theology over scholarly publication.[30] They preached, ministered to their congregations, and produced popular catechisms, devotional tracts, and sermons for publication. Between 1868 and 1870, Horning edited the short-lived weekly *Church Paper for Christians of the Augsburg Confession*, but he used the paper primarily as a means to revive Lutheran orthodoxy, not to document it.[31] Thus, prior to the Franco-Prussian War neither the Pietists nor the orthodox Lutherans had written anything that might contest the histories of the Reformation era proffered by rationalist and liberal scholars.

The Historical Turn in Alsace's Orthodox Lutheran Movement

The passage of Alsace from France to the new German Empire in 1871 hardly altered the region's Protestant churches' legal status or organization. Still, the transition to German rule marked an important turning point in Alsatian Lutheranism.[32] The immigration of many German Protestants into the region after August 1870 bolstered the physical presence of Protantism in the imperial territory (*Reichsland*) of Alsace-Lorraine. The University of Strasbourg's reorganization in 1872 resulted in German theologians being called to the theological faculty, eventually outnumbering the native Alsatians there.[33] That the *Reichsland's* new rulers tended to be Protestants meant that they were less deferential in their exercise of the state's prerogatives vis-à-vis the Protestant churches. From 1871 to 1913, German civil servants were named "governmental commissioner" in the Directory, a tack that aimed to balance out the Alsatian Lutheran Church's overly liberal proclivities.[34] The new administration's support of more conservative church policies failed to satisfy orthodox Lutherans who still clamored—in vain—for the introduction of a decidedly confessional Lutheran regime. Finally, the 1870s was a period of generational transition in the church, affecting liberals, Pietists, and orthodox Lutherans alike. This transition had important consequences for the historical study of Alsatian Protestantism because, unlike his father, William Horning—the new face of orthodox Lutheranism—was convinced that the battle on behalf of orthodox Lutheranism now required challenging liberals' representation of early modern Alsatian Protestantism.

Born in 1843, Wilhelm Horning spent his formative years preparing to follow in his father's footsteps. He took his bachelor of theology degree at Strasbourg in 1864, submitting a thesis that foreshadowed his historical passions: "Holy Ministry: A Dogmatic, Historical, and Critical Review." Ordained a Lutheran minister in 1866, he served as his father's assistant at Young St. Peter's Church, continuing to do so unofficially even after his appointment as Strasbourg's municipal prisons chaplain on the eve of the Franco-Prussian War.[35] In the 1870s, William began to earn a reputation as a polemicist, writing against the liberal church establishment and against the Pietists' "unionist-Methodism."[36] A regular contributor to the orthodox Lutheran weekly, the "Evangelical-Lutheran Messenger of Peace from Alsace-Lorraine," he published the first "Christian Calendar" (1879) for Alsace's confessional Lutherans, having determined that the popular "Good News" Calendar was too "unionistic" and "insufficiently serious."[37] In 1882, Wilhelm succeeded his father at Young St. Peter's, where he continued the fight on behalf of orthodox Lutheranism in Alsace. As a confessional alternative to the Pietist Inner Mission Society and the "insufficiently confessional" Gustav-Adolf Society, he helped found the "Evangelical Lutheran Society for Internal and External Missions in Alsace and Lorraine" in 1883, which aimed to defend Lutheran orthodoxy in rural Alsace. At the turn of the century, he railed against the new hymnal developed by the Alsatian Pastoral Conference and continued to criticize the theological faculty's professors' doctrinal shortcomings.[38] Even after his retirement in 1908, he remained active in church politics, spearheading the confessional Lutheran opposition to the project for Lutheran Church reform between 1908 and 1914.[39]

Although Wilhelm Horning generally held true to his father's ministerial programs, his emergence as a devoted, prodigious church historian represents a significant departure. From the mid-1870s to his death in 1927, he published some eighty-four works, including short pamphlets, journal articles, editions of historical sources, and full-length, scholarly monographs. Horning viewed this activity as intimately connected with the needs of orthodox Lutheranism in Alsace, as is evident from the choice of subject matter. Half of the titles dealt with Lutheran Church history in the sixteenth and seventeenth centuries, while another third chronicled confessional Lutheranism's history in nineteenth-century Alsace. Even the remaining texts, mainly devoted to the history of Strasbourg's Young St. Peter's Church, may be understood as confessional since, with the consecration of the new Catholic Young St. Peter's Church in Strasbourg (1894), the two-hundred-year history of Catholics and Lutherans sharing the church (the *simultaneum*) ended—and to the Lutherans' advantage.[40]

While this extraordinary productivity marked Horning as a passionate historian, his dedication to confessional history writing, in the double sense of writing historical pieces on Alsace's confessional Lutheran community and investigating the past to promote confessional interests in the present, reflects a conviction that history had become an important confessional battleground between Protestants and Catholics and among Protestants (Lutherans). Consequently, he could no longer leave the production of historical narratives to his adversaries. Seen from this perspective, Horning's historical turn is consonant with the broader surge of interest in the age of the Reformation and its aftermath in Imperial Germany. This surge reflected the confessionally oriented contests over the nature of German identity that came to a head during the era of unification and, even more so, during the post-unification culture wars.[41] This penchant for revisiting the past, especially among Protestants, was fueled by opportunity. The four-hundredth anniversaries of the births of such luminaries as Martin Luther, Martin Bucer, and John Calvin all fell during this period, providing powerful occasions to reflect on these men's labors and legacies. Whereas German Protestants and Catholics reworked the past in debating Luther's status as a German national hero in 1883, orthodox Lutherans across the *Kaiserreich* indulged in historical reappraisals to remind Germans (or at least German Protestants) how to respect and honor properly the Lutheran tradition.[42]

A paramount concern in Horning's historical work was to write orthodox Lutheranism back into the narratives on Strasbourg's and Alsace's early modern religious history. In addition to demonstrating that the Reformation in Strasbourg owed more to Martin Luther than "liberal" historians wanted to admit, it involved reframing and extending the entire narrative. Hence, instead of regarding the success of orthodox Lutheranism in 1598 as the moment when the tolerant, Bucerian vision of Protestant reform perished, 1598 became the birth year of Lutheranism's golden age in Strasbourg. Similarly, Horning idealized the seventeenth century, a period extant histories regarded as a period of decline, thanks to orthodoxy's growing sterility and the religious and political pressures created by the Thirty Years' War and its aftermath.

Horning pursued several strategies toward these goals. At the most basic level, he sought to rescue the past by gathering up and publishing its documentary traces. In 1888, he published an edition of letters that the head of Strasbourg's Church Authority (*Kirchenkonvent*), Johann Marbach, exchanged with Lutheran leaders east of the Rhine, notably Philipp Melanchthon.[43] In honor of the four-hundredth anniversary of Martin Bucer's birth, Horning published a collection of texts written by individuals associated with Bucer (e.g., Luther, Capito, and Marbach) or with the post-1598 Lutheran establishment (e.g., Johann Pappus, Johann Schmidt, and Johann Conrad Dannhauer).[44] Shortly after the four-hundredth anniversary of the Reformation in 1917, Horning published a bibliography of Luther's writings that had been printed either in Strasbourg or elsewhere in Alsace.[45] In addition, he organized and published the material he had collected on Strasbourg's Lutheran community from the mid-sixteenth century to the eighteenth century as a series of three "handbooks." These books are thin on narrative but rich in factual information and excerpts from documentary evidence. Each one contains sections on the men and institutions of Strasbourg's Lutheran community and on parish life. But even here Horning showed his confessional colors, including in each volume a section entitled "The Church's Struggles," in which he chronicled how the Lutheran Church met the challenges posed by Catholicism, Calvinism, and various sectarian movements.[46]

Over and above the mere amassing of evidence, Horning sought to broaden scholarly understanding of Strasbourg's Lutheran past by examining the men responsible for establishing and maintaining a "true" Lutheran Church in the sixteenth and seventeenth centuries. He emphasized precisely that history that liberal and rational historians had preferred to forget (or at least downplay): the creation of a rigidly orthodox Lutheran Church in Strasbourg. At the center of this confessional history project stands a series of monographic studies (and occasional articles) on the presidents of Strasbourg's *Kirchenkonvent*, from Marbach to Sebastian Schmidt, and on such seventeenth-century theological stars as Dorsch and Bebel.[47] These monographs reveal Horning to have been an accomplished and even fairly objective historian. Moreover, in the cases of such figures as Marbach, Pappus, Dannhauer, and Johann Schmidt, Horning's remain the only monographic investigations in the scholarly literature.[48]

These works leave little doubt about Horning's partisan agenda. He largely ignored the Reformation's initial decades, concentrating instead on the achievements of his heroes (Marbach and Pappus) and their successors down to the Lutheran Republic of Strasbourg's demise in 1681. Horning's objective was not merely to recenter the history of Strasbourg's confessional age around the era of Lutheran orthodoxy. He wanted to rescue that period and its great men from their latter-day theological despisers. In the preface to the Marbach biography, Horning deplores the smear campaign that rationalist and unionist pastors and professors had long waged against Marbach.[49] Marbach, Horning argued, was a pious man of faith, who worked tirelessly to build a "people's church" in Strasbourg.[50] Similarly, in the preface to his edition of letters exchanged between Marbach and other leading reformers, Horning flatly rejects Roehrich's and Charles Schmidt's negative assessments of Marbach's standing as a theologian; the letters, Horning asserted, made it clear that he was an esteemed and valued colleague of Melanchthon, Johannes Brenz, and Jacobus Andreae.[51] Likewise, in the Pappus study, Horning labeled Roehrich "an opponent of every sort of confessionalism," making him "incapable of understanding Pappus or valuing his accomplishments."[52] Far from being a "zealot" or a blind "*Lutheraner*," Horning describes Pappus as a talented minister and preacher who regarded "dead, inactive orthodoxy" as "an atrocity."[53] Horning emphasized that had it not been for the tireless efforts of Marbach and Pappus, Strasbourg's Lutheran Church, including its rectories, the Protestant *Gymnasium*, and university, would never have survived.[54]

At the same time, Horning's investigations aimed to rebut the argument that the seventeenth century was an age of stagnant and sterile orthodoxy. Horning portrayed the University of Strasbourg as a highly regarded site of Lutheran theological scholarship. In the study of Johann Dannhauer, he notes how students from all across Germany came to Strasbourg to study at the "feet of this man who with his colleagues, the learned Johann Schmidt and Johann Dorsch, formed the so-called 'Trinity of John' [*johanneische Trias*]."[55] Horning interprets Dorsch's call and move to the University of Rostock at the end of his career as an acknowledgment of Strasbourg's significance as a center of Lutheran learning.[56] Thanks to the teaching of such prolific scholars as Bebel and Sebastian Schmidt, Horning maintained, Strasbourg's university was even able to reassert its importance in the decades following the close of the Thirty Years' War.[57] He characterizes Bebel as a close friend of the Pietist Philipp Jakob Spener and as a theologian of truly "European stature" and recognizes Schmidt, Spener's mentor at Strasbourg, as a leading seventeenth-century German exegete.[58] Lastly, by calling attention to the professors' work as ministers, he underscored their encouragement of a sincere, deeply felt faith among Strasbourg's Lutherans. To a man, he asserted, they were active and talented preachers who viewed the sermon as a way to edify their congregations. Pappus's sermons, he noted, were models of clarity, simple depth, and warmth that never failed to attract a devoted audience. Moreover, unlike the homilies delivered by many a modern minister, Pappus's were free of "learned citations" and "rhetorical pomp."[59]

Horning's efforts to rehabilitate Strasbourg's Lutheran leaders and their piety is significant at two levels: the historical and the contemporary-practical. Regarding the former, his studies of the Lutheran Church presidents aimed to counter the prevailing "wisdom" that these men and their obstinate support for orthodoxy were significantly responsible for Strasbourg's failings during the seventeenth century. In recasting the historical image of Lutheran orthodoxy, though, Horning also wished to defend and improve its image in contemporary times. Namely, he held out his cast of early modern characters as examples for present-day Lutherans. In the Dannhauer study's preface, for instance, Horning alludes to the wider purchase of Dannhauer's biography for contemporary audiences by noting that he wrote more with the average lay reader in mind than the scholar.[60] In honor of the 1883 Luther commemoration, Horning wrote a book on Spener's life in Alsace, in which he stressed the deeply Lutheran nature of this seminal Pietist's upbringing, training, and early ministry.[61] But Horning did not just offer up famous individuals as exemplars of good Lutheran faith and living. Several of his publications presented less illustrious, but no less pious individuals to contemporary readers: Joachim Stoll, Spener's pastor in Rappoltsweiler; Caspar Klee, a seventeenth-century Lutheran pastor from Ruprechtsau (a village just outside of Strasbourg); a quartet of seventeenth-century Rappoltsteiner countesses; and Johann Jakob, whom Horning lauds as the "pious [and last] count of Rappoltstein."[62]

The interplay between past deeds and present concerns in Horning's historical oeuvre is especially apparent when we consider one final theme that runs through his publications. Namely, Horning routinely draws attention to the important role that inter- and intraconfessional polemics played in his heroes' activities as theologians and clerics. He devoted over one-third of the Marbach study to his battles against Rome and Catholicism, Zwinglianism, Calvinism, and sectarianism. On the topic of "Dannhauer the Polemicist," Horning reflects, "Could one perhaps describe Dannhauer's polemical zeal as blind? . . . Not in the least. [His] battle against papacy was necessary, and consequently also successful."[63] He rebutted the negative assessments of Dorsch's polemical activity, notably those of Heinrich Holtzmann, a prominent liberal theologian at the University of Strasbourg who branded Dorsch a *Streittheologe* (combative theologian) to disparage most of his theological writing.[64] Horning conceded that Dorsch's devotion to polemics was lamentable, because it came at the cost of his scholarship. Yet, he finds them indispensable. Given the serious internal and external challenges facing Alsatian Lutherans between 1618 and 1648, "it fell on the Lutheran theologians to stand up for the Lutheran faith and rebuff the attacks of its foes."[65] Even at the end of the century, Horning observes, Sebastian Schmidt and Bebel had to defend the church against the "clever attempts of its enemies," "refuting their objections and claims against the Lutheran Church in numerous tracts."[66]

This recourse to history served to legitimate Horning's own polemical campaigns on behalf of Lutheran orthodoxy in late nineteenth-century Alsace. In Horning's eyes, his attacks on church officials who refused to honor the Augsburg Confession, his complaints about theology professors whose teachings and publications deviated from orthodox doctrine, and his constant efforts to thwart the spread of unionism within the Alsatian Lutheran Church were all in keeping with good, Strasbourg Lutheran traditions. Moreover, Horning found history writing a congenial means for advancing his polemical program. His historical texts enabled him to "set the record straight," while also highlighting the silences, distortions, and insufficiencies in accounts by such liberal and unionist theologians as Roehrich, Christian Schmidt, and August Tholuck.[67] Horning even took up the pen to revisit figures and eras beloved by his adversaries. The Spener biography served to distinguish the "Lutheran" Pietism of Spener from the "unionist" Pietism of Johann Hinrich Wichern, Franz Haerter, and their associates. Responding to claims that Calvin and his followers had been poorly treated in Strasbourg, Horning's short tract commemorating the four-hundredth anniversary of Calvin's birth pointed out that just as Calvin saw fit to exclude other Protestant confessions from Geneva, so too did Strasbourg's city fathers have the right to declare it a monodenominational city.[68] Lastly, Horning took advantage of the four-hundredth anniversary of Martin Bucer's birth to publish a tract that documented Bucer's move toward orthodox Lutheranism in the late 1530s, thereby asserting that Strasbourg's Reformation had a decidedly Lutheran character from a very early stage.[69]

Confessional Histories and Confessional Relations in Imperial Germany

History, so the famous dictum goes, is written by the victors. A look at the confessional narratives written in nineteenth-century Alsace and German Europe suggest that we need to be more circumspect about this verdict. For the accounts written and published after 1815, particularly those by clergy and theologians, resembled contributions to an ongoing conflict more than they did an ex post facto tidying up of a narrative to suit the needs of the prevailing side. They were, in short, important contributions to the wars of words and images with which Protestants fought Catholics but also other Protestants during the nineteenth century.[70] Indeed, as the process of historical remembrance and forgetting reached a high point during the Bismarckian era, historical writing on the "confessional age" tended to encourage a binary vision of

Germany's religious landscape that divided the nation into Protestants and Catholics and idealized the restoration of confessional unity in Germany along loosely Protestant lines.[71]

The case of Wilhelm Horning's historical oeuvre encourages us to look anew at this understanding of confessional conflict and coexistence in Germany, an understanding that places a premium on the forgetting of confessional plurality. To be sure, Horning needed no convincing that Roman Catholicism remained a serious threat to contemporary Lutherans and Lutheranism. He shared his heroes' beliefs about Catholicism's doctrinal errors. His personal experiences with the *simultaneum* at Young St. Peter's gave him ample evidence of Catholicism's efforts to undermine the health of present-day Lutheran communities. As recently as 1865, Catholic forces in Strasbourg had conspired to acquire the entire Young St. Peter's Church for Catholicism, a plan derailed only as a result of the Lutheran parish's steadfast opposition.[72] Consequently, as head of Young St. Peter's Lutheran parish and in his various historical and polemical writings, Horning minced few words regarding the danger that Catholicism and papism presented.

Nevertheless, while remaining vigilant with respect to Catholicism, Horning was more alarmed by developments within the Lutheran–Protestant fold. He feared that good Lutheran piety and belief, rooted in the practices of late sixteenth- and seventeenth-century Strasbourg, were at risk of being caught between the Scylla of liberal Lutheranism and the Charybdis of unionist Pietism. Worse still, liberal approaches to the history of Strasbourg's Reformation and its aftermath tended to promote toleration by marginalizing, even ignoring the positive contributions of orthodox Lutheranism. Writing confessional history, in both of its senses, was thus a key element in Horning's strategy for preserving and advocating on behalf of the Lutheran tradition in the long nineteenth century's closing decades. For Horning, this was not a tradition to be invented à la Hobsbawm, but rather one to be recovered from the historical record.[73] Historical study helped to legitimate and celebrate that tradition, while also helping to establish that tradition's claims on the present day. It sought to delegitimize the extant ecclesiastical regime, which failed to recognize the authoritative status of the Augsburg Confession within the church. But, and more positively, it also presented historical figures of the confessional age as models of piety and faith who could inspire Lutherans in contemporary times.

Although the terms of Horning's arguments and the ways in which he strove to promote a more pluralistic historical account to promote narrower polemical and church political ends were specific to the Alsatian context, they are indicative of broader trends in the reanimation of confessional tensions in German Europe during the century following the Congress of Vienna. The need to renegotiate confessional relationships and boundaries after Napoleon's demise was not just a Protestant-Catholic affair, but arguably even more intensely an intra-Protestant matter. In contrast to the early modern situation, the continued existence of Protestantism and Catholicism in Germany was less of an issue after 1815. The new constellation of legal, political, and theological conditions in post-Napoleonic Germany did mean that the diversity within the Protestant fold was very much at stake. Although initially seen as a solution to the problem, the emergence of united churches in the 1810s and 1820s exacerbated intraconfessional relations more than it calmed them. In fact, it is tempting—although this point must remain speculative for now—to explain a good measure of Protestants' anti-Catholic posturing in the nineteenth century as a sign of frustration over the absence of a coherent, stable sense of Protestant identity, rather than viewing it merely as a revival of former anti-Catholic passions. This posturing reflected anxieties within the Protestant community that the diversity that characterized German Protestantism since early modern times would not survive in the modern era. Whereas "modern" histories of the confessional age routinely called into question the very plurality that the Reformation and Counter-Reformation had produced, the historical narratives of churchmen like Wilhelm Horning sought to maintain and defend that plurality, advocating what we might call a confessional application of the principle of "separate but equal," at least with respect to Lutherans and Reformed Protestants. Thus, while they supported a more pluralist, or at least inclusive, history of the confessional age, confessional Lutherans did so as part of a broader call for a less pluralistic, more exclusive vision of Lutheranism in modern times.

Anthony J. Steinhoff is associate professor of history at the Université du Québec à Montréal. A specialist in modern German and French history, he is the author of *The Gods of the City: Protestantism and Religious Culture in Strasbourg, 1870–1914* (Brill, 2008); translator of Rita Kuczynski, *Wall Flower: A Life on the German Border* (University of Toronto Press, 2015); and coeditor of *The Total Work of Art: Foundations, Articulations, Inspirations* (Berghahn, 2016). He is currently writing a cultural history of the Richard Wagner's *Parsifal* and operatic culture in German-speaking Europe (c. 1860–present).

Notes

1. Anthony J. Steinhoff, *The Gods of the City: Protestantism and Religious Culture in Strasbourg, 1870–1914* (Leiden, 2008), 380–82.
2. Wilhelm Horning, *Der Straßburger evangelisch-lutheranische Gemeinde-Anzeiger (Seelsorge Pfr. W. Horning)* (Strasbourg, c. 1890s), esp. 7–10.

3. Wolfgang Reinhard, "Gegenreformation als Modernisierung? Prolegomena zu einer Theorie des konfessionellen Zeitalters," *Archiv für Reformationsgeschichte* 68 (1977): 226–51; Heinz Schilling, "Die Konfessionalisierung im Reich: Religiöser und gesellschaftlicher Wandel in Deutschland zwischen 1555 und 1620," *Historische Zeitschrift* 246 (1988): 1–45; and Thomas A. Brady, Jr., "Confessionalization—The Career of a Concept," in *Confessionalization in Europe 1550–1700: Essays in Honor and Memory of Bodo Nischan,* ed. John M. Headley, Hans J. Hillerbrand, and Anthony J. Papalas (Aldershot, 2004), 1–20.

4. Leopold von Ranke, *Geschichte der Reformation in Deutschland* (Berlin, 1845–47).

5. Kurt Nowak, *Geschichte des Christentums in Deutschland: Religion, Politik und Gesellschaft vom Ende der Aufklärung bis zur Mitte des 20. Jahrhunderts* (Munich, 1995), 65.

6. Compare Wolfgang Altgeld, *Katholizismus, Protestantismus und Judentum: Über religiös begründete Gegensätze und nationalreligiöse Ideen in der Geschichte des deutschen Nationalismus* (Mainz, 1992); Michael Gross, *The War against Catholicism* (Ann Arbor, 2004); and Helmut Walser Smith, *German Nationalism and Religious Conflict: Culture, Ideology, Politics 1870–1914* (Princeton, 1995), esp. 19–49.

7. Anthony J. Steinhoff, "Christianity and the Creation of Germany," in *The Cambridge History of Christianity,* vol. 8, *World Christianities, c. 1814–1914,* ed. Sheridan Gilley and Brian Stanley (Cambridge, 2006), 282–300.

8. Olaf Blaschke, "Das 19. Jahrhundert: Ein Zweites Konfessionnelles Zeitalter?," *Geschichte und Gesellschaft* 26 (2000): 38–75; and Anthony J. Steinhoff, "Ein zweites konfessionelles Zeitalter? Nachdenken über die Religion im langen 19. Jahrhundert," *Geschichte und Gesellschaft* 30 (2004): 549–70.

9. Nigel Aston, *Christianity and Revolutionary Europe c. 1750–1830* (Cambridge, 2002), 211–57.

10. Although ratified on 10 September 1801, the Concordat was not promulgated until 1802.

11. Henri Strohl, *Le Protestantisme en Alsace* (1950; repr., Strasbourg, 2000), 185–286; and Wolfgang Altgeld, "German Catholics," in *The Emancipation of Catholics, Jews, and Protestants: Minorities and the Nation State in Nineteenth-Century Europe,* ed. Rainer Liedtke and Stephan Wendehorst (Manchester, 1999), 100–21, esp. 102–7.

12. René Epp, Marc Lienhard, and Freddy Raphaël, *Catholiques, Protestants, Juifs en Alsace* (Colmar, 1992), 134–35; and Robert Will, "L'Église protestante de Strasbourg sous la Restauration," *Revue d'histoire et de philosophie religieuses* (hereafter *RHPR*) 22 (1942): 240–76, esp. 240–55.

13. Napoleon took similar pains with the Catholics, prohibiting any national or metropolitan gatherings of clergy without the express permission of the French state.

14. André Encrevé, *Protestants français au milieu du XIXe siècle: Les réformés de 1848 à 1870* (Geneva, 1986), 67–82.

15. Strohl, *Protestantisme,* 340–41.

16. Marcel Scheidhauer, *Les Églises luthériennes en France 1800–1815: Alsace-Montbéliard-Paris* (Strasbourg, 1975).

17. Franz Schnabel, *Deutsche Geschichte im 19. Jahrhundert,* vol. 4, *Die religiösen Kräfte* (Freiburg im Breisgau, 1937), 320–58.

18. Gerhard Besier, *Religion Nation Kultur: Die Geschichte der christlichen Kirchen in den gesellschaftlichen Umbrüchen des 19. Jahrhunderts* (Neukirchen-Vluyn, 1992), 18–23.

19. Marie-Joseph Bopp, *Die evangelischen Gemeinden und hohen Schulen in Elsaß und Lothringen von der Reformation bis zur Gegenwart* (Neustadt a. d. Aisch, 1965), 442–46.

20. Robert Will, "L'Église protestante de Strasbourg pendant le Consulat et l'Empire," *RHPR* 21 (1941): 138–76, here 138–52, 165–69; Robert Will, "Les Églises protestantes de Strasbourg sous la Monarchie de Juillet," *RHPR* 24 (1944): 1–60, esp. 8–11; and Strohl, *Protestantisme*, 322–26.

21. Robert M. Bigler, *The Politics of German Protestantism: The Rise of the Protestant Church Elite in Prussia, 1815–1848* (Berkeley and Los Angeles, 1972).

22. Philip Schaff, *Germany: Its Universities, Theology, Religion* (Philadelphia, 1857), 154.

23. Charles Théodore Gérold, *La Faculté de théologie et le Séminaire protestant de Strasbourg (1803–1872): Une page de l'histoire de l'Alsace* (Strasbourg, 1923), 128–29, 164.

24. Will, "Églises protestantes . . . monarchie de Juillet," 45–49.

25. Karl Christian Hackenschmidt, *Haerter und Horning: Beitrag zur Geschichte des Unionspietismus in Straßburg* (Strasbourg, 1888).

26. Robert Will, "Les Églises protestantes de Strasbourg sous le second Empire, II," *RHPR* 28–29 (1948–49): 204–40, here 211–16; Henri Strohl, *Protestantisme*, 391–97; and Wilhelm Horning, *Friedrich Theodor Horning: Pfarrer an der Jungsanktpeterkirche. Lebensbild eines Strassburger evangelisch-lutherischen Bekenners im 19. Jahrhundert* (Strasbourg, 1885). For a discussion of intraconfessional dynamics in pre-1870 Strasbourg, see Steinhoff, *Gods of the City*, 48–55.

27. Timotheus Wilhelm Roehrich, *Geschichte der Reformation im Elsass und besonders in Straßburg, nach gleichzeitig Quellen bearbeitet*, 2 vols. (Strasbourg, 1830–32).

28. I use the term "rationalist-liberal" here because over the course of the 1840s and 1850s, religious rationalism in Alsace gradually evolved into "liberalism," a position that retained rationalism's skepticism toward the symbolic confessions but tended to replace rationalism's intellectualism with a subjective approach to Protestant faith and piety.

29. Charles Schmidt, *La vie et les travaux de Jean Sturm, premier recteur du Gymnase et de l'Académie de Strasbourg* (Strasbourg, 1855); and Johann Wilhelm Baum, *Capito und Bucer, Strassburgs Reformatoren* (Elberfeld, 1860).

30. Franz Haerter, *Die Augsburg. Confession, mit einem Vorberichte u. Anmerkungen* (Strasbourg, 1838).

31. Franz Haerter, *Handbüchlein für Jung und Alt oder Katechismus der evangel. Heilslehre*, 3rd ed. (Strasbourg, 1865); Franz Haerter, *Ich und mein Haus wollen dem Herrn dienen: Eine Aufforderung zur täglichen Haus-Andacht im Familienkreise* (Strasbourg, 1853); Martin Luther, *Der kleine Katechismus*, ed. Franz Haerter (Strasbourg, 1854); Franz Haerter, ed., *Die alte Strassburger Kinderbibel* (Strasbourg, 1854); and Johann Friedrich Lenz, *Geheligter Kinder Gottes Betkämmerlein*, ed. Friedrich Horning (Strasbourg, 1858).

32. Steinhoff, *Gods of the City*, 73–77.

33. John E. Craig, *Scholarship and Nation Building: The Universities of Strasbourg and Alsatian Society, 1870–1939* (Chicago, 1984), esp. 52–56; and Otto Michaelis, *Grenzlandkirche: Eine evangelische Kirchengeschichte Elsaß-Lothringens 1870–1918* (Strasbourg, 1934), 62–64.

34. Steinhoff, *Gods of the City*, esp. 171–224.

35. Personnel file Wilhelm Horning, *Archives départementales du Bas-Rhin* AL 272/50; and Wilhelm Horning, *Köstliche Mühe und Arbeit in Amt, Gemeinde und Kirche 1863–1913*, 4 vols. (Strasbourg, 1913–14), vol. 1, 1–24.

36. Wilhelm Horning, *Zwei Gespräche über die fliegenden Blätter des Herrn Dr Bruch* (Strasbourg, 1871); and Wilhelm Horning, *Etliche Methodistenprediger unrechtliche und unehrliche Missionsschleicherei im Elsaß* (Strasbourg, 1871).

37. Horning, *Köstliche Mühe*, vol. 1, 53–5.

38. Wilhelm Horning, *Neue Gesangbuchsnot: Das zweite Straßburger Konferenzgesangbuch (Gesangbuchkommission: Gerold-Spitta-Redslob) (Entwurf 1898) mit seinen hymnologischen und kirchlichen Schäden* (Strasbourg, 1898); and Wilhelm Horning, *Die Professur der praktischen Theologie, vertreten duch [Friedrich] Spitta und [Julius] Smend: beurteilt u. a. durch Fachgenossen* (Strasbourg, 1904).

39. Wilhelm Horning, *Der evang. luth. Bekenntnißstand der Landeskirche Augsb. Konfession in Elsaß-Lothringen (aus Anlaß der Verfassungsänderungsfrage)* (Strasbourg, 1908); and Wilhelm Horning, *Unliberale Mängel und Lücken in der "Neuen Kirchenordnung" (Landeskirche A.K.)* (Strasbourg, 1910).

40. Franklin L. Ford, *Strasbourg in Transition, 1648–1789* (New York, 1958), 104–5.

41. Smith, *German Nationalism*, 19–49.

42. Stan M. Landry, *Ecumenism, Memory, and German Nationalism, 1817–1917* (Syracuse, NY, 2013), 90–100.

43. Wilhelm Horning, ed., *Aus dem lateinischen Briefwechsel von Melanchton, Brenz, Chemnitz, Jakob Andreä, u. A. mit Dr. Johann Marbach* (Strasbourg, 1888), 3–4.

44. Wilhelm Horning, *Kirchenhistorische Nachlese oder Nachträge zu den "Beiträgen zur Kirchengeschichte des Elsasses" und "Biographieen der Straßburger luth. Theologen: Marbach, Pappus, J. Schmidt, Dannhauer": Festschrift zum 400 jährigen Geburtsjubiläum von Martin Butzer* (Strasbourg, 1891).

45. Wilhelm Horning, *165 Écrits de Luther imprimés à Strasbourg et 34 de ses écrits imprimés à Colmar, Sélestat et Haguenau* (Strasbourg, 1919).

46. Wilhelm Horning, *Handbuch der Geschichte der evang. Luth. Kirche in Strassburg unter Marbach und Pappus. XVI. Jahrhundert* (2. Hälfte) (Strasbourg, 1903); Wilhelm Horning, *Handbuch der Geschichte der evang.-luth. Kirche im 17. Jahrh.* (Strasbourg, 1903); Wilhelm Horning, *Zur Strassburger Kirchengeschichte im XVIII Jahrhundert* (Strasbourg, 1907). For a similar documentary project concerning rural Alsace, see Wilhelm Horning, *Versuch einer Gemeindekunde in kirchengeschichtlichen Daten aus allen Stadt- und Landgemeinden der Landeskirche Augsburger Konfession (ausgenommen Strassburg), 1517–1912*, 2 vols. (Strasbourg, 1913–15).

47. Wilhelm Horning, *Dr. Johann Marbach, Pfarrer zu St. Nikolai, Münsterprediger, Professor und Präsident des luth. Kirchenkonvents in Straßburg (1545–1581)* (Strasbourg, 1887); Wilhelm Horning, *Dr. Joh. Pappus von Lindau, 1549–1610, Münsterprediger, Universitätsprofessor und Präses des Kirchenkonvents zu Straßburg* (Strasbourg, 1891); Wilhelm Horning, *Dr. Johann Conrad Dannhauer, der Straßburger Universitätsprofessor, Münsterprediger und Präsident des Kirchenkonvents (†1666)* (Strasbourg, 1883); Wilhelm Horning, *Dr. Sebastian Schmidt von Lampertheim, Professor, Präses des Kirchenkonvents und Münsterprediger in Straßburg (†1696)* (Strasbourg, 1885); Wilhelm Horning, *Dr. Balthasar Bebel, Professor der Theologie und Münsterprediger zu Straßburg im 17. Jahrhundert* (Strasbourg, 1886); and Wilhelm Horning, *Dr. Johann Dorsch, Professor der Theologie und Münsterprediger zu Straßburg im 17. Jahrhundert: Ein Lebenszeuge der lutherische Kirche* (Strasbourg, 1886).

48. Lorna Jane Abray, *The People's Reformation: Magistrates, Clergy, and Commons in Strasbourg 1500–1598* (Ithaca, 1985), 76; and Johannes Wallmann, "Die Eigenart der Straßburger lutherischen Orthodoxie im 17. Jahrhundert: Apokalyptisches

Endzeitbewußtsein und konfessionnelle Polemik bei Johann Dannhauer," in *Theologie und Frömmigkeit im Zeitalter des Barock: Gesammelte Aufsätze* (Tübingen, 1995), 87–104.

49. Roehrich, *Geschichte der Reformation*; and Heinrich Holtzmann, "Marbach, Johann," in *Allgemeine Deutsche Biographie (ADB)*, 56 vols. (Leipzig, 1875–1912), vol. 20, 289–90 (1884). Both Roehrich and Holtzman, a noted proponent of Protestant liberalism in the Strasbourg's Faculty of Protestant Theology, exhibit this negative view of Marbach.

50. Horning, *Marbach*, 1.

51. Horning, *Aus dem lateinischen Briefwechsel*, 3–4.

52. Horning, *Pappus*, 1–2.

53. Richard Otto Zoepffel, "Johann Pappus," in *ADB*, vol. 25, 163–64 (1887); and Horning, *Pappus*, 286. Zoepffel calls Pappus a "Lutheraner," a label with considerable negative connotations at the time.

54. Horning, *Pappus*, 318. Founded in 1566, the Strasbourg Academy was elevated to the status of a university in 1621 (which existed until 1793). Although Horning carefully distinguishes between the two stages of this institution's existence in his writings, in referring more generally to its importance as a place of higher learning I have chosen to refer only to the University of Strasbourg.

55. Horning, *Dannhauer*, 129.

56. Horning, *Dorsch*, 1.

57. Horning, *Bebel*, 25.

58. Zoepffel, "Pappus," 66; and Horning, *Schmidt*, 37.

59. Horning, *Pappus*, 286.

60. Horning, *Dannhauer*, 2.

61. Wilhelm Horning, *Philipp Jacob Spener in Rappoltsweiler, Colmar und Strassburg. Bilder aus Haus, Schule und Kirche im 17. Jahrh.* (Strasbourg, 1883), here 41, 105.

62. Wilhelm Horning, *Joachim Stoll, Hofprediger der gräfl. Herrschaft von Rappoltsweier* (Strasbourg, 1889); Wilhelm Horning, "Caspar Klee, Pfr. in der Ruprechtsau (bei Straßburg)," *Beiträge zur Kirchengeschichte des Elsaß* (1881, 1882); Wilhelm Horning, *Johann Jakob, der letzte Derer von Rapoltstein, ein frommer luth. Graf im Elsass (1598–1673)* (Rappoltsweiler, 1890); and Wilhelm Horning, *Ein Kleeblatt Rappolsteinischer Gräfinnen aus dem 17. Jahrhundert: Beitrag zur Geschichte des Verhältnisses des elsässischen Adels zur ev.-luth. Kirche* (Strasbourg, 1886).

63. Horning, *Dannhauer*, 151.

64. Heinrich Holtzmann, "Dorsche, Johann Georg," in *ADB*, vol. 5, 363 (1877).

65. Horning, *Dorsch*, 65.

66. Horning, *Bebel*, 34.

67. August Tholuck, *Das akademische Leben des siebzehnten Jahrhunderts mit besonderer Beziehung auf die protestantisch-theologischen Fakultäten Deutschlands* (Halle, 1853); Horning, *Dannhauer*, 2; and Horning, *Dorsch*, 2. Although generally appreciative of Tholuck, Horning accuses him of not discussing Dannhauer sufficiently and "casting shadows of a united nature on Dannhauer, especially where his spirit shone most brightly."

68. Wilhelm Horning, *Calvin's Amtieren in der luth. Kirche Straßburg's. Drei ergänzende und korrigierende Kapitel: Zu Calvin's 400jährigem Jubliäum* (Strasbourg, 1909), esp. 17–18, 27.

69. Wilhelm Horning, *Zum 400jährigen Geburtsjubiläum von Martin Butzer, dem Reformator Strassburgs*, 2nd ed. (Strasbourg, 1891).
70. Margaret Lavinia Anderson, "Afterword: Living Apart and Together in Germany," in *Protestants, Catholics, and Jews in Germany, 1800–1914*, ed. Helmut Walser Smith (Oxford, 2001), 319–32, here 325–26.
71. On the function of remembering and forgetting in interconfessional relations, see Helmut Walser Smith, *The Continuities of German History* (Cambridge, 2008), esp. 74–114. On Protestant-Catholic relations during the 1860s and 1870s, see Smith, *German Nationalism*, 20–49; and Gross, *War against Catholicism*.
72. Robert Will, "Les Églises protestantes de Strasbourg sous le second Empire, I," *RHPR* 27 (1947): 64–90, here 85–87.
73. Eric Hobsbawm and Terence Ringer, ed., *The Invention of Tradition* (Cambridge, 1983), 1–14.

Bibliography

Abray, Lorna Jane. *The People's Reformation: Magistrates, Clergy, and Commons in Strasbourg, 1500–1598*. Cornell, 1985.

Altgeld, Wolfgang. "German Catholics." In *The Emancipation of Catholics, Jews, and Protestants: Minorities and the Nation State in Nineteenth-Century Europe*, edited by Rainer Liedtke and Stephan Wendehorst, 100–21. Manchester, 1999.

———. *Katholizismus, Protestantismus und Judentum: Über religiös begründete Gegensätze und nationalreligiöse Ideen in der Geschichte des deutschen Nationalismus*. Mainz, 1992.

Anderson, Margaret Lavinia. "Afterword: Living Apart and Together in Germany." In *Protestants, Catholics, and Jews in Germany, 1800–1914*, edited by Helmut Walser Smith, 319–32. Oxford, 2001.

Aston, Nigel. *Christianity and Revolutionary Europe c. 1750–1830*. Cambridge, 2002.

Baum, Johann Wilhelm. *Capito und Bucer, Strassburgs Reformatoren*. Elberfeld, 1860.

Besier, Gerhard. *Religion Nation Kultur: Die Geschichte der christlichen Kirchen in den gesellschaftlichen Umbrüchen des 19. Jahrhunderts*. Neukirchen-Vluyn, 1992.

Bigler, Robert M. *The Politics of German Protestantism: The Rise of the Protestant Church Elite in Prussia, 1815–1848*. Berkeley, 1972.

Blaschke, Olaf. "Das 19. Jahrhundert: Ein Zweites Konfessionelles Zeitalter?" *Geschichte und Gesellschaft* 26 (2000): 38–75.

Bopp, Marie-Joseph. *Die evangelischen Gemeinden und hohen Schulen in Elsaß und Lothringen von der Reformation bis zur Gegenwart*. Neustadt a. d. Aisch, 1965.

Brady, Thomas A. "Confessionalization—The Career of a Concept." In *Confessionalization in Europe, 1555–1700: Essays in Honor and Memory of Bodo Nischan*, edited by John M. Headley, Hans J. Hillerbrand, and Anthony J. Papalas, 1–20. Burlington, 2004.

Craig, John E. *Scholarship and Nation Building: The Universities of Strasbourg and Alsatian Society, 1870–1939*. Chicago, 1984.

Encrevé, André. *Protestants français au milieu du XIXe siècle: Les réformés de 1848 à 1870*. Geneva, 1986.

Epp, René, Marc Lienhard, and Freddy Raphaël. *Catholiques, Protestants, Juifs en Alsace*. Colmar, 1992.

Ford, Franklin L. *Strasbourg in Transition, 1648–1789*. New York, 1958.

Gérold, Charles Théodore. *La Faculté de théologie et le Séminaire protestant de Strasbourg (1803–1872): Une page de l'histoire de l'Alsace*. Strasbourg, 1923.

Gross, Michael B. *The War against Catholicism: Liberalism and the Anti-Catholic Imagination in Nineteenth-Century Germany*. Ann Arbor, 2004.

Hackenschmidt, Karl Christian. *Haerter und Horning: Beitrag zur Geschichte des Unionspietismus in Straßburg*. Strasbourg, 1888.

Haerter, Franz. *Die Augsburg. Confession, mit einem Vorberichte u. Anmerkungen*. Strasbourg, 1838.

———. *Handbüchlein für Jung und Alt oder Katechismus der evangel. Heilslehre*. 3rd ed. Strasbourg, 1865.

———. *Ich und mein Haus wollen dem Herrn dienen: Eine Aufforderung zur täglichen Haus-Andacht im Familienkreise*. Strasbourg, 1853.

———, ed. *Die alte Strassburger Kinderbibel*. Strasbourg, 1854.

Hobsbawm, Eric, and Terence Ringer, ed. *The Invention of Tradition*. Cambridge, 1983.

Holtzmann, Heinrich. "Dorsche, Johann Georg." In *Allgemeine Deutsche Biographie*, vol. 5, 363. Leipzig, 1877.

———. "Marbach, Johann." In *Allgemeine Deutsche Biographie*, vol. 20, 289–90. Leipzig, 1884.

Horning, Wilhelm. *165 Écrits de Luther imprimés à Strasbourg et 34 de ses écrits imprimés à Colmar, Sélestat et Haguenau*. Strasbourg, 1919.

———. *Calvin's Amtieren in der luth. Kirche Straßburg's. Drei ergänzende und korrigierende Kapitel: Zu Calvin's 400jährigem Jubliäum*. Strasbourg, 1909.

———. *"Caspar Klee, Pfr. in der Ruprechtsau (bei Straßburg)." Beiträge zur Kirchengeschichte des Elsaß* (1881, 1882).

———. *Dr. Balthasar Bebel, Professor der Theologie und Münsterprediger zu Straßburg im 17. Jahrhundert*. Strasbourg, 1886.

———. *Dr. Johann Conrad Dannhauer, der Straßburger Universitätsprofessor, Münsterprediger und Präsident des Kirchenkonvents (†1666)*. Strasbourg, 1883.

———. *Dr. Johann Dorsch, Professor der Theologie und Münsterprediger zu Straßburg im 17. Jahrhundert: Ein Lebenszeuge der lutherische Kirche*. Strasbourg, 1886.

———. *Dr. Johann Marbach, Pfarrer zu St. Nikolai, Münsterprediger, Professor und Präsident des luth. Kirchenkonvents in Straßburg (1545–1581)*. Strasbourg, 1887.

———. *Dr. Joh. Pappus von Lindau, 1549–1610, Münsterprediger, Universitätsprofessor und Präses des Kirchenkonvents zu Straßburg*. Strasbourg, 1891.

———. *Etliche Methodistenprediger unrechtliche und unehrliche Missionsschleicherei im Elsaß*. Strasbourg, 1871.

———. *Der evang. luth. Bekenntnißstand der Landeskirche Augsb. Konfession in Elsaß-Lothringen (aus Anlaß der Verfassungsänderungsfrage)*. Strasbourg, 1908.

———. *Friedrich Theodor Horning: Pfarrer an der Jungsanktpeterkirche. Lebensbild eines Strassburger evangelisch-lutherischen Bekenners im 19. Jahrhundert*. Strasbourg, 1885.

———. *Handbuch der Geschichte der evang.-luth. Kirche im 17. Jahrh*. Strasbourg, 1903.

———. *Handbuch der Geschichte der evang. Luth. Kirche in Strassburg unter Marbach und Pappus. XVI. Jahrhundert* (2. Hälfte). Strasbourg, 1903.

———. *Joachim Stoll, Hofprediger der gräfl. Herrschaft von Rappoltsweier.* Strasbourg, 1889.

———. *Johann Jakob, der letzte Derer von Rapoltstein, ein frommer luth. Graf im Elsass (1598–1673).* Rappoltsweiler, 1890.

———. *Kirchenhistorische Nachlese oder Nachträge zu den "Beiträgen zur Kirchengeschichte des Elsasses" und "Biographieen der Straßburger luth. Theologen: Marbach, Pappus, J. Schmidt, Dannhauer": Festschrift zum 400 jährigen Geburtsjubiläum von Martin Butzer.* Strasbourg, 1891.

———. *Ein Kleeblatt Rappoltsteinischer Gräfinnen aus dem 17. Jahrhundert: Beitrag zur Geschichte des Verhältnisses des elsässischen Adels zur ev.-luth. Kirche.* Strasbourg, 1886.

———. *Köstliche Mühe und Arbeit in Amt, Gemeinde und Kirche 1863–1913.* 4 vols. Strasbourg, 1913–14.

———. *Neue Gesangbuchsnot: Das zweite Straßburger Konferenzgesangbuch (Gesangsbuchkommission: Gerold-Spitta-Redslob) (Entwurf 1898) mit seinen hymnologischen und kirchlichen Schäden.* Strasbourg, 1898.

———. *Philipp Jacob Spener in Rappoltsweiler, Colmar und Strassburg. Bilder aus Haus, Schule und Kirche im 17. Jahrh.* Strasbourg, 1883.

———. *Die Professur der praktischen Theologie, vertreten duch [Friedrich] Spitta und [Julius] Smend: beurteilt u. a. durch Fachgenossen.* Strasbourg, 1904.

———. *Dr. Sebastian Schmidt von Lampertheim, Professor, Präses des Kirchenkonvents und Münsterprediger in Straßburg (†1696).* Strasbourg, 1885.

———. *Der Straßburger evangelisch-lutherische Gemeinde-Anzeiger (Seelsorge Pfr. W. Horning.* Strasbourg, [c. 1890s].

———. *Unliberale Mängel und Lücken in der 'Neuen Kirchenordnung' (Landeskirche A.K.).* Strasbourg, 1910.

———. *Versuch einer Gemeindekunde in kirchengeschichtlichen Daten aus allen Stadt- und Landgemeinden der Landeskirche Augsburger Konfession (ausgenommen Strassburg), 1517–1912.* 2 vols. Strasbourg, 1913–15.

———. *Zum 400jährigen Geburtsjubiläum von Martin Butzer, dem Reformator Strassburgs.* 2nd ed. Strasbourg, 1891.

———. *Zur Strassburger Kirchengeschichte im XVIII Jahrhundert.* Strasbourg, 1907.

———. *Zwei Gespräche über die fliegenden Blätter des Herrn Dr Bruch.* Strasbourg, 1871.

———, ed. *Aus dem lateinischen Briefwechsel von Melanchton, Brenz, Chemnitz, Jakob Andreä, u. A. mit Dr. Johann Marbach.* Strasbourg, 1888.

Landry, Stan M. *Ecumenism, Memory, and German Nationalism, 1817–1917.* Syracuse, NY, 2013.

Nowak, Kurt. *Geschichte des Christentums in Deutschland: Religion, Politik und Gesellschaft vom Ende der Aufklärung bis zur Mitte des 20. Jahrhunderts.* Munich, 1995.

Ranke, Leopold von. *Deutsche Geschichte im Zeitalter der Reformation.* 5 vols. Berlin, 1839–43.

Reinhard, Wolfgang. "Gegenreformation als Modernisierung? Prolegomena zu einer Theorie des konfessionellen Zeitalters." *Archiv für Reformationsgeschichte* 68 (1977): 226–51.

Roehrich, Timotheus Wilhelm, *Geschichte der Reformation im Elsass und besonders in Straßburg, nach gleichzeitig Quellen bearbeitet*. 2 vols. Strasbourg, 1830–32.

Schaff, Philip. *Germany: Its Universities, Theology, Religion*. Philadelphia, 1857.

Scheidhauer, Marcel. *Les Églises luthériennes en France 1800–1815: Alsace-Montbéliard-Paris*. Strasbourg, 1975.

Schilling, Heinz. "Die Konfessionalisierung im Reich: Religiöser und gesellschaftlicher Wandel in Deutschland zwischen 1555 und 1620." *Historische Zeitschrift* 246 (1988): 1–45.

Schmidt, Charles. *La vie et les travaux de Jean Sturm, premier recteur du Gymnase et de l'Académie de Strasbourg*. Strasbourg, 1855.

Schnabel, Franz. *Deutsche Geschichte im 19. Jahrhundert*. Vol. 4, *Die religiösen Kräfte*. Freiburg im Breisgau, 1937.

Smith, Helmut Walser. *The Continuities of German History: Nation, Religion, and Race across the Long Nineteenth Century*. Cambridge, 2008.

———. *German Nationalism and Religious Conflict: Culture, Ideology, Politics 1870–1914*. Princeton, 1995.

Steinhoff, Anthony J. "Christianity and the Creation of Germany." In *The Cambridge History of Christianity*. Vol. 8, *World Christianities, c. 1814–1914*, edited by Sheridan Gilley and Brian Stanley, 282–300. Cambridge, 2006.

———. *The Gods of the City: Protestantism and Religious Culture in Strasbourg, 1870–1914*. Leiden, 2008.

———. "Ein zweites konfessionelles Zeitalter? Nachdenken über die Religion im langen 19. Jahrhundert." *Geschichte und Gesellschaft* 30 (2004): 549–70.

Strohl, Henri. *Le Protestantisme en Alsace*. 1950; reprint, Strasbourg, 2000.

Tholuck, August. *Das akademische Leben des siebzehnten Jahrhunderts mit besonderer Beziehung auf die protestantisch-theologischen Fakultäten Deutschlands*. Halle, 1853.

Wallmann, Johannes. "Die Eigenart der Straßburger lutherischen Orthodoxie im 17. Jahrhundert: Apokalyptisches Endzeitbewußtsein und konfessionnelle Polemik bei Johann Dannhauer." In *Gesammelte Aufsätze*, vol. 3, 87–104. Tübingen, 1995.

Will, Robert. "L'Église protestante de Strasbourg pendant le Consulat et l'Empire." *Revue d'histoire et de philosophie religieuses* 21 (1941): 138–76.

———. "Les Églises protestantes de Strasbourg sous la Monarchie de Juillet." *Revue d'histoire et de philosophie religieuses* 24 (1944): 1–60.

———. "L'Église protestante de Strasbourg sous la Restauration." *Revue d'histoire et de philosophie religieuses* 22 (1942): 240–76.

———. "Les Églises protestantes de Strasbourg sous le second Empire, I." *Revue d'histoire et de philosophie religieuses* 27 (1947): 64–90.

———. "Les Églises protestantes de Strasbourg sous le second Empire, II." *Revue d'histoire et de philosophie religieuses* 28/29 (1948–49): 204–40.

Zoepffel, Richard Otto. "Johann Pappus." In *Allgemeine Deutsche Biographie*, vol. 25, 163–64. Leipzig, 1887.

CHAPTER FOUR

Confessional Histories of Women and the Reformation from the Eighteenth to the Twenty-First Century

MERRY WIESNER-HANKS

Women disappeared from scholarly studies of the Reformation at about the same time that they disappeared from scholarly history in general. In the mid-nineteenth century, the seminar held by a professor initially in his home and later at a university became the central institution in the newly professionalizing field of "scientific" history. The primary goal of this scientific history was objectivity, or in the words of Lord Acton, one of its most prominent proponents, history written so that "nothing shall reveal the country, the religion, or the party to which the writers belong."[1] Such objective history was to be based on intensive archival research, where, as Leopold von Ranke noted, documents waited like "so many princesses, possibly beautiful and needing to be saved."[2] As Ranke's comment suggests, and as Bonnie Smith, Lisa Des Jardins, Peter Novick, and others have demonstrated, this professionalization was gendered (and also racialized) in terms of both practitioners and subject matter, as the "manly work" of seminar debates and archival research was limited to men and the most important topic of research became the political and constitutional history of the Western state.[3]

Church historians of the late nineteenth century continued to write from a confessional viewpoint, so generally did not share this quest for objectivity. In gigantic tomes and smaller works, Heinrich Denifle and Hartmann Grisar presented the Catholic perspectives, and Adolf von Harnack, Erich and Reinhold Seeberg, and a host of others, the Protestant. Like their secular colleagues, however, they increasingly highlighted official institutional and intellectual developments and paid less attention to popular practices or individuals who were not major figures. They occasionally included men's ideas about family and private life in their purview, but they left actual women out of the story. Luther's ideas about marriage were an important thread in these debates, but actual women were largely absent, and women's actions were nowhere to be found. Despite the increasingly iconic nature of the Luther marriage in German Lutheran teachings, even Katharina von Bora was rarely granted more than a few paragraphs of blame or praise.

Women continued as subjects of a different type of history, however: the "amateur history" that often appeared as biography, prosopography, or social and cultural studies of specific locales, both nearby and exotically foreign. Much of this amateur history was patriotic and moral, with dramatic narratives full of heroes and villains designed to provide spiritual uplift. Its authors were not trained in seminars, though they might be quite learned, and they included women.[4] Because scholarly histories of the Reformation in the nineteenth and most of the twentieth century left women out—other than the obligatory mention of a few queens and reformers' wives—amateur history was for decades the only place that any women could be found. In its assignment of praise and blame, and its inclusion of women, amateur history continued a pattern found in some of the confessional histories written during the eighteenth century. This essay examines the ways in which the story of women, and later gender, and the Reformation has been told in confessional histories over the last several centuries. It begins with a brief look at the eighteenth century, then traces religious confessionalism in nineteenth-century amateur histories and in studies of the Reformation and marriage produced by professionally trained church historians from the late nineteenth century onward. This essay also uses the idea of confessionalism in a broader sense, tracing various "confessions" that have emerged in women's and gender history itself, particularly since the dramatic increase in women's and gender history that resulted from the women's movement of the 1970s.

Linking eighteenth-century confessional history, amateur history of the late nineteenth century, and the sharply confessional history of the early twentieth century with the scholarly women's and gender history of the late twentieth and early twenty-first centuries might appear to demean the last of these, but there are striking parallels. The most influential of the amateur histories was the Scottish Presbyterian reverend James Anderson's two-volume *Ladies of the Reformation: Memoirs of Distinguished Female Characters*, which appeared in 1855 and 1857.[5] Anderson explains his purpose:

> Such a work seems to offer an opportunity to present various of the leading facts in the history of the Reformation in a somewhat new connection, as well as of introducing notices of the characteristics of the period, and of episodes

in real life, altogether omitted or only slightly touched upon, in general history, though partaking sometimes even of a romantic interest.[6]

If one substituted "sexual nature" or "gendered structure" for his Victorian phrase "romantic interest," that motivation has hardly changed. Whatever their perspective, whether eighteenth-century confessional history or nineteenth-century moral tome or twenty-first-century scholarly analysis, studies of women and gender and the Reformation all want to present "a somewhat new connection," and most also discuss "episodes in real life." And until very, very recently, their findings have continued to be "omitted or only slightly touched upon, in general or scholarly history."

Women in Confessional Histories of the Eighteenth Century

Confessional histories written during the eighteenth century sometimes highlighted the role of women, who appear most often as a way to attack certain groups, with authors using women's influence as proof of a group's demonic or, at the very least, misguided nature. That idea had a long history. Saint Bernard of Clairvaux attacked the Cathars and other heretics of his day for—among other things—listening to women, and among the "errors, heresies, blasphemies and pernicious practices of the sectaries," described by the English Puritan preacher Thomas Edwards in his polemical treatise *Gangraena* (1646), was the fact that they allowed women to preach.[7] The prolific German Lutheran theologian Johann Feustking turned his attention entirely to women in *Gynaeceum Haeretico Fanaticum* (1704), spending nearly seven hundred pages describing, as his full title reads, the "false prophetesses, Quakers, fanatics and other sectarian and frenzied female persons through whom God's church is disturbed."[8] He began with women in the Bible and early church who had led men astray and included a few medieval abbesses and nuns who were visionaries. He then worked alphabetically through a long list of women from the sixteenth and seventeenth centuries, beginning with the English Quaker Alida Ambrosia, who had founded several meetings despite persecution, and ending with the Dutch Catholic activist Helena Wouteria, who had hung crosses and rosaries around people's necks and urged them to return to allegiance to the pope. In between were about a hundred Anabaptists and enthusiasts, millenarians and mystics, prophets and Pietists, quietists and Quakers from all over Europe and even a few from the American colonies. In some cases, Feustking is the only published historical source that mentions the women's names and actions, for he regarded the obscure and prominent alike as dangerous.

Feustking wrote from within a long tradition of attacks on women, but the proximate cause of his catalog of female horrors was the publication in 1700 of the German Pietist Gottfried Arnold's *Impartial History of the Church and Heretics from the Beginning of the New Testament until 1688 A.D.*, a twelve-hundred-page sympathetic history of "church and heretics" that included a long list of "blessed women who showed the way to the truth, or who suffered greatly, or who were amazingly gifted, enlightened or directed by God."[9] Although most of Arnold's biographical entries are brief, and some do not even include the woman's name but identify her simply by place, a few are quite long. The seventeenth-century French mystic and reformer Antoinette Bourignon, who believed spiritual rebirth was more important than baptism so that Jews and Muslims might also be resurrected, and who refused to be associated with any group, gets more than twenty pages. So does the Franconian visionary Anna Vetterin, who made political predictions and wrote letters exhorting the residents of Nuremberg and Ansbach to repent. Arnold views some of the more extravagant visionaries a bit skeptically and suggests that illness might have contributed to their visions and trances, but in general he judges women's actions positively, as heroic signs of God operating through the least of his creatures. He equates the Lutheran theologians who forced Bourignon to flee with the Spanish Inquisition and describes Vetterin's attempt to feed her family by sewing and selling bread as brave.

A few women received even more detailed treatment from confessional historians. Among the many polemical works published by Michael Kuen, an Augustinian canon and provost of Stift Wengen in Ulm who published under the name Eusebius Engelhard, was *Lucifer Wittenbergensis*, which presents, as the subtitle indicates, the "complete life of Katharina von Bora, the so-called wife of Martin Luther, in which all her pretended virtues, fictitious achievements, false visions, and pitiful miracles . . . are related at length." Not content with the 346 pages of the first edition of 1747, two years later Kuen issued a second edition, noting that it was "new, expanded and improved."[10] Kuen was answered in 1751 by the even more prolific Lutheran theologian Christian Wilhelm Franz Walch, whose *True History of the Revered Catharina von Bora, Dr. Martin Luther's Wife*, initially a mere 286 pages, also went through several ever-larger editions, presenting stories and myths from Luther lore to show Katharine in a near-saintly light.[11]

Arnold, Feustking, Kuen, and Walch were polemicists, but they were also university-trained theologians and church historians, and they directed even their polemical works to a highly learned audience. They do seem to have been more concerned about women than were confessional historians and biographers outside of Germany in the eighteenth century, perhaps because of the number of women who were active in early Pietism.[12] English Quakers used examples of biblical women who preached and prophesied in their defenses of women's speech, and the eighteenth-century reprints of John Foxe's *Book of Martyrs* of course included women, but there is nothing comparable to Feust-king outside of Germany."

Amateur Histories of Women and the Reformation, 1850–1900

By the middle of the nineteenth century, discussions of women and the Reformation had moved to the realm of amateurs, who, like Gottfried Arnold a century earlier, focused on heroic actions in the face of suffering, a common theme among amateur historians of any subject and era. Among the numerous works of the evangelical Anglican novelist, editor, and writer Charlotte Elizabeth Tonna, writing under the name Charlotte Elizabeth, was the 1844 *The Female Martyrs of the English Reformation*, with stories she had pulled from Foxe's *Book of Martyrs*, of which she had earlier made an abridged edition.[13] Like many of her other works, Tonna envisioned this to be appropriate reading for adolescents, especially for young women, and for readers of the religious magazines that she edited, which included *The Protestant Annual* and *The Christian Lady's Magazine*. Its stories were retold by Rev. Henry Clissold, rector of the parish church in Chelmondiston, Suffolk, in *Last Hours of Christian Women*, published in 1853, and in other popular histories of Protestant martyrs.[14] As one would expect, all of these were overtly anti-Catholic—Tonna lived in Ireland for a while and wrote and edited works that defended the Orange Order along with sentimental fiction and children's literature.

Tonna's work, like Foxe's, was a series of biographical sketches, a popular genre for amateur historians in the late nineteenth century who understood that their readers—like those who read popular histories in the twenty-first century—wanted history that was character driven. Anderson's *Ladies of the Reformation* was also in this genre, though it went beyond martyrs to focus on "distinguished females in the principal countries of Europe who supported or contributed to this great revolution by sympathetic action, or heroic suffering."[15] The first of Anderson's seven-hundred-page volumes presents women from England, Scotland, and the Netherlands, and his second volume focuses on women from Germany, Switzerland, France, Italy, and Spain. His motivation for publishing was explicitly confessional: "From recent events in England, particularly the progress of Oxford Tractarianism, and the Papal aggressions, the study of this great revolution has become anew important, that under a deeper impression of the benefits we have received from it, our gratitude may be quickened."[16] Thus, like Feustking, Anderson had been provoked to gather his biographies and publish them by a specific local development.

Anderson's confessional purpose leads him to *celebrate* plurality among Protestants rather than forget it as did authors considered in other essays in this volume, however, and he includes women from a wide range of Protestant confessions and groups. In the first volume he tells the stories of Dutch Anabaptists along with those of English noblewomen and the wives of various Scottish reformers, noting that although they were "not equally enlightened in their views on divine truth, and they held different sentiments on some religious points . . . they were united on many great important truths about God's Word, which are denied or corrupted by Popery."[17] In the second volume, he includes German Lutherans, French Calvinists, Spanish Alumbrados, and Italian freethinkers.

Anderson's book was translated into French, and it also served as the basis for similar works in other languages by Protestant authors, including Elisabeth Hasebroek's *De vrouwen der hervorming* published in Amsterdam in 1859, the anonymous *Quelques femmes de la Réforme: recueil biographique* published in Lausanne in 1859, Ernestine Dietsch Diethoff's *Edle Frauen der Reformation und der Zeit der Glaubenskämpfe in Lebens- und Zeitbildern* (*Noble women of the Reformation and the Religious War in Biographical Sketches and as Portraits of an Era*) published in Leipzig in 1875, and many others.[18] Each of these books arranges the biographies so that those of the country in which the book was published came first and adds a few local figures that are not found in the others. Certain "women worthies" are in all of them, however: Katharina von Bora, Argula von Grumbach, Elisabeth of Braunschweig-Lüneburg, Anne Askew, Jeanne d'Albret. Whether written by male or female authors, they are inclusive in terms of Protestant confessions, as are the American versions of such works, including Emma Louise Parry's 1882 *Woman in the Reformation* and Annie Wittenmyer's 1885 *The Women of the Reformation*.[19] In addition to these, there were also a few individual biographies of women worthies, primarily wives of reformers.

These collections of biographical sketches are mind-numbing in their similarity—unsurprising, since they all copy freely from Anderson—and hagiographic in tone. Because neither continental Europeans nor Americans were particularly concerned with Oxford Tractarians and creeping popery the way the Scottish Presbyterian Anderson was, however, they have slightly different confessional purposes than did his collection. Wittenmyer's preface, in fact, sets out an explicitly non-confessional or even anti-confessional and ecumenical aim: "If this book shall inspire its readers to a deeper and more unselfish consecration to God and humanity, and to a broader, richer, Christian charity, that will, without regard to name, or creed, or nationality, accord *the largest religious liberty to all*, its mission will not have been in vain."[20] Wittenmyer had directly experienced sectarian conflict, as she had worked among the Union troops during the Civil War as part of the Women's Relief Corps trying to improve food and sanitation. Her distinctly American emphasis on religious liberty is expressed even more strongly in the book's dedicatory introduction, written by the poet Kate Brownlee Sherwood, which notes that the book is for those who "trace back their ancestry to the heroic men and women . . . who have helped to found in this New World an impregnable structure, based upon the rights of man and the liberty of thought and conscience."[21]

Both Anderson and Wittenmyer, and their many imitators, envision women among their readers. In the preface to his second volume, Anderson comments, "To the attention of Woman especially, it may be hoped that these Biographies will commend themselves," and Sherwood's introduction notes that Wittenmyer's book is "a gracious bequest to mothers and daughters of America."[22] Anderson sours his gift, however, with the comment that one of the "blessings" that have "descended richly" on women as a result of the Reformation is the fact that "it has delivered her from the superstitious terrors by which, from the sensibility of her nature, she is so liable to be enthralled."[23] Wittenmyer makes no such comments about women's weakness, and her version of the story is completely women-centered. For example, the first thirty pages of Anderson's second volume are devoted to Luther, without a woman in sight. In Wittenmyer, by contrast, Luther does not show up until page 361, in a relatively short chapter on Katharina von Bora; here he is given only several paragraphs and described simply as "the most conspicuous figure in the great contest with Romanism." The German Lutheran author Ernestine Dietsch Diethoff also explicitly addresses her book to female readers, and especially to "the female youth of the present" and "maidens and youthful mothers."[24] She mentions Luther only within the biography of Katharina von Bora and includes several "female thinkers" (*Denkerinnen*), such as the seventeenth-century Dutch polymath Anna Maria van Schurman, along with the usual wives, martyrs, and queens.

Despite writing for a popular audience, Wittenmyer does give a nod to scientific history. She thanks Anderson for "important historical data which have been used freely" but also says, "But years of careful research found among old records, found only in the largest libraries, have been necessary to secure and verify the facts of history."[25] How she found the time to do this research while also being the first president of the National Women's Christian Temperance Union is unclear, but at least she knows that in good Rankean fashion, to be taken seriously history requires research.

Ranke himself, and the other German academics who were creating scientific history at the same time that Tonna, Anderson, and Wittenmyer were publishing, paid no attention to amateur works, of course. They also refused to allow women into their seminars and led the fight to keep women out of universities in Germany. Heinrich von Treitschke, who at the end of the nineteenth century held the chair that had been Ranke's at the University of Berlin, declared that "for half a millennium German universities have been designed for men, and I will not help destroy them."[26] Such attitudes even shaped popular histories. Along with the introduction written by Diethoff herself, *Noble Women of the Reformation* includes a preface written by the Lutheran pastor Karl Zimmerman, in which he notes that the publisher specifically asked him, "as a man" (*als Mannesperson*) to check the book over for accuracy.[27]

Women *were* being trained elsewhere in scientific history—the first woman to obtain a doctorate in history was Kate Everest, at the University of Wisconsin in 1893—but they did not focus their attention on the Reformation. Most concentrated on modern history, although some, such as Florence Griswold Buckstaff, Eileen Power, and Lina Eckenstein, did examine the Middle Ages.[28] The most important scientific history on women in the early modern period produced in the era before World War I was written by women associated with the London School of Economics, which had been coeducational since its founding in 1895. Here Eileen Power and Lillian Knowles were professors of history, and Alice Clark received a fellowship to conduct research for what would become her classic study *Working Life of Women in the Seventeenth Century*. Faculty and students at LSE—female and male—were among those creating the new field of economic history, which incorporated social history as well.[29] Many early economic historians were active in social reform movements, and religious history was not among their concerns; it was also often the province of church history or theology departments, which were even less open to women than were departments of history.

Confessional Histories of the Reformation and Marriage, 1850–2000

At the same time that popular histories were telling one confessional story involving women and the Reformation, academic studies of the reformers'— especially Luther's—ideas about marriage were telling another, and here the author's confessional stance is even more evident than it is among the amateur historians. These began with the Protestant legal historian H. L. von Strampff's 1857 *Luther on Marriage* (*Luther über die Ehe*), largely a compendium of Luther's writings on marriage viewed very positively.[30] The Magdeburg journalist, art historian, and cultural commentator Friedrich Waldemar Kawerau built on this theme in his 1892 *The Reformation and Marriage* (*Die Reformation und die Ehe*), which examines marriage in various types of literature in the sixteenth century. Kawerau ends with a ringing endorsement of Luther, who "eradicated marriage from the stain of unholiness" and "showed how the highest callings of the Christian life could be performed within the household and family," thus setting in motion a "moral renewal" as a "quiet train of victory that could not be stopped."[31] Kawerau (and all other fans of Luther) were answered in the general attacks on Protestant ideas by Denifle and Grisar in the 1900s and in the more focused *Luther's Teachings on Marriage* (*Luthers Lehre von der Ehe*) published by the Catholic scholar Sigmund Baranowski in 1913.[32] Compared to most authors, Baranowski is relatively moderate: "His [Luther's] judgment of women is not exactly as ideal as some would have us believe. . . . The brutal openness with which he thrusts women into the 'natural' law of sexual life. . . . degraded female honor and dignity much more than simple vulgar satires did."[33] Denifle, Grisar, and Baranowski were answered by Werner Elert and Erich and Rheinhold Seeberg in the 1920s, who largely repeat Kawerau's assertions, as does Julius Boehmer in his giant 1935 *Luther's Book on Marriage* (*Luthers Ehebuch*), another compendium.[34]

One of the few women to be involved in this debate, the Catholic religious historian Lilly Zarncke, weighed in with "The Natural View of Marriage of the Young Luther" ("Die naturhafte Eheanschauung des jungen Luther") published in 1935, in which she describes Luther's "natural" view of marriage as leading to its "coarsening and darkening" when compared with the "deeper and more spiritualized" Catholic view.[35] The Finnish Lutheran theologian Olavi Lähteenmaki answered this in his 1955 *Sexuality and Marriage in Luther* (*Sexus und Ehe bei Luther*), which asserts that Luther's "new marriage ethics," rather than that of the Catholics, was the more spiritual because it was "grounded in the Gospel" and "freed humans caught in a net of doubts."[36]

Protestant intellectual and church historians writing in the 1960s in both Germany and the United States continued the line of argument begun a century earlier in which the Protestant Reformation rescued marriage from its degradation in late medieval monastic culture. In *Luther on the Christian Home*, William Lazareth asserts that Luther's own marriage combined with his ideas about marriage led to "the rebirth of a genuinely Christian ethos in home and community" and to the "liberation and transformation of Christian daily life."[37] This idea was largely repeated in the 1980s and again in 2001 by Steven Ozment.[38] And Catholic historians also show remarkable continuity, with Brad Gregory recently weighing in about the dire consequences of "widespread challenges to the very meaning of family and marriage" that originated—as did most of our other contemporary ills, in Gregory's view—in the Protestant Reformation.[39]

Luther's presence is overpowering in all of these studies, whether from the nineteenth century or the twenty-first, with the ideas of other reformers and differences among Protestants receiving relatively little attention. The plurality of Protestant opinions on marriage was lost in the sharp Catholic/Protestant confessional split.

Women's and Gender History and the Reformation, 1970–2010

As the debate about the Reformation and marriage was continuing on well-trodden confessional paths, other scholars went in new directions. Advocates of women's rights in the late 1960s, the "second wave" of the women's movement, looked at what was taught about the past—as well as what was taught in every other discipline—and realized it was only half the story. They asserted that history that did not include women's experiences was incomplete, and they began to investigate the lives of women in the past, unearthing these from new sources in archives and libraries and rereading more traditional sources to discover or highlight what they said about women.

Studies focusing on the Reformation appeared fairly early in this new wave of women's history. The first volume of the American Protestant Roland Bainton's *Women of the Reformation* appeared in 1971, with the second and third volumes following in 1973 and 1977.[40] Like the amateur histories of the nineteenth century, these were collections of biographical sketches with a somewhat hagiographic tone: among his "reasons for undertaking this study," Bainton explains in the first of these books, "is that we have here magnificent examples of courage."[41] Unlike the nineteenth-century histories, however, these include Catholic women along with Protestant, reflecting Bainton's concerns for toleration and religious liberty; in the section on Spain, even Teresa of Avila is given a substantial chapter, rather than simply Spanish Alumbrados and Erasmians. Bainton does not write from a feminist perspective, of course—his prefaces have comments that would have been at home in Anderson's preface a century earlier—but he does briefly mention the studies that were just then beginning to appear on women and the Reformation. These included the first articles on women and the Reformation by Miriam Chrisman, Nancy Roelker, and Charmarie Blaisdell, published in a special issue of the *Archive for Reformation History* in 1972. Other early studies included Jane Dempsey Douglass's chapter on women and the continental Reformation in Rosemary Radford Ruether's *Religion and Sexism* (1974), and Natalie Davis's *Society and Culture in Early Modern France* (1975), which included two chapters about women.[42]

None of the works on women and the Reformation published in the 1970s had the stridently confessional slant of Anderson's work or of the studies of Luther's writings on marriage, but implicitly they did have a confessional message, as they almost all focused on Protestant women, including Marguerite of Navarre, Renée de France, and Katharina Zell. Even in Bainton's works, Protestants vastly outnumbered Catholics. This focus suggested that Protestant women's lives were more worthy of note than those of Catholic women, that somehow the Reformation had provided women with more opportunities. To use a word that was becoming key to historical analysis, Protestant women had more agency.

This positive view of the impact of the Protestant Reformation on women was countered in the 1980s by other scholars, however, such as Lyndal Roper, Susan Karant-Nunn, Sigrid Brauner, and me, who tended to view the impact of Protestant ideas more negatively.[43] They stressed that viewing *marriage* in a positive light, as the Protestant reformers did, is not the same as viewing *women* positively and may, in fact, have contributed to suspicion of unmarried women—and, to lesser degree, unmarried men—as deviant and dangerous. Scholarship on the radical Reformation was also divided about whether the ideas and practices of Anabaptists, spiritualists, and other radicals were positive or negative toward women. G. H. Williams argued that radical groups offered women more opportunities than did magisterials or Catholics, and Claus-Peter Clasen that they were more restrictive and patriarchal.[44]

This difference of opinion created what we might term a "confessional period" in the history of scholarship on women and the Reformation, during which it was important to make clear exactly whether one regarded the Protestant Reformation as good or bad for women. This "confessional" split did not map onto a Protestant/Catholic split in terms of the religious identity of the historian, but it did roughly correspond to the place of training and historical emphasis: social historians or literary scholars trained outside of Germany tended to see the impact of the Reformation as more negative, intellectual historians trained in Germany as more positive. Questions about the effects of a particular change on women—what a friend of mine calls the Glinda test, from the good witch in the Wizard of Oz who asks Dorothy whether she is a good witch or a bad witch—were not limited to Reformation history, however. Such questions were quite common in women's history as a whole at this point, asked about Christianity, virginity, the Enlightenment, democracy, labor unions, pornography, and many other topics as well. Because value judgments so often underlay periodization—the "golden age" of Athens, the Dark Ages, the Renaissance, modernity—the Glinda test was also applied to historical periods.

At the same time that historians of women were assessing whether events and eras had positive or negative consequences for women, they also increasingly began to discuss the ways in which systems of sexual differentiation affected both women and men and by the early 1980s to use the word "gender" to describe these systems. At that point, they differentiated primarily between "sex," by which they meant physical, morphological, and anatomical differences (what are often called "biological differences"), and "gender," by which they meant a culturally constructed, historically changing, and often unstable system of differences. Most of the studies with "gender" in the title still focused on women—and women's history continued as its own field—but a few looked equally at both sexes or concentrated on the male experience, calling their work "men's history" or the "new men's studies."

Scholars in many fields increasingly switched from "sex" to "gender" as the acceptable terminology: "sex roles" became "gender roles," "sex distinctions" became "gender distinctions," and so on. Historians interested in this new perspective asserted that gender was an appropriate category of analysis when looking at *all* historical developments, not simply those involving women or the family. *Every* political, intellectual, religious, economic, social, and even military change had an impact on the actions and roles of men and women, and conversely, a culture's gender structures influenced every other structure or development.

Though not exactly in the forefront, the Reformation was fairly well represented in the new scholarship on gender. Lyndal Roper's article "'The Common Man,' 'The Common Good,' 'Common Women': Reflections on Gender and Meaning in the Reformation German Commune," appeared in 1987, and Jean Brink, Allison Coudert, and Maryanne Horowitz's *The Politics of Gender in Early Modern Europe* in 1989.[45] In general, those who framed their studies as gender analysis rather than women's history or religious history tended to have a more negative view of the Protestant Reformation, viewing it as limiting rather than liberating.

The late 1980s also saw the beginning of another historiographical trend that had a strong impact on views of women and the Reformation: a dramatic growth in the history of convents and women religious. In part this development was a function of sources, for convents housed literate women, controlled property and people, and were often linked with powerful families, all of which means they have frequently left extensive records. Historians, art historians, and literary scholars shaped by the women's movement began to examine convents in Germany that fought the Reformation; nuns and holy women in Spain (most prominently Teresa of Avila) who established or reformed institutions; abbesses in many places who patronized the visual arts and music and shaped family dynamics and political life; individuals and groups throughout Europe, such as Mary Ward or the Ursulines, who attempted to create an active religious vocation for women out in the world. In Italy, Gabriella Zarri at the University of Bologna directed teams of researchers exploring convents, holy women, and hagiographical texts and sponsored regular conferences on these topics.[46] Many of the abbesses and other female religious wrote extensively, and their works began to see modern editions and translations or in some cases the first appearance of their words in print.[47] Works by Protestant women also began to appear in new editions, but in terms of sources *by* women about religious issues, those from educated nuns in the sixteenth century far outweigh those from laywomen, Protestant or Catholic.[48]

This new convent history is continuing, contributing to the sense that it was Catholic women, rather than Protestant women, who had more agency and more options during this period: they had, as long recognized, *maritus aut murus* (marriage or the convent) but also various in-between forms, limited and criticized though these were. Those studying Teresa, or convents, or women striving to be Jesuits do not argue this explicitly, as they are very careful to talk about the many constraints within which women acted. But the sheer number of studies—whatever their tone or conclusions—makes it appear as if Catholic women were more likely than Protestant to have lives and ideas worthy of note or at least that any study of women and the Reformation cannot focus on Protestants alone.

This widening of focus is representative of more general developments in women's and gender history over the last several decades. Debating whether certain developments were good or bad for women has generally fallen out of favor, in large part because of the stress on difference and diversity—which women? Where? When? Married or single? Old or young? Urban or rural? Mothers or childless? It has also fallen out of favor as more research explicitly focuses on gender and includes men in its purview. Intensive archival research in many parts of Europe has meant that most scholars are less willing to make general conclusions about the impact of the Protestant or Catholic Reformation on *all* women or on ideas about gender in *all* of Europe than they were several decades ago.

Along with emphasizing complexity and variety, scholars are also de-emphasizing the role of the Protestant Reformation *alone* in changing women's lives or gender structures. Heide Wunder, for example, points to a "familialization of work and life" before the sixteenth century, in which the marital pair became the basic production and consumption unit. Thus Reformation ideas about the family did not create the bourgeois family, but resulted from it. This was one of the reasons that Protestant arguments in favor of marriage as the "natural" vocation of women and an acceptable life for men were accepted so easily across much of Europe and readily adopted, with a few modifications, by Catholics.[49] Beate Schuster similarly sees praise of the male-headed bourgeois household as part of a new "morality of settledness" that emerged out of an urban context before the Reformation, and I have argued that gendered ideas about men as workers and women as "helpmeets" emerged in craft and journeymen's guilds before they become part of Reformation ideology.[50]

There has also been increasing emphasis on continuities across the great divide of 1517. Christine Peters finds continuities in patterns of piety centering on Christ and ideals for women extending from the fifteenth through the seventeenth centuries, and Kathleen Crowther-Heyck finds not much difference between Protestants and Catholics in terms of ideas about reproduction and childbirth.[51] Ulinka Rublack has noted that even the Protestant reformers' choice of dress, often black gowns lined with fur or red to emphasize their stature as scholars, continues a pattern in male clothing established by scholars in the century preceding the Reformation.[52]

Thus in most lines of research, the history of women and/or gender and the Reformation has moved out of its confessional period into one in which the key emphasis is on diversity, variety, and complexity and on the intersection of categories of analysis. It has exploded in volume and no longer tells a single story of advance or decline, but emphasizes the differences between the ideas and ideals of religious reformers and the institutions that were established and ended, highlights women's agency and the actions of men supporting and restricting that agency, and discusses the great differences between rural and urban, rich and poor. It has developed new theoretical and methodological directions and also presented new ways to look at more "old-fashioned topics," such as the lives of great women and the ideas of great men. Historians of the Reformation are beginning to examine reformers' ideas about men as men more systematically and also to study the way men responded to or ignored those ideas.[53] Following the lead of the new scholarship on masculinity in more recent periods (which tends to speak of "masculinities" in the plural), they have emphasized variety and diversity in both ideals of manhood and their actualization.

Conclusion

Were Johann Feustking to come back from the dead and see what has happened to the history of women and the Reformation in the three centuries since he wrote, he would probably scurry instantly back to his coffin in horror. Prophetesses and "other sectarian female persons through whom God's church is disturbed" are certainly still there, but their ideas, writings, and actions are now carefully analyzed rather than simply denounced. Were James Anderson to come back from the dead, he would probably retreat less quickly and might well recognize the descendants of his books in popular and scholarly histories of women and the Reformation that present "various of the leading facts in the history of the Reformation in a somewhat new connection."[54] According to what I know about Roland Bainton from my colleagues and friends who were his students (and from the one time I met him myself), he might be surprised but would not retreat at all.

What *might* surprise Bainton, who forty years ago recognized that a new research area was developing in Reformation history, is how long it has taken for this research to move beyond journals, collections of articles, and monographs and into general histories of the Reformation. In the 1980s, most surveys of the Reformation followed the pattern identified by Anderson more than a century earlier, with discussions of women or gender (or sexuality) "altogether omitted or only slightly touched upon." In the 1990s, a few began to include at least a few pages on women and marriage, generally introduced in the section on Luther's own marriage and the debate over clerical celibacy, but that is all. Only Jonathan W. Zophy's *A Short History of Renaissance and Reformation Europe* and later Ulinka Rublack's *Reformation Europe* included more than these tiny sections or began to integrate material on women, gender, or sexuality.[55] Scholars, even those at the senior level, focusing on women were criticized for ignoring topics judged more significant. Elsie McKee, for example, told me she was both teased and reproved for spending time producing her edition and biography of Katharina Schütz Zell instead of concentrating on her "important" editions of Calvin.

This imbalance can also be found in works on broader Christian history. A much-advertised and lavishly produced source reader in Christian history published in 2001 by Wiley-Blackwell, Alister McGrath's *Christian Literature: An Anthology*, includes writings by only two women, Julian of Norwich and Dorothy Sayers, along with those of eighty-nine men, including Shakespeare, Trollope, and Garrison Keillor. As Elizabeth Clark commented in the same year about Christian history in general, "the hoped-for 'paradigm shift'" has had "less than overwhelming success."[56]

That shift may finally be happening. Kirsi Stjerna begins her 2009 book on women and the Reformation designed for undergraduates and seminarians as follows: "Teaching courses on the Reformation is no longer feasible without the inclusion of women as subjects in the story of the Reformation and its evaluation."[57] Stjerna is a pastor, church historian, and the director of the Institute for Luther Studies at the Lutheran Theological Seminary at Gettysburg, the oldest continuing Lutheran seminary in the Americas. She thus writes from the perspective of mainstream Protestant theological training, not primarily from the perspective of women's history or gender studies. That sentence is still more of a wish than a statement of fact, but books like Stjerna's, together with the continuing expansion of research now under way, may help the next generation of historians to transform her opening sentence into reality. Such a gender-inclusive history might seem novel, and it certainly would have seemed bizarre to most confessional and scientific historians. It might not to Gottfried Arnold, my favorite among all the authors I have considered here. Though trained at Wittenberg and for a time a professor of church history at Giessen, Arnold developed a view of Christianity's past that never forgot its plurality in any era, nor forgot that women were part of nearly every group. Were *he* to come back from the grave, he might very well see the last forty years of research on women as simply a continuation of what he began.

Merry Wiesner-Hanks is Distinguished Professor of History and Women's and Gender Studies at the University of Wisconsin–Milwaukee. She is the senior editor of the *Sixteenth Century Journal*, editor of the *Journal of Global History*, and the editor-in-chief of the nine-volume *Cambridge World History* (2015). She is an author or editor of more than thirty books and nearly one hundred articles that have appeared in English, German, French, Italian, Spanish, Greek, Chinese, Turkish, and Korean. Her research has been supported by grants from the Fulbright and Guggenheim Foundations, among others.

Notes

1. John Acton, letter to contributors to the *Cambridge Modern History,* quoted in Bonnie G. Smith, *The Gender of History: Men, Women, and Historical Practice* (Cambridge, MA, 1998), 127.
2. Leopold von Ranke, letter to Bettina von Arnim, quoted in Smith, *Gender of History*, 116.
3. Smith, *Gender of History*; Julie Des Jardins, *Women and the Historical Enterprise in America: Gender, Race, and the Politics of Memory, 1880–1945* (Chapel Hill, 2003); and Peter Novick, *That Noble Dream: The "Objectivity Question" and the American Historical Profession* (New York, 1988).
4. On amateur history, see Smith, *Gender of History*, esp. chap. 6; and Mary Spongberg, *Writing Women's History since the Renaissance* (Houndmills, Basingstoke, 2002), esp. chap. 5.
5. James Anderson, *Ladies of the Reformation: Memoirs of Distinguished Female Characters, belonging to the Reformation in the Sixteenth Century* (Glasgow, 1855 and 1857).
6. Anderson, *Ladies of the Reformation,* vi.
7. Thomas Edwards, *Gangraena* (London, 1646). The quotation is from the long subtitle.
8. Johann Feustking, *Gynaeceum Haeretico Fanaticum* (Frankfurt am Main and Leipzig, 1704).
9. Gottfried Arnold, *Unpartheiische Kirchen und Ketzerhistorie: Von Anfang des Neuen Testaments biß auf das Jahr Christi 1688* (Frankfurt am Main, 1729), 1108; my translation.
10. Eusebius Engelhard [Michael Kuen], *Lucifer Wittenbergensis, oder, Der Morgen-Stern von Wittemberg. Das ist: Vollständiger Lebens-Lauff Catharinae von Bore, Des vermaynten Ehe-Weibs D. Martini Lutheri* (Landsperg, 1747; 2nd ed., 1749).
11. Christian Wilhelm Franz Walch, *Wahrhaftige Geschichte der seligen Frau Catharina von Bora, D. Martin Luthers Ehegattin, wieder Eusebii Engelhards Morgenstern zu Wittenberg* (Halle, 1751; 2nd ed., 2 vols., 1752–54).
12. See Barbara Hoffman, *Radikalpietismus um 1700: Der Streit um das Recht auf eine neue Gesellschaft* (Frankfurt am Main, 1996); and Ulrike Witt, *Bekehrung, Bildung und Biographie: Frauen im Umkreis des Halleschen Pietismus* (Halle, 1996).
13. Charlotte Elizabeth Tonna, *The Female Martyrs of the English Reformation* (London, 1844).
14. Henry Clissold, *Last Hours of Christian Women, or, An Account of the Deaths of Some Eminent Christian Women of the Church of England: From the Period of the Reforma-*

tion to the Beginning of the Present Century (London, 1853); and Walter Walsh, *The Women Martyrs of the Reformation* (London, 1911).

15. Anderson, *Ladies of the Reformation,* vi.

16. Anderson, *Ladies of the Reformation,* iv.

17. Anderson, *Ladies of the Reformation,* ix.

18. James Anderson, *Les femmes de la réformation,* 3 vols. (Paris, 1865–69); Elisabeth Hasebroek, *De vrouwen der hervorming* (Amsterdam, 1859); *Quelques femmes de la Réforme: recueil biographique* (Lausanne, 1859); Ernestine Dietsch Diethoff, *Edle Frauen der Reformation und der Zeit der Glaubenskämpfe in Lebens- und Zeitbildern* (Leipzig, 1875); Ellen Creathorne Needham, *Women of the Reformation, Their Lives, Faith and Trials* (London, 1861); William Chapman, *Notable Women of the Reformation* (London, 1884); J. I. Good, *Famous Women of the Reformed Faith* (Philadelphia, 1901); and Christopher Hare [Marian Andrews], *Men and Women of the Italian Reformation* (London, 1914).

19. Emma Louise Parry, *Woman in the Reformation* (Philadelphia, 1882); and Annie Wittenmyer, *The Women of the Reformation* (New York, 1885).

20. Wittenmyer, *The Women of the Reformation,* 6; her emphasis.

21. Wittenmyer, *The Women of the Reformation,* ix.

22. Anderson, *Ladies of the Reformation,* ix; and Wittenmyer, *The Women of the Reformation,* x.

23. Anderson, *Ladies of the Reformation,* ix.

24. Diethoff, *Edle Frauen,* 8.

25. Wittenmyer, *The Women of the Reformation,* 6.

26. Quoted in James C. Albisetti, *Schooling German Women and Girls: Secondary and Higher Education in the Nineteenth Century* (Princeton, 1989), 228. See also Patricia M. Mazón, *Gender and the Modern Research University: The Admission of Women to German Higher Education, 1865–1914* (Stanford, 2003).

27. Diethoff, *Edle Frauen,* v.

28. See Susan Mosher Stuard, ed., *Women in Medieval History and Historiography* (Philadelphia, 1986).

29. Maxine Berg, "The First Women Economic Historians," *Economic History Review* 45 (1992): 308–12.

30. H. L. von Strampff, *Luther über die Ehe* (Berlin, 1857).

31. Walter Kawerau, *Die Reformation und die Ehe: Ein Beitrag zur Kulturgeschichte des sechzehnten Jahrhunderts* (Halle, 1892), 86.

32. Heinrich Denifle, *Luther und Luthertum in der ersten Entwickelung: Quellenmässig dargestellt* (Mainz, 1904–9); Hartmann Grisar, *Luther* (Freiburg in Breisgau, 1911–12); and Sigmund Baranowski, *Luthers Lehre von der Ehe* (Münster, 1913).

33. Baranowski, *Luthers Lehre,* 198–99.

34. Werner Elert, *Die Ehe in Luthertum* (Erlangen, 1927); Erich Seeberg, *Luthers Ehe: Vortrag gelegentlich der 29. Generalversammlung des Evang. Bundes zur Wahrung der deutsch-protestantischen Interessen gehalten am 29. Juni 1925* (Berlin, 1925); Reinhold Seeberg, *Luthers Anschauung von dem Geschlechtsleben und der Ehe und ihre geschichtliche Stellung* (Berlin, 1929); and Julius Boehmer, *Luthers Ehebuch* (Zwickau, 1935).

35. Lilly Zarncke, "Die naturhafte Eheanschauung des jungen Luther," *Archiv für Kulturgeschichte* 25 (1935): 281–305, esp. 304.

36. Olavi Lähteenmaki, *Sexus und Ehe bei Luther* (Turku, 1955), 175.

37. Willliam Lazareth, *Luther on the Christian Home* (Philadelphia, 1960), vii.

38. Steven Ozment, *When Fathers Ruled: Family Life in Reformation Europe* (Cambridge, MA, 1983); and Steven Ozment, *Ancestors: The Loving Family of Old Europe* (Cambridge, MA, 2001). For a less celebratory interpretation from a Protestant perspective, see Scott Hendrix, "Luther on Marriage," *Lutheran Quarterly* 14 (2000): 335–50.
39. Brad S. Gregory, *The Unintended Reformation* (Cambridge, MA, 2012), 176.
40. Roland Bainton, *Women of the Reformation*, 3 vols. (Minneapolis, 1971–79).
41. Bainton, *Women of the Reformation*, vol. 1, 14.
42. Miriam Chrisman, "Women of the Reformation in Strassburg, 1490–1530," *Archiv für Reformationsgeschichte* 63 (1972): 143–68; Nancy Roelker, "The Role of Noblewomen in the French Reformation," *Archiv für Reformationsgeschichte* 63 (1972): 168–95; Charmarie Blaisdell, "Renée de France between Reform and Counter-Reform," *Archiv für Reformationsgeschichte* 63 (1972): 196–226; Jane Dempsey Douglass, "Women and the Continental Reformation," in *Religion and Sexism: Images of Woman in the Jewish and Christian Traditions*, ed. Rosemary Radford Ruether (New York, 1974), 292–318; and Natalie Davis, *Society and Culture in Early Modern France* (Stanford, 1975).
43. Lyndal Roper, "'The Common Man,' 'the Common Good,' 'Common Women': Reflections on Gender and Meaning in the Reformation German Commune," *Social History* 12 (1987): 1–21; Roper, *The Holy Household: Women and Morals in Reformation Augsburg* (Oxford, 1989); Susan C. Karant-Nunn, "Continuity and Change: Some Effects of the Reformation on the Women of Zwickau," *Sixteenth Century Journal* 13 (1982): 17–42; Susan Karant-Nunn, "The Transmission of Luther's Teachings on Women and Matrimony: The Case of Zwickau," *Archiv für Reformationsgeschichte* 77 (1986): 31–46; Sigrid Brauner, *Fearless Wives and Frightened Shrews: The Construction of the Witch in Early Modern Germany* (Amherst, 1994); and Merry Wiesner, "Luther and Women: The Death of Two Marys," in *Disciplines of Faith: Religion, Patriarchy and Politics*, ed. Raphael Samuel, James Obelkevich, and Lyndal Roper (London, 1987), 295–310.
44. G. H. Williams, *The Radical Reformation* (Philadelphia, 1962), 506–7; and Claus-Peter Clasen, *Anabaptism: A Social History, 1525–1618* (Ithaca, 1972), 207.
45. Roper, "Common Man"; and Jean Brink, Allison Coudert, and Maryanne Horowitz, ed., *The Politics of Gender in Early Modern Europe* (Kirksville, 1989).
46. Zarri has also edited the proceedings of many of these conferences. See Gabriella Zarri, ed., *Donna, disciplina, creanza cristiana dal XV al XVII secolo: studi e testi a stampa* (Rome, 1996), which has a very large bibliography of early modern works by and about religious women; and Gabriella Zarri, *Ordini religiosi, santità e culti: prospettive di ricerca tra Europa e America Latina: atti del Seminario di Roma, 21–22 giugno 2001* (Galatina, 2003).
47. Many of these texts appeared in the series The Other Voice in Early Modern Europe, edited by Margaret King and Albert Rabil, Jr., which was initially published by the University of Chicago Press and in 2010 moved to the University of Toronto Press. In addition, the Reformation Texts with Translation (1350–1600): Women of the Reformation series, edited by Kenneth Hagen and Merry Wiesner-Hanks and published by Marquette University Press, has issued several books with works by female religious.
48. Elsie Anne McKee, *Katharina Schütz Zell* (Leiden, 1999) includes one volume of biography and interpretation (vol. 1, *The Life and Thought of a Sixteenth-Century Reformer*) and one of edited texts (vol. 2, *The Writings: A Critical Edition*); and Peter Matheson,

Argula von Grumbach: A Woman's Voice in the Reformation (Edinburgh, 1995). For Dutch Anabaptist women, see Hermoine Joldersma and Louis Grijp, ed. and trans., *Elisabeth's Manly Courage: Testimonials and Songs by and about Martyred Anabaptist Women* (Milwaukee, 2001).

49. Heide Wunder, *Er ist die Sonn', sie ist der Mond: Frauen in der frühen Neuzeit* (Munich, 1992). English edition: *He Is the Sun, She Is the Moon: Women in Early Modern Germany*, trans. Thomas Dunlap (Cambridge, MA, 1998).

50. Beate Schuster, *Die freie Frauen: Dirnen und Frauenhäuser in 15. und 16. Jahrhundert* (Frankfurt am Main, 1995); Merry Wiesner-Hanks, "The Religious Dimensions of Guild Notions of Honor in Reformation Germany," in *Ehrkonzepte in der Frühen Neuzeit: Identitäten und Abgrenzungen*, ed. Sibylle Backmann, Hans-Jörg Künast, Sabine Ullman, and B. Ann Tlusty, Colloquia Augustana 8 (Berlin, 1998), 223–33.

51. Christine Peters, *Patterns of Piety: Women, Gender, and Religion in Late Medieval and Reformation England* (Cambridge, 2003); and Kathleen Crowther-Heyck, "'Be Fruitful and Multiply': Genesis and Generation in Reformation Germany," *Renaissance Quarterly* 55 (2002): 904–35.

52. Ulinka Rublack, *Dressing Up: Cultural Identity in Renaissance Europe* (Oxford, 2010), esp. chap. 3.

53. Scott H. Hendrix and Susan C. Karant-Nunn, ed., *Masculinity in the Reformation Era* (Kirksville, 2008).

54. For example, see C. Arnold Snyder and Linda A. Huebert Hecht, *Profiles of Anabaptist Women: Sixteenth-Century Reforming Pioneers* (Waterloo, Ontario, 1996); Paul F. L. Zahl, *Five Women of the English Reformation* (Grand Rapids, MI, 2001); and Jeni Hiett Umble and Linda Huebert Hecht, ed., *Strangers at Home: Amish and Mennonite Women in History* (Baltimore, 2002).

55. Jonathan W. Zophy, *A Short History of Renaissance and Reformation Europe* (Upper Saddle River, NJ, 1996; 4th ed., 2008); and Ulinka Rublack, *Reformation Europe* (Cambridge, 2005).

56. Elizabeth A. Clark, "Women, Gender, and the Study of Christian History," *Church History* 70 (2001): 395–426, esp. 395.

57. Kirsi Stjerna, *Women and the Reformation* (London, 2009), esp. 1.

Bibliography

Albisetti, James C. *Schooling German Women and Girls: Secondary and Higher Education in the Nineteenth Century*. Princeton, 1989.

Anderson, James. *Les femmes de la réformation*. 3 vols. Paris, 1865–69.

———. *Ladies of the Reformation: Memoirs of Distinguished Female Characters, Belonging to the Reformation in the Sixteenth Century*. Glasgow, 1855 and 1857.

Arnold, Gottfried. *Die Unparteyische Kirchen- und Ketzer-Historie: Vom Anfang des Neuen Testaments bis auff das Jahr Christi 1688*. Frankfurt am Main, 1729.

Bainton, Roland. *Women of the Reformation*. 3 vols. Minneapolis, 1971–79.

Baranowski, Sigmund. *Luthers Lehre von der Ehe*. Münster, 1913.

Berg, Maxine. "The First Women Economic Historians." *Economic History Review* 45, no. 2 (1992): 308–12.

Blaisdell, Charmarie. "Renée de France between Reform and Counter-Reform." *Archiv für Reformationsgeschichte* 63 (1972): 196–226.

Boehmer Julius. *Luthers Ehebuch*. Zwickau, 1935.

Brauner, Sigrid. *Fearless Wives and Frightened Shrews: The Construction of the Witch in Early Modern Germany*. Amherst, 1994.

Brink, Jean, Allison Coudert, and Maryanne Horowitz, ed. *The Politics of Gender in Early Modern Europe*. Kirksville, 1989.

Chapman, William. *Notable Women of the Reformation*. London, 1884.

Chrisman, Miriam. "Women of the Reformation in Strassburg, 1490–1530." *Archiv für Reformationsgeschichte* 63 (1972): 143–68.

Clark, Elizabeth A. "Women, Gender, and the Study of Christian History." *Church History* 70 (2001): 395–426.

Clasen, Claus-Peter. *Anabaptism: A Social History, 1525–1618*. Ithaca, 1972.

Clissold, Henry. *Last Hours of Christian Women, or, An Account of the Deaths of Some Eminent Christian Women of the Church of England: From the Period of the Reformation to the Beginning of the Present Century*. London, 1853.

Crowther-Heyck, Kathleen. "'Be Fruitful and Multiply': Genesis and Generation in Reformation Germany." *Renaissance Quarterly* 55 (2002): 904–35.

Davis, Natalie Zemon. *Society and Culture in Early Modern France*. Stanford, 1975.

Denifle, Heinrich. *Luther und Luthertum in der ersten Entwickelung: Quellenmässig dargestellt*. Mainz, 1904–9.

Des Jardins, Julie. *Women and the Historical Enterprise in America: Gender, Race, and the Politics of Memory, 1880–1945*. Chapel Hill, 2003.

Diethoff, Ernestine Dietsch. *Edle Frauen der Reformation und der Zeit der Glaubenskämpfe in Lebens- und Zeitbildern*. Leipzig, 1875.

Douglass, Jane Dempsey. "Women and the Continental Reformation." In *Religion and Sexism: Images of Woman in the Jewish and Christian Traditions*, edited by Rosemary Radford Ruether, 292–319. New York, 1974.

Edwards, Thomas. *Gangraena*. London, 1646.

Elert, Werner. *Die Ehe in Luthertum*. Erlangen, 1927.

Engelhard, Eusebius [Michael Kuen]. *Lucifer Wittenbergensis, oder, Der Morgen-Stern von Wittemberg. Das ist: Vollständiger Lebens-Lauff Catharinae von Bore, Des vermaynten Ehe-Weibs D. Martini Lutheri*. Landsperg, 1747; 2nd ed., 1749.

Feustking, Johann. *Gynaeceum Haeretico Fanaticum*. Frankfurt am Main and Leipzig, 1704.

Good, J. I. *Famous Women of the Reformed Faith*. Philadelphia, 1901.

Gregory, Brad S. *The Unintended Reformation*. Cambridge, MA, 2012.

Grisar, Hartmann. *Luther*. Freiburg in Breisgau, 1911–12.

Hare, Christopher [Marian Andrews]. *Men and Women of the Italian Reformation*. London, 1914.

Hasebroek, Elisabeth. *De vrouwen der hervorming*. Amsterdam, 1859.

Hendrix, Scott H. "Luther on Marriage." *Lutheran Quarterly* 14 (2000): 335–50.

Hendrix, Scott H., and Susan C. Karant-Nunn, ed. *Masculinity in the Reformation Era*. Kirksville, 2008.

Hoffman, Barbara. *Radikalpietismus um 1700: Der Streit um das Recht auf eine neue Gesellschaft*. Frankfurt am Main, 1996.

Joldersma, Hermoine, and Louis Grijp, ed. *Elisabeth's Manly Courage: Testimonials and Songs by and about Martyred Anabaptist Women.* Milwaukee, 2001.

Karant-Nunn, Susan C. "Continuity and Change: Some Effects of the Reformation on the Women of Zwickau." *Sixteenth Century Journal* 13 (1982): 17–42.

———. "The Transmission of Luther's Teachings on Women and Matrimony: The Case of Zwickau." *Archiv für Reformationsgeschichte* 77 (1986): 31–46.

Kawerau, Walter. *Die Reformation und die Ehe: Ein Beitrag zur Kulturgeschichte des sechzehnten Jahrhunderts.* Halle, 1892.

Lähteenmaki, Olavi. *Sexus und Ehe bei Luther.* Turku, 1955.

Lazareth, Willliam. *Luther on the Christian Home.* Philadelphia, 1960.

Matheson, Peter. *Argula von Grumbach: A Woman's Voice in the Reformation.* Edinburgh, 1995.

Mazón, Patricia M. *Gender and the Modern Research University: The Admission of Women to German Higher Education, 1865–1914.* Stanford, 2003.

McKee, Elsie Anne. *Katharina Schütz Zell.* 2 vols. Leiden, 1999.

Needham, Ellen Creathorne. *Women of the Reformation, Their Lives, Faith and Trials.* London, 1861.

Novick, Peter. *That Noble Dream: The "Objectivity Question" and the American Historical Profession.* New York, 1988.

Ozment, Steven. *Ancestors: The Loving Family of Old Europe.* Cambridge, MA, 2001.

———. *When Fathers Ruled: Family Life in Reformation Europe.* Cambridge, MA, 1983.

Parry, Emma Louise. *Woman in the Reformation.* Philadelphia, 1882.

Peters, Christine. *Patterns of Piety: Women, Gender, and Religion in Late Medieval and Reformation England.* Cambridge, 2003.

Quelques femmes de la Réforme: recueil biographique. Lausanne, 1859.

Roelker, Nancy. "The Role of Noblewomen in the French Reformation." *Archiv für Reformationsgeschichte* 63 (1972): 168–95.

Roper, Lyndal. "'The Common Man,' 'the Common Good,' 'Common Women': Reflections on Gender and Meaning in the Reformation German Commune." *Social History* 12 (1987): 1–22.

———. *The Holy Household: Women and Morals in Reformation Augsburg.* Oxford, 1989.

Rublack, Ulinka. *Dressing Up: Cultural Identity in Renaissance Europe.* Oxford, 2010.

———. *Reformation Europe.* Cambridge, 2005.

Schuster, Beate. *Die freie Frauen: Dirnen und Frauenhäuser in 15. und 16. Jahrhundert.* Frankfurt am Main, 1995.

Seeberg, Erich. *Luthers Ehe: Vortrag gelegentlich der 29. Generalversammlung des Evang. Bundes zur Wahrung der deutsch-protestantischen Interessen gehalten am 29. Juni 1925.* Berlin, 1925.

Seeberg, Reinhold. *Luthers Anschauung von dem Geschlechtsleben und der Ehe und ihre geschichtliche Stellung.* Berlin, 1929.

Smith, Bonnie G. *The Gender of History: Men, Women, and Historical Practice.* Cambridge, MA, 1998.

Snyder, C. Arnold, and Linda A. Huebert Hecht. *Profiles of Anabaptist Women: Sixteenth-Century Reforming Pioneers*. Waterloo, Ontario, 1996.

Spongberg, Mary. *Writing Women's History since the Renaissance*. Houndmills, Basingstoke, 2002.

Stjerna, Kirsi. *Women and the Reformation*. London, 2009.

Stuard, Susan Mosher, ed. *Women in Medieval History and Historiography*. Philadelphia, 1986.

Strampff, H. L. von. *Luther über die Ehe*. Berlin, 1857.

Tonna, Charlotte Elizabeth. *The Female Martyrs of the English Reformation*. London, 1844.

Umble, Jeni Hiett, and Linda Huebert Hecht, ed. *Strangers at Home: Amish and Mennonite Women in History*. Baltimore, 2002.

Walch, Christian Wilhelm Franz. *Wahrhaftige Geschichte der seligen Frau Catharina von Bora, D. Martin Luthers Ehegattin, wieder Eusebii Engelhards Morgenstern zu Wittenberg*. Halle, 1751; 2nd ed., 2 vols., 1752–54.

Walsh, Walter. *The Women Martyrs of the Reformation*. London, 1911.

Wiesner, Merry. "Luther and Women: The Death of Two Marys." In *Disciplines of Faith: Religion, Patriarchy and Politics*, edited by Raphael Samuel, James Obelkevich, and Lyndal Roper, 295–310. London, 1987.

Wiesner-Hanks, Merry. "The Religious Dimensions of Guild Notions of Honor in Reformation Germany." In *Ehrkonzepte in der Frühen Neuzeit: Identitäten und Abgrenzungen*, edited by Sibylle Backmann, Hans-Jörg Künast, Sabine Ullman, and B. Ann Tlusty, 223–33. Berlin, 1998.

Williams, George Hunston. *The Radical Reformation*. Philadelphia, 1962; reprint, Kirksville, 2000.

Witt, Ulrike. *Bekehrung, Bildung und Biographie: Frauen im Umkries des Halleschen Pietismus*. Halle, 1996.

Wittenmyer, Annie. *The Women of the Reformation*. New York, 1885.

Wunder, Heide, *Er ist die Sonn', sie ist der Mond: Frauen in der frühen Neuzeit*. Munich, 1992.

———. *He Is the Sun, She Is the Moon: Women in Early Modern Germany*. Translated by Thomas Dunlap. Cambridge, MA, 1998.

Zahl, Paul F. L. *Five Women of the English Reformation*. Grand Rapids, MI, 2001.

Zarncke, Lilly. "Die naturhafte Eheanschauung des jungen Luther." *Archiv für Kulturgeschichte* 25 (1935): 281–305.

Zarri, Gabriella. *Ordini religiosi, santità e culti: prospettive di ricerca tra Europa e America Latina: atti del Seminario di Roma, 21–22 giugno 2001*. Galatina, 2003.

———, ed. *Donna, disciplina, creanza cristiana dal XV al XVII secolo: studi e testi a stampa*. Rome, 1996.

Zophy, Jonathan W. *A Short History of Renaissance and Reformation Europe*. Upper Saddle River, NJ, 1996; 4th ed., 2008.

CHAPTER FIVE

Catholics as Foreign Bodies
The County of Mark as a Protestant Territory in Nineteenth- and Twentieth-Century Prussian Historiography

RALF-PETER FUCHS

"There was a grand movement in our lands. The people felt the power of truth and could not withstand it. . . . The years from 1560 to 1580 were the years of the Reformation in the parishes."[1] In this manner, the renowned church historian Hugo Rothert began his 1909 history of the church in the county of Mark. Rothert produced his work in celebration of the jubilee of the three-hundred-year alliance of the county of Mark with the Protestant ruling house of Hohenzollern, commemorated by many regional historians as having begun in 1609. In this year in accordance with the terms of the Treaty of Dortmund, two rulers claimed possession of the county of Mark as well as the territories of the duchies of Kleve, Jülich, and Berg, the county of Ravensberg, and the lordship of Ravenstein. From this moment on, both Lutheran princes, often designated as the Possessors (*Possidierende*), tried to safeguard their interests in the region first and foremost by acting in opposition to one another. The electoral prince of Brandenburg and the count Palatinate-Neuburg each maintained their claim of ownership over the entire territory for decades, despite signing the Treaty of Xanten, which had divided up the territories in 1614. The count of Palatinate-Neuburg obtained the duchies of Jülich and Berg and the lordship of Ravenstein. The elector of Brandenburg obtained Kleve, Mark, and Ravensberg.[2] Nonetheless, both princes considered the Treaty of Xanten only as a provisional treaty, not as a resolution of their claims.

Regional historians repeatedly have ignored the provisional character of the Treaty of Xanten. They also have ignored the way in which political authority penetrated the region through the interplay of the two sides during the decades following this treaty. Religion played an important role. In 1613, the count of Palatinate-Neuburg became a Catholic, followed swiftly by the conversion of the elector of Brandenburg to Calvinism. Each of the princes regularly took advantage of the multiconfessional situation in the territories of Jülich-Kleve, where people of different confessions lived, to reclaim sovereignty over their co-religious church ministers and parishioners of the other by providing them religious protection.[3]

The instability of the political situation created by the Treaty of Xanten became apparent soon after its conclusion. During the Thirty Years' War, Wolfgang Wilhelm, count of Palatinate-Neuburg, seized temporary political power in the county of Mark with the help of Spanish troops after they captured most of the towns in 1622, followed by the most important fortresses Lippstadt and Soest in 1623.[4] Although the Dutch and Brandenburg troops successfully reconquered some towns in 1624, the count of Palatinate-Neuburg and his allies retained control over a large part of the territory.[5] He used Italian mercenaries and other troops to maintain military control.

This outcome was to have significant implications for religious policy. The Spanish troops expelled most Lutheran and Reformed priests. In 1623, they set fire to the Lutheran church in Bochum and tortured the pastor. Wolfgang Wilhelm implemented Catholicism in a systematic, bureaucratic manner. He appointed a Catholic as his local magistrate (*Landdrost*) responsible for contributions and grievances of the subjects (*Gravamina*).[6] He required each priest to get his qualifications. While the actions of the troops were spontaneous, the official transformations were not. Nonetheless, neither method led to an enduring change. The majority of the population remained Protestant in most towns. In some places, however, Catholicism was strengthened during the war. In Blankenstein, where Catholic bailiffs had influenced local church services since the early seventeenth century, Catholic priests remained in office even after the Spanish occupation ended.[7]

In 1629 and in 1630, the rival princes tried again to reach new agreements but instead signed renewed provisional contracts. Even after Wolfgang Wilhelm finished his occupation of the county of Mark in accordance with the Treaty of The Hague in 1630, the estates and subjects of the region still had to deal with Catholic authorities. Imperial and Catholic League troops were billeted in many towns from 1632 onward. In 1636, Johann, count of Götz, was the commander-in-chief of the imperial army that ravaged the territory, which had gained a reputation as containing traitors to the emperor.[8] Brandenburg rule was not even firmly reestablished in many regions before 1644 when Elector Friedrich Wilhelm finally sent in his troops. In 1647 he was able to conclude a new provisional treaty with the count of Palatinate-Neuburg, granting the duchy of Kleve and the counties of Mark and Ravensberg to himself and the duchies of Jülich and Berg to Wolfgang Wilhelm. In 1651, the county of Mark once again became the center of conflict when Friedrich Wilhelm unsuccessfully tried to seize the duchy of Berg by force.[9] After 1651, both princes repeatedly negotiated the rules of possession. During each incident, the interests of the inhabitants of disputed parishes, especially those of different confessions, played an important role. In 1666 and again in 1672/73, treaties were negotiated to settle the differences. In 1682, an official diplomatic resolution was reached at the conference of Rheinberg. Even afterward, the kings of Prussia and the Electoral Palatines, the descendants of the so-called Possessors, repeatedly became embroiled in the conflicts between Lutherans, Reformed, and Catholics living in the territories well into the eighteenth century.[10]

When regional historians of the county of Mark wrote their texts for the three-hundred-year Hohenzollern Jubilee in 1909, they avoided discussing all those problems stemming from this uncertain and complex political situation after 1609. Instead, Hugo Rothert portrayed the story of a Protestant county of Mark, focusing on its roots and foundation. When he spoke of a "Reformation of the church" in this context, he obviously was inspired by the national historical tradition established by Leopold von Ranke that recognized only one genuine Reformation in Germany.

Thomas A. Brady recently has argued for an alternative thesis. In place of Ranke's "German History in the Age of Reformation" with Martin Luther in a central position, Brady has proposed "German Histories in the Age of Reformations."[11] If I understand this new direction of Reformation history, I see an increased awareness of the plurality of the concepts of Reformation held by contemporaries during the sixteenth and seventeenth centuries than Ranke's focus on the central position of Martin Luther would indicate. Diarmaid MacCulloch points out that "in fact there were many different Reformations, nearly all of which would have said that they were simply aimed at creating authentic Catholic Christianity."[12] Finally, many American historians, including most recently Lee Palmer Wandel and Thomas Max Safley, have emphasized the diversity in the perception of what "Reformation" meant in the late Middle Ages and early modern era.[13] Furthermore, researchers have become interested in those territories with mixed confessions within the Holy Roman Empire, exploring how the coexistence of groups with different religious identities was possible.[14] Against this background of a paradigm shift, the efforts of Hugo Rothert and other earlier historians to deal with such plurality has drawn new interest. How did they handle differences within confessions, and how did they handle the coexistence of Lutherans, Calvinists, and Catholics living in the county of Mark?

Catholics as Strangers

The preconditions to produce a history of Reformation in the county of Mark as a uniform story of the triumph of Protestantism, let alone Lutheranism, were rather unfavorable. Historians could not deny or ignore the coexistence of Lutherans, Calvinists, and Catholics living in the region and attending diverse forms of divine services during the sixteenth, seventeenth, and eighteenth centuries. When the Lutheran pastor Johann Dietrich von Steinen wrote his *History of Westphalia* in the mid-eighteenth century, he already had to concede that people of all the confessions permitted in the Holy Roman Empire were represented in many localities within the county of Mark. He also remarked that although Lutherans remained the majority confession, in some towns such as Kamen, it was the Reformed subjects, not the Lutheran, who possessed the central churches.[15]

Some members of Lutheran groups producing church histories concentrated on their own parishes and patterns of connection between parishes, ignoring the existence of multiconfessionalism completely. One of the first such texts was Johann Friedrich Dahlenkamp's report *On the External Establishment of a Lutheran Religious Society in the County of Mark* published in 1798. For him, Luther was the origin of all: "The people of the county of Mark were ready for Luther and his Reformation when he started. . . . His ideas . . . were acclaimed. So the Augsburg Confession was adopted in all of the churches and parishes during the sixteenth century."[16] The Lutheran success presupposed here provided the justification for a Lutheran church history as the central church history of Mark.[17] Dahlenkamp viewed the first synod, organized by the count of Palatinate-Neuburg's court chaplain, Georg Heilbrunner, in 1612, as the starting point for an orderly development of parishes under the auspices of evangelical princes.[18] He made no mention of the elector's Calvinism when he identified Friedrich Wilhelm of Brandenburg as the ruler who accomplished the establishment of the Lutheran church.[19]

Nevertheless historians knew that the county of Mark was a multiconfessional territory. Having discovered the conflicts surrounding the Jülich-Kleve Succession Crisis as a precursor to the Thirty Years' War, they could not ignore that these same conflicts continued after 1648. In his *Reformation History* (1826), Johann Peter Berg published documents from 1665 concerning the partition of church property between Catholics and Protestants, without commentary. Later in the work, Berg wrote that he intended to comment only on those "problems of the Reformation."[20] Some years later, in 1845, Friedrich Char described the negotiations after the Thirty Years' War between the elector of Brandenburg and the count of Palatinate-Neuburg regulating the cohabitation of subjects of different confession. He emphasized that the imperial commissioners tried to find a solution using the Peace of Westphalia as the norm for determining confessional identity for each area.[21]

The struggles of the Jülich-Kleve Succession Crisis attracted more attention when the jubilee of Prussian rulership of the duchy of Kleve and the county of Mark was celebrated for the first time in 1859. These events undeniably brought the religious controversies in the associated territories to the forefront of historical consideration. E. von Schaumburg, a retired colonel, underscored the importance of the house of Hohenzollern on the development of the territories and declared his confidence that his "booklet would find kind reception even among the Catholic public."[22] He stated his intention to maintain an unbiased assessment when dealing with religious matters. The validity of his avowed neutrality was called into question by several confessionally subjective statements, including his positive evaluation of the Brandenburgian discriminations of Catholics in Kleve and Mark. He described those political measures simply as a reaction to repression of Protestants living in the territories of the count of Palatinate-Neuburg. Overall, he presented the Brandenburgian measures against the Catholics as modest in comparison to the politics of suppression in Jülich and Berg.[23]

Gustav Natorp, a *Gymnasium* teacher, also published a book in 1859 praising the reign of Brandenburg-Prussia.[24] Using the same approach as Dahlenkamp, Natorp described how the Reformation had been adopted first by "enlightened men," then by the citizens in cities during the sixteenth century, and finally finding its way into the villages, where it developed "roots that were deep in some locations and superficial in others."[25] When he turned his attention to the last dukes of Jülich-Kleve, Natorp argued they had allowed the movement to spread undisturbed, sometimes even supporting it, until Catholicism "had been brought down to a subordinated position."[26]

Natorp, however, did not deny that Catholics continued to reside in the territory of the county of Mark but undercut their importance in how he presented the Catholic contributions. We can observe narrative patterns focusing on negative Catholic characters in Natorp's extensive discussion of the years between 1622 and 1630, which he described as a time of distress under Spanish-Neuburgian occupation. In retelling an episode previously circulated in the eighteenth century and published by King Frederick II of Prussia in his *Memoirs of the House of Brandenburg*, Natorp focused on Wolfgang Wilhelm, count of Palatinate-Neuburg, as a central villain in the events of the occupation. According to the story, Wolfgang Wilhelm swore revenge after being slapped in the face by Johann Sigismund of Brandenburg during a dispute in 1613. Natorp presented Wolfgang Wilhelm's subsequent conversion to Catholicism and his alliance with the Spaniards as a payback for this humiliation.[27] Furthermore, he declared Wolfgang Wilhelm's eagerness to bring the subjects of the county of Mark to the Catholic belief as typical of all proselytes.[28]

Natorp presented intolerance as a characteristic feature of the adherents of the old religion, among a series of other archetypes that repeatedly appear in other historical writings. Catholics living in the county of Mark during the Spanish-Neuburgian occupation are depicted as people giving "vigorous support" to systematic oppression.[29] They are portrayed as willing to make a pact with foreign powers in order to gain advantages for themselves and their belief. In trying to force their religious identity upon their neighbors, Natorp characterized the Catholics as ready to destroy all of the fruits of the Reformation despite the fact that the vast majority of the people were adherents of this Reformation. Most Catholics appearing in Natorp's narratives had no names. Occasionally a Catholic priest is named when he praises his own success in re-catholicizing the county by assuming the parish of a forcibly removed evangelical pastor.[30] Natorp describes the election of the unqualified, ordinary craftsmen Erasmus Schmid, a dyer, and Wilhelm Wihoff, a baker, as mayors in Hamm, the capital of the county of Mark. In naming them, he sought to demonstrate how absurd the situation had become during this era of repression and disorder.[31]

In short, Natorp's juxtaposition of Protestants and Catholics is significant. For Natorp, the differences between Lutheran and Reformed subjects living in Mark are insignificant; the two groups form a united whole. In contrast, he presented the behavior of Catholics as bizarre and different. They walk in processions holding up wooden crucifixes and banners under the protection of the Spanish warriors.[32] Should they be considered traitors? Natorp reports that the Catholics in Lippstadt had to deny the rumors that they had invited the Spaniards.[33] As a historian, however, he does not go so far as to confirm this suspicion. When the stories are considered as a whole, we get the impression that all Catholics described by Natorp must have been strangers in their own native country.

Protestantism and Modernity

During the German Kulturkampf, another author, a historian who emerged as influential in the German Empire, became important for how Protestant historiography dealt with the early modern multiconfessionalism in the lands of Jülich-Kleve. Max Lehmann published the first part of *Prussia and the Catholic Church since 1640* in 1878.[34] Though Lehmann would later come into conflict with his contemporaries for holding an ideal of a more impartial historiography, he created a stir among the Catholics with his first volumes. Otto von Bismarck sought to calm the waves by asking Heinrich von Sybel to

exert his influence on Lehmann and his writings in order to avoid a confrontation with the German Center Party (*Zentrumspartei*).[35]

For Lehmann, multiconfessionalism in the lands of Jülich-Kleve first was
the result of the politics of Wilhelm VI, the second to last duke. Like previous historians, Lehmann mentioned the influence of Konrad von Heresbach,
a disciple of Erasmus, within the territory and described church politics in
the court as taking an Erasmian course between Protestantism and Catholicism.[36] Lehmann stated that Heresbach's contemporaries were unable to
determine his confession, and he described an atmosphere at the duke's court
more shaped through "enlightenment" than through "institutional religion."[37]
Lehmann saw a political and ecclesiastical development in the lands of Jülich-
Kleve as differing entirely from the rest of Germany.[38] He described how the
Lutheran movement arrived from the east, the Reformed movement as introduced by refugees from the west, and even the old church had survived because
the dukes had not favored the Reformation. The outcome was, as Lehmann
called it, a religiously mixed society.[39]

Lehmann sought to establish a strong connection between those principles of "enlightenment" characteristic of Duke Wilhelm's court in the mid-
sixteenth century and Protestantism. He argued that the Protestant estates of
Jülich, Berg, Kleve, and Mark served a bridging function in preserving those
ideals of religious freedom. He also saw the territorial estates as a significant
factor in preserving the Augsburg Confession when the Spaniards and adherents of the Counter-Reformation gained influence at the ducal court in the
last decades of Wilhelm's reign.[40]

In 1609 the Lutheran princes, the elector of Brandenburg and the count
of Palatinate-Neuburg, confirmed those rights. Multiconfessionalism was
guaranteed in the so-called *Reversalien*, which granted the territorial estates
the freedom to practice the Catholic belief and all other Christian religions.
In comparing this agreement to the Letter of Majesty (*Majestätsbrief*) in
Bohemia granted to the Protestant estates by the Habsburgs in the same year
as the *Reversalien*, Lehmann found a fundamental difference. He concluded
that the Protestant Hohenzollern princes proved themselves to be more successful defenders of religious freedom than the Catholic Habsburgs in the
subsequent decades.[41] Lehmann argued that Protestantism promoted this
principle of toleration, concluding that "no one other than evangelical princes
could have kept the promise of 1609." He made the truth of this statement
immediately apparent by stating that Wolfgang Wilhelm, count of Palatinate-
Neuburg, broke this promise after his conversion to Catholicism.[42]

Lehmann's view that only Protestantism made multiconfessional politics
possible is most clearly demonstrated in his portrait of Friedrich Wilhelm
of Brandenburg. For him the elector adhered to the only "true, reformed religion," which included the principle of "tolerance for all other confessors to

the gospel in the common battle against papism."[43] Lehmann emphasized that Friedrich Wilhelm, for political reasons, allowed even Catholic "superstitious belief" within his territories and treated all of his subjects as equal, regardless of confession, whether Lutheran, Reformed, or Catholic.[44] In order to make the contrast clear, Lehmann exhaustively enumerated the repressive measures undertaken by the count of Palatinate-Neuburg against the Protestant minorities in his territories.[45] These descriptions provoked at least one Catholic historian, Heinrich Joseph Floß, to respond by reporting the reprisals against Catholics in the county of Mark, citing the grievances of Catholic subjects under Brandenburg-Prussia in 1663.[46]

Overall, Lehmann's understanding of church history removed Catholics. Similar to the debates emerging during the German Kulturkampf in the 1870s, Catholicism was depicted as a religion belonging to a superstitious past, while Protestantism was pictured as a progressive movement and a wise policy of rulers. Lehmann saw the Protestantism of the sixteenth and seventeenth centuries as a foundation for future developments including the Enlightenment and secular state politics. In this context, he connected Protestantism with the methods used by the Brandenburgian-Prussian rulers. Moreover, Lehmann's concept of a "true reformed religion" obviously mirrored the 1817 unification of the two Protestant churches, Lutheran and Reformed, into a United Evangelical Church decreed by law in Prussia. In Lehmann's portrait of Friedrich Wilhelm we can observe that he saw the elector as a force preparing for this unity. In his work, Lehman downplayed any conflicts between the ruler and the Lutherans living in his territories and at the same time he emphasized the Friedrich Wilhelm's efforts to get the adherents of the Reformed confession under the protection of the imperial peace as members of the Augsburg Confession (*Confessio Augustana*) in 1648.[47]

Creating Jubilees

Although anti-Catholic polemics declined during the last decade of the nineteenth century, the focus on the importance of Protestantism in the county of Mark did not. In 1892 and 1893, Franz Darpe, a *Gymnasium* teacher in Bochum who was a Catholic, published his description of the negotiations between Brandenburg and Palatinate-Neuburg that led to the agreement that resolved remaining church conflicts after the Thirty Years' War.[48] In his summaries of the relevant documents, Darpe presented many illustrations of multiconfessionalism in the county of Mark and provided the different viewpoints of Lutherans, Reformed, and even Catholics. Darpe, however, viewed the primary relevance of his work as showing evidence of the "beginnings of the Reformation" in the county of Mark.[49] The numerous witness statements he cited recount how and when parishes had been converted to the Reformation, along with other documentations of Protestants in the territory. These examples provided concrete evidence for the progress of the Reformed movement. In collecting those dates of conversion for Reformation jubilees, he consolidated the notion of the county of Mark as entirely a Protestant territory.

When Gerrit Haren, a teacher from Witten, studied the commission papers of Brandenburg in 1911, he transcribed the Catholics' testimonies in a similar way.[50] Even in Haren's text, the Protestant perspective dominated the Catholic view in large part because his work largely replicated the records produced by Brandenburgian commissions. Those commissions had organized the papers following an obvious intent of creating dramatic tension. Often they had placed a Catholic statement first, which was immediately contradicted and invalidated by a subsequent Protestant statement. In this way, Haren's works, as well as those of others who followed similar methodologies, demonstrated the superiority of Protestantism, particularly the Lutherans. This trend is especially evident in Hugo Rothert's "Official Reports" published in the *Journal of Westphalian Church History* (*Zeitschrift für westfälische Kirchengeschichte*) after 1909, which reproduced the testimonies word for word.[51]

We have already observed how the date of the great Prussian jubilee in 1909 was used as an opportunity to celebrate the Lutheran Reformation in the county of Mark. Hugo Rothert described this as a popular movement.[52] In doing so, he intensively portrayed the function of pamphlets and other writing supporting the spread of Luther's ideas.[53] Rothert considered the Reformation as a period of educational formation, which he described as a time of "Sturm und Drang."[54] Rothert's heroes were the Lutherans. His narrative concerning the Reformed movement gaining ground since the mid-sixteenth century is a distanced one. Against the background of increasing religious pluralization, he does not consider those religious refugees fleeing England and the Netherlands for this region of the empire as influential in spreading Protestantism, as many other historians had done.[55] In this context, Rothert characterized the Lutheran theologians as navigators in times of change. First, he portrayed Hermann Hamelmann (1526–95) as a new kind of Hercules due to his success in consolidating the prominent position of the Lutheranism in the county of Mark.[56] In contrast to Hamelmann, adherents of the Reformed confession organizing their first synod in the county of Mark (1611) before the Lutherans appear only as faceless characters.[57] Catholics, such as Gerhard von Kleinsorgen, are mentioned only as figures losing terrain in the face of Hamelmann's success.[58]

The Catholic population tolerated by rulers and the Protestant majority emerged in sharper relief in the *Festschrift* written in 1909 to commemorate the three-hundred-year anniversary of the Treaty of Dortmund. Rothert characterized the treaties of 1672/73 between Brandenburg and Neuburg as acts of complaisance by the Protestants.[59] In another article on the political history of the county of Mark, Karl Spannagel sought to demonstrate how the multiconfessional balance of the early modern age paralleled the contemporary situation. In his text, he pointed out the "considerable shift in confessional balance in favor of the Catholics" since the late nineteenth century.[60] He noted that while the proportion of Protestants to Catholics had averaged 3:1 in 1825, now (in 1905) it averaged 3:2. For Spannagel, the Catholic immigrants arriving from Poland and Silesia since the mid-nineteenth century were still foreigners, unlikely to assimilate in the near future. He warned that the government "should prepare itself for those dangers that threatened it, especially the foreign immigrants now comprising the bulk of the Social Democratic working class."[61]

We should not assume that the authors of the 1909 *Festschrift* looked at the contemporary demographic developments only with the romanticized view of the past. Even Hugo Rothert pleaded for more mutual understanding between the confessions in his "church history."[62] That the county of Mark in 1909 was still a Protestant territory was for these authors completely beyond debate. This interpretation would be confirmed in the next decades. Subsequent church histories still dealt with Protestant parishes and not with Catholic ones.[63] More interest in the integration and cohabitation of the Catholic elements in the county of Mark emerged very late in the studies of Oliver Becher over the "autonomous confessionalization."[64]

Conclusion

Regional historians of the nineteenth and the early twentieth centuries regarded the county of Mark as a Protestant territory. In the late eighteenth century, the histories sought to ignore Catholicism completely. The coexistence of Lutheran, Reformed, and Catholic parishes in the early modern period, however, could not remain completely invisible. Subsequently, Protestant authors explained the persistence of Catholicism as a result of the particular geographic situation and the complexity of international history during the confessional age.[65] In particular, they attributed the situation to the presence of Spanish politicians and troops since the late sixteenth century and the forceful Counter-Reformation during the Thirty Years' War. Historians saw the evolution of an evangelical, and especially Lutheran, territory and the path of the population to evangelical belief as hindered by these circumstances. In contrast, the Catholics living in the county of Mark during this time were depicted as foreigners in their own homelands. They were described as characters seeking to establish their belief against the will of the majority with the help of foreign troops.

During the nineteenth century, Prussia became a central subject for historians dealing with the church history of the territories of Jülich-Kleve, including the county of Mark. Max Lehmann identified the rule of Brandenburg-Prussia in the seventeenth century with religious policies of toleration, which paved the way for the Enlightenment. Influenced by debates emerging out of the German Kulturkampf, he saw the ability to act with religious tolerance as an exclusive attribute of Protestantism. Catholics presented as a group benefited from Protestant tolerance but were unable to be tolerant themselves. For these authors, multiconfessionalism existing in the county of Mark since the sixteenth century was a manifestation of Protestant superiority and an example of Catholic shame.

Around 1900, we can observe efforts to avoid anti-Catholic polemics in the historiography of the county of Mark. The works of Franz Darpe, Gerrit Haren, and Hugo Rothert covering the struggles over the churches of Jülich-Kleve after the Thirty Years' War mostly only paraphrased the archival records. They used the records of witness hearings, for instance, to construct a narrative for the local Reformation jubilees. As a whole these works reflect the standpoints of the Protestants as more intensive than the views of the Catholics. The jubilee of 1909 provided another occasion to retell the history of the Lutheran and the Reformed Reformations in the county of Mark. Hugo Rothert emphasized the thesis that it had been the will of the people of the county of Mark to establish an evangelical Reformation during the sixteenth and seventeenth centuries. This was seen as a solid foundation for the close bond between the inhabitants and the house of Hohenzollern. Even the historian Karl Spannagel appealed strictly to this tradition. As Catholic immigration increased, multiconfessionalism reemerged as a modern problem leading to renewed irritations and fear in Protestant circles.

During the last two decades of the twentieth century, historians have discovered multiconfessionalism as a fascinating aspect of the history of the early modern age.[66] They have asked new questions concerning the mentalities of the people living in towns and villages of the sixteenth and seventeenth centuries and how they cohabitated with people of different beliefs. In this context, even the multiplicity of concepts of Reformation came into focus. In contrast to Leopold von Ranke, Tom Brady has shown how the Holy Roman Empire's structure of political particularism enabled the formation of multiple reformations and the emergence of a system of coexistence of people with diverse confessions. He does not deny that heated conflicts arose from confessional diversities, but he also emphasizes that tendencies to harden oppositions led to increased confessional rigidity in Germany after the Peace of Westphalia, which he calls "confessionalism." This was the background for historians of the nineteenth and the early twentieth centuries dealing with the county of Mark. They saw multiconfessionalism as hindering national progress and modernity, not promoting it.

Ralf-Peter Fuchs is chair of the Historical Institute/University Duisburg-Essen (History of the Rhine-Maas-Region). He is author of many books and articles on the history of witchcraft, on the history of honor, and on the reception of jazz in postwar Germany. He also studies early modern concepts of time and the practical knowledge of early modern farmers and craftsmen. His more recent publications deal with peacemaking concepts during and after the Thirty Years' War, including *Ein 'Medium' zum Frieden. Die Normaljahrsregel und die Beendigung des Dreißigjährigen Krieges* (Munich, 2010) and "Lutherans, Calvinists and the Road to a Normative Year," in *The Ashgate Research Companion of the Thirty Years' War*, ed. Olaf Asbach and Peter Schröder (Farnham 2014).

Notes

1. "Eine gewaltige Volksbewegung ging auch durch unsere Gauen. Man fühlte die Macht der Wahrheit, der man nicht widerstehen konnte. . . . Gerade die Jahre 1560–80 sind die der Reformation in den märkischen Gemeinden." Hugo Rothert, "Märkische Kirchengeschichte," in *Die Grafschaft Mark: Festschrift zum Gedächtnis der 300jährigen Vereinigung mit Brandenburg-Preußen*, ed. Aloys Meister (Dortmund, 1909), vol. 1, 207–62.

2. Heribert Smolinsky, "Jülich-Kleve-Berg," in *Die Territorien des Reichs im Zeitalter der Reformation und Konfessionalisierung. Land und Konfession 1500–1650*, ed. Anton Schindling and Walter Ziegler, 2nd ed., 7 vols. (Münster, 1995), vol. 3, 86–107, here 101.

3. See Ralf-Peter Fuchs, "Verschiedene Normaljahre und die gemeinsame Autorität zweier Fürsten im jülich-klevischen Kirchenstreit," in *Autorität der Form—Autorisierungen—Institutionelle Autorität*, ed. Wulf Oesterreicher, Gerhard Regn, and Winifred Schulze (Münster, 2003), 309–22, here 320.

4. Ralf-Peter Fuchs, "Der Dreißigjährige Krieg und die Grafschaft Mark," *Märkisches Jahrbuch für Geschichte* 100 (2000): 103–38, here 111.

5. Stefan Ehrenpreis, "Brandenburgische Herrschaft und Kriegsalltag in der Grafschaft Mark 1618–1648," in *Das Amt Wetter im Dreißigjährigen Krieg*, ed. Dietrich Thier (Wetter, 1998), 7–26, here 14.

6. Fuchs, "Der Dreißigjährige Krieg," 111.

7. Heinrich Schoppmeyer, "Zur Geschichte der katholischen Pfarrei in Blankenstein," *Märkisches Jahrbuch für Geschichte* 91 (1993): 33–97, here 49.

8. Ralf-Peter Fuchs, "Claesgen von Wildt und seine Bande. 'Landzwinger' und die Ehre der Grafschaft Mark während des Aufenthaltes von Grimmelshausen in Soest," in *Grimmelshausen und Simplicissimus in Westfalen*, ed. Peter Heßelmann (Bern, 2006), 119–37.

9. Ralf-Peter Fuchs, "1609, 1612 oder 1624? Der Normaljahrskrieg von 1651 in der Grafschaft Mark und die Rolle des Reichshofrates," *Westfälische Forschungen* 59 (2009): 297–311.

10. Landesarchiv NRW, Abt. Westfalen, Münster, KMR, Landessachen 155, Gravamina of the Catholics in Kleve-Mark concerning the parish in Ostönne.

11. Thomas A. Brady, *German Histories in the Age of Reformations (1400–1650)* (New York, 2009).

12. Diarmaid MacCulloch, *Reformation: Europe's House Divided, 1490–1700* (London 2003), xix.
13. Rolf Kießling, Thomas Max Safley, and Lee Palmer Wandel, ed., *Im Ringen um die Reformation: Kirchen und Prädikanten, Rat und Gemeinden in Augsburg* (Tübingen, 2011).
14. Scott Dixon, Dagmar Freist, and Mark Greengrass, ed., *Living with Religious Diversity in Early-Modern Europe* (Farnham, 2009); and Howard Louthan, Gary B. Cohen, and Franz A. J. Szabo, ed., *Diversity and Dissent: Negotiating Religious Difference in Central Europe, 1500–1800* (New York, 2011).
15. "Alle im Röm. Reich geduldete Religionen haben zwar hierselbst ihren öffentlichen Gottesdienst, die Ev. Reformierte aber haben die Pfarr-Kirch und machen den grössesten Hauffen aus." Johann Diederich von Steinen, *Westphälische Geschichte*, 4 vols. (Lemgo, 1755–60), vol. 3, 21–22.
16. "Das Volk der Grafschaft Mark war, als Luther die Reformation begann, dazu reif. Seine Ideen wurden durch seine Schriften, durch hiesige von Adel, die in Wittenberg seine Hausgenossen gewesen waren, durch Handelsverkehr mit Obersachsen, durch Volkslieder und durch, der Religion wegen, aus den Niederlanden Vertriebene, die man willkommner und herzlicher, als jetzo Auswanderer, annahm. früh, schnell, und allgemein in der Grafschaft Mark verbreitet, und fanden dergestallt Beyfall, dass im sechzehnten Jahrhundert, eine längere oder kürzere Zeit, in allen Kirchen und von allen Gemeinen in der Grafschaft Mark die Augsburgische Konfession ist angenommen worden." Johann Friedrich Dahlenkamp, *Ueber die äußere Einrichtung der lutherischen Religions-Gesellschaft in der Grafschaft Mark* (n.p., 1798), 4.
17. D. Bädeker, ed., *Ueber die Einführung der Reformation in die evangelischen Gemeinen der Grafschaft Mark beider Confessionen: Mit Einschluß von Limburg und Werden. Kurze alphabetisch geordnete Uebersicht. Nebst einem Anhange betreffend die Reformation in Dortmund, Essen, Soest und Lippstadt* (Dortmund, 1838); and F. G. H. J. Bädeker and Heinrich Heppe, ed., *Geschichte der Evangelischen Gemeinden der Grafschaft Mark und der benachbarten Gemeinden von Dortmund, Soest, Lippstadt, Essen, rc.* (Iserlohn, 1870).
18. Dahlenkamp, *Ueber die äußere Einrichtung*, 6–10.
19. "Vollendet wurde die jetzige Verfassung der evang. Kirchen und Gemeinen durch den großen, und für die Grafschaft Mark in vieler Rücksicht merkwürdigen Churfürsten Friedrich Wilhelm." Dahlenkamp, *Ueber die äußere Einrichtung*, 7.
20. "Widrigkeiten der Reformation." J. P. Berg, *Reformationsgeschichte der Länder Jülich, Cleve, Berg, Mark, Ravensberg und Lippe*, ed. Ludwig Troß (Hamm, 1826), 190. The book was published posthumously in 1800.
21. Friedrich Char, *Geschichte des Herzogthums Cleve, seit der ersten historischen Kenntnis bis auf unsere Zeit. Mit besonderer Rücksicht auf die Hauptstadt Cleve* (Kleve, 1845), 230.
22. E. von Schaumburg, *Die Begründung der Brandenburg-Preußischen Herrschaft am Niederrhein und in Westfalen oder der Jülich-Clevische Erbfolgestreit. Nebst einer geographischen und historischen Uebersicht der Herzogthümer Jülich, Cleve, Berg, der Grafschaften Mark und Ravensberg, der Herrschaft Ravenstein, rc, mit Karte und genealogischer Tabelle. Zur zweihundertfünfzigjährigen Denkfeier des Erbanfalles dieser Länder an Brandenburg-Preußen, nach älteren Quellen bearbeitet* (Wesel, 1859), viii.
23. "Daß diese Maßnahmen auf der anderen Seite ähnliche Maßregeln gegen die Katholiken hervorriefen, liegt auf der Hand, doch sind dieselben—nach dem Zeugnisse aller unparteiischen Schriftsteller über jene Zeit—durchaus nicht zu jener Höhe getrieben worden." Schaumburg, *Die Begründung der Brandenburg-Preußischen Herrschaft*, 235–36.

24. Gustav Natorp, *Die Grafschaft Mark: Denkschrift zur Feier des zweihundertundfünf-zigsten Jahrestages ihrer Vereinigung mit der Brandenburgisch-Preussischen Monarchie* (Iserlohn, 1859).

25. "Von den Städten hatte sich der protestantische Glaube allmählich auf das Land ver-breitet, und hier tiefer, dort oberflächlicher Wurzeln gefaßt." Natorp, *Die Grafschaft Mark*, 43.

26. "Die letzten Herzöge von Cleve hatten diese Umwältzung entweder sich ungestört entwickeln lassen oder auch selbst unterstützt, und so war der Katholicismus zu einer untergeordneten Stellung herabgedrückt worden." Natorp, *Die Grafschaft Mark*, 43.

27. Natorp, *Die Grafschaft Mark*, 40.

28. "Der Pfalzgraf verfolgte mit dem fanatischen Eifer, welcher Proselyten eigen zu sein pflegt, neben der Absicht, sich den Besitz der Grafschaft zu sichern, den Zweck, ihre Bewohner zu jenem Glauben zurückzuführen, zu dem er selbst zurückgekehrt war." Natorp, *Die Grafschaft Mark*, 43.

29. "Bei diesem Streben fand er in dem Theile der Bevölkerung, welcher dem alten Glauben treu geblieben war und sich durch den um sich greifenden Protestantismus bedrängt sah, lebhafte Unterstützung und es entwickelte sich im Innern des Landes die gehässigste Verfolgungssucht und religiöse Unduldsamkeit." Natorp, *Die Graf-schaft Mark*, 43.

30. Natorp, *Die Grafschaft Mark*, 44–45.

31. Natorp, *Die Grafschaft Mark*, 46.

32. "Durch die Strassen zogen wieder Processionen mit hölzernen Crucifixen und Fahnen." Natorp, *Die Grafschaft Mark*, 48.

33. Natorp, *Die Grafschaft Mark*, 47–48.

34. Max Lehmann, *Preußen und die katholische Kirche seit 1640: Bis 1897 nach den Acten des geheimen Staatsarchivs*, 8 vols. (Leipzig, 1878–1902).

35. Rüdiger von Bruch, "Lehmann, Max," *Neue Deutsche Biographie*, 25 vols. (Berlin, 1985), vol. 14, 88–90, here 89.

36. Char, *Geschichte des Herzogthums Cleve*, 147; and Berg, *Reformationsgeschichte der Länder Jülich*, 55. On the contrary, Berg considered Heresbach a Protestant.

37. "Ein Schüler von ihm [Erasmus] war jener Konrad von Heresbach, von welchem die Zeitgenossen nicht wußten, ob er Katholik, Lutheraner oder Calvinist sei. . . . Dieser Hof lebte nicht der Religion, sondern der Wissenschaft; er stellte die Aufklärung höher als den Kirchenglauben, die Freiheit vom Bekenntnis höher als das Bekennt-niss, den Frieden höher als den Krieg." Lehmann, *Preußen und die katholische Kirche*, vol. 1, 23.

38. "[K]irchliche Zustände, welche ihres Gleichen nicht hatten in Deutschland." Leh-mann, *Preußen und die katholische Kirche*, vol. 1: 23.

39. "[E]in konfessionell gemischtes Gemeinwesen." Lehmann, *Preußen und die katholische Kirche*, vol. 1, 28.

40. Lehmann, *Preußen und die katholische Kirche*, vol. 1: 29.

41. "[D]iesen [the Hohenzollern] wurde die confessionelle Mischung der Bevölkerung ein neuer Sporn zu duldsamer Kirchenpolitik, jenen [the Habsburgs] galt sie als ein möglichst schnell zu besitigendes Ärgerniss." Lehmann, *Preußen und die katholische Kirche*, vol. 1: 31.

42. "[E]r [Protestantism] war doch immer noch dem Gedanken der Duldung zugäng-licher als die Schüler der Jesuiten . . . andere als evangelische Fürsten hätten das Ver-

sprechen von 1609 nicht halten können. . . . Dasselbe wurde auf der Stelle hinfällig, als einer der Spondenten, der Pfalzgraf, katholisch wurde." Lehmann, *Preußen und die katholische Kirche*, vol. 1: 31.

43. "Duldung der übrigen Bekenner des Evangeliums, gemeinsame[r] Kampf gegen den Papismus" as "'wahre' reformirte Religion." Lehmann, *Preußen und die katholische Kirche*, vol. 1, 43.

44. "Zulassung ihres abergläubischen Glaubens." Lehmann, *Preußen und die katholische Kirche*, vol. 1, 58.

45. Lehmann, *Preußen und die katholische Kirche*, vol. 1, 61–66.

46. Heinrich Joseph Floß, *Zum Clevisch-Märkischen Kirchenstreit: (Eine Erinnerung aus der früheren Geschichte des Kulturkampfes)* (Bonn, 1883), 16–44.

47. Lehmann, *Preußen und die katholische Kirche*, vol. 1, 44–45.

48. Franz Darpe, "Die Anfänge der Reformation und der Streit über das Kirchenvermögen in der Grafschaft Mark: Amtliche Berichte des 17. Jahrhunderts," *Zeitschrift für Vaterländische Geschichte und Alterthumskunde* 50 (1892): 1–68 (part 1); 51 (1893): 1–89 (part 2). On Franz Darpe, see also S. Pätzold, "Franz Darpe (1842–1911) und die historische Forschung seiner Zeit," *Märkisches Jahrbuch für Geschichte* 111 (2011): 209–32.

49. Darpe, "Die Anfänge der Reformation," part 1, 1–2.

50. Gerrit Haren, "Auseinandersetzungen hinsichtlich des Kirchenvermögens zwischen Evangelischen und Katholischen der Grafschaft Mark nach beendetem Jülich-Clevischen Erbfolgestreit," *Märkisches Jahrbuch für Geschichte* 15 (1900–1): 3–48.

51. [Hugo Rothert], "Die amtlichen Erkundigungen aus den Jahren 1664–1667," *Jahrbuch für westfälische Kirchengeschichte* 11–12 (1909–10): 183–303; 13 (1911): 225–36; 14 (1912): 176–231; 15 (1913): 162–89; and 16 (1914–15): 303–35.

52. "Aber das ist nun das Besondere an der westfälischen Reformationsgeschichte, daß wir, wenn von den Mitteln, wodurch die evangelische Religion sich ausbreitete, die Rede ist, in keinster Weise der staatlichen Gewalt zu gedenken haben . . . die Dinge gingen ihren Gang nach dem ihnen eingeborenen Gesetz und nicht nach dem Wunsch wohlmeinender Doktrinäre." Rothert, "Märkische Kirchengeschichte," 247.

53. Rothert, "Märkische Kirchengeschichte," 243–47.

54. Rothert, "Märkische Kirchengeschichte," 247.

55. "Hier aber tragen sie zunächst nicht dazu bei, das ringende Chaos zu entwirren." Rothert, "Märkische Kirchengeschichte," 249. On the influence of the refugees, see chapter 13 in this volume.

56. "So steht Hamelmann da inmitten des tobenden Chaos, fest und sicher steuert er das Schifflein der Kirche durch Tiefen und Untiefen . . . er war ein neuer Herkules." Rothert, "Märkische Kirchengeschichte," 251.

57. Rothert, "Märkische Kirchengeschichte," 254.

58. "[D]er katholische v. Kleinsorgen aber sagt kleinlaut, daß infolge dieser Angelegenheit durch Hamelmanns Eifer 'Unna, Kamen, Duisburg, Essen und fast die ganze Grafschaft Mark und das Herzogtum Berg' evangelisch geworden seien." Rothert, "Märkische Kirchengeschichte," 250.

59. Rothert, "Märkische Kirchengeschichte," 261.

60. Karl Spannagel, "Die Grafschaft Mark als Teil des brandenburgisch-preußischen Staates," in *Die Grafschaft Mark. Festschrift zum Gedächtnis der 300 jährigen Vereinigung mit Brandenburg-Preußen*, ed. Alois Meister, 2 vols. (Dortmund, 1909) vol. 1, 25–76, here 71.

61. "[G]egen die Gefahren zu wappnen, die ihr von den zu einem großen Teil aus der Fremde eingewanderten sozialdemokratischen Arbeitermassen drohen." Karl Spannagel, "Die Grafschaft Mark," vol. 1, 71.
62. "Auch das Nebeneinander beider christlicher Konfessionen können wir nicht bedauern, sofern ein gegenseitiges Verständnis und reger Wetteifer in allem Guten dadurch gefördert und der Friede gewahrt wird." Rothert, "Märkische Kirchengeschichte," 262.
63. Hugo Rothert, *Festschrift zur 300jährigen Gedächtnis-Feier der ersten märkischen lutherischen Generalsynode. 2. u. 3. Oktober 1612/1912 in Unna* (Witten, 1912); and Ewald Dresbach, *Pragmatische Kirchengeschichte der preussischen Provinzen Rheinland und Westfalen* (Meinerzhagen, 1931).
64. Oliver Becher, *Herrschaft und autonome Konfessionalisierung. Politik, Religion und Modernisierung in der frühneuzeitlichen Grafschaft Mark* (Essen, 2006).
65. Berg, *Reformationsgeschichte der Länder*, 97–100. Berg saw the emperor's defeat of Wilhelm V, duke of Kleve, in the Gueldarian Wars and the subsequent Treaty of Venlo (1543) as essential.
66. Paul Warmbrunn, *Zwei Konfessionen in einer Stadt: Das Zusammenleben von Katholiken und Protestanten in den paritätischen Reichsstädten Augsburg, Biberach, Ravensburg und Dinkelsbühl von 1548 bis 1648* (Wiesbaden, 1983); and Etienne François, *Die unsichtbare Grenze: Protestanten und Katholiken in Augsburg* (Sigmaringen, 1991)

Bibliography

Bädeker, D., ed. *Ueber die Einführung der Reformation in die evangelischen Gemeinen der Grafschaft Mark beider Confessionen: Mit Einschluß von Limburg und Werden. Kurze alphabetisch geordnete Uebersicht. Nebst einem Anhange betreffend die Reformation in Dortmund, Essen, Soest und Lippstadt.* Dortmund, 1838.

Bädeker, F. G. H. J., and Heinrich Heppe, ed. *Geschichte der Evangelischen Gemeinden der Grafschaft Mark und der benachbarten Gemeinden von Dortmund, Soest, Lippstadt, Essen, rc.* Iserlohn, 1870.

Becher, Oliver. *Herrschaft und autonome Konfessionalisierung. Politik, Religion und Modernisierung in der frühneuzeitlichen Grafschaft Mark.* Essen, 2006.

Berg, J. P. *Reformationsgeschichte der Länder Jülich, Cleve, Berg, Mark, Ravensberg und Lippe,* ed. Ludwig Troß. Hamm, 1826.

Brady, Thomas A. *German Histories in the Age of Reformations (1400–1650).* New York, 2009.

Bruch, Rüdiger von. "Lehmann, Max." In *Neue Deutsche Biographie,* vol. 14, 88–90. Berlin, 1985.

Char, Friedrich. *Geschichte des Herzogthums Cleve, seit der ersten historischen Kenntnis bis auf unsere Zeit. Mit besonderer Rücksicht auf die Hauptstadt Cleve.* Kleve, 1845.

Dahlenkamp, Johann Friederich. *Ueber die äußere Einrichtung der lutherischen Religions-Gesellschaft in der Grafschaft Mark.* N.p., 1798.

Darpe, Franz. "Die Anfänge der Reformation und der Streit über das Kirchenvermögen in der Grafschaft Mark: Amtliche Berichte des 17. Jahrhunderts." *Zeitschrift für Vaterländische Geschichte und Alterthumskunde* 50 (1892): 1–68 (part 1); 51 (1893): 1–89 (part 2).

Dixon, C. Scott, Dagmar Freist, and Mark Greengrass, ed. *Living with Religious Diversity in Early-Modern Europe.* Farnham, 2009.

Dresbach, Ewald. *Pragmatische Kirchengeschichte der preussischen Provinzen Rheinland und Westfalen.* Meinerzhagen, 1931.

Ehrenpreis, Stefan. "Brandenburgische Herrschaft und Kriegsalltag in der Grafschaft Mark 1618–1648." In *Das Amt Wetter im Dreißigjährigen Krieg,* edited by Dietrich Their, 7–26. Wetter, 1998.

Floß, Heinrich Joseph. *Zum Clevisch-Märkischen Kirchenstreit: (Eine Erinnerung aus der früheren Geschichte des Kulturkampfes).* Bonn, 1883.

François, Etienne. *Die unsichtbare Grenze: Protestanten und Katholiken in Augsburg 1648–1806.* Sigmaringen, 1991.

Fuchs, Ralf-Peter. "1609, 1612 oder 1624? Der Normaljahrskrieg von 1651 in der Grafschaft Mark und die Rolle des Reichshofrates." *Westfälische Forschungen* 59 (2009): 297–311.

———. "Claesgen von Wildt und seine Bande. 'Landzwinger' und die Ehre der Grafschaft Mark während des Aufenthaltes von Grimmelshausen in Soest." In *Grimmelshausen und Simplicissimus in Westfalen,* edited by Peter Heßelmann, 119–37. Bern, 2006.

———. "Der Dreißigjährige Krieg und die Grafschaft Mark." *Märkisches Jahrbuch für Geschichte* 100 (2000): 103–38.

———. *Ein Medium zum Frieden: Die Normaljahrsregel und die Beendigung des Dreissigjährigen Krieges.* Munich, 2010.

———. "Verschiedene Normaljahre und die gemeinsame Autorität zweier Fürsten im jülich-klevischen Kirchenstreit." In *Autorität der Form—Autorisierungen—Institutionelle Autorität,* edited by Wulf Oesterreicher, Gerhard Regn, and Winifred Schulze, 309–22. Münster, 2003.

Haren, Gerrit. "Auseinandersetzungen hinsichtlich des Kirchenvermögens zwischen Evangelischen und Katholischen der Grafschaft Mark nach beendetem Jülich-Clevischen Erbfolgestreit." *Märkisches Jahrbuch für Geschichte* 15 (1900–1901): 3–48.

Kießling, Rolf, Thomas Max Safley, and Lee Palmer Wandel, ed. *Im Ringen um die Reformation: Kirchen und Prädikanten, Rat und Gemeinden in Augsburg.* Tübingen, 2011.

Lehmann, Max. *Preußen und die katholische Kirche seit 1640: Bis 1897 nach den Acten des geheimen Staatsarchivs.* 8 vols. Leipzig, 1878–1902.

Louthan, Howard, Gary B. Cohen, and Franz A. J. Szabo, ed. *Diversity and Dissent: Negotiating Religious Difference in Central Europe, 1500–1800.* New York, 2011.

MacCulloch, Diarmaid. *Reformation: Europe's House Divided, 1490–1700.* London, 2003.

Meister, Aloys, ed. *Die Grafschaft Mark: Festschrift zum Gedächtnis der 300jährigen Vereinigung mit Brandenburg-Preußen.* Dortmund, 1909.

Natorp, Gustav. *Die Grafschaft Mark: Denkschrift zur Feier des zweihundertundfünfzigsten Jahrestages ihrer Vereinigung mit der Brandenburgisch-Preussischen Monarchie.* Iserlohn, 1859.

Pätzold, S. "Franz Darpe (1842–1911) und die historische Forschung seiner Zeit." *Märkisches Jahrbuch für Geschichte* 111 (2011): 209–32.

Rothert, Hugo. *Festschrift zur 300jährigen Gedächtnis-Feier der ersten märkischen lutherischen Generalsynode. 2. u. 3. Oktober 1612/1912 in Unna.* Witten, 1912.

[Rothert, Hugo]. "Die amtlichen Erkundigungen aus den Jahren 1664–1667." *Jahrbuch für westfälische Kirchengeschichte* 11–12 (1909–10): 183–303; 13 (1911): 225–36; 14 (1912): 176 –231; 15 (1913): 162–89; and 16 (1914–15): 303–35.

Schaumburg, E. von. *Die Begründung der Brandenburg-Preußischen Herrschaft am Niederrhein und in Westfalen oder der Jülich-Clevische Erbfolgestreit. Nebst einer geographischen und historischen Uebersicht der Herzogthümer Jülich, Cleve, Berg, der Grafschaften Mark und Ravensberg, der Herrschaft Ravenstein, rc, mit Karte und genealogischer Tabelle. Zur zweihundertfünfzigjährigen Denkfeier des Erbanfalles dieser Länder an Brandenburg-Preußen, nach älteren Quellen bearbeitet.* Wesel, 1859.

Schoppmeyer, Heinrich. "Zur Geschichte der katholischen Pfarrei in Blankenstein." *Märkisches Jahrbuch für Geschichte* 91 (1993): 33–97.

Smolinsky, Heribert. "Jülich-Kleve-Berg." In *Die Territorien des Reichs im Zeitalter der Reformation und Konfessionalisierung. Land und Konfession 1500–1650*, ed. Anton Schindling and Walter Ziegler, 2nd ed., vol. 3, 86–107. Münster, 1995.

Spannagel, Karl. "Die Grafschaft Mark als Teil des brandenburgisch-preußischen Staates." In *Die Grafschaft Mark. Festschrift zum Gedächtnis der 300 jährigen Vereinigung mit Brandenburg-Preußen*, edited by Alois Meister, vol. 1, 25–76. Dortmund, 1909.

Steinen, Johann Diederich von. *Westphälische Geschichte*. 4 vols. Lemgo, 1755–60.

Warmbrunn, Paul. *Zwei Konfessionen in einer Stadt: Das Zusammenleben von Katholiken und Protestanten in den paritätischen Reichsstädten Augsburg, Biberach, Ravensburg und Dinkelsbühl von 1548 bis 1648.* Wiesbaden, 1983.

II

Recovering Plurality

CHAPTER SIX

A Catholic Genealogy
of Protestant Reason

RICHARD SCHAEFER

Religious polemic strikes a discordant note for many of us today. The denigration of one faith or denomination by another is not only out of step with the pluralism that is common in many Western societies, but seems willfully ignorant of the historical record. What could be plainer, after all, than the fact that religious bigotry breeds intolerance, social division, and, in certain cases, violence?[1] From this perspective, it might seem strange to want to take a more positive approach to polemics, one that does not simply point to what is narrow-minded and mean-spirited in religious polemics, but seeks to tease out how polemic might serve as a generative context for more constructive processes of identity formation and self-fashioning. And yet that is precisely what this essay does. This essay explores the anti-Protestant writing of four German Catholic writers in the 1820s and argues that this polemic was formative for how German Catholics sought to mobilize their faith to meet the challenges of the day. A less well-known chapter in the larger Protestant-Catholic conflict, this polemic is significant because it features a largely Catholic minority attacking a Protestant majority and so falls outside of what John Wolffe has recently identified as the two main approaches to framing the conflict, namely, anti-Catholicism and religious war.[2] As such, it helps revise our image of "Catholics as primarily passive targets of antagonism and prejudice rather than as active agents" and illuminates the parallel and diverging tactics Catholics used to attack their Protestant enemies.[3]

This essay also contributes to the growing literature devoted to exploring the formative role of the Protestant-Catholic conflict in German history, an area that offers significant potential for illuminating some of the interconnections between confessional conflict, religious-secular animosity, anti-Semitism, and nationalism.[4] This literature, which emerged in the 1980s, established itself as a critical rejoinder to earlier research rooted in assumptions about modernization that only ever saw religion as either atavistic or proper to the subfield of church history. This new scholarship capitalized on techniques of cultural history that explored how religion, and symbolic interaction more generally, was not merely epiphenomenal of more concrete material and social structures, but, as Helmut Walser Smith and Christopher Clark put it, a "motor of historical change" that was especially salient for understanding instances of "cultural cooperation, collision, and contention."[5] Indeed, as Smith and Clark point out in their introduction to the important collection *Protestants, Catholics, and Jews in Germany 1800–1914*, the nineteenth century saw "culture" become a battleground precisely because culture is never merely self-referential or self-contained but a domain in which mutual self-understanding and misunderstanding clash in the pursuit of power. Seen in this way, the plurality of religious groups in Germany—within Protestant, Catholic, and Jewish communities as much as between them—offer particularly interesting opportunities for further research into heterogeneous symbolic networks out of which discursive constructions of purity (e.g., national, cultural, gendered) sought to extricate themselves. Far from being marginal to the main currents of modern German history, therefore, as Smith and Clark so aptly put it, "cultural differentiation constituted the center."[6]

That Catholics attacked Protestants with new vigor in the nineteenth century has long been noted by historians. In the late 1970s, Heinrich Lutz noted this fact in his overview of the four phases of Catholic approaches to Luther: (1) anti-Luther writings of the Reformation era, (2) a conciliatory effort during the Enlightenment, (3) a militant resurgence in anti-Protestant polemic in the nineteenth century, and (4) a new irenic approach post-1930s. More recently, Olaf Blaschke cited this polemic as among the constellation of factors that suggest how we might see the nineteenth century as a "second confessional era," during which confessional issues of the sixteenth century were not so much repeated as refracted through distinctly nineteenth-century issues such as nationalism, industrialization, and the rise of science.[7] But in seeking to understand the significance of Catholic attacks on Protestants in the nineteenth century, the 1820s has received little scholarly attention.[8] And yet the 1820s are important as a decade in which Catholics took stock of their situation and the decisive changes ushered in by the Napoleonic Wars, which upset the earlier Westphalian order and transferred millions into states where others of a different confession now ruled them.[9] In 1803, the Enactment of the Delegates of the Empire (*Reichsdeputationshauptschluss*) officially brought the imperial church to an end and set in motion the secularization of massive amounts of church property. Influential prince-bishoprics and imperial abbeys were dissolved, and scores of religious orders were expelled and had their property appropriated. And perhaps most demoralizing of all, in 1808,

Napoleon even imprisoned Pope Pius VII for refusing to grant him control over the Papal States.[10] The loss of church property and the reorganization of ecclesiastical boundaries that resulted from these changes altered decisively the material basis of Catholic life and encouraged Catholic intellectuals to reflect on new strategies for defending their communities and how to sustain a distinctly Catholic way of life.

In the wake of the Napoleonic era, Catholics also struggled with how to reconcile their confessional identity with a growing nationalism that favored Protestantism. Indeed, the intensification of German nationalism in opposition to French hegemony during the conflict forced Catholics into a difficult position. No less interested in being "good Germans" or beating back the French than their Protestant compatriots, Catholics were often at pains to justify their loyalty to the nation, given the growing imbrication of "German" with "Protestant."[11] Whether it was Johann Gottlieb Fichte's singular focus on Protestant virtues in his 1807 *Addresses to the German Nation* or the 1817 tercentenary of Martin Luther's attack on Rome, celebrated at the Wartburg Festival, many Catholics resented the way that distinctly Protestant history and symbols were being used to define German culture.[12] Even the more conciliatory atmosphere of Romanticism, which revalued the medieval and "catholic" past and inspired some to dream of reconciling confessional differences on a higher plane, foundered on the rocks of reality. High-profile conversions, like those of Graf Leopold von Stolberg and Dorothea and Friedrich von Schlegel, confirmed many in their fear that Catholicism remained a clear and present danger. Practical issues, like the simmering dispute over mixed marriages between Protestants and Catholics, and the conflict over requiring Protestants serving in the Bavarian army to genuflect before public displays of the Catholic Eucharist, thwarted any easy solutions to the problems besetting confessional diversity. That Catholics found it difficult to endorse German nationalism unreservedly should not, of course, lead us to follow in the footsteps of so many Protestant critics who, at the time, accused Catholics of sacrificing nation to confession. A much better approach, as Wolfgang Altgeld argues, is to reframe the issue from "one of a homogeneous national movement vis-à-vis national and anti-national forces," to a struggle between "competing national forces . . . center[ing] on which older cultural facts and points of orientation the nation should take up, and which it should exclude."[13] Indeed, for our purposes, it is this perspective that motivates the attempt here to reassess the anti-Protestant polemic of the 1820s.

In response to a cultural nationalism that increasingly equated "Protestant" with "German," Catholics pursued a variety of strategies aimed at legitimizing their place in the nation. One strategy involved claiming for Catholicism otherwise key figures from the Protestant canon. Though frequently overlooked, German Catholic attempts to claim Shakespeare, Goethe, Leibniz,

and even Spinoza for Catholicism were a regular feature of Catholic writing
in the nineteenth century.[14] Another strategy involved formulating a distinctly
Catholic approach to scholarship. If the flowering of humanistic scholarship and other sciences in Germany owed much to hermeneutics and other
techniques of reading that were thought by many to be distinctly Protestant,
Catholics lobbied hard for a *katholische Wissenschaft* capable of redressing
the deficiencies of a scholarship whose alleged objectivity actually advanced
the ideological agenda of one particular community over against another.[15]
By far the most popular strategy for dealing with cultural Protestantism,
however, was the attempt to discredit Protestantism by showing how it was
responsible for a wide array of "modern" problems, from revolution to moral
indifference. In numerous pamphlets, articles, and books, Catholic authors
attacked the Reformation for placing the individual ahead of the community
and for undermining all legitimate authority. By tracing these problems back
to a prior disorder in Protestant thinking, Catholics undertook a genealogy of
Protestant reason whose goal was to identify the deep roots of alleged social
pathologies and reinforce the absolute necessity of a return to "Catholic life."[16]
One of the effects of this particular strategy was to elide the entire spectrum
of non-Catholic Christianity under an all-encompassing "Protestantism." As
Heinrich Lutz points out, the strident anti-Protestantism of the nineteenth
century elided the differences between Protestant groups and offered "an
increasingly uniform historical picture of world historical decadence: Luther's
Reformation became the first phase of the red revolution, and the beginning
of the de-Christianization of the modern world."[17] By willfully forgetting the
diversity of post-Reformation history, this line of Catholic attack was particularly effective insofar as the scourge of a monolithic "Protestantism" seemed
to justify the need for an equally powerful, monolithic, and world-historical
Catholic antidote.

In what follows, I look at how four Catholic theologians contributed to this
image of Protestantism. These thinkers, who number among the leading lights
of Catholic thought in the early part of the nineteenth century, were not exclusively, or even mainly, polemicists, and it is not my intention to paint them
thus. In the excerpts analyzed below, the goal is to show their tendency to view
recent German philosophy as the tainted fruit of Protestant reason. German
philosophy had, of course, reached a new zenith in the first decades of the
nineteenth century, with the achievements of the great idealist philosophers.
Though tremendously complex, idealism held that consciousness was foundational in the order of things. Philosophy, if correctly understood, was thus a
method of understanding the basic architecture of the world, in all of its various dimensions, including nature, society, culture, religion, and politics. More
than that, however, the act of understanding the interconnections between
these otherwise separate spheres transformed philosophy itself into an instru-

ment of reconciliation. Aimed principally at the one-sided rationalism of the Enlightenment, whose analysis of phenomena was locked into a dichotomy between subject and object, idealism presented itself as a medium that provided a divided consciousness with moments of insight into the original self-identity of things. When it came to religion, idealism offered an especially powerful critique of the religious divisions besetting the German nation and keeping it from achieving political unity. While some idealists favored a return to the pre-Reformation unity of Christendom, more favored the idea that Protestantism represented a significant and desirable development that Catholics and others should follow. Hegel, reflecting on the course of idealism from Kant to Fichte, thus famously declared that "the great form of the world spirit that has come to cognizance of itself in these great philosophies, is the principle of the North, and from the religious point of view, of Protestantism."[18] In view of this and similar kind of claims, many Catholic scholars strived to show how Catholicism was compatible with German nationalism and undermine the equation of German culture with Protestantism. By showing how philosophers like Immanuel Kant and Georg Wilhelm Friedrich Hegel were envoys of distinctly Protestant habits of thought, Catholic critics sought to expose what claimed to be universal systems of reason as tendentious and confessionally biased. Though not always as explicit, this desire to expose contemporary philosophy as the outgrowth of a disorder in Protestant thinking also aimed at articulating standards for what counted as healthy "Catholic" alternatives. Some readers might find calling this effort "genealogy" odd, given the obvious disparity between the politics of Friedrich Nietzsche and Michel Foucault and the politics of nineteenth-century Catholics. Nevertheless, German Catholic polemicists' selective approach to the Protestant past was no less politically motivated and no less iconoclastic in seeking to expose the dynamics of power. Indeed, it was firmly committed to the same kind of unmasking of ideal origins and to showing how supposedly universally accepted facts were in fact nothing more than an expression of particular interests.[19]

Catholic intellectual historians traditionally depict Franz Baader as a religious moderate, embodying the reconciliatory spirit often associated with Romanticism that prioritized Christian unity over confessional differences.[20] An incredible polymath, Baader was a physician and engineer and later a professor of philosophy and speculative theology at the University of Munich. Though associated with the circle around Friedrich Wilhelm Joseph Schelling, Baader was no mere disciple, and he was not convinced that unity could be purchased at the cost of staying true to one's principles. Indeed, in 1824 Baader published two articles that took a severely critical approach to Protestant reason. In his essay "On Catholicism and Protestantism," Baader stated in no uncertain terms that the Reformation was a revolutionary moment that promoted an attack on all authority. He pointed to the fact that "[e]very quarrel between the bourgeois and religious of society that developed at the time of the Reformation was, inasmuch as the reformers thought to settle them radically, for that reason transformed into a radical contradiction or break. Instead of truly grasping the principle of reform they grasped that of revolution." All revolutions were self-defeating precisely because they always turned against their initial aims, and Baader called "revolutionary that tendency of any activity that, instead of proceeding from its foundations, turns and rises up against them as though they were an obstruction."[21] This was true of both the Reformation and the French Revolution, and it was also true of the revolution in modern philosophy. That Catholics took a sharply critical view of revolution in the aftermath of the French Revolution and Napoleonic Wars is well known. Given the massive expropriation of church land and deep upheavals of that turbulent period, it is surprising that any Catholics at all favored revolution, though of course some did. In his *Catholics on the Barricades?*, Bernhard Schneider analyzes the complex spectrum of opinion surrounding revolution among German Catholics in the first half of the century. But by focusing on the politics of revolution Schneider misses how Catholics like Baader saw revolution in much broader terms than simply a change in political leadership or system of government.[22] Indeed, according to Baader, revolution had as much to do with habits of mind as with political demands. To understand better these habits of mind—their origins in the Reformation and their influence in German culture—Baader drew attention to what he saw as a fundamental homology between Reformation thought and recent German philosophy.

In "On Catholicism and Protestantism," Baader traced the effects of the Reformation's revolutionary thrust on contemporary German philosophy. He argued that Kant's critical philosophy was the model for how reason attacked its own foundations in a revolutionary way. By dividing reason into self-regulating theoretical and practical domains, and restricting valid propositions to only those that could be deduced consistently from domain-specific premises, Kant's investigations into the conditions of any possible knowledge turned reason against itself. This was particularly dangerous because it undermined reason's role in promoting salvation. Since salvation necessarily involved the totality of existence, reason could not be divided into autonomous sciences nor divorced from issues of everyday practice without incurring serious consequences. Baader also attacked Kant's philosophy for the way it isolated the lone thinking subject and made this subject the arbiter of reason. This severed the individual from the community and from traditions of thought whose validity and vitality might simply not "fit" the Kantian scheme. In a second essay published in 1824, "On the Need for an Inner Unification of Science and Religion for Our Times," Baader accused recent German philosophy of encouraging people to think that religion was essentially irrational and reason inherently irreligious. Pointing again to Kantian philosophy, Baader blamed "the development of that new moral philosophy, which is built on the concept of absolute autonomy, or, what is the same, the absolute sovereignty of the person."[23] With its ideal of a self-regulating moral system free from external authority, Kant's moral philosophy in particular deformed the vital role of knowledge in life and appealed to the destructive impulse (*Zerstörungstrieb*) in people. When detached from its role in the pursuit of vital questions such as those raised by religion, reason that seeks only to be autonomous limits itself from intervening in the important affairs of life.

Baader's contemporary Carl J. H. Windischmann similarly combined the practical vocation of physician with the speculative profession of philosopher to offer up a diagnosis of the ills of Protestant reason.[24] Professor of history, philosophy, and medicine at the University of Bonn, Windischmann was friends with Friedrich Schlegel. Though substantially interested in Hegel's philosophy and that of other idealists, he opposed the more overtly Kantian direction championed by Georg Hermes, his colleague in faculty of Catholic theology at Bonn.[25] Although Hermes himself envisioned the Kantian method of absolute doubt as a means to overcoming all doubt of God, his work was condemned in 1835 by Pope Gregory XVI. In his *On the Subject of What the Healing Arts Need*, published in 1824, Windischmann outlined what he took to be the potential of philosophy to be a healing art and contrasted this with the dominant mode of idealist subject-philosophy.[26] For Windischmann, this consisted in freeing the mind from the idolatry of its own finite subjectivity and adopting a "Catholic perspective" (*katholische Gesichtspunkt*) capable of thinking through questions according to both their subjective and objective dimensions.[27] Like Baader, Windischmann believed that reason's primary purpose was to help achieve salvation and that Protestantism obscured this truth by subjectivizing reason. This perversion of reason's purpose was reflected in the superficiality of recent philosophical terminology. According to Windischmann, language served "as the voice of reason," and "comprehend[ed] in itself the entire history of . . . all that it felt, perceived, sensed, formed, presented, desired, and willed." As the medium of reason, language contains within it "the continually imminent, easily vanishing, but always ready to definitely establish itself Word."[28] Given the salvific potential of language, Windischmann railed against modern philosophy's "talk of chaotic subjectivity in merely external and inorganically constructed verbal formulations."[29] By focusing its energy on verbal performance, philosophy distracted from the saving mission of reason and made the external aspect of language into an "idol" (*Abgott*). Taking aim squarely at Hegel's philosophy, he lamented:

> It is no great leap for such a way of thinking to take the empty word and raise it to the level of the concept, and then turn it into the intellectual contents of reason comprehending itself. . . . It is a consequence of these high pretensions that merely formal constructions, the weaving with words, the grasping and

combination of presentations (what only in a general, though not philosophical, sense might be called "thinking," even though it may seem like real and effective thought, if only superficially), that the results are only linguistic and, at most subjective, fragments of thoughts. Such fragments will have some sense, and will be able to move and delight men, being of them, but only at the expense of a lack of spirit.[30]

But if philosophy's superficial and one-sided terminology was symptomatic of a deeper and more dangerous egoism, Windischmann was doubtful whether this fact was widely understood by either philosophers or the educated public, Protestant and Catholic alike. In his 1825 *Critical Observations on the Fate of Philosophy in Recent Times and Its Entry into a New Epoch*, Windischmann analyzed the particular effects of sickness on consciousness in detail. What was "unique about the massive, life-encompassing sickness-process," he asserted, "is that it excites the whole person to the last fibers of his body and to the depths of his soul so that, disunited in himself, he becomes the object of torment and his whole existence comes to passionate self-consciousness."[31] Sickness "doesn't leave him any rest or peace until it fully runs its course and the unity and truth of the affected community of all members is restored."[32] To the extent that modern philosophy's preoccupation with consciousness, and more specifically with the reconciliation of a consciousness that was divided in itself (*pace* Fichte, Hegel, and Schelling), could be read as a sign that reason had turned as far enough in on itself as it could, Windischmann concluded that a breakthrough was at hand. Indeed, he concluded that the "critical perturbation in the philosophizing of the most recent period" portended a new "epoch of regeneration" (*Epoche der Regeneration*) and the imminent triumph of the "Catholic principle" (*katholisches Princip*).

Even more than Baader or Windischmann, the Catholic theologian Johann Adam Möhler galvanized the polemic between Protestants and Catholics by articulating their differences in a systematic way. Professor of theology and church history at Tübingen, Möhler was part of a historic encounter between Catholics and Protestants. Württemberg, having acquired a portion of Upper Swabia under the Napoleonic reorganization of Europe, attempted to make provision for its new Catholic population by establishing a Catholic school of theology at Ellwangen in 1812. This faculty was then transferred to the university at Tübingen in 1817, where it was forced to contend with the rival claims of the important Protestant theologians established there. Brought into such close proximity in this way, both faculties made interconfessional differences the basis for a productive and sustained exchange in which Möhler was at the forefront. Like other Catholic polemicists, Möhler charged Protestantism with breeding a disorder in thinking. Though its motives of reform may have been sincere and even laudable, Protestantism embodied a willful and subjectivist impulse that was the paradigm for all revolutionary rejections of authority. In his first major work, *The Unity of the Church*, published in 1825, Möhler drew attention to the foundational role of the early Christian community, arguing that this community provided the inviolable foundation for any real knowledge of Christ.[33] In opposition to the Protestant principle of *sola scriptura* and to the subjectivist approach encouraged by modern philosophy that he believed it engendered, Möhler insisted that salvation was only available in the community united by Spirit. The presence of the divine Spirit, he maintained, was first imparted to humanity in and through the community of apostles, who received it directly and whose lives were thereby suffused with divine purpose. Because this distinct moment of divine transformation by the Spirit was a communal one, it was only in community with those connected to the original apostolic community that one could receive the Spirit. In Möhler's view, the unbroken tradition of all who received the Spirit from the apostles down to the present day comprised a community of believers and a living incarnation of the "Catholic principle." The encounter with the Spirit was not simply hearing the divine message, but acquiring a direct imprint in himself or herself that, in turn, guided action. By "direct contemplation one is to make the experience of the church one's own, to beget in oneself holy thought and action."[34] According to Möhler, "Christianity is no mere concept but a matter to be understood as grasping the whole person and having rooted itself in that person's life."[35] Only by direct appropriation in community with other Christians was one capable of receiving the knowledge of salvation that is Spirit. Möhler thus defined heresy as any "attempt to discover Christianity by mere thought . . . without consideration for the Christian life and that which arises from it."[36] Heretics were those who wanted to construct a Christian community based merely on concepts, that is to say, by setting out principles in advance of practice. Like the pagan philosophers of old, they endeavored to work on life by a system of concepts. Christianity, on the other hand, imparted to the world a creative power, able to beget a new life to its adherents.

Because Möhler believed that Christianity emerged alongside older Greek philosophical schools, like Platonism and Aristotelianism, it was forced since its inception to distinguish itself from those schools, even among those who called themselves Christians. Indeed, Möhler argued that Christianity was all too frequently misunderstood by those steeped in these traditions, especially when construed in various ways as a mere system of concepts by those who still did not know its Spirit deeply enough. This temptation was as much to be found in the church as outside of it. He saw heresy thus as part of a continuum linking pagan thought with both Protestant theology and contemporary philosophy. Möhler warned that heresy could take any of the following forms: (1) holding that Christianity must be sought, or that it was somehow lost or could pass away; (2) asserting that Christianity could be grasped aside from any church community; (3) believing that one could possess community without faith, and thus separate Christian knowledge from the church; (4) taking the letter of Scripture as the one and only principle of the faith; and (5) "designating primitive Christianity as the point to which one must return."[37] Each of these activities treated Christianity as something aging, or even dead, and in need of reviving through the activity of the human mind. For Möhler, then, the pagan, the Protestant, and the modern philosopher all failed to grasp the truth of Christianity precisely because they set out to "learn" this truth according to concepts and other instruments of the understanding alone. Reformers who sought the renewal of Christianity by a rational act of interpretation or appraisal thus took an unduly narrow and individual approach to reason and denied the continued vitality of Christ's church as it lived on in traditions of thought and interpretation that transcended individual systems of thought. For Möhler, to be a Catholic meant knowing oneself to be part of a continuing community of Spirit, which shapes life and knowledge in a comprehensive way. Instead of searching for truth, Catholics testify to it by acknowledging the pre-rational hold of Spirit in and through the community.

Möhler was aware of the potential for confessional polemic to sound a sour note. Indeed, he acknowledged that the differences between the confessions had in modern times given rise to violent sallies on the part of many Protestants against Catholics and vice versa. It was all too common, he admitted, to accuse Catholics of "hierarchical arrogance" and Protestants of a "frivolous love of independence." Möhler argued that "it would betoken a very great narrowness of mind if the duration of the mighty religious contest were not sought for in deeper causes." One must look beyond everyday polemics therefore to where "deep interests are defended." In his 1832 book *Symbolism*, he tried to locate such deep interests in the "symbolic" texts of the different confessions, namely, texts in which "the public faith is expressed."[38] Using what he called a "Christian anthropology" to explore the fundamentally different ways Catholics and Protestants understood the original, or primitive, state of man before the Fall, Möhler took particular aim at Luther's naturalism. Luther held that God created Adam in a way that was entirely pleasing and acceptable to him. He held that "the pure nature of man, as it sprang forth at the omnipotent word of the Creator, comprised absolutely in itself all the conditions to render it pleasing unto God" and that "without any supernatural aid, he truly knew God."[39] To this, Möhler responded that it was indisputable that Adam was made by God and was therefore good. Being made in the "image of God," Adam was also capable of knowing God. However, Möhler insisted that for Adam to actually know God required God's grace. Being made in the "image of God" was insufficient and therefore one needed to distinguish "between the bare faculty itself and the exercise of that faculty in correspondence to the divine will." Möhler maintained that "a relation to God . . . is no wise to be attained and upheld by natural powers," but "a special condescension of the Almighty is required thereto." For "no finite being can exist in a living moral communion with the Deity, save by the communion of the self-same Holy Spirit. This relation of Adam to God, which exalted him above human nature and made him participate in the divine nature, is hence termed . . . a supernatural gift of divine grace, super-added to the endowments of nature."[40]

Möhler concluded that the "image of God" that Adam possessed was thus only prerequisite to receiving the "likeness unto God" necessary for him to relate to God. This was significant, for by thoroughly naturalizing the human relationship to God, Luther dispensed with the divine grace necessary for being in communion with God, the grace that was requisite after Adam's fall. According to Möhler, this put Protestants in an extremely difficult position, since they had to explain Adam's fallen state by saying he was no longer able to exercise what were, originally, purely natural powers. As a result of their mistaken anthropology, Protestants were thus forced to hold that "fallen man can neither think, believe, nor will, anything having reference to divine and spiritual concerns; that he is utterly dead to all good, and no longer possesses any, even the least spark of spiritual powers." In the end, "to that faculty of the human mind, which it terms reason, it assigns merely the finite world as the sphere of activity."[41] Möhler thus concluded that since Protestant reason could no longer claim knowledge of divine things, it had nothing left but philosophy. This insight was relevant to Catholics too, of course. To the extent that Catholics were becoming increasingly intent on trying to out-reason philosophers, he warned that some Catholics too were succumbing to the same temptation to articulate a philosophical grasp of faith. Möhler acknowledged that

> there is within us an irrepressible longing after comprehension: it is the same which in its excess leads to the denial of everything above comprehension. This very longing to comprehend, like the fact, that we are surrounded by incomprehensible mysteries, points to the distraction which has convulsed our nature, to the wound inflicted on our reason—to a lost intuition, and, in so far, to an unhappy past.[42]

As the "wound inflicted on our reason," philosophy had become part of the age, and Catholic thought was not immune to its sires or difficulties. In spite of their faith, Catholics were deeply enmeshed in the same quest to bring reality before the court of human reason.

Like Möhler, Joseph Görres recognized that Catholics and Protestants were in the same intellectual predicament to some extent. The onetime political radical and founder of *Der Rheinsche Merkur*, Görres spent much of his later life rejuvenating Catholic intellectual life. As a professor of history at the University of Munich, Görres attracted a number of important Catholic intellectuals to his circle, including Ignaz Döllinger, Johann Ringseis, and Johann Adam Möhler. Görres devoted most of his scholarly career to studies of mythology and mysticism, but also weighed in on confessional issues, and he was much more aggressive than Möhler in flaunting Protestantism's inability to defend itself against the scourge of rationalism. With no little irony, Görres pointed to the fact that Protestants were now forced to defend themselves against the rationalism they had themselves unleashed. Indeed, Protestants were now in the same position as Catholics had been during the Reformation, having to defend themselves against charges of radical individualism on the one hand and of dogmatism on the other. In their defense, Protestants were grabbing hold of the same arguments they themselves rejected three hundred years earlier, namely, the authority of certain dogmas and biblical interpretations as the living core of the church. In light of this twist of historical fate, Görres argued that the only sure weapon against rationalism was Catholicism.

Görres illustrated the superiority of the Catholic position by returning to the theological debate over justification and showing how Catholic and Protestant theologians diverged on justification because of fundamentally different perspectives on the meaning of subjective and objective. To the Protestant theologian, it was axiomatic that "[e]verything that conflicts with or departs from the rule of the righteousness of God, which is revealed in the law, is sin."[43] To the Catholic theologian, however,

> this last determination has as its ground the confusion between the objectively bad with the subjectively sinful, which is justified in figurative usage, but which is entirely inadmissible for logical definitions and the deduction of definite propositions. God is pure good, and so what deviates from the norm of his law is bad and derives from evil. In order for the objectively bad to become subjectively sinful, another subjective condition must necessarily be added, that can only lie in the freedom of human will. . . . Error is in the soul, desire in the heart, uncleanness in the body, but sin alone in the will, and just as error, so also desire and such bodily disturbances first become sin, and therefore punishable, when, through free acceptance they are imprinted with the character of guilt.[44]

It was not simply breaking the law, therefore, that made something a sin—it was a particular disposition of the will. Sinning involved two separate acts: the act of contravention and the act which "through free acceptance . . . [it is] imprinted with the character of guilt." With respect to the doctrine of justification, therefore,

> the fundamental error is the same . . . which enthralled the reformers in most of their dogmatic innovations. For it is as they say: grace is a free gift, without which no justification can occur. But, this is only the objective moment of the same, the indispensable condition of its possibility. In order for it, as our subjective justification, to become real, the action of God *on us* (the free act of grace) must link up with another act *in us* that appropriates it to our individuality, and transfers that small portion meant for us from the wellspring of blessedness.[45]

According to Görres, the "fundamental error" of Reformation theology rested on the confusion of subjective and objective. For the sixteenth-century reformers, it was God's act alone that justified each individual; the individual could have no role in meriting God's grace. For Catholics, however, justification consisted of both the free act of God in giving grace and the act of the human person in appropriating that grace on the individual level. In order for God's act of grace "to become real" it needed to "link up" with an act in the individual. In this way, "objective grace" found its counterpart in "subjective justification," thereby completing the "objectivity" of the act. The fundamental error of Protestantism was thus a mistaken use of "subject" and "object." This, in turn, promoted a "contradiction-ridden web of human ways of thinking" clearly evident in the "subjectivist" influence in contemporary philosophy.[46] As a child of the Reformation, modern philosophy made a virtue out of radical doubt and the view that "subjects" can no longer aspire to certainty over objects. Görres countered, however, that this drew an impenetrable veil of uncertainty around the lone thinking subject that obscured the subjective dimension of all objective knowledge. Indeed, Görres insisted that for any perception (*Wahrnehmung*), whether of the mundane or the divine, to occur "one must open oneself to it. One must . . . first turn one's attention toward the light, and then clean the receiving organ from as much murkiness as possible."[47] Perception required subjective preparation and participation in order to succeed.

Nineteenth-century Catholics have typically been seen as withdrawing into an intellectual ghetto of their own making, celebrating precisely those ritualistic and supernatural aspects of the faith considered most out of step with rational, enlightened society.[48] The veneration of relics like the Holy Coat of Trier, as well as the dramatic surge in the number of Marian apparitions throughout the century, only confirmed many (Protestants and others) in their belief that Catholicism was incapable of adapting to the changing times. The dogmatization of the Immaculate Conception and of papal infallibility, as well as papal pronouncements such as the "Syllabus of Errors," seemingly gave official stamp to the view that the Catholic Church was in principle irreconcilable with modern society. Further, Catholic scientific, industrial, and professional "backwardness"—that is to say, both the real and imagined disparity between non-Catholics and Catholics in schools and in the workplace—seemed to many indicative of a deep discrepancy between Catholic practices and modern rhythms of life. A steady stream of anti-Catholic writing throughout the century reinforced this image and helped define German culture and national identity as fundamentally Protestant. From this perspective, Catholic polemic in the 1820s might be read as the mirror image of slurs and stereotypes that Protestants and others were hurling at Catholics.[49] But as this essay has tried to show, the Catholic genealogy of Protestant reason was not just a case of mudslinging.

Motivated by a growing dissatisfaction with the rising tide of cultural Protestantism, the Catholic polemicists analyzed here did not just defend themselves against Protestant attacks. They analyzed what they took to be increasingly influential "Protestant" habits of mind and offered Catholicism as an important corrective. That they appeared roughly one decade before the outbreak of the so-called *Kölner Wirren* is significant. This incident, which saw the archbishop of Cologne arrested for standing firm against Prussian authorities over the issue of mixed marriages, is typically seen as the crucial impetus for the political mobilization of German Catholics and for the broader Catholic revival movement that took root in the second half of the nineteenth century.[50] Without disputing the importance of the event or its influence, a focus on the episode tends to reinforce an image of Catholics as only ever reactive when fighting for their rights. In contrast, the polemic of the 1820s shows that Catholics were just as capable of being proactive and even aggressive, and that they were active participants in shaping the discourse of modernity, even though—and precisely to the extent—that they were explicitly hostile to it. Indeed, the texts under investigation here show clearly that Catholics were staunchly, and even militantly, confident in their ability to turn the tide against cultural Protestantism. While this might seem naïve in retrospect, this should not lead us to portray Catholic polemics as historically fated to playing catch-up with their Protestant and secular counterparts. On the contrary, the Catholic assault on Protestantism offers an important perspective on how confessional conflict encouraged innovative modes of self-articulation in the public sphere.[51] One of the most innovative of these was the effort to locate a distinctly Protestant impulse in history, an impulse that was not merely the effect of the Reformation, but the cause of the Reformation and a range of other threats.

The Catholic genealogy of Protestant reason displayed a growing confidence that Catholicism had something important to offer German culture. In contrast to the reckless and capricious iconoclasm of Protestant thought (and its philosophical offshoots), Catholicism was presented in these polemics as a way of life and thought that encouraged respect for authority and tradition. Because it put the community ahead of the individual, Catholicism advanced a decidedly different and healthier alternative to the arrogance of egotism (whether religious, philosophical, or political) and was thus heralded as a particularly effective matrix for promoting loyalty. Of course, to achieve this image of a positive and somewhat monolithic Catholic community, it is important to note that the same elision of all varieties of Protestant thought into one overarching category of Protestantism was matched by an equally strategic elision of all varieties of Catholic thought and opinion. Thus, there is virtually no mention in the 1820s of the many positive Catholic appropriations of Kant and Hegel, nor is there mention of the Catholic Enlightenment, which prior to the French Revolution had made important inroads into Catholic thought.[52] By documenting what they took to be an insidious cultural impulse whose transhistorical influence could be read backward to pagan times and forward to modern socialism, what Catholic polemicists did therefore was define Catholicism as an equal and opposite culture. Recasting Protestantism in this way served Catholic polemicists as a way of justifying confessional polemics as a necessary, and almost Manichean, struggle between equal and opposed transhistorical impulses. For if the Protestant principle was much more than a historically specific desire for Christian reform located in the sixteenth century, then the "Catholic principle" must also be progenitive of facets of experience and history far beyond merely the institutional church and its doctrines. The genealogy of Protestant reason thus prepared the way for a much more comprehensive stocktaking of Catholicism's cultural impact, past and present.[53] This insight is especially important if we are to understand the evolution of dominant strands of Catholic thought, like "traditionalism" and "neo-scholasticism" in the second half of the nineteenth century, neither of which were foreordained to take precedence over alternatives that were eventually silenced.

Richard Schaefer is associate professor of history and religious studies at the State University of New York, College at Plattsburgh. Trained in modern European intellectual history, Schaefer received the PhD from Cornell University in 2005. His current research focuses on the role of scholars in the Catholic revival movement in the nineteenth century, and he has published articles on that topic in *Modern Intellectual History*, the *Journal of the History of Ideas*, and the *Catholic Historical Review*.

Notes

1. For an important critique of "religious violence," see William T. Cavanaugh, *The Myth of Religious Violence: Secular Ideology and the Roots of Modern Conflict* (Oxford, 2009).
2. Of course, as Golo Mann has pointed out, we need to take care when discussing Catholics as a minority prior to the founding of the German nation state in 1871. In cities, regions, and states (like the kingdom of Bavaria) Catholics were majorities. Golo Mann, *Deutsche Geschichte des 19. und 20. Jahrhunderts* (Frankfurt am Main, 1999).
3. John Wolffe, *Protestant-Catholic Conflict from the Reformation to the Twenty-First Century: The Dynamics of Religious Difference* (Basingstoke, 2013), 7.
4. Some important books in this new literature include Dagmar Herzog, *Intimacy and Exclusion: Religious Politics in Pre-Revolutionary Baden* (Princeton, 1996); Helmut Walser Smith, *German Nationalism and Religious Conflict: Culture, Ideology, Politics, 1870–1914* (Princeton, 1995); Michael B. Gross, *The War against Catholicism: Liberalism and the Anti-Catholic Imagination in Nineteenth-Century Germany* (Ann Arbor, 2004); and Manuel Borutta, *Antikatholizismus: Deutschland und Italien im Zeitalter der Europäischen Kulturkämpfe* (Göttingen, 2010).

5. Helmut Walser Smith and Christopher Clark, "The Fate of Nathan," in *Protestants, Catholics, and Jews in Germany, 1800–1914*, ed. Helmut Walser Smith (New York, 2001), 3–29, here 14.

6. Smith and Clark, "The Fate of Nathan," 16.

7. Olaf Blaschke, "Das 19. Jahrhundert: Ein Zweites Konfessionelles Zeitalter?" *Geschichte und Gesellschaft* 26 (2000): 38–75. For more on this issue, see chapter 3 in this volume.

8. Andreas Holzem, *Kirchenreform und Sektenstiftung: Deutschkatholiken, Reformkatholiken und Ultramontane am Oberrhein 1844–1866* (Paderborn, 1994); and Christoph Weber, *Aufklärung und Orthodoxie im Mittelrhein 1820–1850* (Munich, 1973).

9. The *Reichsdeputationshauptschluss* resulted in the transfer of church property into secular hands and the dissolution of religious houses and institutions. For more details, see Rudolf Lill, "Reichskirche—Säkularisation—Katholische Bewegung," in *Der Soziale und Politische Katholizismus. Entwicklungslinien in Deutschland 1803–1963*, ed. Anton Rauscher, 2 vols. (Munich, 1981), vol. 1.

10. E. E. Y. Hales, *Revolution and the Papacy 1769–1846* (London, 1960).

11. David Blackbourn, *The Long Nineteenth Century: A History of Germany, 1780–1918* (New York, 1998).

12. Wichmann von Meding, "Das Wartburgfest im Rahmen des Reformationjubiläums 1817," *Zeitschrift für Kirchengeschichte* 95 (1986): 205–36.

13. Wolfgang Altgeld, "Religion, Denomination and Nationalism in Nineteenth-Century Germany," in Smith, *Protestants, Catholics, and Jews in Germany*, 51.

14. Wilhelm Fels, *Spinoza der Grosse Philosoph, als er Roemisch-Katholisch Werden Sollte* (Leipzig, 1829); Gottlob Ernst Schulze, *Ueber die Entdeckung, dass Leibnitz ein Katholik gewesen sey* (Göttingen, 1827); and Wilhelm von Schuetz, *Goethe's Faust und der Protestantismus: Manuscript für Katholiken und Freunde* (Bamberg, 1844).

15. Richard Schaefer, "Program for a New Catholic Wissenschaft: Devotional Activism and Catholic Modernity in the Nineteenth Century," *Modern Intellectual History* 4 (2007): 433–62.

16. For the most part, it should be noted, Catholic writers elided the different Protestant denominations and spoke in general terms about *Protestantismus*. The only exception among the authors treated here was Johann Adam Möhler, although he too treated Luther as emblematic of "German Protestantism."

17. Heinrich Lutz, "Zum Wandel der Katholischen Lutherinterpretation," in *Objektivität und Parteilichkeit in der Geschichtswissenschaft*, ed. Reinhart Koselleck and Wolfgang J. Mommsen, (Berlin, 1977), 190.

18. G. W. F. Hegel, *Faith and Knowledge*, ed. H. S. Harris and Walter Cerf (Albany, NY, 1977), 57.

19. Michel Foucault, "Nietzsche, Genealogy, History," in *The Foucault Reader*, ed. Paul Rabinow (New York, 1984), 76–100.

20. Thomas F. O'Meara, *Romantic Idealism and Roman Catholicism: Schelling and the Theologians* (Notre Dame, 1982). For German Catholic ecumenicists of this era, see chapter 2 in this volume.

21. Franz Baader, "Über Katholizismus und Protestantismus," in *Sämmtliche Werke*, ed. Franz Hoffman, 16 vols. (Leipzig, 1824), vol. 1, 76. This and all other translations are the author's, unless otherwise indicated.

22. Bernhard Schneider, *Katholiken auf die Barrikaden? Europäische Revolutionen und deutsche katholische Presse 1815–1848* (Paderborn, 1998).

23. Franz Baader, "Über das durch unsere Zeit herbeigeführte Bedürfniss einer innigeren Vereinigung der Wissenschaft und der Religion," in Hoffman, *Sämmtliche Werke*, vol. 1, 84.

24. The early nineteenth century saw a number of Catholics combining medicine and faith to perform and explain miracles. An important exponent of the idea that miracles had a real scientific basis was Johann Nepomuk von Ringseis, rector of the University of Munich. Windischmann claimed to have been "healed" of a vision ailment due to the intercession of the healer Prince Alexander von Hohenlohe, a miracle that even Hegel conceded. See Heribert Raab, "'Katholische Wissenschaft'—Ein Postulat und seine Variationen in der wissenschafts- und bildungspolitik deutscher Katholiken während des 19. Jahrhunderts," in *Katholizismus, Bildung und Wissenschaft im 19. und 20. Jahrhundert*, ed. Anton Rauscher (Munich, 1987), 61–91.

25. Ludwig Lenhart, *Die erste Mainzer Theologenschule des 19. Jahrhunderts (1805–30)* (Mainz, 1956).

26. Carl J. H. Windischmann, *Ueber etwas, das der Heilkunst Noth thut: Ein Versuch zur Vereinigung dieser Kunst mit der christlichen Philosophie* (Leipzig, 1824).

27. Windischmann, *Heilkunst Noth*, l–li.

28. Windischmann, *Heilkunst Noth*, xii–xiii.

29. Windischmann, *Heilkunst Noth*, xv.

30. Windischmann, *Heilkunst Noth*, xv.

31. Carl J. H. Windischmann, *Kritische Betrachtungen über die Schicksale der Philosophie in der neueren Zeit und den Eintritt einer neuen Epoche in Derselben* (Frankfurt am Main, 1825), 11.

32. Windischmann, *Kritische Betrachtungen*, 11.

33. Johann Adam Möhler and E. J. Vierneisel, *Die Einheit in der Kirche: Oder das Prinzip des Katholicismus, dargestellt im Geiste der Kirchenväter der drei ersten Jahrhunderte* (Mainz, 1925), 5.

34. Möhler and Vierneisel, *Die Einheit in der Kirche*, 12.

35. Möhler and Vierneisel, *Die Einheit in der Kirche*, 15.

36. Möhler and Vierneisel, *Die Einheit in der Kirche*, 59.

37. Möhler and Vierneisel, *Die Einheit in der Kirche*, 62.

38. Johann Adam Möhler, *Symbolism: Or, Exposition of the Doctrinal Differences between Catholics and Protestants as Evidenced by Their Symbolical Writings* (New York, 1844). Since it is the standard in scholarship on Möhler, I use Robertson's translation. I have reviewed all of the translations used in the text.

39. Möhler, *Symbolism*, 30.

40. Möhler, *Symbolism*, 26–27.

41. Möhler, *Symbolism*, 54–57.

42. Möhler, *Symbolism*, 52.

43. Joseph von Görres, "Katholizismus, Protestantismus und Rationalismus," in *Schriften der Strassburger Exilszeit, 1824–1827: Aufsätze und Beiträge im 'Katholik,'* ed. Heribert Raab (Paderborn, 1987), 78.

44. Görres, "Katholizismus, Protestantismus und Rationalismus," 78.

45. Görres, "Katholizismus, Protestantismus und Rationalismus," 80.

46. Görres, "Katholizismus, Protestantismus und Rationalismus," 85.

47. Görres, "Katholizismus, Protestantismus und Rationalismus," 80.

48. Thomas Nipperdey, *Germany from Napoleon to Bismarck, 1800–1866* (Dublin, 1996).

49. These polemics also reinforced a much more militant Christian anti-Semitism. For more: Olaf Blaschke, *Katholizismus und Antisemitismus im Deutschen Kaiserreich* (Göttingen, 1997).
50. Friedrich Keinemann, *Das Kölner Ereigniss: Sein Wiederhall in der Rheinprovinz und in Westfalen* (Münster, 1974).
51. I follow Robert Wuthnow in using "self-articulation" to describe the discursive underpinnings of identity formation. In his analysis of different "discourse communities," Wuthnow employs these concepts in order to discuss the production, selection, and institutionalization of elements of "[a] discursive field . . . [that] provides the fundamental categories in which thinking can take place . . . [and] establishes the limits of discussion and defines the range of problems that can be addressed." Robert Wuthnow, *Communities of Discourse: Ideology and Social Structure in the Reformation, the Enlightenment, and European Socialism* (Cambridge, 1989), 22–23.
52. Norbert Fischer, *Kant und der Katholizismus: Stationen einer wechselhaften Geschichte* (Freiburg im Breisgau, 2005).
53. Matthias Klug, *Rückwendung zum Mittelalter? Geschichtsbilder und historische Argumentation im Politischen Katholizismus des Vormärz* (Paderborn, 1995).

Bibliography

Altgeld, Wolfgang. "Religion, Denomination and Nationalism in Nineteenth Century Germany." In *Protestants, Catholics, and Jews in Germany*, edited by Helmut Walser Smith, 49–66. New York, 2001.

Baader, Franz. "Über das durch unsere Zeit herbeigeführte Bedürfniss einer innigeren Vereinigung der Wissenschaft und der Religion." In *Sämmtliche Werke*, edited by Franz Hoffman, vol. 1, 81–96. Leipzig, 1824.

———. "Über Katholizismus und Protestantismus." In *Sämmtliche Werke*, edited by Franz Hoffman, vol. 1, 71–80. Leipzig, 1824.

Blackbourn, David. *The Long Nineteenth Century: A History of Germany, 1780–1918*. New York, 1998.

Blaschke, Olaf. *Katholizismus und Antisemitismus im Deutschen Kaiserreich*. Göttingen, 1997.

———. "Das 19. Jahrhundert: Ein Zweites Konfessionelles Zeitalter?" *Geschichte und Gesellschaft* 26 (2000): 38–75

Borutta, Manuel. *Antikatholizismus: Deutschland und Italien im Zeitalter der Europäischen Kulturkämpfe*. Göttingen, 2010.

Cavanaugh, William T. *The Myth of Religious Violence: Secular Ideology and the Roots of Modern Conflict*. Oxford, 2009.

Fels, Wilhelm. *Spinoza der Grosse Philosoph, als er Roemisch-Katholisch Werden Sollte*. Leipzig, 1829.

Fischer, Norbert. *Kant und der Katholizismus: Stationen einer wechselhaften Geschichte*. Freiburg, 2005.

Foucault, Michel. "Nietzsche, Genealogy, History." In *Language, Counter-memory, Practice: Selected Essays and Interviews*, edited by Paul Rabinow, 139–64. Ithaca, 1977.

Görres, Joseph von. "Katholizismus, Protestantismus und Rationalismus." In *Gesammelte Schriften / Schriften der Strassburger Exilszeit, 1824–1827: Aufsätze und Beiträge im "Katholik,"* edited by Heribert Raab, 71–87. Paderborn, 1987.

Gross, Michael B. *The War against Catholicism: Liberalism and the Anti-Catholic Imagination in Nineteenth-Century Germany.* Ann Arbor, 2004.

Hales, E. E. Y. *Revolution and the Papacy 1769–1846.* London, 1960.

Hegel, G. W. F. *Faith and Knowledge.* Edited by H. S. Harris and Walter Cerf. Albany, NY, 1977.

Herzog, Dagmar. *Intimacy and Exclusion: Religious Politics in Pre-Revolutionary Baden.* Princeton, 1996.

Holzem, Andreas. *Kirchenreform und Sektenstiftung: Deutschkatholiken, Reformkatholiken und Ultramontane am Oberrhein 1844–1866.* Paderborn, 1994.

Keinemann, Friedrich. *Das Kölner Ereigniss: Sein Wiederhall in der Rheinprovinz und in Westfalen.* Münster, 1974.

Klug, Matthias. *Rückwendung zum Mittelalter? Geschichtsbilder und historische Argumentation im Politischen Katholizismus des Vormärz.* Paderborn, 1995.

Lenhart, Ludwig. *Die erste Mainzer Theologenschule des 19. Jahrhunderts (1805–30).* Mainz, 1956.

Lill, Rudolf. "Reichskirche—Säkularisation—Katholische Bewegung." In *Der Soziale und Politische Katholizismus. Entwicklungslinien in Deutschland 1803–1963,* edited by Anton Rauscher, vol. 1, 15–45. Munich, 1981.

Lutz, Heinrich. "Zum Wandel Des Katholischen Lutherinterpretation." In *Objektivität und Parteilichkeit in der Geschichtswissenschaft,* edited by Reinhart Koselleck and Wolfgang J. Mommsen, 173–98. Berlin, 1977.

Mann, Golo. *Deutsche Geschichte des 19. und 20. Jahrhunderts.* Frankfurt am Main, 1999.

Meding, Wichmann von. "Das Wartburgfest im Rahmen des Reformationsjubiläums 1817." *Zeitschrift für Kirchengeschichte* 96 (1986): 203–36.

Möhler, Johann Adam. *Symbolism: Or, Exposition of the Doctrinal Differences between Catholics and Protestants as Evidenced by Their Symbolical Writings.* New York, 1844.

——— and E. J. Vierneisel. *Die Einheit in der Kirche: Oder das Prinzip des Katholicismus, dargestellt im Geiste der Kirchenväter der drei ersten Jahrhunderte.* Mainz, 1925.

Nipperdey, Thomas. *Germany from Napoleon to Bismarck, 1800–1866.* Dublin, 1996.

O'Meara, Thomas F. *Romantic Idealism and Roman Catholicism: Schelling and the Theologians.* Notre Dame, 1982.

Raab, Heribert. "'Katholische Wissenschaft'—Ein Postulat und seine Variationen in der wissenschafts und bildungspolitik deutscher Katholiken während des 19. Jahrhunderts." In *Katholizismus, Bildung und Wissenschaft im 19. und 20. Jahrhundert,* edited by Anton Rauscher, 61–91. Munich, 1987.

Schaefer, Richard. "Program for a New Catholic Wissenschaft: Devotional Activism and Catholic Modernity in the Nineteenth Century." *Modern Intellectual History* 4 (2007): 433–62.

Schneider, Bernhard. *Katholiken auf die Barrikaden? Europäische Revolutionen und deutsche katholische Presse 1815–1848.* Paderborn, 1998.

Schuetz, Wilhelm von. *Goethe's Faust und der Protestantismus: Manuscript für Katholiken und Freunde*. Bamberg, 1844.

Smith, Helmut Walser. *German Nationalism and Religious Conflict: Culture, Ideology, Politics 1870–1914*. Princeton, 1995.

Smith, Helmut Walser, and Christopher Clark. "The Fate of Nathan." In *Protestants, Catholics, and Jews in Germany, 1800–1914*, edited by Helmut Walser Smith, 3–29. New York, 2001.

Weber, Christoph. *Aufklärung und Orthodoxie im Mittelrhein 1820–1850*. Munich, 1973.

Windischmann, Carl J. H. *Kritische Betrachtungen über die Schicksale der Philosophie in der neueren Zeit und den Eintritt einer neuen Epoche in Derselben*. Frankfurt am Main, 1825.

———. *Ueber etwas, das der Heilkunst Noth thut: Ein Versuch zur Vereinigung dieser Kunst mit der christlichen Philosophie*. Leipzig, 1824.

Wolffe, John. *Protestant-Catholic Conflict from the Reformation to the Twenty-First Century: The Dynamics of Religious Difference*. Basingstoke, 2013.

Wuthnow, Robert. *Communities of Discourse: Ideology and Social Structure in the Reformation, the Enlightenment, and European Socialism*. Cambridge, 1989.

CHAPTER SEVEN

Fighting or Fostering Confessional Plurality?
Ernst Salomon Cyprian as a Historian of Lutheranism in the Early Eighteenth Century

ALEXANDER SCHUNKA

Confessional polemics are closely connected to the confessional ruptures of Europe following the Reformation. Written polemics were numerous and ranged among the most popular ways of coping with competing religious truths. While polemical writings seemed to aim at changing the minds of opponents, they often contributed to solidifying the views of the authors' supporters. Points of contention were not only continuously present between the large confessional denominations but, in the course of the early modern era, increasingly within Protestantism itself. Quarrels between orthodox Lutherans, Reformed irenicists, and Lutheran Pietists featured prominently in the late seventeenth and early eighteenth centuries. This confessional plurality itself was, to a great extent, shaped by polemical argument: Pietism largely evolved as a distinct movement of spiritual reform from the struggle between Lutheran church critics and orthodox theologians, and while irenicism aimed at uniting different Protestant doctrines, it was both anti-Catholic and opposed to the strict Lutheranism laid down in the Formula of Concord of 1577.[1]

Polemicist quarrels among Protestants gained in momentum in the later decades of the seventeenth century not only because new arguments had evolved since the Reformation, but also due to changing structures in politics and communication. The Peace of Westphalia in 1648 had put an end to religious warfare and officially recognized three different faiths in the Holy Roman Empire. While this institutionalized heterogeneity of the empire fostered interconfessional dialogue, it also contributed to new strife, often originating from theologians in conjunction with the political interests of their rulers. In the years around 1700, an expanding print market and new literary genres such as the periodical journal provided new battlegrounds for confessional arguments and quickly impacted the mechanisms of writing and distributing polemic.[2]

Polemics of the earlier eighteenth century often appeared as small pamphlets but sometimes also in voluminous works. Their sheer number is enormous. Normally they were written in German as opposed to Latin, which suggests that they aimed at a large, nonspecialist audience of opponents and followers alike. By creating in-groups and ostracizing out-groups, polemics often simplified confessional truths in order to create a clear scenario of orthodoxy and dissent, stressing certain facts at the expense of downplaying, omitting, or deliberately "forgetting" others.

If one were to draw a map of Protestant polemical agitation in early eighteenth-century Germany, its capital cities would be the strongholds of Lutheran orthodoxy: Wittenberg and Leipzig, Hamburg and Gotha. These centers of polemicism often gained their notoriety from the influence of specific scholarly theologians and pastors. A number of authors disputed certain arguments or subjected their confessional opponents to *ad hominem* attacks. While they were generally well-educated and highly erudite, these authors were also frequently accused by their adversaries as being mere hell-raisers who lacked the virtues of Christian love and forbearance.

Ernst Salomon Cyprian (1673–1745) was arguably the most notorious orthodox Lutheran polemicist of early eighteenth-century Germany. In the course of his long career, he agitated against Roman Catholicism, Lutheran Pietism, and Protestant irenicism, as well as against what he sometimes called atheism, naturalism, or "Thomasian disbelief" (*Thomasianischen Unglauben*).[3] Cyprian was a theologian, though he was never ordained as a pastor. From 1713 until his death he held the position of librarian and ecclesiastical adviser (*Kirchenrat*) for Duke Friedrich II of Saxe-Gotha. In his spare time he compiled historical documents and composed Reformation histories as well as corresponded with numerous other theologians. His agitations made him a well-known and hotly controversial figure within early eighteenth-century German Protestantism. Some diplomats at the Perpetual Diet of Regensburg firmly believed that Cyprian alone could bring the complete political work of all Protestant estates of the Holy Roman Empire to a halt.[4] From his outpost at the duchy of Saxe-Gotha, he diagnosed a decline of Lutheran traditions, as could be seen not only in the rise of Pietism, Protestant irenicism, and the religious criticism of the early Enlightenment, but also in the conversion of Augustus the Strong and his son, rulers of Gotha's powerful neighbor Electoral Saxony (1697 and 1712, respectively). He therefore believed that Saxe-Gotha remained the only true stronghold of the Reformation. Cyprian's confessional polemics not only affected his ruler's dynastic politics, but also influenced the political as well as the public spheres of the Holy Roman Empire, as the debates and controversies between 1715 and 1730 illustrate.

Together with his contemporaries, the Saxon theologian Valentin Ernst Löscher (1673–1749) and the two Hamburg-based authors Erdmann Neumeister (1671–1756) and Sebastian Edzard (1672–1736), Cyprian stood at the center of a network of polemicists who constituted the core figures in early eighteenth-century German Lutheran orthodoxy. Their close collaboration, evident in the well-preserved and as yet almost fully neglected correspondence between these churchmen, hints at their pivotal role within Lutheran polemics and church politics in the empire of the earlier eighteenth century. While Löscher specialized in the publication of theological treatises and periodicals and Edzard and Neumeister focused on short polemics, the Gotha theologian tried to preserve what he understood as true Lutheranism not with doctrinal but with historical arguments.[5] As a renowned scholar of his day, Cyprian blended his own polemical aspirations with the genre of Protestant historiography and based it on the accurate analysis of historical, even archival sources. In doing so, he became one of the most important eighteenth-century apologists of the Reformation as the restoration of a true and pure faith. He defended this idea of the Lutheran reform as a turning point not only against Roman Catholicism but more so against those other Protestants who either considered the Reformation incomplete and were doubtful about the role of institutional churches (such as Pietists) or who tried to resolve the schisms between Lutheranism and the Reformed faith (such as irenicists).

In recent decades, scholars in a range of disciplines have given increasing attention to understanding polemics as a tool of confessional communication. They have addressed the topic from the perspective of communication and media and have offered studies of certain conflicts or authors, of their particular milieus and infrastructures.[6] However, as is the case with German orthodox Lutheranism in general, the historian and polemicist Cyprian remains a distinctly under-researched figure, especially considering the impressive amount of still extant material such as letters and prints. In a recent article, Scott Dixon has focused on Cyprian's relationship with Gottfried Arnold. He has argued that the Gotha *Kirchenrat*, as an inherently conservative preserver of the Reformation, dedicated a significant part of his life to fight Arnoldian Pietism because he considered Arnold's *Impartial History of the Church and Heretics* immensely disturbing to the Reformation heritage.[7] The present chapter situates Cyprian's struggle against Pietism in a broader framework of historiography and identity formation among the Lutheran orthodoxy of the early eighteenth century. The polemicism against Arnold was thus more than just a defensive battle: it was part of a larger strategy to promote the achievements of the Reformation and to carry them into a new age of religious and intellectual pluralism, in order to serve the contemporary needs of Cyprian's Ernestine ruler and Lutheranism in the empire. By defining and fighting deviations from what he saw as pure Lutheranism, Cyprian highlighted and clarified the gaps between different confessional strands and inadvertently contributed to the forging of pluralist Protestant confessional cultures in eighteenth-century Germany.[8] The remainder of this essay addresses Cyprian as a polemicist historian and illustrates how his historiographical interests related to contemporary polemics, to the traditions and standards of history writing among Protestants of the early eighteenth century, to the politics of the Holy Roman Empire as well as the duchy of Saxe-Gotha, and to Lutheran identity formation vis-à-vis an evolving religious plurality of the early Enlightenment.

The Life of a Polemicist Historian

Cyprian was born in the town of Ostheim in the Rhön Mountains, which used to be part of Ernestine Saxony. He was educated at the Lutheran University of Jena and eventually followed his teacher, the church historian Johann Andreas Schmidt (1652–1726), to Helmstedt. Schmidt supervised his dissertation, which dealt with the history of the omophor, a shoulder scarf of Greek Christian bishops in the early church. This choice of topic already sheds light upon Cyprian's use of church history to prove religious truths: following in the footsteps of Schmidt, Cyprian argued that this particular piece of garment was sufficient evidence for the fact that the pope had an unjustified claim to be head of the Roman Catholic Church.[9] In Helmstedt he got into personal quarrels surrounding his polemics against Gottfried Arnold's *Impartial History*. Soon after, he left for Coburg, where he became head of the *Gymnasium*. This brought him into direct contact with Friedrich II of Saxe-Gotha.[10] After some time traveling and obtaining another doctorate in theology at the University of Wittenberg, he went to the capital of Gotha in 1713 as a librarian, vice president of the consistory, and ecclesiastical adviser.[11]

Apart from his studies at Helmstedt, most of Cyprian's life illustrates his rootedness in Ernestine Saxony. At the same time, he was well-connected with renowned Protestant scholars of his age, exchanging letters with the philosopher and Hanoverian court councilor Gottfried Wilhelm Leibniz, as well as with contemporary theologians as diverse as the Reformed irenicist court preacher Daniel Ernst Jablonski in Berlin, the irenicist theologian Jean-Alphonse Turrettini of Geneva, but also the Pietists Gottfried Arnold in Quedlinburg (later in Allstedt) and August Hermann Francke in Halle.[12] His contacts with Leibniz and Jablonski, for instance, contributed to his membership in the Berlin Academy of Sciences in 1703.[13] Furthermore, Cyprian entertained an impressive communication network with numerous pastors, writers, and teachers, which resulted in about eleven thousand pages of letters that are still preserved in the Library of Gotha.

What is important here is that Cyprian maintained an extensive correspondence with his fellow orthodox Lutherans Edzard and Neumeister. From the ducal court in Gotha, Cyprian led the fierce Lutheran resistance to the politics of toleration and irenicism at the Perpetual Diet of Regensburg in the early 1720s and in due course became the favorite enemy of rulers, politicians, and churchmen, especially in the powerful Protestant German states of Hanover and Prussia.[14] In the 1730s, Cyprian acted as a theological adviser in the negotiations between Saxe-Gotha and the British Hanoverian dynasties that resulted in the marriage of Princess Augusta of Saxe-Gotha to Frederick Louis, the Prince of Wales, in 1736. A number of similar dynastic alliances between the Ernestine duchy and European royal families were sealed in the following decades, later inspiring German chancellor Otto von Bismarck to mock Saxe-Gotha as the "stud farm of Europe."[15]

Apart from his political responsibilities, librarianship, and scholarly networking, Cyprian published lengthy historical works, in which, among other topics, he touched on the history of the Reformation, on Protestant irenicism, and on the institution of the papacy. Others of his writings were published anonymously or printed posthumously by collaborators under their own name, such as the still authoritative "biography" by Erdmann Rudolf Fischer, which is in fact rather an autobiography largely written by Cyprian himself before his death.[16] Judging from the number of printed editions of his works as well as from reviews and quotes in prints and letters of contemporaries, Cyprian's works gained a wide impact in the eighteenth century.

Altogether, Cyprian's personal productivity can hardly be underestimated, even considering the fact that as an author and editor he sometimes relied on the assistance of a number of collaborators.[17] Whereas he usually wrote his letters in Latin, he published most of his books in German, which guaranteed a broader public. This was an increasingly common strategy among eighteenth-century polemicists, including most importantly, Pietists. In Cyprian's mind, the fact that Lutheran Pietists wrote in the vernacular made them powerful but also dangerous.[18]

Cyprian as a Historian

Traditional narratives of early modern German historiography have long concentrated on secular, courtly, and dynastic histories as well as on a more "scientific" (*wissenschaftlich*) historiography evolving from the universities of the Enlightenment. Contrary to its enormous output, the period between 1648 and 1750 was largely forgotten.[19] This period, however, witnessed an impressive revival of Lutheran history writing.

Cyprian's works belong to a tradition of Lutheran ecclesiastical history dating back to the sixteenth century and to its most famous piece of Lutheran historical scholarship, the *Magdeburg Centuries*. From its stronghold in the lands of Saxony, Lutheran historiography was revived at the court of Gotha in the seventeenth century. The works of Friedrich Hortleder, Caspar Sagittarius, Veit Ludwig von Seckendorff, Wilhelm Ernst Tentzel, Tobias Pfanner, and other Ernestine authors of the seventeenth and early eighteenth centuries often served apologetical interests of their rulers by dealing with a combination of church history and political history. Just like Cyprian, most of these historians had served the dukes of Saxe-Gotha as political advisers.[20] Their works increasingly relied upon archival sources and linked a more traditional ecclesiastical history with the antiquarian standards of contemporary scholarship.

In recent years, the general significance of confessional historiography for the evolution of more "modern" historical standards has been acknowledged. Catholic historiographers such as the Bollandists developed new methodological approaches from the treatment of seemingly old-fashioned ecclesiastical topics such as hagiographies of saints.[21] Even though the works of their Lutheran contemporaries at the courts of Gotha and elsewhere (who were, of course, not interested in Catholic saints) have not been equally well researched, scholars as early as Hans Holl have convincingly stressed their instrumental role in Germany's catching up with the more advanced historical methodology of Western Europe.[22]

As is evident from post-1648 Lutheran historiography, history writing could be intrinsically connected to polemics, but this does not justify the common conclusion that it was poor scholarship. Lutheran confessional historiography deserves to be seen not just as a *"Hilfswissenschaft* for polemics," but rather as one important, albeit still largely missing link between the historiography in the Reformation era and the Enlightenment.[23] Under circumstances that differed greatly from the sixteenth century, historiography continued to be an important tool to preserve, strengthen, and update a Lutheran identity, and it also served political needs. As a reaction to the increased plurality of faiths and to the rise of historical knowledge in general, church history had to be based on hitherto unknown archival documents and on an appropriate methodology.

This is where Cyprian as a historiographer needs to be situated. He continued a tradition of manuscript-based history writing that had evolved around the Gotha court, publishing a good number of hitherto unedited documents from the impressive holdings of his duke's library and archives. Cyprian, as an antiquarian collector of historical evidence, also rearranged and even significantly enlarged his ruler's library by acquiring numerous manuscripts and prints pertaining to the Reformation—a fact that makes the Gotha library's holdings significant for Reformation research even today.[24] In his books, the Gotha *Kirchenrat* usually presents documentary evidence in the text, in footnotes, or in appendices. Contrary to history writing that came before him (and even contrary to Gottfried Arnold and Johann Lorenz von Mosheim), Cyprian arranged his works thematically rather than strictly chronologically.[25] His point of view as a historian was clear from the start: he did not reflect on the need for objectivity, because there was no need for such reflections—the documents spoke for themselves, and they demonstrated the relevance of Reformation history for contemporaries and later generations.

The Gotha theologian benefited greatly from his close proximity to the library and archives, which put him at the forefront of Lutheran scholarship, emphasizing the importance of original and previously unseen documents and their most authentic and exact reproductions in print. Apart from the quality of Reformation material in Gotha, its sheer presence could be turned into a polemical argument. Cyprian not only praised the extensive ducal collections, which he considered an important contribution to the duke's fame, but he also spoke highly of the accessibility of the duke's library and archives for scholars such as himself. The duke's allegedly transparent information policy, Cyprian claimed, rendered a unique "authority" to the ducal archives as far as the history of the Reformation was concerned.[26] However, it would have been difficult for others to gain access to Cyprian's sources in such a privileged fashion in order to verify his work.

Cyprian's goal as a historian was primarily one of "protecting the Church" of the Reformation, as Scott Dixon has maintained.[27] At the same time, his historiography served the politics of his ruler in a territorial and an imperial perspective and aimed at supporting Lutheranism in the empire. In one of his shorter treatises, for instance, Cyprian advocated the introduction of primogeniture among the Ernestine-Saxon territories. This advocacy contributed to a highly disputed topic among the Wettin dynasty against the backdrop of the enormous political fragmentation within the Thuringian territories around 1700.[28] Cyprian's apologetical work was always closely connected to his rulers' contemporary politics.

Even Cyprian's prefaces of source editions were turned into political and polemical statements, as can be seen in his publications of material relating to Luther's companions Georg Spalatin (1484–1545) and Friedrich Myconius (1490–1546). Here, the *Kirchenrat* tried to revive an interest in the Reformation among his readers and also took a stance on the contemporary debates surrounding the toleration of religious minorities. In addition, he criticized the allegedly arcane character of Roman Catholicism where, contrary to the Lutherans, a publication of similar historic sources would not be possible because Catholics, according to Cyprian, had so much to hide.[29]

Sometimes the Gotha scholar emerged as a political actor in his own right through his historical writings, as can be illustrated, for instance, in his 1722 work on Protestant irenicism, the *Abgetrungener Unterricht*. This work was closely linked to the politics of Protestant unity in the Corpus Evangelicorum at the Diet of Regensburg; it resulted in lengthy debates leading to an official resolution of the Protestant estates to put forward unity between Lutherans and Calvinists and in the condemnation of Cyprian as a disturber of confessional peace in the empire.[30] Even if the practical results of these statements were meager, Cyprian and his Lutheran orthodox collaborators involuntarily contributed to the promotion of Protestant irenicism and intraconfessional toleration in the empire.

The Gotha scholar often advocated or even crafted his ruler's image as the true protector of the Reformation heritage—as opposed to the princes of the neighboring and more powerful Electoral Saxony, Friedrich August I (known as Augustus the Strong) and his son by the same name, who, after all, had both renounced Lutheranism and turned Roman Catholic. The fact that Friedrich August II's conversion was made public only days before the important two-hundredth anniversary of the Reformation in October 1717 corresponded nicely with Cyprian's efforts to present Saxe-Gotha, rather than its original homeland in Electoral Saxony, as the real stronghold of the Reformation. His voluminous 1719 documentation of the bicentennial, *Hilaria evangelica*, is an impressive source collection that illustrates how the Lutheran orthodox editor instrumentalized the writing of confessional *Zeitgeschichte*. More than just documenting the anniversary (and thus, as Cyprian makes clear in a military jargon, the victory of Lutheranism in a confessional battle), the *Hilaria evangelica* combined dynastic panegyrics with the aim to "serve posterity as a reinforcement of their faith."[31]

Cyprian's selection of historical material frequently tended toward procuring evidence that served his polemical aims. In addition, he did not refrain from quoting at length the documents of his supposed opponents in order to beat them at their own game. Thus he integrated Calvinist and Jesuit writings to direct them against either Calvinism or the Roman Catholic Church, respectively. This method, he believed, combined with the sheer length of his books, made it almost impossible for his adversaries to refute his historical accounts. In his 1719 treatise *Origins of the Papacy* (*Ursprung des Papsttums*), which, judging from the number of later editions and translations, turned out to be one of his most successful works, he stated that refuting it would make any possible enemy turn old and gray before he could work through its more than one thousand pages. According to Cyprian, "my book is irrefutable," in part because it was based on the Bible, in part because it was grounded in historical evidence that both Protestants and Catholics alike valued, and not least because of its physical length.[32]

While Cyprian seems to have been accurate in presenting his evidence, he did select from sources creatively to support his polemical agenda. For instance, he sometimes used minority opinions or rather bizarre passages instead of quotes taken from Lutheran celebrities, probably because he expected esoteric sources to be more widely accepted, less likely discounted, and thus more useful for his arguments. In the context of imperial politics at the Diet of Regensburg, the Hanoverian envoy Rudolf Johann von Wrisberg, a strong supporter of a Protestant irenicism, considered Cyprian not as a forger of sources, but as someone who twisted the facts.[33] Such practices were, of course, quite common among scholars of the early eighteenth century. As Scott Dixon has illuminated, at times Cyprian himself accused others of quoting overly esoteric documents, similar to Leibniz, who raised the same charge against Cyprian's archenemy Gottfried Arnold's *Impartial History*.[34]

Cyprian's critics were undoubtedly correct that his historical method served apologetical ends in order to defend his own understanding of Lutheranism and the nature of the Reformation. However, the Gotha historian was not cut off from the early Enlightenment, but rather had to face up to its new theological and intellectual developments. Therefore, the challenges of the Enlightenment provided another battleground for the Gotha theologian. A sound knowledge of history, that is, church history, was the prerequisite of being a good Lutheran, and this knowledge also served as a protection from enlightened aberrations. Thus, regarding the bicentennial celebrations of the Augsburg Confession in 1730, he remarked, "Whoever has no idea of history or is even an atheist will not be able to appreciate our celebration."[35] Implicitly addressing the Lockean idea of a "reasonableness of Christianity" and the deist attempts to strip Christian religion from its mysteries, he maintained that revealing the secrets of Christian religion worked "not against, but above reason."[36] It is quite probable that even a number of Catholic historians of his age would have agreed with him.

Cyprian's Reformation

Incorporating the intellectual developments of his day, Cyprian's point of departure nevertheless remained the Lutheran Reformation. He presented his central view of the Reformation in a nutshell in the opening sentence of his preface of the lengthy *History of the Reformation*, published 1730, on the occasion of the bicentennial of the *Confessio Augustana*. The Roman Church, according to Cyprian, had needed a reformation "because it was so very corrupted" (*weil sie sehr verderbet war*). The Reformation had therefore been inevitable. At the same time it had doubtless been a success, because it was directed by God.[37] This was why sharing the history of the Reformation with his readers in Cyprian's own day served the glory of God.[38] Proving the success of the Reformation with the help of historical documentation was a lifelong task of the Gotha theologian. In doing so, he aimed at Pietists, and particularly at Gottfried Arnold, who considered the Reformation as incomplete and deficient. The true Christians were, according to this more radical stance of Pietism, the ones who advocated a spiritual, non-institutional Christianity and had thus remained beyond the established churches. However, Cyprian's sociological interpretation of his own group of real (sc., Lutheran orthodox) Christians did not differ much from that of the Pietists; he, too, saw his age as a period with only a small group of believers left who were surrounded by numerous enemies of the true faith. Whereas Arnold and other radical Pietists considered it necessary to defend the few real Christians against an institutional church, Cyprian tried to protect his Lutheran followers against "popery," Calvinism, confessional indifference such as irenicism,[39] and atheism, but most of all against Pietism and all overtly individualistic forms of piety and devotion that neglected the importance of doctrines and institutions. Therefore his history writing served to legitimize the events around 1517, while it largely disregarded earlier epochs.

Furthermore, Cyprian's Reformation turns out to have been an almost purely German phenomenon. The theologian only implicitly considered the manifold movements for religious reform around the sixteenth century as contributions to a revival of the universal Christian church. Accordingly, the enemies of the true Reformation were situated in Rome, Geneva, and the Netherlands, from where all dangerous religious deviations or even explicit unbelief had infiltrated Germany. In addition to his claim that an unjustified papal authority was usurped by the bishop of Rome, he also argued that foreigners had been instrumental in introducing Calvin's teachings to the Holy Roman Empire. Thus it came as no surprise that the rigid Calvinism of the Synod of Dordt contradicted not only imperial law, as expressed in the peace treaties of Augsburg (1555) and Westphalia (1648), but also what Cyprian called a "natural equity" (*natürliche Billigkeit*). Calvinism was thus not only un-German, but also opposed to the principles of human nature themselves.[40] However, the Gotha *Kirchenrat* was a political pragmatist who did not generally call into question the guarantee of multiple faiths in the empire.

Cyprian's Lutheran patriotism reflected a particularly German outlook on church history and theological scholarship, which he shared with a number of orthodox Lutheran writers of his age. One way to see his German alignment is by looking at his correspondence network, which had a considerably less international scope than, for instance, the letters of his Reformed contemporaries Jean-Alphonse Turrettini or Daniel Ernst Jablonski. Cyprian nevertheless did not consider himself to be a particularly parochial scholar. He rather seemed to imitate a cosmopolitan habitus of the Republic of Letters, taking pride, for instance, in his alleged visit to Pierre Bayle in the Netherlands[41] and publishing some of his own works in translation or abroad; one of Cyprian's treatises was even printed in London—with the help of the local Lutheran orthodox pastor of one of the German churches in the British capital.[42] At the same time, his rather negligible international network of correspondents included Lutheran pastors of German-speaking congregations in London or Geneva as well as a few Lutherans in Scandinavia.[43] Even his use of foreign scholarly literature sometimes appears rather provincial, particularly considering the fact that Cyprian's primary occupation was that of a ducal librarian.[44] Thus, compared to the cosmopolitan outlook of Calvinist scholars in the early eighteenth century, orthodox Lutherans like Cyprian seem much more oriented toward their German *Heimat*.

Cyprian's institutional affiliations and the fact that he was employed and paid by the duke of Saxe-Gotha are clearly reflected in his work. His allegiances are not only visible in the numerous dedications of his books to Duke Friedrich II, but also in political statements within his history writing. He appears, for instance, as a loyal advocate of the Holy Roman emperor, beginning with Charles V. Emperor Charles, according to Cyprian, could have easily extinguished the Reformation in 1547 but had refrained from doing so, because even a German emperor knew he could benefit from the Augsburg Confession as well as from Lutherans' genuine loyalty toward their rulers.[45] Thus, a certain Lutheran *Reichspatriotismus* did not necessarily contradict Cyprian's confessional anti-Catholicism.[46]

However, Cyprian's imperial patriotism came to its limits with regard to his ruler's dynasty. It comes as no surprise that due to his position and loyalty at court, the Gotha historian felt much more attached to the dynasty of Wettin and in particular to its Ernestine branch at Saxe-Gotha.[47] The memory of the Reformation was largely coincident with the fame of its eminent dynasty of the Reformation period, namely the House of Wettin whose rulers had championed the Reformation and protected the reformers in the sixteenth century. Unfortunately, the most renowned branch of the Wettin rulers, Friedrich August I in Dresden, had converted to Roman Catholicism in 1697 in order to become king of Poland, putting himself into a problematic position as champion of the Reformation cause and head of the Protestant estates at the Corpus Evangelicorum of the Diet of Regensburg.[48] The Ernestine branch of the Wettin dynasty, based in Gotha, had long suffered from a loss of prestige to its more powerful neighbor and now seemed to seize its chance to become the true protector of Lutheranism among the Saxon territories and even in the empire overall. It was therefore an important task of Cyprian's employer, Friedrich II of Saxe-Gotha, to celebrate the heritage of the Reformation—not just for Saxony but also among the Lutherans of the Holy Roman Empire. According to Cyprian, the tiny remaining group of the true evangelical (i.e.,

Lutheran) believers had to watch out carefully and maybe even take up arms in order not to be marginalized.[49]

From his letters and prints, it is quite striking how Cyprian tried to construct not only a small group of true, orthodox believers, but also created other out-groups by excluding their supporters from being proper adherents to the Protestant faith. Whenever he attacked particular individuals, his opponents figured as part of a large group of antagonists who threaten the true believers. Similar rhetorical techniques were used by his opponents, of course: when Gottfried Arnold, for instance, attacked Cyprian for his polemics, he referred not to the Gotha historian alone but to "those gentlemen" (*die Herren*) for whom he allegedly spoke.[50] Likewise, other opponents mentioned Cyprian together with "his knaves" (*seine Gesellen*), which referred to his orthodox Lutheran allies, such as Löscher, Neumeister, and Edzard.[51] Numerous juxtapositions of "ours" and "the others" (*die unsrigen / die anderen*) in the correspondence of Cyprian and other committed theologians around 1700 illustrate that orthodox Lutheran polemicists such as Cyprian as well as renowned Pietists and irenicists all considered one another not just as cantankerous individuals, but as representatives of larger groups within continental Protestantism.

The creation of small, seemingly persecuted "in-groups" threatened by considerably larger, though (at least partly) fictitious "out-groups" of enemies resembles the evolution of early modern conspiracy theories.[52] Such a polarizing rhetoric was not only widespread within the anti-Catholicism of Protestant Europe around 1700, but similar techniques were employed by polemicists to define one Protestant group against another. These strategies have influenced later interpretations of early eighteenth-century Protestant groups as well. Here lies one important reason why the so-called "late Lutheran orthodoxy" has generally received a rather bad press for centuries among scholars of German church history.[53] In fact, history writing like that of Cyprian played an important role in this rhetorical polarization of confessional camps. At the same time, Cyprian's attacks on his opponents along with their sharp replies contributed to the propagation not just of his own worldview, but of theirs.

It should not be forgotten that Cyprian was as much a polemicist and historian of the Reformation as he was a church politician who advocated the characteristic Lutheran unity of church and state, based on clear hierarchies and confessional doctrines.[54] In his work, he linked the Lutheran Reformation in Germany with the political authority of the dynasty that employed him. These motivations converged in his battles over a number of confessional adversaries, such as Catholicism (because it seemed a non-German as well as a non-territorial phenomenon), Protestant irenicism (because it appeared dangerously international, trans-confessional, and doctrinally weak), radical Pietism (because it questioned the institution of the church and the importance of the Reformation), and finally "atheism," which, too, opposed the doctrines and the setup of a confessional church.[55] In this respect, Cyprian can be seen as an eighteenth-century advocate of what some modern researchers would term the princely confessionalization of church and state, originating from the Reformation, but against the backdrop of a plurality of beliefs. Cyprian was well aware of the fact that the established confessional realities of his time did not allow a return to the Reformation era. Thus, more than just preserving the Reformation, Cyprian tried to adapt and update it to meet the needs of a confessional pluralism—while involuntarily making Lutheran orthodoxy part of it.

Conclusion: Fighting and Fostering Confessional Plurality

Cyprian's impact on later generations has not been undisputed. Even the nineteenth-century Gotha patriot scholar August Beck considered him "all too rigorous" and of a rather problematic character.[56] While, with some revisionist exceptions, Lutheran orthodoxy has received a bad press for many decades, today's scholars increasingly value Cyprian's role as a collector, preserver, and editor of Reformation sources. Still it would be misleading to assume from a teleological perspective that Cyprian and the protagonists of a "late Lutheran orthodoxy" were simply backward-oriented conservatives who stood in contrast to the allegedly more modern and open-minded spirits of the Enlightenment. Cyprian's historical method, after all, was quite advanced compared to the standards of his day. He also published his works mostly in German, just as some of his opponents did. The Gotha scholar managed to use contemporary media quite cleverly in order to address a large audience with his writings, as can be seen in the political debates of the 1720s. He engaged in imperial politics and sometimes exerted significant influence on his ruler.[57] Further, his personal notion of piety was sometimes remarkably close to that of Lutheran Pietists, and while he engaged in a lifelong fight against Gottfried Arnold, he was much more lenient toward the Halle Pietist leader August Hermann Francke.[58] Cyprian's interest in foreign churches was not as extensive as that of the Reformed irenicists whom he criticized, but he was still informed about certain developments within an international Protestantism. He even tried several times to connect to a larger Protestant network via his correspondence with theological celebrities such as Daniel Ernst Jablonski and Jean-Alphonse Turrettini.[59] While he focused on the history and memory of the Reformation, especially surrounding its bicentenary celebrations, he struggled to update sixteenth-century Lutheranism to meet the needs of his own time and to create a powerful force against its suspected enemies—in complete opposition, of course, to Pietists like Gottfried Arnold who refused to accept the institutional churches of the Reformation as a watershed between a corrupt church and a renewed one. As opposed to Pietists and particularly to many Reformed irenicists of his day, Cyprian's increasing fear, though, was not a revival of Catholicism at the expense of the Protestant faiths, but the growth of atheism. It was his desire to combat this danger in the present and into the future that led him to write Lutheran histories. His *Reformation History* was thus meant to provide such orientation for the next one hundred years.[60]

Finally, by defining and fighting the deviations from what he considered to be pure Lutheranism, Cyprian, together with his orthodox Lutheran contemporaries, highlighted the differences between Protestant camps and thus featured the confessional pluralism of eighteenth-century Germany. By quarreling with his opponents both in print and in letters, he promoted not just his own opinion but theirs, and he strengthened the group coherence of his enemies and therefore added to the propagation of not one, but multiple religious options. In this respect, Gottfried Arnold, Christoph Matthaeus Pfaff, Daniel Ernst Jablonski, and many other renowned contemporary theologians should have perhaps been grateful to Cyprian instead of making him the bogeyman of early eighteenth-century Protestantism.

Alexander Schunka is professor of early modern history at the Freie Universität Berlin. He received his doctorate in history at the Ludwig-Maximilians-Universität München in 2004 and has since taught early modern history at the Universities of Stuttgart and Erfurt. He specializes in the cultural and religious history of early modern Europe, with a focus on the history of migrations and on Protestantism. His publications include *Soziales Wissen und dörfliche Welt* (2000), *Gäste, die bleiben* (2006), *Migrations in the German Lands, 1500–2000* (2016, co-edited with Jason Coy and Jared Poley), and a number of articles. His forthcoming book will be on the relationship between Protestantism and the birth of German Anglophilia in the eighteenth century.

Notes

1. On Pietism and orthodoxy, see Martin Gierl, *Pietismus und Aufklärung: Theologische Polemik und die Kommunikationsreform der Wissenschaft am Ende des 17. Jahrhunderts* (Göttingen, 1997). On irenicism, see Howard Hotson, "Irenicism in the Confessional Age: The Holy Roman Empire, 1563–1648," in *Conciliation and Confession: The Struggle for Unity in the Age of Reform, 1415–1648*, ed. Howard P. Louthan and Randall C. Zachman (Notre Dame, 2004), 228–85.
2. On confessional quarrels in the post-1648 Holy Roman Empire, see Joachim Whaley, *Germany and the Holy Roman Empire*, vol. 2, *From the Peace of Westphalia to the Dissolution of the Reich, 1648–1806* (Oxford, 2012). On confessional polemics and the periodical press, see Christopher Voigt-Goy, "Valentin Ernst Löschers Unschuldige Nachrichten als Institution im Konflikt zwischen Frühaufklärung und Pietismus,"

in *Gelehrte Polemik: Intellektuelle Konfliktverschärfungen um 1700*, ed. Kai Bremer and Carlos Spoerhase (Frankfurt am Main, 2011), 312–24.

3. This was aimed at the enlightened scholar Christian Thomasius. See Gustav Adolf Benrath, "Ernst Salomon Cyprian als Reformationshistoriker," in *Ernst Salomon Cyprian (1673–1745) zwischen Orthodoxie, Pietismus und Frühaufklärung*, ed. Ernst Koch and Johannes Wallmann (Gotha, 1996), 36–48, here 44. In respect to Valentin Ernst Löscher, see C. Scott Dixon, "Faith and History on the Eve of Enlightenment: Ernst Salomon Cyprian, Gottfried Arnold, and the *History of Heretics*," *Journal of Ecclesiastical History* 57 (2006): 33–54, here 45.

4. See, for instance, the statements of Hanoverian diplomat Johann Rudolf von Wrisberg, such as in Niedersächsisches Hauptstaatsarchiv Hannover, Cal.Br. 11/2993, Relation no. 93, 17 November 1721, fol. 415r. On Cyprian, see Erdmann Rudolf Fischer, *Das Leben Ernst Salomon Cyprians, der heil: Schrifft Doctors, und des Gothaischen Ober–Consistorii Vice–Präsidentens, zum Preiß der göttlichen Vorsorge und Barmhertzigkeit* (Leipzig, 1749); and Koch and Wallmann, *Ernst Salomon Cyprian*.

5. Benrath, "Cyprian," 44. On "Spätorthodoxie" from a theological point of view, see Jan Rohls, *Protestantische Theologie der Neuzeit*, 2 vols. (Tübingen, 1997), vol. 1, 147–56.

6. See, among others, Gierl, *Pietismus und Aufklärung*; Christoph Böttigheimer, *Zwischen Polemik und Irenik: Die Theologie der einen Kirche bei Georg Calixt* (Münster, 1996); Markus Friedrich, *Die Grenzen der Vernunft: Theologie, Philosophie und gelehrte Konflikte am Beispiel des Helmstedter Hofmannstreits und seiner Wirkungen auf das Luthertum um 1600* (Göttingen, 2004); and Marian Füssel, *Gelehrtenkultur als symbolische Praxis: Rang, Ritual und Konflikt an der Universität der Frühen Neuzeit* (Darmstadt, 2006).

7. Dixon, "Faith."

8. On the notion of "confessional cultures" (*Konfessionskulturen*), see Thomas Kaufmann, "Lutherische Konfessionskultur in Deutschland: Eine historiographische Standortbestimmung," in *Konfession und Kultur: Lutherischer Protestantismus in der zweiten Hälfte des Reformationsjahrhunderts* (Tübingen, 2006), 3–26.

9. Johann Andreas Schmidt and Ernst Salomon Cyprian, *De Omophorio Episcoporum Graecorum* (Helmstedt, 1698).

10. See Annette Gerlach, "Das Sammeln, Bewahren und Erschließen reformationshistorischen Quellenmaterials durch den Gothaer Bibliotheksdirektor Ernst Salomon Cyprian (1673–1745)" (unpublished diss., Berlin, 1981), 6f.

11. Fischer, *Cyprian*, 16–17; and Herbert Oppel, "D. Ernst Salomon Cyprian, Direktor des Gymnasium Casimirianum Academicum zu Coburg (1700–1713), und sein Briefwechsel mit Gottfried Wilhelm Leibniz," *Jahrbuch der Coburger Landesstiftung* 23 (1978): 38–82, here 52, 55.

12. The voluminous correspondence is preserved in Universitätsbibliothek Erfurt/Forschungsbibliothek Gotha, Manuscripts, Chart. A 422–47.

13. Gerlach, "Sammeln," 6; and Oppel, *Cyprian*, 46 following Fischer, *Cyprian*, 17. See Staatsbibliothek Berlin preußischer Kulturbesitz, Manuscripts, Nachlass August Hermann Francke, 11,2/14 no. 34, Daniel Ernst Jablonski to Ernst Salomon Cyprian, Berlin 13 January 1703; and ibid., no. 50, Berlin 29 December 1703.

14. Wolf-Friedrich Schäufele, *Christoph Matthäus Pfaff und die Kirchenunionsbestrebungen des Corpus Evangelicorum 1717–1726* (Mainz, 1998), 181–88.

15. Quoted in Anne–Sophie Knöfel, *Dynastie und Prestige: Die Heiratspolitik der Wettiner* (Cologne, 2009), 378.

16. Fischer, *Cyprian*, preface, B2r; the same applies to Georg Grosch, *Nothwendige Vertheidigung der evangelischen Kirche wider die Arnoldische Ketzerhistorie . . .* (Frankfurt am Main and Leipzig, 1745). See Dixon, "Faith," 34, 52.

17. Cyprian himself sheds light upon this practice in Ernst Salomon Cyprian, ed., *Georgii Spalatini Annales Reformationis Oder Jahr–Bücher von der Reformation Lvtheri . . .* (Leipzig, 1718), preface, A6r.

18. Dixon, "Faith," 51; Cyprian's role in the irenicist quarrels was popularized by the respective translations from Latin into German, see Ernst Salomon Cyprian and Christoph Matthäus Pfaff, *Herrn D. Salomon Ernst Cyprians und Herrn D. Christoph Matthäi Pfaffens Brief–Wechsel Von der Vereinigung Der Evangelisch–Lutherischen und Reformirten Religion: Denen Ungelehrten zum Besten Teutsch übersetzet* (Tübingen, 1721); cf. Wolf-Friedrich Schäufele, "Ernst Salomon Cyprian, Christoph Matthäus Pfaff und die Regensburger Kirchenunionsbestrebungen," in Koch and Wallmann, *Ernst Salomon Cyprian*, 187–201.

19. For a very brief treatment of seventeenth-century Lutheran ecclesiastical historiography, see A. G. Dickens and John Tonkin, *The Reformation in Historical Thought* (Cambridge, MA, 1985), 116–18. A more recent example of a similar neglect is Markus Völkel, *Geschichtsschreibung: Eine Einführung in globaler Perspektive* (Cologne, 2006).

20. On seventeenth-century archival historiography in the duchy of Saxe-Gotha, see Solveig Strauch, *Veit Ludwig von Seckendorff (1626–1692): Reformationsgeschichtsschreibung—Reformation des Lebens—Selbstbestimmung zwischen lutherischer Orthodoxie, Pietismus und Frühaufklärung* (Münster, 2005), 15–21; and Dixon, "Faith," 37–38. The uses of archives in early modern historiography, with numerous references to Ernestine Saxony, are described by Markus Friedrich, *Die Geburt des Archivs: Eine Wissensgeschichte* (Munich, 2013).

21. Most recently: Jan Marco Sawilla, *Antiquarianismus, Hagiographie und Historie im 17. Jahrhundert: Zum Werk der Bollandisten. Ein wissenschaftshistorischer Versuch* (Tübingen, 2009).

22. Karl Holl, "Die Bedeutung der großen Kriege für das religiöse und kirchliche Leben innerhalb des deutschen Protestantismus [1917]," in *Gesammelte Aufsätze zur Kirchengeschichte*, vol. 3, *Der Westen* (Tübingen, 1928), 302–84, here 312.

23. The quote is from Dirk Fleischer, "Der Strukturwandel der evangelischen Kirchengeschichtsschreibung im 18. Jahrhundert," in *Aufklärung und Historik: Aufsätze zur Entwicklung der Geschichtswissenschaft, Kirchengeschichte und Geschichtstheorie in der deutschen Aufklärung*, ed. Horst Walter Blanke and Dirk Fleischer (Waltrop, 1991), 141–59, here 142.

24. Gerlach, *Sammeln*, esp. 10–14; and Gertraud Zaepernick, *Verzeichnis der Handschriftenbestände pietistischer, spiritualistischer und separatistischer Autoren des 17. und 18. Jahrhunderts in der Landesbibliothek Gotha, sowie in anderen Handschriftensammlungen und Archiven in Gotha und Erfurt* (Halle, n.d.).

25. On the use of chronological models of periodization (including Arnold and Mosheim) see Fleischer, "Strukturwandel," 154–55.

26. Cyprian, ed., *Georgii Spalatini Annales Reformationis*, A6v; cf. Gerlach, *Sammeln*, 19.

27. Dixon, "Faith," 44. On Lutheran ecclesiastical history and Protestant identity in the confessional age, see Matthias Pohlig, *Zwischen Gelehrsamkeit und konfessioneller Identitätsstiftung: Lutherische Kirchen- und Universalgeschichtsschreibung 1546–1617* (Tübingen, 2007).

28. According to current library catalogues, its second edition was much more influential than the first: Ernst Salomon Cyprian, *Unpartheyischer Bericht vom Vorrecht der Erstgebohrnen in illustren Familien*, 2nd ed. (Gotha, 1727). Saxe-Gotha had introduced primogeniture under Duke Friedrich I in 1685.
29. See the prefaces of Ernst Salomon Cyprian, ed., *Friderici Myconii Historia Reformationis, vom Jahr Christi 1517 bis 1542* (Gotha, 1715); and Cyprian, ed., *Georgii Spalatini Annales Reformationis*.
30. Ernst Salomon Cyprian, *Abgetrungener Unterricht von kirchlicher Vereinigung der Protestanten aus Liebe zur nothleidenden Warheit abgefasset mit historischen Original–Documenten bestärcket und allen Evangelischen Lehrern zur Prüfung übergeben* (Frankfurt am Main and Leipzig, 1722). On this book and the ensuing debates at the Diet of Regensburg, see Schäufele, *Pfaff*, 265–67. The relevant "Conclusa" are printed in Eberhard Christian Wilhelm von Schauroth, *Vollständige Sammlung Aller Conclusorum Schreiben und anderer übrigen Verhandlungen Des Hochpreißlichen Corporis Evangelicorum . . .* , vol. 2 (Regensburg, 1751), 495–96.
31. Ernst Salomon Cyprian, ed., *Hilaria Evangelica, Oder Theologisch–Historischer Bericht Vom Andern Evangelischen Jubel-Fest* (Gotha and Leipzig, 1719), introduction. Cf. Hans–Jürgen Schönstädt, "Das Reformationsjubiläum 1717: Beiträge zur Geschichte seiner Entstehung im Spiegel landesherrlicher Verordnungen," *Zeitschrift für Kirchengeschichte* 93 (1982): 58–118; Wolfgang Flügel, *Konfession und Jubiläum: Zur Institutionalisierung der lutherischen Gedenkkultur in Sachsen 1617–1830* (Leipzig, 2005), 125–67; and Harm Cordes, *Hilaria evangelica academica: Das Reformationsjubiläum von 1717 an den deutschen lutherischen Universitäten* (Göttingen, 2006).
32. Ernst Salomon Cyprian, *Uberzeugende Belehrung vom Ursprung und Wachsthum des Pabstthums: Nebst einer Schutz-Schrifft vor die Reformation* (Gotha, 1719), C2v. Translations appeared, for instance, in Dutch: Cyprian, *Grondig onderrecht van den oorsprong en wasdom des pausschaps* (The Hague, 1731); and Czech: Cyprian, *Naucenj o Půwodu a Zrůstu Papežstwa spolu s Obranau Obnoweni Cyrkwe* (Wittenberg, 1744).
33. See, for instance, Niedersächsisches Hauptstaatsarchiv Hannover, Cal.Br 11/2994, Relation Wrisberg no. 6, 19 January 1722, appendix 4, fols. 122–24; and ibid., 11/2995, Relation Wrisberg, 2 April 1722, appendix, fols. 102r–103r.
34. Dixon, "Faith," 47. Similarly, Leibniz criticized Arnold for using the wrong sources. See Gerlach, *Sammeln*, 5, following Oppel, "Cyprian," 41 and 76n44.
35. Ernst Salomon Cyprian, *Historia der Augspurgischen Confession* (Gotha, 1730), 11.
36. Cyprian, *Ursprung und Wachsthum des Pabstthums*, dedication to Duke Friedrich II of Saxe-Gotha (unpag.).
37. Cyprian, *Historia der Augspurgischen Confession*, 109, quoted in Dixon, "Faith," 52. See Klaus Wetzel, *Theologische Kirchengeschichtsschreibung im deutschen Protestantismus, 1660–1760* (Gießen, 1983), 302–8, which highlights a similar argument in Cyprian's *Schutzschrift für die Reformation* (the appendix of Cyprian, *Ursprung und Wachsthum des Pabstthums*).
38. Dixon, "Faith," 45f.
39. The *Historia der Augspurgischen Confession* can be seen as an anti-irenical piece in the light of Cyprian's attacks against Melanchthon and the *Confessio Augustana Variata*. See Benrath, "Cyprian," 43.
40. Ernst Salomon Cyprian, *Abgetrungener Unterricht*, C2r.
41. Fischer, *Leben*, 19.

42. Ernst Salomon Cyprian, *Dissertatio de propagatione hæresium per cantilenas: Accedit Cunr. Theodorici oratio de mixta hæreticorum prudentia* (London, 1720). Cyprian's connections to London's Lutheran Orthodox German (formerly "Swedish") Church are evident from his correspondence.

43. See Ernst Koch, "Die Evangelisch-Lutherische Kirche in Genf und der Gothaer Hof," in *Kommunikationsstrukturen im europäischen Luthertum der Frühen Neuzeit*, ed. Wolfgang Sommer (Gütersloh, 2005), 51–69; and Pentti Laasonen, "Die Rezeption der deutschen Spätorthodoxie im Norden: Ernst Salomon Cyprian und Erik Benzelius d.J.," in Koch and Wallmann, *Ernst Salomon Cyprian*, 71–83.

44. This is evident considering, for instance, Cyprian's references to the rather outdated book by Anglican author William Nicholls, *Defensio Ecclesiæ anglicanæ: In qua vindicantur omnia, quæ ab adversariis in doctrina, cultu, & disciplina ejus, improbantur* (London, 1707), which was popular among German Protestants not least because it was published in Latin instead of English.

45. Cyprian, *Historia der Augspurgischen Confession*, 11.

46. On *Reichspatriotismus* of earlier decades, see, for instance, Alexander Schmidt, *Vaterlandsliebe und Religionskonflikt: Politische Diskurse im Alten Reich (1555–1648)* (Leiden, 2007).

47. On the relationship between the Gotha territories and the Holy Roman emperor, see Siegrid Westphal, *Kaiserliche Rechtsprechung und herrschaftliche Stabilisierung: Reichsgerichtsbarkeit in den thüringischen Territorialstaaten 1648–1806* (Cologne, 2002). On dynastic self-representations within the Ernestine branch of Saxony, see Westphal, "Nach dem Verlust der Kurwürde: Die Ausbildung konfessioneller Identität anstelle politischer Macht bei den Ernestinern," in *Zwischen Schande und Ehre: Erinnerungsbrüche und die Kontinuität des Hauses, Legitimationsmuster und Traditionsverständnis des frühneuzeitlichen Adels in Umbruch und Krise*, ed. Martin Wrede and Horst Carl (Mainz, 2007), 173–92.

48. Jochen Vötsch, *Kursachsen, das Reich und der mitteldeutsche Raum zu Beginn des 18. Jahrhunderts* (Frankfurt am Main, 2003); and Dagmar Freist, "Religionssicherheiten und Gefahren für das Seelenheil: Religiös-politische Befindlichkeiten in Kursachsen seit dem Übertritt Augusts des Starken zum Katholizismus," in *Konfession und Konflikt: Religiöse Pluralisierung in Kursachsen im 18. und 19. Jahrhundert*, ed. Ulrich Rosseaux and Gerhard Poppe (Münster, 2012), 35–53.

49. See, for instance, Cyprian, *Abgetrungener Unterricht*, 63, as well as Cyprian's analogies to celebrations of military victories in the preface of Cyprian, ed., *Hilaria Evangelica*.

50. Universitätsbibliothek Erfurt/Forschungsbibliothek Gotha, Manuscripts, Chart. A 423, fols. 186–87, Gottfried Arnold to Ernst Salomon Cyprian, 16 May 1700.

51. Niedersächsisches Hauptstaatsarchiv Hannover, Cal.Br. 11/2994, Relation Wrisberg no. 15, 19 February 1722, fol. 308r.

52. I am grateful to Dr. Andrew McKenzie-McHarg at Cambridge University, who is currently preparing a history of early modern conspiracy theories, for our discussions on this point.

53. For a fairer evaluation of post-1648 Lutheran orthodoxy, which has largely been forgotten since the Second World War, see already Holl, "Bedeutung," 312–13; and Hans Leube, *Die Reformideen in der deutschen lutherischen Kirche zur Zeit der Orthodoxie* (Leipzig, 1924).

54. Dixon, "Faith," 50, who relies upon Grosch, *Vertheidigung*, preface, xvi.

55. See Dixon, "Faith," 48.
56. August Beck, "Cyprian, Ernst Salomon," *Allgemeine deutsche Biographie*, 4 (1876): 667–69.
57. Schäufele, *Pfaff*, 209–36.
58. Johannes Wallmann, "Pietas contra Pietismus: Zum Frömmigkeitsverständnis der lutherischen Orthodoxie," in Wallmann, *Gesammelte Aufsätze*, vol. 2, *Pietismus–Studien* (Tübingen, 2008), 105–17.
59. This is evident, for instance, in Staatsbibliothek Berlin preußischer Kulturbesitz, Manuscripts, Nachlass August Hermann Francke, 11,2/14 no. 12, Daniel Ernst Jablonski to Ernst Salomon Cyprian, Berlin 15 June 1701.
60. Benrath, "Cyprian," 44.

Bibliography

Beck, August. "Cyprian, Ernst Salomon." In *Allgemeine Deutsche Biographie* 4 (1876): 667–69.

Benrath, Gustav Adolf. "Ernst Salomon Cyprian als Reformationshistoriker." In *Ernst Salomon Cyprian (1673–1745) zwischen Orthodoxie, Pietismus und Frühaufklärung*, edited by Ernst Koch and Johannes Wallmann, 36–48. Gotha, 1996.

Böttigheimer, Christoph. *Zwischen Polemik und Irenik: Die Theologie der einen Kirche bei Georg Calixt*. Münster, 1996.

Cordes, Harm. *Hilaria evangelica academica: Das Reformationsjubiläum von 1717 an den deutschen lutherischen Universitäten*. Göttingen, 2006.

Cyprian, Ernst Salomon. *Abgetrungener Unterricht von kirchlicher Vereinigung der Protestanten aus Liebe zur nothleidenden Warheit abgefasset mit historischen Original–Documenten bestärcket und allen Evangelischen Lehrern zur Prüfung übergeben*. Frankfurt am Main and Leipzig, 1722.

———. *Dissertatio de propagatione hæresium per cantilenas: Accedit Cunr. Theodorici oratio de mixta hæreticorum prudentia*. London, 1720.

———. *Grondig onderrecht van den oorsprong en wasdom des pausschaps*. The Hague, 1731.

———. *Historia der Augspurgischen Confession*. Gotha, 1730.

———. *Naucenj o Půwodu a Zrůstu Papežstwa spolu s Obranau Obnoweni Cyrkwe*. Wittenberg, 1744.

———. *Uberzeugende Belehrung vom Ursprung und Wachsthum des Pabstthums: Nebst einer Schutz-Schrifft vor die Reformation*. Gotha, 1719.

———. *Unpartheyischer Bericht vom Vorrecht der Erstgebohrnen in illustren Familien*. 2nd ed. Gotha, 1727.

———, ed. *Friderici Myconii Historia Reformationis, vom Jahr Christi 1517 bis 1542*. Gotha, 1715.

———, ed. *Georgii Spalatini Annales Reformationis Oder Jahr–Bücher von der Reformation Lvtheri. . . .* Leipzig, 1718.

———, ed. *Hilaria Evangelica, Oder Theologisch–Historischer Bericht vom Andern Evangelischen Jubel-Fest*. Gotha and Leipzig, 1719.

Cyprian, Ernst Salomon, and Christoph Matthäus Pfaff. *Herrn D. Salomon Ernst Cyprians und Herrn D. Christoph Matthäi Pfaffens Brief–Wechsel Von der Vereinigung Der Evangelisch–Lutherischen und Reformirten Religion: Denen Ungelehrten zum Besten Teutsch übersetzet.* Tübingen, 1721.

Dickens, A. G., and John Tonkin. *The Reformation in Historical Thought.* Cambridge, MA, 1985.

Dixon, C. Scott. "Faith and History on the Eve of Enlightenment: Ernst Salomon Cyprian, Gottfried Arnold, and the *History of Heretics.*" *Journal of Ecclesiastical History* 57 (2006): 33–54.

Fischer, Erdmann Rudolf. *Das Leben Ernst Salomon Cyprians, der heil: Schrifft Doctors, und des Gothaischen Ober–Consistorii Vice–Präsidentens, zum Preiß der göttlichen Vorsorge und Barmhertzigkeit.* Leipzig, 1749.

Fleischer, Dirk. "Der Strukturwandel der evangelischen Kirchengeschichtsschreibung im 18. Jahrhundert." In *Aufklärung und Historik: Aufsätze zur Entwicklung der Geschichtswissenschaft, Kirchengeschichte und Geschichtstheorie in der deutschen Aufklärung,* edited by Horst Walter Blanke and Dirk Fleischer, 141–59. Waltrop, 1991.

Flügel, Wolfgang. *Konfession und Jubiläum: Zur Institutionalisierung der lutherischen Gedenkkultur in Sachsen 1617–1830.* Leipzig, 2005.

Freist, Dagmar. "Religionssicherheiten und Gefahren für das Seelenheil: Religiöspolitische Befindlichkeiten in Kursachsen seit dem Übertritt Augusts des Starken zum Katholizismus." In *Konfession und Konflikt: Religiöse Pluralisierung in Kursachsen im 18. und 19. Jahrhundert,* edited by Ulrich Rosseaux and Gerhard Poppe, 35–53. Münster, 2012.

Friedrich, Markus. *Die Geburt des Archivs: Eine Wissensgeschichte.* Munich 2013.

———. *Die Grenzen der Vernunft: Theologie, Philosophie und gelehrte Konflikte am Beispiel des Helmstedter Hofmannstreits und seiner Wirkungen auf das Luthertum um 1600.* Göttingen, 2004.

Füssel, Marian. *Gelehrtenkultur als symbolische Praxis: Rang, Ritual und Konflikt an der Universität der Frühen Neuzeit.* Darmstadt, 2006.

Gerlach, Annette. "Das Sammeln, Bewahren und Erschließen reformationshistorischen Quellenmaterials durch den Gothaer Bibliotheksdirektor Ernst Salomon Cyprian (1673–1745)." Unpublished dissertation. Berlin, 1981.

Gierl, Martin. *Pietismus und Aufklärung: Theologische Polemik und die Kommunikationsreform der Wissenschaft am Ende des 17. Jahrhunderts.* Göttingen, 1997.

Grosch, Georg. *Nothwendige Vertheidigung der evangelischen Kirche wider die Arnoldische Ketzerhistorie. . . .* Frankfurt am Main and Leipzig, 1745.

Holl, Karl. "Die Bedeutung der großen Kriege für das religiöse und kirchliche Leben innerhalb des deutschen Protestantismus [1917]." In *Gesammelte Aufsätze zur Kirchengeschichte,* vol. 3, *Der Westen,* 302–84. Tübingen, 1928.

Hotson, Howard. "Irenicism in the Confessional Age: The Holy Roman Empire, 1563–1648." In *Conciliation and Confession: The Struggle for Unity in the Age of Reform, 1415–1648,* edited by Howard P. Louthan and Randall C. Zachman, 228–85. Notre Dame, 2004.

Kaufmann, Thomas. "Lutherische Konfessionskultur in Deutschland: Eine historiographische Standortbestimmung." In *Konfession und Kultur: Lutherischer Protestantismus in der zweiten Hälfte des Reformationsjahrhunderts*, 3–26. Tübingen, 2006.

Knöfel, Anne-Sophie. *Dynastie und Prestige: Die Heiratspolitik der Wettiner*. Cologne, 2009.

Koch, Ernst. "Die Evangelisch-Lutherische Kirche in Genf und der Gothaer Hof." In *Kommunikationsstrukturen im europäischen Luthertum der Frühen Neuzeit*, edited by Wolfgang Sommer, 51–69. Gütersloh, 2005.

Koch, Ernst, and Johannes Wallmann, ed. *Ernst Salomon Cyprian (1673–1745) zwischen Orthodoxie, Pietismus und Frühaufklärung*. Gotha, 1996.

Laasonen, Pentti. "Die Rezeption der deutschen Spätorthodoxie im Norden: Ernst Salomon Cyprian und Erik Benzelius d. J." In *Ernst Salomon Cyprian (1673–1745) zwischen Orthodoxie, Pietismus und Frühaufklärung*, edited by Ernst Koch and Johannes Wallmann, 71–83. Gotha, 1996.

Leube, Hans. *Die Reformideen in der deutschen lutherischen Kirche zur Zeit der Orthodoxie*. Leipzig, 1924.

Nicholls, William. *Defensio Ecclesiæ anglicanæ: In qua vindicantur omnia, quæ ab adversariis in doctrina, cultu, & disciplina ejus, improbantur*. London, 1707.

Oppel, Herbert. "D. Ernst Salomon Cyprian, Direktor des Gymnasium Casimirianum Academicum zu Coburg (1700–1713), und sein Briefwechsel mit Gottfried Wilhelm Leibniz." *Jahrbuch der Coburger Landesstiftung* 23 (1978): 38–82.

Pohlig, Matthias. *Zwischen Gelehrsamkeit und konfessioneller Identitätsstiftung: Lutherische Kirchen- und Universalgeschichtsschreibung 1546–1617*. Tübingen, 2007.

Rohls, Jan. *Protestantische Theologie der Neuzeit*. Vol. 1. Tübingen, 1997.

Sawilla, Jan Marco. *Antiquarianismus, Hagiographie und Historie im 17. Jahrhundert: Zum Werk der Bollandisten. Ein wissenschaftshistorischer Versuch*. Tübingen, 2009.

Schäufele, Wolf-Friedrich. *Christoph Matthäus Pfaff und die Kirchenunionsbestrebungen des Corpus Evangelicorum 1717–1726*. Mainz, 1998.

———. "Ernst Salomon Cyprian, Christoph Matthäus Pfaff und die Regensburger Kirchenunionsbestrebungen." In *Ernst Salomon Cyprian (1673–1745) zwischen Orthodoxie, Pietismus und Frühaufklärung*, edited by Ernst Koch and Johannes Wallmann, 187–201. Gotha, 1996.

Schauroth, Eberhard Christian Wilhelm von. *Vollständige Sammlung Aller Conclusorum Schreiben und anderer übrigen Verhandlungen Des Hochpreißlichen Corporis Evangelicorum. . . .* Vol. 2. Regensburg, 1751.

Schmidt, Alexander. *Vaterlandsliebe und Religionskonflikt: Politische Diskurse im Alten Reich (1555–1648)*. Leiden, 2007.

Schmidt, Johann Andreas and Ernst Salomon Cyprian. *De Omophorio Episcoporum Graecorum*. Helmstedt, 1698.

Schönstädt, Hans-Jürgen. "Das Reformationsjubiläum 1717: Beiträge zur Geschichte seiner Entstehung im Spiegel landesherrlicher Verordnungen." *Zeitschrift für Kirchengeschichte* 93 (1982): 58–118.

Strauch, Solveig. *Veit Ludwig von Seckendorff (1626–1692): Reformationsgeschichts-schreibung —Reformation des Lebens—Selbstbestimmung zwischen lutherischer Orthodoxie, Pietismus und Frühaufklärung.* Münster, 2005.

Voigt-Goy, Christopher. "Valentin Ernst Löschers Unschuldige Nachrichten als Institution im Konflikt zwischen Frühaufklärung und Pietismus." In *Gelehrte Polemik: Intellektuelle Konfliktverschärfungen um 1700,* edited by Kai Bremer and Carlos Spoerhase, 312–24. Frankfurt am Main, 2011.

Völkel, Markus. *Geschichtsschreibung: Eine Einführung in globaler Perspektive.* Cologne, 2006.

Vötsch, Jochen. *Kursachsen, das Reich und der mitteldeutsche Raum zu Beginn des 18. Jahrhunderts.* Frankfurt am Main, 2003.

Wallmann, Johannes. "Pietas contra Pietismus: Zum Frömmigkeitsverständnis der lutherischen Orthodoxie." In *Gesammelte Aufsätze,* vol. 2, 105–17. Tübingen, 2008.

Westphal, Siegrid. *Kaiserliche Rechtsprechung und herrschaftliche Stabilisierung: Reichsgerichtsbarkeit in den thüringischen Territorialstaaten 1648–1806.* Cologne, 2002.

———. "Nach dem Verlust der Kurwürde: Die Ausbildung konfessioneller Identität anstelle politischer Macht bei den Ernestinern." In *Zwischen Schande und Ehre: Erinnerungsbrüche und die Kontinuität des Hauses, Legitimationsmuster und Traditionsverständnis des frühneuzeitlichen Adels in Umbruch und Krise,* edited by Martin Wrede and Horst Carl, 173–92. Mainz, 2007.

Wetzel, Klaus. *Theologische Kirchengeschichtsschreibung im deutschen Protestantismus, 1660–1760.* Gießen, 1983.

Whaley, Joachim. *Germany and the Holy Roman Empire.* 2 vols. Oxford, 2012.

Zaepernick, Gertraud. *Verzeichnis der Handschriftenbestände pietistischer, spiritualistischer und separatistischer Autoren des 17. und 18. Jahrhunderts in der Landesbibliothek Gotha, sowie in anderen Handschriftensammlungen und Archiven in Gotha und Erfurt.* Halle, n.d.

CHAPTER EIGHT

Heresy and the Protestant Enlightenment
Johann Lorenz von Mosheim's History of Michael Servetus

MICHAEL PRINTY

"Michael Servetus," wrote Roland Bainton, "has the singular distinction of having been burned by the Catholics in effigy and by the Protestants in actuality."[1] Born in Spain around 1509 and executed in Geneva in 1553, Servetus has been described as "the complete heretic." Seeking a return to ante-Nicene Christianity, he rejected Rome, Wittenberg, and Geneva. His repudiation of orthodox Christian doctrines shared by Catholics and (magisterial) Protestants went much deeper than merely rejecting the Trinity: Servetus considered infant baptism, original sin, the humanity of Christ, and possibly the immortality of the soul to be without biblical foundation.[2] Despite scattered pleas for tolerance from such figures as Sebastian Castellio, the overwhelming response of the Reformed communities was to endorse the execution. In a rare moment of agreement, the three magisterial confessions agreed that Servetus's teachings threatened the foundations of Christianity.[3] Justice, in the eyes of most contemporaries, was served in that the "duty of intolerance" obliged Christian magistrates to protect the faith and their subjects with deadly force.[4]

Yet by the middle of the eighteenth century, the question of justice had been flipped on its head. Where once Catholic Lyon and Reformed Geneva could agree that the execution of heretics was as necessary as it was just, by the 1750s this proposition had been repudiated in enlightened circles. Servetus had come to be seen as an archetypical victim of unjust religious persecution. A key figure in this posthumous reassessment was the theologian and historian Johann Lorenz von Mosheim. The story of Servetus's unfortunate confrontation with Calvin occupied center stage of the second volume of his "impartial and thorough" history of heresy published in 1748. Mosheim did not seek to glorify Servetus or to redeem him. Instead he sought to strike a historical balance between the needs of correct doctrine and the desire to advocate for a tolerant, enlightened Protestant Christianity. For Mosheim, the greatest threat to contemporary Christianity came not from anti-Trinitarians or other heretics, but from deism and unbelief. The historical intolerance of the Protestant confessions, Mosheim was well aware, only fueled radical criticism of Christianity. In revisiting this history of heresy and persecution, Mosheim sought to acknowledge as well as to historicize past persecution. At the same time, he put forth a robust defense of the values of moderation he saw as the key to Christianity's place in the modern world. Mosheim's *History of Heresy* may thus be considered a confessional history, albeit one that made a claim to be above confession in the interest of historical truth.

Heresy and the history of heresy belong to a larger story about tolerance and intolerance, a story that was central to the Enlightenment and its participants' perception of themselves as the exponents of individual freedom. This theme had both legal-political as well as historical aspects. From a legal and political perspective, the question of the toleration of dissenters and schismatics, as well as of heretics strictly defined, touched on the nature of the Christian state and its relationship to secular authority. At stake was the basic question of whether Christian values and norms should dominate social life, or whether religion was a private matter, protected by the state but separate from civil society. By the early eighteenth century an intellectual program for toleration emerged among the scholars and writers who shaped the public sphere. While this new program of toleration was hardly embraced universally, acts of state persecution had become the exception. No serious political thinker envisioned a return to the confessional state of the late sixteenth and seventeenth centuries.

As a historical question, however, concerning the relationship of Christianity's persecuting and intolerant past to the current age of moderation, heresy and the history of heresy were as yet uncharted. It is to this story that Mosheim's *History of Heresy* belongs. By the eighteenth century, exponents of enlightened Protestantism had come to view their faith as heir to a proud legacy of religious liberty. From this perspective, Calvin's complicity in the execution of Servetus was an embarrassment. By dealing with Servetus so prominently, Mosheim grasped the nettle firmly. Toleration and freedom of thought were essential to enlightened Protestants' self-image, and only through an act of historical reconciliation could this modern version of Protestantism be brought in line with its actual past. As part of an intellectual defense of the possibility of a Protestant Enlightenment, Mosheim had to integrate Protestantism's past into a narrative of moderation and toleration without at the same time abandoning basic Christian tenets. To do so, Mosheim made the lesson of the history of heresy about the need for careful investigation, modesty, and sobriety.

In arguing that Mosheim's *History of Michael Servetus* should be considered a confessional history of the Protestant Enlightenment, this essay will point to two moments of historical amnesia. The first required effacing magisterial Protestantism's unapologetic willingness to kill in defense of orthodoxy. The second moment relates to the historiography of modern Protestantism. Post-Enlightenment historians have implicitly accepted the narrative of Servetus as a victim of unfortunate religious enthusiasm. But they have overlooked the way that narrative was constructed in an attempt to align Protestant-ism's past with its aspirations to be seen as a religion of tolerance, freedom, and progress. In order to show how Mosheim's historical work functioned, this essay will first look at Mosheim's great predecessor, Gottfried Arnold, whose vernacular *Impartial History of the Church and Heretics* (*Unparteiische Kirchen- und Ketzerhistorie*) of 1699/1700 laid the groundwork for a reevalu-ation of heterodoxy and dissent in German Protestantism. Second, the essay will explore Mosheim's *History of Michael Servetus* in the context of his larger history of heresy and show how he sought to reconcile Protestantism's perse-cuting past with its Enlightenment present. Finally, the essay will examine the ways in which Mosheim sought to integrate his historical apologetics into the emerging Protestant public sphere and thus helped establish a foundation for modern Protestant historical consciousness.

Gottfried Arnold: Pietism, Heresy, and the Oppression of Truth

In Germany, the roots of an enlightened approach to the history of heresy and intolerance lay not in the religious criticism of a skeptical or materialist radi-cal Enlightenment but in radical Pietism. More precisely, the new approach that Mosheim constructed responded to the dominant narrative provided by the radical Pietist theologian and historian Gottfried Arnold (1666–1714). Influenced by Philipp Jakob Spener, the author of *Pia Desideria* (1675) and "father" of German Pietism, Arnold turned against the orthodox Lutheran-ism in which he had been raised. Taking up a position in Quedlinburg, he turned to a mystical and spiritual form of Pietism, renounced marriage and clerical offices, and devoted himself to theology. In this time, he wrote and published a long history of the early church, *The First Love of the Congregations of Jesus Christ* (1696).[5] The book extolled the first centuries of the church when Christianity did not yet know clergy, hierarchy, or dogma. On the strength of his work, which was well received among Pietists, Arnold was named a professor of history at Giessen in 1697, where the university was in Pietist control. Within a year, he renounced his professorial and clerical offices and soon thereafter published his large history of heresy and the church.[6]

Constantine, in Arnold's view, transformed Christianity by enabling the institutionalization of dogma and a persecuting church and clergy. Arnold saw any confessional church (that is, one that relies on authority of any kind) as contrary to the spirit of Christianity. Thus the history of heresy and, more importantly, heresy-persecution is told as a story of the suppression of piety.[7] But Arnold did not simply stand received values on their head. Heretical and separatist groups were not seen as signs of a "true church" in the manner of the *Magdeburg Centuries* (1559–74).[8] For Arnold, the pre-Constantinian church was the era when the gospel alone reigned supreme, without the corrupting influence of hierarchy, clergy, and dogma. Arnold's method, while based on careful reading of the sources, is above all rooted in a religious conviction to present details and stories that had long been repressed or pushed aside and to test all that has happened against God's word, not the authority of worldly doctrines or hierarchies.[9] Arnold could write a history that cast established Christianity in such a bad light because he was motivated by a deep conviction that the work would awaken true piety.

The book's purpose required that it could be read beyond a narrow circle of scholars. "It is written in [German]," Arnold states, "so that . . . those outside of the schools, among whom there is much wisdom, can make their own judgments and derive something from it."[10] This passage links two key aspects of Arnold's work, namely the dedication to recovering a "true" Christianity that has been suffocated under worldly dogma and authority and the equal and related desire to bringing these truths to light and sharing them as widely as possible. Arnold's commitment to spreading his message makes his history not only part of Pietism, but also a part of the early German Enlightenment, specifically in its use of history as a moral and pedagogical instrument. Indeed, Arnold shared these aspirations with the traditional "father" of the German Enlightenment, Christian Thomasius.

Thomasius greeted Arnold's book as the "best and most useful book" of its genre and told his students to buy it, "even if they have to spend less money on food or even beg."[11] Thomasius was at the forefront of the campaign to end the prosecution of heresy. As Ian Hunter has argued, Thomasius's two important works of 1697, *Is Heresy a Punishable Crime?* and *The Right of Princes regarding Heretics*—subsequently translated into German in 1705—were part of his larger concern with strengthening the power of the territorial prince in order to prevent confessional conflict.[12] According to Hunter, Thomasius defended the rights of putative heretics in order to assert the rights and responsibility of a civil authority whose sole purpose was the maintenance of peace and stability, not the pursuit of higher truths.[13] Thomasius's juridical approach, however, did not exclude religious commitments. Indeed, as Thomas Ahnert argues, Thomasius shared with Arnold "'enthusiastic,' spiritualist religious beliefs" that alienated them from the orthodox ecclesiastical establishment.[14] In the eyes of both men, the post-Constantinian institutionalization of doctrine had corrupted Christianity. Arnold and Thomasius put their historical and juridical critiques of the church's approach to heresy in the service of a heartfelt renewal of piety at the same time that they responded to the growth of religious dissent in Europe toward the end of the seventeenth century.[15]

The early Enlightenment approach to heresy represented by Arnold and Thomasius emerged from a series of debates about orthodoxy and political power and about the repression of religious dissenters. While these issues had by no means been fully resolved by the time Mosheim published his *History of Heresy*, the ground had considerably shifted. Arnold offered a vigorous defense of history's "heretics" as part of a pious critique of the corrupting influence of the world. His book also partook of an early Enlightenment discourse of toleration that had, intellectually at least, been settled by the mid-eighteenth century.[16] Like Arnold and Thomasius, Mosheim did not think heresy should be punished as a crime. He shared with them a skepticism toward post-Constantinian Christianity, fearing that the official acceptance of Christianity by the state had not always been beneficial. However, he did not reject clergy and hierarchy; their influence on the history of Christianity was to be regarded skeptically, but not rejected. Most importantly, Mosheim was able to combine his sincere Lutheran beliefs with a notion that the history of manners demonstrated improvement in human affairs. In this, Mosheim's historical works, and especially his history of heresy, provided a framework for a modern Protestant piety that balanced liberal Enlightenment values with traditional Christian forms.

Mosheim's *History of Heresy* as a Confessional History of the Protestant Enlightenment

Arnold's *Impartial History* set the stage for a reconsideration of heresy, but its anti-intellectualism made this vernacular history ill-suited for the Protestant Enlightenment's attempt to reconcile faith and reason. By the 1740s, when Mosheim turned to writing his history of heresy, the debates about toleration and heresy that had raged at the end of the seventeenth century had entered a new phase. Although episodes such as the revolt of the Camisards (1702–15) and the Salzburg expulsion (1731) demonstrated that religious intolerance was still an active tool in the arsenal of domestic rule, few believed that heterodoxy and dissent could overthrow entire states. Instead, a new and more visible threat was apparent in the spread of deism and unbelief. Mosheim's development of a thorough scholarly method was in part due to the need to refute the radical attacks on Christianity that based themselves on reinterpreting Scripture and early church history. Thus Mosheim used history as part of an apologetical tool for a modern, polite Christianity aimed at unbelievers and enthusiasts alike.

Since the mid-sixteenth century, history had been central to the building of Protestant identity. It shored up the spirits of a confession under siege and responded to the Catholic accusation that the churches that had broken away from Rome could not claim continuity with the early church.[17] While history was employed within a larger atmosphere of theological disputation, such disputes spurred technical innovations in the study of sources and the writing of history. As contending parties sought to answer their opponents' accounts and accusations, historians continued a process of source-critical scholarship and other methodological innovations whose roots lie in Renaissance humanism. Thus religious dispute and the formation of confessional identity served as a motor of historiographical innovation.

By the eighteenth century, confessional identity could still motivate historiographical innovation, even if the confessional context had considerably shifted. Whereas seventeenth-century confessional history was largely waged between and among Lutherans, Calvinists, and Catholics, now deists and materialists were employing the same scholarly techniques to undermine Christianity.[18] This new group of critics waged a two-pronged historical attack on orthodox Christianity and the institutional church. An epistemological line of attack went after the believability of biblical revelation and the miracles of Jesus Christ or, somewhat less confrontationally, against the purported miracles of the early church. A second line of attack was moral. It took on the history of persecution in the church in order to undermine Christianity's claim to be a religion of love that could flourish in an age of toleration and civil society. Protestants could usually duck the question of persecution by prioritizing the pre-Constantinian church or by extolling the virtues of a church freed of the papal spirit of domination. But the execution of Michael Servetus for heresy was a stumbling block. By taking up this episode so prominently, Mosheim sought to reconcile the Christian past with modern values of toleration and the emergence of a post-confessional state.

"The history of heresy," Mosheim emphasized, "is written above all . . . so that we can recognize the weakness of our nature." The confrontation between Calvin and Servetus presents us with the drama of "two of the most learned, clever men of their age, who overstepped the boundaries of truth and the main principles of piety in their enthusiasm [*Hitze*]. The one searched for the lost truth and became a dreamer; the other fought for the affronted truth and became a killer. What a piteous and instructive tragedy! I hope it instructs as much as it moves the spectators."[19] This desire to "instruct as much as move" his readers led Mosheim to write a history that was as learned as it was eloquent. Servetus's story was the longest of the three heretical episodes in his *History of Heresy*, but all three contained, for Mosheim, important lessons for the present. Questioning Arnold's supposed impartiality, Mosheim wrote that most histories of heresy strongly lean toward one side or the other, either as defenses of the putative heretics or as attacks on the heretics on the part of orthodoxy. Alternately, such histories can serve as surrogates for other struggles. Thomas Long's *History of the Donatists* (1677), Mosheim suggested, was as much about the disruptive effect of latter-day Presbyterians and Independents as it was about the fourth century.[20] Mosheim sought to develop a style of historical writing that would move beyond the problems that plagued earlier histories of heresy.

Unlike previous historians and theologians, Mosheim did not argue that there was one particular thread that bound the various historical heresies together. The word "heresy"—derived from the Greek word for choice—indicated a "willful choice" on the part of a minority to turn away from the accepted teaching of the Christian community, even once instructed of its error. By emphasizing that heresy was a "choice" (and not just a misunderstanding or plain ignorance), the origin of heresy could be explained by other causes rooted in disobedience, concupiscence, or pride. Sin (and for some, the devil) was thus at the heart of heresy, and the writing of its history—from an orthodox perspective—had an instructive purpose. Similarly, Arnold's history showed how power had corrupted the church since the days of Constantine—heresy hunting itself was the greatest sin. But for Mosheim, heresy had no single cause, and he sought to show how particular circumstances and conditions led to it. In order to do so, he selected three episodes that illustrate, respectively, heresy in the early church, the Middle Ages, and the modern (post-Reformation) period.

For the early church, Mosheim wrote about the snake-worshiping cult of the Ophites. Heresy in the medieval church is represented by the Apostolic Brothers, who rejected the papal church's wealth and power. "The history of these two communities," he commented, "can serve as an introduction to ancient and medieval heresy. At the same time, it can serve as a telescope [*Fernglas*] through which one can see the different groups that have torn apart the kingdom of our savior."[21] The Ophites, or Snake-Brothers, represent one of the many varieties of Gnosticism. Mosheim studied their particular doctrine in detail. He thought them worthy of study because consideration of their beliefs leads to larger questions about how seemingly reasonable people could have such preposterous opinions. The myths of the Ophites also served as a case study of how of one of the oldest "natural doctrines" of an "oriental nation" was subsequently transformed into religion.[22] Likewise, the Apostolic Brothers stand in for one of many heretical groups to attack the wealth and power of the papacy and the clergy. Together, these various medieval poverty groups represented "a tree with a common root, which nonetheless produced various fruit."[23] Mosheim argued that the historian ought to pay careful attention to the actual teaching of heretical groups, and to do this one needed to refrain from taking sides.

At the conclusion of his history of the Ophites, Mosheim observed that for all their fantastical mythology of a good and an evil god, they still held some basic Christian tenets, even if they were too heavily influenced by "oriental" superstition.[24] In his "impartial" history, Mosheim certainly did not advocate for the Ophites. However, his account offered the lesson that, while a superstitious culture is hard to overcome, heresy itself was rooted not in corrupt hearts or vice, but in human culture. It was thus historically specific and also teaches us that we must be aware of our own limits and those of our culture:

> As blind, contemptible and ridiculous as these people were, still they were in a certain way witnesses to the truth. . . . But the unreasonable [*ungereimte*] belief in which they were born and raised, and the supposed oriental wisdom [*vermeinte Morgenländische Weisheit*] concerning the nature of the world, the sources of the soul, the origins of evil and other things, with which they were familiar from the earliest youth, were too deeply ingrained.[25]

Mosheim's "impartiality" here did not consist in finding some golden mean between orthodoxy and the heresy of the Ophites. As he noted elsewhere, many of those "who were scolded for heresy deserved no better name."[26]

However, Mosheim's emphasis on the culture in which heretics were embedded—if not quite trapped—served as a warning that anyone can err. Even medieval inquisitors—long the bogeymen of the Protestant imagination—were given their due as sincere men. Mosheim asserted this in justifying his use of inquisitorial writings as valid historical sources, especially vital because they may be the only record—however distorted—of the beliefs of heretics. He damned their office, but not necessarily the people themselves. Having long studied the history of heresy, his "conscience . . . cannot allow that I treat all [the inquisitors] as shameless liars and those they pursued as holy and innocent souls. Christianity has never lacked for dreamers, crackpots, and confused minds."[27]

One such confused mind was of course Michael Servetus, whose history occupies the entire second volume of Mosheim's *History of Heresy*. With his discussion of Servetus, Mosheim tackled a set of related problems that were key to the Protestant Enlightenment's attitude to the Reformation era and to the history of Christianity more generally. First, Servetus's death posed the challenge of dogma and toleration: while toleration was a core conviction, adherents of the moderate religious Enlightenment nonetheless asked themselves how far it should extend. What was still to be considered within the realm Christianity, they asked, and how could one reconcile Protestant proclamations of the freedom of conscience with a history of persecution and intolerance, of which Servetus was the most recognizable and infamous victim?[28] The second problem raised by the case of Servetus was that his beliefs were well beyond the theological pale of every established Christian church; if Servetus was not worthy of persecution, no one was. Then there was the added threat that Servetus anticipated the deism of Mosheim's contemporaries.[29] With his history of Servetus, as with the larger effort to write an "impartial and thorough history of heresy," Mosheim wrestled with a fundamental problem of the Protestant Enlightenment's approach to the history of Christianity.

But if these core themes of toleration, dogma, and the history of persecution were the key underlying issues in his account, the bulk of his rhetorical efforts aimed as much at comportment and attitude as wayward ideas. At a key moment in his history, Mosheim related Servetus's own proclamation on his Spanish countrymen: "though naturally intelligent, they do not apply themselves very much to learning. Those among them who are half educated think themselves to be learned, and try to convince others through rhetoric and pretense that they have more wisdom than they actually possess. In their language and customs much remains raw and barbaric, and in superstition they surpass all nations." "If only," Mosheim reflected, "Servetus had been able to put aside these vices as well as he had put aside his love for his own people and country, he would have been a great man." If he had only taken the care to see in himself the same violent and unruly nature he criticized in his countrymen, Mosheim continued, "how calmly he would have been able to lead his life. The best minds, who quickly see deficiencies in others, usually do not recognize their own faults. Self-love blinds so strongly."[30]

Mosheim combined this moralizing critique of self-love and enthusiasm with a technically sophisticated historical reconstruction of Servetus's life and thought. *The History of Michael Servetus* is divided into three books. The first recounts Servetus's life from his early years until the publication of his *Restitution of Christianity* (1553).[31] The second book begins with the publication of the *Restitution* and proceeds to a detailed account of his path to Geneva, confrontation with Calvin, trial, and death at the stake. The third book offers an extensive reading of Servetus's works, expanding on Mosheim's remarks throughout the text as well as exploring works attributed to Servetus. To each section Mosheim appended a series of notes exploring controversial points and sources. The book thus swings between stretches of thorough scholarly examination of conflicting sources and detailed reconstructions of dramatic moments of conflict. A constant theme is Servetus's "excitability," which is revealed not only in his rash decisions, but also in his disorganized writing. This disorganization, Mosheim observed, was apparent from his earliest known work, *The Errors of the Trinity*.[32] Commenting on one extravagant passage about God giving us spirit from his inner heart, Mosheim exclaimed, "Who understands this dishonest nonsense [*unlautere Geschwätze*]? If Servetus thought that he himself understood it, then he was enchanted by his own imagination."[33] For Mosheim, it was "too bad that such a rare mind could not overcome self-love." He continues by reflecting that his is a general human weakness, and we must learn to rely on the help of others; learning and moderation require modesty.[34] Servetus's belief that he was called by God only increased as time went on. Living under the name Michael de Villanova in Lyon, he earned his living as a physician, but the more he contemplated the Book of Revelation "and the signs of the times, and the more he observed the abuses of the Roman Church, the more inflamed his soul became and his understanding deteriorated." Mosheim set up the composition of the *Restitution of Christianity* as the dramatic end-point of the first book. The introduction to this work revealed "that he took up his pen in the deepest conviction that God had illuminated him in a special way and called him to be his witness to the deceived world."[35]

The second book opens with the publication at Vienne (near Lyon) of Servetus's *Restitution of Christianity* in 1553, setting in motion a course of events that ended with his death at the stake. Servetus was jailed in Catholic Vienne but managed to escape and was burned in effigy by order of the bishop. He decided to go to Naples, passing through Geneva on the way. He had earlier engaged in a correspondence with Calvin—indeed the two may have even known each other in Paris in 1534 and had arranged a debate, which did not take place.[36] Not surprisingly, Servetus's basic nature and character as revealed in his early writings shaped his interactions with Calvin. Mosheim wrote that Calvin revealed some of the same character traits. This was due both to their individual nature, as well as the times. "Almost everyone in their age believed that it would seem to be indifference to the truth if one handled opponents with mildness and piety."[37] Both Calvin and Servetus were "fierce and full of gall" and used base language.[38]

After a painstaking and scholarly reconstruction of Servetus's trial, Mosheim concluded in a dramatic mode with an account of Servetus's death. This account is followed by a reflection on his character and beliefs, as well as those of Calvin. The effect of this series of episodes is to highlight the differences between the sixteenth and the eighteenth centuries in terms that represent an implicit plea for Mosheim's values of moderation and sobriety, but which at the same time seem to fit into a story of progress. The combination of moderateness and a belief in social progress makes Mosheim's history of Servetus a key text in understanding the modern Protestant approach to the history of the Reformation era.

According to Mosheim, Servetus's dying words to "Jesus, the son of the eternal God" proved that he sincerely held his anti-Trinitarian beliefs to the end. In this sense, "Servetus was indeed a martyr at least in this regard, according to Calvin's view that the duty of a martyr is to die confessing the doctrine in which he believes."[39] "How happy he would have been," Mosheim wrote, "if he could have united these good qualities with a reasonable skepticism toward his own powers, with humility, modesty, and gentleness. But pride, which held more sway over him than any other tendency in his nature, was mainly responsible that his real talents and inner motivation led to misfortune rather than happiness."[40]

Mosheim's criticisms of Servetus's character provide an implicit contrast to what he considered to be good qualities and practices in a theologian and scholar. Servetus had only talked to important theologians after he had already made up his mind. His "main error," Mosheim noted, "was that he . . . did not use it to purify his heart . . . and overcome the unruly drives of his nature, which was industrious and lively in mind but weak in will. If only he had submitted his soul at the outset to the gospel" he would have been better able to "distinguish light from darkness and human rules from divine truths."[41] Thus Servetus's fate can still serve as a valuable lesson for the Christian scholar, a model that Mosheim presumably sought himself to fulfill.

Mosheim concluded the second book with a comparison of Calvin and Servetus, noting that they were both "extraordinary and unique men," although the former "was much more useful to the church than the latter."[42] Calvin's error, Mosheim postulated, was that he thought that Servetus's heresy stemmed from an unruly and godless life. In this, he was stuck with an older view of heresy and did not recognize that Servetus's heresy originated in a lack of understanding.[43] Each attacked the other with equal vehemence. They were unfortunately paired by circumstance, and the whole affair might not have ended in death if Oecolampadius or Melanchthon had stood in Calvin's place.[44] With this stylized conclusion, Mosheim stepped beyond the rigorous attention to detail that otherwise characterized the book, and indeed which he claimed was central to its "impartiality." In fact, in the last paragraph of the second book, he attempted a sort of historical reconciliation between the unhappy men:

> For all their weaknesses, Calvin and Servetus were both upright and pious. This is demonstrated by their respective ends. They both died as people justified [*Gerechte*], suffering no remorse of conscience. Servetus even acknowledged the injustices he had done to Calvin and asked him for forgiveness before he was executed. Let us out of love believe that Calvin, before he took leave of this world, also repented of the mistakes he made with regard to Servetus. *Love hopes all things*. If it seems objectionable to presume that God graced both souls with Jesus, to whom both appealed with their dying breath, then this presumption is not harmful to the truth. It is a weakness of love, that love itself will easily overlook.[45]

In this remarkable passage, Mosheim moved far beyond the pose of the rigorous, impartial historian and revealed most clearly the type of enlightened, Protestant piety that his new style of historiography was to serve. It was not an act of forgetting. Instead, Mosheim offered a frank coming to terms with a persecuting past. But this coming to terms served a larger, contemporary purpose of historicizing Protestantism's past in order to fit a new, enlightened self-image. If Protestantism, and the Reformation with it, was to be put in the genealogy of progress and toleration, then it would also require a process of historical reconciliation for the old mistakes and errors of the past to be overcome. While Mosheim's invocation of love and hope echoed the heartfelt religion of Arnold and his Pietist fellows, it differed profoundly from the latter in that it was forward-looking. Mosheim's Christianity did not reject the world; it was convinced that an enlightened Christianity was both possible and necessary.

Confessional History and the Protestant Public

In revisiting Mosheim's role in the formation of a narrative of Protestant reconciliation, we can uncover a second process of historical forgetting, namely in a modern historiography that has overlooked the ways in which eighteenth-century Protestants were in the process of recasting their religion and its history as part of a genealogy of progress and reason. Mosheim's rejoinder to Arnold's history was part of a larger program of engaging a learned public that was confronted with a growing corpus of literary options. Many of these were hostile to Nicene Christianity. Mosheim saw himself first and foremost as a pastor and theologian whose job it was to defend Christianity and care for souls. Theologians, he wrote in a set of posthumously published lectures, must be universal scholars, able to engage the world and confront the doubters and critics. A theologian must also maintain a positive image in society, "and here," he wrote, "there are no other means than cleverness, understanding, and skill." If he possesses these qualities, "then he will be listened to and read, and thus readers will be more readily convinced of the truth."[46] The task of the scholar, in Mosheim's view, was to reach beyond his study and communicate his message of a tolerant, polite Christianity. In this, Mosheim's historical work was a continuation of his preaching.

Mosheim's public apologetics proceeded on multiple fronts, balancing between European ideals of scholarship and a pastor's need to directly engage his audience.[47] Much of his strictly scholarly work was in Latin, including an earlier history of Michael Servetus that he later admitted to be flawed.[48] The overwhelming concern in these Latin works was careful scholarship, as in his account of the life and writings of John Toland.[49] Likewise, his two great general studies of church history, *Commentaries on the Affairs of the Christians before the Time of Constantine the Great* and the *Institutes of Ecclesiastical History*, were published in Latin.[50] In turning to German, Mosheim the preacher was also turning to the emerging Protestant public sphere, the power and vitality of which came from a deft use of the vernacular.

Mosheim's *Servetus*, in the words of one of its author's most important students, Johann Matthias Schroeckh, was "one of the most beautiful historical works ever published in our language." If only he had written more works in German, Schroeckh continued, "then the German taste in historical works, which was just beginning to blossom, would have begun sooner."[51] The comment about style, marginal though it might seem to the central questions of heresy and toleration, points to a key feature of Mosheim's *History of Heresy*. Enlightenment theology both fueled and fed off the growth of a Protestant reading public, and it was to this public that the formation of an enlightened Protestant confessional identity appealed.[52] The language of this public sphere was not the learned Latin of scholarship, nor even the elaborate and scholarly German of Christian Wolff, but a German that was emerging, in the words of Eric Blackall, into a "literary language."[53]

Mosheim's *Ketzergeschichte* did not achieve the same kind of popularity or readership as many of his other works. Unlike his *Institutes*, which was enormously influential in Germany and beyond (especially in Archibald Maclaine's annotated English edition), his *History of Heresy* was not reprinted or translated.[54] Nonetheless, it was important for scholars and was appreciated for its refined style as much for its scholarly ambition. One contemporary reviewer noted the remarkable ending passage of the second section of *Servetus*, where Mosheim expressed his wish for a transhistorical reconciliation between Servetus and Calvin.[55] Schroeckh's endorsement was high praise, given that history, secular as well as sacred, had emerged as one of the most popular genres for the reading public by the second half of the century. It was also a discipline in flux. History did not have a permanent home in the university and was taught in different faculties (such as law, theology, or philosophy). Historians as such were not appointed to highly paid chairs and indeed often used their positions as stepping-stones to more prestigious ones in other disciplines. Because of the shifting boundaries and emerging institutional parameters, a profusion of textbooks and other historical works flooded the market as historians sought to supplement their income and establish themselves.[56]

This same process of institutionalization and growth of the print market applied to church history as well. After Mosheim, Protestant church historiography in Germany continued to grow in depth and sophistication, and became an important subject at German universities.[57] Schroeckh's *Christian Church History* (1768–1803) would reach some thirty-five volumes, plus ten more volumes for post-Reformation church history. Far less prolix, and for that more accessible, was Ludwig Timothäus Spittler's single-volume *Outline of the History of the Christian Church* (1782). "Church history is a type of universal history," Spittler declared. A secular Göttingen historian influential in the rise of pragmatic history, Spittler did not see the history of the church as a catalog of darkness and error. He was keenly aware of the major "revolution" in Protestant theology since the middle of the century and greeted it with approval as "one of the most brilliant periods of Lutheran Church history."[58] Thus Protestant church history became more than a specific discipline of theology. It became part of the essential historical background to the cultural moment and was quite often invoked not only as a subdiscipline of theology but as part of general cultural awareness.

As Spittler indicated, the sense of newness and innovation emerging in Protestant theology seemed to have a significance for the Enlightenment and the moral improvement of humankind that reached far beyond theology's immediate ecclesiastical context. In 1790, Heinrich Philipp Conrad Henke declared triumphantly that "in no other age have such powerful and bold advances in human culture been taken." These have been applied to the benefit of religion and have restored "the natural and necessary connection between reason and Christianity."[59] Although Henke's optimism may have been somewhat misplaced given the unrest that was about to sweep through Europe, his exclamation nonetheless captured an essential element of enlightened Protestantism's sense of its place in history.

From the eighteenth century on, modern Protestantism was fueled by an intense consideration of its own past. Because the question was never settled—nor could it ever really be settled—this consideration of the past constituted a core feature of its dynamism. At the same time, the restless reconsideration of the past always posed a threat to Protestantism's sense of continuity and threatened to dissolve the intellectual coherence of Enlightenment Protestantism. Thus the attempt to reconcile Christianity's persecuting past with a vision of enlightened moderate Christianity stands at the origin of a key theme in modern Protestantism. Mosheim still hewed to Nicene doctrine, as did Arnold. But the search for a reconciliation of Protestant Christianity with modern life and values became part of modern Protestantism from that point forth. Until the "anti-historical revolution" of the 1920s, the fact that this reconciliation always needed to be rethought did not seem to disturb the belief that Protestantism could be brought into accord with modern life and values.[60] As Mosheim, quoting Luther's translation of 1 Corinthians, would write, "Love hopes all things."[61]

Michael Printy is the librarian for Western European Humanities at Yale University. He is the author of *Enlightenment and the Creation of German Catholicism* (Cambridge, 2009), as well as journal articles on the Protestant Enlightenment in *The Journal of the History of Ideas* and *Modern Intellectual History*. Research for the essay in this volume has been made possible by fellowships from the Alexander von Humboldt Foundation, the American Council of Learned Societies, and the National Endowment for the Humanities.

Notes

1. Roland Bainton, *Hunted Heretic: The Life and Death of Michael Servetus, 1511–1533* (Boston, 1953), 3.

2. Jerome Friedman, *Michael Servetus: A Case Study in Total Heresy* (Geneva, 1978), 133. For a biography see Bainton, *Hunted Heretic*. On Servetus's place in the radical Reformation, see George Hunston Williams, *The Radical Reformation*, 3rd ed. (Kirksville, 2000), 52–59, 307–9, 401–4, 467–68, 924–34.

3. Benjamin Kaplan, *Divided by Faith: Religious Conflict and the Practice of Toleration in Early Modern Europe* (Cambridge, MA, 2007), 21.

4. Brad S. Gregory, *Salvation at Stake: Christian Martyrdom in Early Modern Europe* (Cambridge, MA, 2001).

5. Gottfried Arnold, *Die erste Liebe der Gemeinen Jesu Christi*, 2 vols. (Frankfurt am Main, 1696).

6. Hans Schneider, "Der radikale Pietismus in 17. Jahrhundert," in *Geschichte des Pietismus*, ed. Martin Brecht, 4 vols. (Göttingen, 1993), vol. 1, 410–16, here 412. On the end of Arnold's radical phase, see W. R. Ward, "Is Martyrdom Mandatory? The Case of Gottfried Arnold," in *Faith and Faction* (London, 1993), 377–84.

7. John Christian Laursen, "What Is Impartiality? Arnold on Spinoza, Mosheim on Servetus," in *Heresy in Transition: Transforming Ideas of Heresy in Medieval and Early Modern Europe*, ed. Ian Hunter, John Christian Laursen, and Cary J. Nederman (Aldershot, 2005), 143–54.

8. Hermann Dörries, *Geist und Geschichte bei Gottfried Arnold* (Göttingen, 1963), 13–19.

9. Gottfried Arnold, *Unparteyische Kirchen- und Ketzer-Historie: Vom Anfang des Neuen Testaments bis auff das Jahr Christi 1688* (Frankfurt am Main, 1700), n.p., §25. Hereafter Arnold, *Ketzer-Historie*.

10. Arnold, *Ketzer-Historie*, §41.

11. Christian Thomasius, *Erinnerung . . . über den vierten Teil seiner Grund-Lehren* (Halle, 1701), 7f. Excerpted in Dörries, *Geist und Geschichte*, 205.

12. Christian Thomasius, *De jure principis circa haereticos* (Halle, 1697); and Thomasius, *An haeresis sit crimen* (Halle, 1697). For a modern English translation of the former, see the appendix to Ian Hunter, *The Secularisation of the Confessional State: The Political Thought of Christian Thomasius* (Cambridge, 2007).

13. Ian Hunter, "Thomasius on the Toleration of Heresy," in Hunter, Laursen, and Nederman, *Heresy in Transition*, 155–67, here 167.

14. Thomas Ahnert, *Religion and the Origins of the German Enlightenment: Faith and the Reform of Learning in the Thought of Christian Thomasius* (Rochester, 2006). See also Martin Pott, "Christian Thomasius und Gottfried Arnold," in *Gottfried Arnold (1666–1714)*, ed. Dietrich Blaufuß and Friedrich Niewöhner (Wiesbaden, 1995), 247–66.

15. Thomas Ahnert, "Historicizing Heresy in the Early Enlightenment," in Hunter, Laursen, and Nederman, *Heresy in Transition*, 129–42, here 142.
16. John Marshall, *John Locke, Toleration and Early Enlightenment Culture* (Cambridge, 2006).
17. Bruce Gordon, "The Changing Face of Protestant History and Identity in the Sixteenth Century," in *Protestant History and Identity in Sixteenth-Century Europe*, ed. Bruce Gordon, 2 vols. (Aldershot, 1996), vol. 1, 1–22.
18. On the use of history in deist criticism, see Justin Champion, *The Pillars of Priestcraft Shaken: The Church of England and Its Enemies* (Cambridge, 1992). On ecclesiastical history, see J. G. A. Pocock, *Barbarism and Religion*, vol. 5, *Religion: The First Triumph* (Cambridge, 2010).
19. Johann Lorenz von Mosheim, *Anderweitiger Versuch einer unparteiischen und gründlichen Ketzergeschichte: Geschichte des berühmten Spanischen Artztes Michael Serveto* (Helmstedt, 1748), 28 (preface). Hereafter: Mosheim, *Servetus*. The pagination restarts at 1 after the preface. See Martin Mulsow, "Eine 'Rettung' des Servet und der Ophiten? Der junge Mosheim und die häretische Tradition," in Mulsow et al., *Johann Lorenz Mosheim*, 45–92, here 58.
20. Mosheim, *Versuch einer unparteiischen und gründlichen Ketzergeschichte* (Helmstedt, 1746; reprint, Hildesheim, 1998), 37.
21. Mosheim, *Ketzergeschichte*, 40.
22. Mosheim, *Ketzergeschichte*, 50–51.
23. Mosheim, *Ketzergeschichte*, 41.
24. Knowledge about Gnosticism and Gnostic cults was radically transformed by the discovery of the Nag Hammadi texts in 1945. I have not attempted to compare Mosheim's account with that of later scholarship. For a recent study, see Tuomas Rasimus, *Paradise Reconsidered in Gnostic Mythmaking: Rethinking Sethianism in Light of the Ophite Evidence* (Leiden, 2009).
25. Mosheim, *Ketzergeschichte*, 111–12.
26. Mosheim, *Ketzergeschichte*, 203.
27. Mosheim, *Ketzergeschichte*, 202–3.
28. It goes without saying that only much later would peasants, witches, and other marginal groups be added to the list of unjustly abused victims.
29. For the argument that Servetus's ideas cannot be reduced to anti-Trinitarianism and that he can be considered a "total heretic," see Friedman, *Michael Servetus*, 17–20.
30. Mosheim, *Servetus*, 63.
31. Michael Servetus, *Christianismi restitutio* (n.p., 1553).
32. Michael Servetus, *De Trinitatis erroribus libri septem* (n.p., 1531).
33. Mosheim, *Servetus*, 27.
34. Mosheim, *Servetus*, 30.
35. Mosheim, *Servetus*, 93. Mosheim remarked on the following page, however, that with respect to Servetus's message, it is difficult to believe that God would hide such a necessary truth for so long and that it would be understood by so few.
36. Mosheim, *Servetus*, 59.
37. Mosheim, *Servetus*, 70.
38. Mosheim, *Servetus*, 157.
39. Mosheim, *Servetus*, 229.
40. Mosheim, *Servetus*, 243.
41. Mosheim, *Servetus*, 243, 245.

42. Mosheim, *Servetus*, 255.

43. Mosheim, *Servetus*, 246f.

44. Mosheim, *Servetus*, 257.

45. Mosheim, *Servetus*, 258.

46. Johann Lorenz Mosheim, *Kurze Anweisung, die Gottesgelahrtheit vernünftig zu erlernen, in Academischen Vorlesungen vorgetragen* (Helmstedt, 1756), 171–72.

47. Even as English and French writers turned increasingly to their respective vernaculars for scholarly communication, German had not yet become established as an international scholarly language.

48. Mosheim had been interested in the heretical tradition from the early years of his career. He had once envisioned a project entitled the *Bibliotheca Vulcani* on the history of burned books. Mosheim first wrote on Servetus in a Latin dissertation coauthored with his student Heinrich von Allwoerden (Heinrich von Allwoerden and Johann Lorenz Mosheim, *Historia Michaelis Serveti* [Helmstedt, 1727]). He later wrote that this work was "not worthy to be called a *history*" because it was only a "moderately successful account of the main events that Servetus experienced until his end" (*Servetus*, 7, preface). As Mulsow notes, Mosheim was motivated by the critical reception of this book to find a "method" that would move beyond the "dualistic pattern of apology and accusation." See Mulsow, "Rettung," 49.

49. Johann Lorenz von Mosheim, *De vita, fatis, et scriptis celeberrimi viri, Ioannis Tolandi, Hiberni, commentatio* (Hamburg, 1722). See Henning Graf Raventlow, "Johann Lorenz Mosheims Auseinandersetzung mit John Toland," in Mulsow et al., *Johann Lorenz Mosheim*, 93–110.

50. *De rebus Christianorum ante Constantinum Magnum Commentarii* (Helmstedt, 1753) and his *Institutiones historiæ christianæ antiquioris et recentioris*, 2nd ed. (Helmstedt, 1755). See Mulsow, "Rettung," 86; see also J. G. A. Pocock, "Clergy and Commerce: The Conservative Enlightenment in England," in *L'Età dei Lumi: studi storici sul settecento europeo in onore di Franco Venturi*, ed. Raffaele Ajello, E. Cortese, and Vincenzo Piano Mortari, 2 vols. (Naples, 1985), vol. 2, 523–62.

51. Johann Matthias Schroeckh, *Christliche Kirchengeschichte*, 2nd ed., 35 vols. (Leipzig, 1768–1803), vol. 1, 198.

52. On the emergence and significance of the Protestant public sphere, see Michael Printy, "The Determination of Man: Johann Joachim Spalding and the Protestant Enlightenment," *Journal of the History of Ideas* 72 (2013): 189–212.

53. Eric Blackall, *The Emergence of German as a Literary Language 1700–1775* (Cambridge, 1959).

54. Johann Lorenz von Mosheim, *An Ecclesiastical History, Antient* [*sic*] *and Modern*, trans. Archibald Maclaine (London, 1768).

55. Anon., "Johann Lorenz von Mosheims . . . anderweitiger Versuch einer vollständigen und unpartheyischen Ketzergeschichte," *Zuverlässige Nachrichten von dem gegenwärtigen Zustande, Veränderung und Wachsthum der Wissenschaften* 10 (1749): 37–38.

56. Konrad Jarausch, "The Institutionalization of History in Eighteenth-Century Germany," in *Aufklärung und Geschichte*, ed. Hans Erich Bödeker, Georg G. Iggers, Peter Hanns Reill, and Jonathan B. Knudsen (Göttingen, 1986), 36–41. See also Otto Dann, "Das historische Interesse in der deutschen Gesellschaft des 18. Jahrhunderts. Geschichte und historische Forschung in den zeitgenössichen Zeitschriften," in *Historische Forschung im 18. Jahrhundert. Organisation-Zielsetzung-Ergebnisse*, ed. Karl Hammer and Jürgen Voss (Bonn, 1976), 386–415.

57. See John Stroup, "Protestant Church Historians in the German Enlightenment," in Bödeker, *Aufklärung und Geschichte*, 169–92; and Dirk Fleischer, *Zwischen Tradition und Fortschritt: Der Strukturwandel der protestantischen Kirchengeschichtsschreibung im deutschsprachigen Diskurs der Aufklärung* (Waltrop, 2006).

58. Ludwig Timothäus Spittler, *Grudriß der Geschichte der christlichen Kirche* (Göttingen, 1782), 466.

59. Heinrich Philipp Conrad Henke, *Frohe Aussichten für die Religion in die Zukunft. Eine Rede, bey der Einführung Herrn August Christian Barthels, als Abts zu Riddagshausen am 8tn Jenner 1790 in der Klosterkirche daselbst gehalten*, 2nd ed. (Helmstedt, 1801).

60. Friedrich Wilhelm Graf, "Die 'antihistorische Revolution' in die protestantischen Theologie der zwanziger Jahre," in *Vernunft des Glaubens: Wissenschaftliche Theologie und kirchliche Lehre*, ed. Jan Rohls and Gunther Wenz (Göttingen, 1988), 377–405.

61. Mosheim, *Servetus*, 258 (citing 1 Cor. 17:3).

Bibliography

Ahnert, Thomas. "Historicizing Heresy in the Early Enlightenment." In *Heresy in Transition: Transforming Ideas of Heresy in Medieval and Early Modern Europe*, edited by Ian Hunter, Christian Laursen, and Cary J. Nederman, 129–42. Aldershot, 2005.

———. *Religion and the Origins of the German Enlightenment: Faith and the Reform of Learning in the Thought of Christian Thomasius*. Rochester, 2006.

Anonymous. "Johann Lorenz von Mosheims . . . anderweitiger Versuch einer vollständigen und unpartheyischen Ketzergeschichte." *Zuverlässige Nachrichten von dem gegenwärtigen Zustande, Veränderung und Wachsthum der Wissenschaften* 10 (1749): 37–38.

Arnold, Gottfried. *Die erste Liebe der Gemeinen Jesu Christi*. 2 vols. Frankfurt am Main, 1696.

———. *Unparteyische Kirchen- und Ketzer-Historie: Vom Anfang des Neuen Testaments bis auff das Jahr Christi 1688*. Frankfurt am Main, 1700, 1729.

Bainton, Roland. *Hunted Heretic: The Life and Death of Michael Servetus, 1511–1533*. Boston, 1953.

Blackall, Eric. *The Emergence of German as a Literary Language 1700–1775*. Cambridge, 1959.

Champion, Justin. *The Pillars of Priestcraft Shaken: The Church of England and Its Enemies*. Cambridge, 1992.

Dann, Otto. "Das historische Interesse in der deutschen Gesellschaft des 18. Jahrhunderts. Geschichte und historische Forschung in den zeitgenössischen Zeitschriften." In *Historische Forschung im 18. Jahrhundert. Organisation-Zielsetzung-Ergebnisse*, edited by Karl Hammer and Jürgen Voss, 386–415. Bonn, 1976.

Dörries, Hermann. *Geist und Geschichte bei Gottfried Arnold*. Göttingen, 1963.

Fleischer, Dirk. *Zwischen Tradition und Fortschritt: Der Strukturwandel der protestantischen Kirchengeschichtsschreibung im deutschsprachigen Diskurs der Aufklärung*. Waltrop, 2006.

Friedman, Jerome. *Michael Servetus: A Case Study in Total Heresy*. Geneva, 1978.

Gordon, Bruce. "The Changing Face of Protestant History and Identity in the Six-teenth Century." In *Protestant History and Identity in Sixteenth-Century Europe*, edited by Bruce Gordon, vol. 1, 1–22. Aldershot, 1996.

Graf, Friedrich Wilhelm. "Die 'antihistorische Revolution' in der protestantischen Theologie der zwanziger Jahre." In *Vernunft des Glaubens: Wissenschaftliche Theologie und kirchliche Lehre*, edited by Jan Rohls and Gunther Wenz, 377–405. Göttingen, 1988.

Gregory, Brad S. *Salvation at Stake: Christian Martyrdom in Early Modern Europe.* Cambridge, MA, 1999.

Henke, Heinrich Philipp Conrad. *Frohe Aussichten für die Religion in die Zukunft. Eine Rede, bey der Einführung Herrn August Christian Barthels, als Abts zu Riddagshausen am 8tn Jenner 1790 in der Klosterkirche daselbst gehalten.* 2nd ed. Helmstedt, 1801.

Hunter, Ian. *The Secularisation of the Confessional State: The Political Thought of Christian Thomasius.* Cambridge, 2007.

Jarausch, Konrad. "The Institutionalization of History in Eighteenth-Century Germany." In *Aufklärung und Geschichte*, edited by Hans Erich Bödeker, Georg G. Iggers, Peter Hanns Reill, and Jonathan B. Knudsen, 36–41. Göttingen, 1986.

Kaplan, Benjamin. *Divided by Faith: Religious Conflict and the Practice of Toleration in Early Modern Europe.* Cambridge, MA, 2007.

Laursen, John Christian. "What Is Impartiality? Arnold on Spinoza, Mosheim on Servetus." In *Heresy in Transition: Transforming Ideas of Heresy in Medieval and Early Modern Europe*, edited by Ian Hunter, Christian Laursen, and Cary J. Nederman, 143–54. Aldershot, 2005.

Marshall, John. *John Locke, Toleration and Early Enlightenment Culture.* Cambridge, 2006.

Mosheim, Johann Lorenz. *Anderweitiger Versuch einer unparteiischen und gründlichen Ketzergeschichte: Geschichte des berühmten Spanischen Artztes Michael Serveto.* Helmstedt, 1748.

———. *An Ecclesiastical History, Antient [sic] and Modern.* Translated by Archibald Maclaine. London, 1768.

———. *Institutiones historiæ christianæ antiquioris et recentioris.* 2nd ed. Helmstedt, 1755.

———. *Kurze Anweisung, die Gottesgelahrtheit vernünftig zu erlernen, in Academischen Vorlesungen vorgetragen.* Helmstedt, 1756.

———. *De rebus Christianorum ante Constantinum Magnum Commentarii.* Helmstedt, 1753.

———. *Versuch einer unparteiischen und gründlichen Ketzergeschichte.* Helmstedt, 1746; reprint, Hildesheim, 1998.

———. *De vita, fatis, et scriptis celeberrimi viri, Ioannis Tolandi, Hiberni, commentatio.* Hamburg, 1722.

——— and Heinrich von Allwoerden. *Historia Michaelis Serveti.* Helmstedt, 1727.

Mulsow, Martin. "Eine 'Rettung' des Servet und der Ophiten? Der junge Mosheim und die häretische Tradition." In *Johann Lorenz Mosheim (1693–1755): Theologie im Spannungsfeld von Philosophie, Philologie und Geschichte*, edited by Martin Mulsow, Ralph Häfner, Florian Neumann, and Helmut Zedelmaier, 45–92. Wiesbaden, 1997.

Pocock, J. G. A. *Barbarism and Religion*. Vol. 5, *Religion: The First Triumph*. Cambridge, 2010.

———. "Clergy and Commerce: The Conservative Enlightenment in England." In *L'Età dei Lumi: studi storici sul settecento europeo in onore di Franco Venturi*, edited by Raffaele Ajello, E. Cortese, and Vincenzo Piano Mortari, vol. 2, 523–62. Naples, 1985.

Pott, Martin. "Christian Thomasius und Gottfried Arnold." In *Gottfried Arnold (1666–1714)*, edited by Dietrich Blaufuß and Friedrich Niewöhner, 247–66. Wiesbaden, 1995.

Printy, Michael. "The Determination of Man: Johann Joachim Spalding and the Protestant Enlightenment." *Journal of the History of Ideas* 72 (2013): 189–212.

Rasimus, Tuomas. *Paradise Reconsidered in Gnostic Mythmaking: Rethinking Sethianism in Light of the Ophite Evidence*. Leiden, 2009.

Raventlow, Henning Graf. "Johann Lorenz Mosheims Auseinandersetzung mit John Toland." In *Johann Lorenz Mosheim (1693–1755): Theologie im Spannungsfeld von Philosophie, Philologie und Geschichte*, edited by Martin Mulsow, Ralph Häfner, Florian Neumann, and Helmut Zedelmaier, 93–110. Wiesbaden, 1997.

Schneider, Hans. "Der radikale Pietismus in 17. Jahrhundert." In *Geschichte des Pietismus*, edited by Martin Brecht, vol. 1, 410–16. Göttingen, 1993.

Schroeckh, Johann Matthias. *Christliche Kirchengeschichte*, 2nd ed, vol. 1. Leipzig, 1768.

Servetus, Michael. *Christianismi restitutio*. N.p., 1553.

———. *De Trinitatis erroribus libri septem*. N.p., 1531.

Spittler, Ludwig Timothäus. *Grudriß der Geschichte der christlichen Kirche*. Göttingen, 1782.

Stroup, John. "Protestant Church Historians in the German Enlightenment." In *Aufklärung und Geschichte*, edited by Hans Erich Bödeker, Georg G. Iggers, Peter Hanns Reill, and Jonathan B. Knudsen, 169–92. Göttingen, 1986.

Thomasius, Christian. *An haeresis sit crimen*. Halle, 1697.

———. *De jure principis circa haereticos*. Halle, 1697.

———. *Erinnerung . . . über den vierten Teil seiner Grund-Lehren*. Halle, 1701.

Ward, W. R. "Is Martyrdom Mandatory? The Case of Gottfried Arnold." In *Faith and Faction*, 377–84. London, 1993.

Williams, George Hunston. *The Radical Reformation*. Philadelphia, 1962; reprint, Kirksville, 2000.

CHAPTER NINE

The Great Fire of 1711
Reconceptualizing the Jewish Ghetto and Jewish–Christian Relations in Early Modern Frankfurt am Main

DEAN PHILLIP BELL

Disasters—natural or human-induced, unexpected or recurring—can open valuable windows onto otherwise unseen cultural structures, latent social tensions, and a full range of intergroup relations in different historical contexts. Such events may both reinforce and challenge existing norms and behaviors. How they are perceived and remembered can have a great deal to do with the perspectives and concerns of the individuals and communities that experience them, whether in person or even at a temporal or geographical distance. In this essay I examine the well-known fire that devastated the Jewish ghetto in Frankfurt am Main in 1711. The event garnered a broad range of Jewish and Christian responses that shaped Jewish community agendas and Jewish and Christian interactions for many years. Specifically, I ask how the various responses to this dramatic fire allow us to understand religious identities and interreligious relationships in early modern Germany.

While many responses to the fire drew from traditional religious texts and arguments about divine punishment for sin—thus casting the disaster as divine vengeance against the Jews and reinforcing many traditional anti-Jewish accusations and motifs—other responses provide evidence of more pragmatic and positive interactions between Jews and Christians that may force us to reevaluate the normative historical narratives that emphasize Jewish and Christian otherness and opposition. As we will see, some of the textual responses—in the form of historical accounts and liturgy—and some pointed political and economic debates at the time of the fire strengthened perceived religious differences, while other writings and discussions revealed more nuanced, and at times friendly, daily encounters between Jews and

Christians. Recounting the fire could serve both as a means to reinforce identity and perceptions and challenge extant conditions for both Jews and Christians. Jewish writers, for example, leveraged the event to connect and cope with the challenges and crises facing Jews in Frankfurt and beyond throughout history and in their own day. At the same time, in narrating and memorializing the fire, Jewish authors also called for religious introspection and communal improvement. Similarly, for Christian writers, the fire could reinforce anti-Jewish sensibilities that labeled Jews as rejected by God and outsiders fomenting against Christian society. Still, many Christian authors were forced to notice the positive behavior of the Jews—among themselves and in their relationships with Christians—at a time of crisis. What is more, despite a good deal of local debate, the city council and the imperial authorities maintained a rather balanced response, protecting the Jews and their property and facilitating reconstruction of the Jewish ghetto. Of course, this response also revealed the position of the authorities that could not see beyond the spatial marginalization and legal circumscription of the Jews.

In evaluating the great fire of 1711, the confessionalization paradigm is quite beneficial.[1] The fire proved to be a key event in the history of the Frankfurt Jewish community around which Jews could develop cohesive customs and liturgy, moralize behavior and censure dissidence, concretize responses (including theological, physical, and political) to crisis, and reorganize communal space and institutions. From a Christian perspective as well, confessionalization provides a useful tool for analysis. The fire offered an opportunity for the consolidation of Christian identity in opposition to what was perceived as the divine rejection of the Jews and the defeat of an alleged Jewish threat. At the same time, the fire sparked discussion about religious and social boundaries (maintaining borders and separation), and it served as a wake-up call for Christians, who realized that they could also be punished by God, through fire and other catastrophes, for their own misbehavior and religious and moral shortcomings.

The fire of 1711, however, was not simply a confessional battlefield that could be used to consolidate internal identity or bolster marginalization and sharpen separation. A wide range of contemporary documents noted a degree of integration of Jews into broader early modern German society. Such integration was probably never thorough, but it did allow Jews to find housing after the destruction of the ghetto, and it did result in the reconstruction of the Jewish space—still separated by walls—within the city. Aside from the important and nuanced work of the prolific historian of Frankfurt Jewry Isidor Kracauer (1852–1923), the fire of 1711 has garnered little sustained scholarly attention. When the event is referenced, it is generally within the context of the anti-Jewish sensibilities of early modern Christian writers, who saw the fire as punishment for the Jews' rejection of Christianity or as evidence of

Jewish (kabbalistic) plotting against Christianity gone awry. In no small measure, such brief accounts assume a general lachrymose sense of Jewish history, one that entailed a long and difficult path of Jewish liminality and suffering. Still, some historians have pointed out that the recurrence of fires throughout early modern Frankfurt helped to remove any specifically anti-Jewish message in the long run, proving that God was angry at the entire city and not just the Jews.[2] Other historians, reading the event in the context of the later eighteenth-century Enlightenment, have argued that the interaction between Jews, seeking temporary housing after the fire, and Christians revealed to the latter a high level of culture among the Jews.[3] Indeed, as the following analysis will make clear, Jewish and Christian relations, at times of crisis and normalcy, were much more complex than generally explained in historical accounts that focus primarily on religious differences and theological debate, economic competition, or uneven and meandering toleration that largely served other political purposes.

The fiery destruction of the Jewish ghetto in early eighteenth-century Frankfurt provides the opportunity to trace the construction of religious and communal identity that was anchored in the past and responsive to practical realities of the present and potential developments in the future. This essay builds upon and expands my previous work on natural disasters (such as floods, earthquakes, and severe weather) as a profitable laboratory in which to examine Jewish and Christian relations in early modern Germany.[4] It provides a useful way to test traditional understandings of Jewish and Christian interactions and to suggest new ways to approach early modern Jewish history.

Early Modern Fires

Harnessed for important domestic and industrial purposes, fire has been essential for human social development. Not surprisingly, fire was seen by the philosopher scientists of antiquity as a primal element (along with earth, air, and water) and a self-generating and key force of change.[5] Even when downgraded from "elemental status," fire remained a central process and key theme for reflection, investigation, and application.[6] Uncontrolled and wild fires, by contrast, while serving many natural functions, have at times devastated human communities. The ubiquity of fire in early modern society naturally fueled the chances for the spread of fire, and nearly every urban area was scorched at some point in its history. Indeed, fire has been seen as the greatest threat to early modern cities.[7] Whether the result of lightning strikes, dry weather conditions, or human actions (accidentally according to early modern writers or as a part of crime or warfare), fire could have devastating effects on cities and towns comprised of houses and buildings that were constructed largely from wood and that often lacked conscious planning and the development of fire prevention. Although the deaths that resulted from fires might be fewer than from other disasters, the broader damage and economic and social impact could be much greater.[8] Fires destroyed houses and other buildings; this destruction as well as the process of rebuilding could escalate latent economic and social tensions or confirm traditional social rules and privileges. Fires could reveal societal vulnerabilities and resiliencies. They could challenge, recalibrate, or reinforce social, economic, and political hierarchies.[9]

In describing fires, early modern Germans drew from a well of biblical, theological, scientific, and historical sources. The Hebrew Bible, for example, abounds with positive and negative images of fire that early modern writers frequently referenced. These texts were related to God's presence (e.g., burning bush, pillar of fire guiding the Israelites through the desert, reception of the Torah on Mount Sinai) and various rituals, including those related to the sacrificial offerings. Biblical fires could also descend from heaven to consume evil or transgressive individuals. In either case they represented God's power and control of both natural and supernatural forces. Similar imagery could also be found throughout the New Testament.[10] From a biblical perspective, then, fire could be multivalent, representing religious practice and connection to God and simultaneously cast as divine punishment for human sin.[11]

Most early modern accounts of fires were brief and rather general. Typical of such reports was the entry for 1539, in which the Jewish historian and scientist David Gans recorded, "Also in this year, in the year [5]399, 1539 according to the Christians, there was by the hand of God in the city Embach, which is in the territory of Saxony, a fire that consumed the entire city to the ground and there was not a single house left there and it was not known who ignited it."[12] But fires might excite a range of literary productions beyond historical chronicling. Among the most famous was Andreas Gryphius's poem "Freistadt in Flames" (*Fewrige Freystadt*) of 1637, which described the dry conditions and the results of the conflagration in that city.

Early modern chroniclers often did not specify who or what caused fires. At times they simply did not know. The lack of agency, however, also allowed writers to associate anonymity with divine punishment. For many medieval and early modern people, fires were often part of a panoply of wonder signs and punishments from heaven, frequently seen in an apocalyptic vein. Johannes Merclius, for example, in his *Heavenly Fire Signs* (*Himlische Fewerzeichen*), published in 1560, discussed a great light in the skies on 30 January 1560 (in the evening between six and seven o'clock) in the village of Reichenau (a mile from Camitz) and throughout Bohemia and Moravia, signaling to some the onset of the Day of Judgment and the resurrection of the dead.[13] Merclius placed this event in the category of other signs—including solar and lunar eclipses; rains of fire, brimstone, and blood; bloody snow; terrible winds and storms; earthquakes; and even locust infestations—all of which portended misfortune and divine punishment for an unrepentant and godless world. The polemicist used the opportunity toward the end of the pamphlet to parallel what he termed the "eclipse of the papacy."[14]

Similarly for Kaspar Goldwurm (d. 1559), the Lutheran theologian who served for a time as an adviser to Count Wilhelm of Nassau-Dillenburg and who chronicled wondrous signs, fire was one of the elements—the others being water and wind—that appeared as wondrous works from the biblical period until his own day. Like many others, Goldwurm associated fire with the thunder and lightning recorded in biblical passages such as those describing the events in Sodom, the punishments of Nadab, Abihu, Datan, Aviron, and Korach, as well as those described in other stories from the Prophets.[15] Goldwurm referenced historical occurrences, such as the fiery heavens in Rome in the seventh century, the eruption of Mount Vesuvius, and other medieval events.[16] He narrated these events in a rather matter-of-fact way, but he presented all of them under the broader category of wondrous and terrifying forms and events that appeared in the sky and clouds and associated them with the broader warning signs that God was providing to people through unusual events. Goldwurm recounted such events in his own time as well, in France, Naples, and parts of south Germany throughout the first four decades of the sixteenth century. He saw these fiery appearances, as well as a wide range of other unusual occurrences in nature (such as strange creatures and various heavenly sights), as signs of God's displeasure and powerful opportunities for moral upbraiding and criticism of particular social groups or confessions.[17]

Explanations of and responses to fires could take many forms. In the midst of the August 1677 conflagration that devastated the city of Rostock, for example, the local pastor excoriated his congregation for their un-Christian lifestyle and called for repentance as the only way to placate God and extinguish the flames.[18] Indeed, sermons of this sort frequently sought both to console and to moralize against sinning and particular transgressions such as haughtiness, blasphemy, desecration of the Sabbath, and unchasteness.[19] Well-trained preachers could leverage such events to warn of possible further disasters. Similarly, civic and religious authorities (Christian or Jewish) might address religious concerns by instituting designated days of fasting and penance, which in some communities persisted for decades after a major fire.[20]

Authorities could take more administrative steps in response to urban fires as well.[21] The fire that ravaged Rostock fifteen years later (1692) led to calls for the implementation of new methods for firefighting—the use of extinguishers and the creation of firehouses, for example—and preventative measures to keep fires from breaking out in the first place.[22] Such practical measures became increasingly common in the seventeenth century, at times in place of or, more often, in conjunction with religious measures.[23]

In seeking assistance from other cities or communities or in an effort to maintain order, civic governments might issue a range of edicts and ordinances regarding the measures necessary to prevent fire. These included construction regulations, the relocation of businesses or industries utilizing fire to less densely populated parts of town or even outside the city walls, precautions to be taken against wind and severe weather as well as candles at night, techniques to protect key structures such as bridges, and the development of surveillance and warning systems. Many ordinances stipulated the specific measures to be taken in the event of an actual conflagration: the types of machinery to be employed to battle the flames; the use of lights at night; fire watches, horn blasts, and other means to notify people of fires; measures to safeguard the food supply; and protocols for rescue efforts. Social and communal responses were at times likewise standardized, as with regulations governing the collection of alms.[24] The early modern response to fires also included the development of fire guilds and fire insurance.[25]

Fires often led to increased regulation of daily life and industry, and by the seventeenth century they broadly influenced architecture and urban planning, including even the selection of building materials (e.g., stone).[26] The prophylactic attempt to prevent fires from beginning or spreading once they did could itself be expensive, with the investment in equipment and supplies, the creation of watchtowers, digging of wells, and the need to staff various communal positions.[27] A great deal of money could also be required to respond to damages caused by fires, and as a result special taxes might be collected to fund the reconstruction projects in cities.[28]

The particular response to a fire could vary by location and specific conditions but often entailed a mix of theological and practical responses.[29] However, the question of where to lay blame for the outbreak of a fire was important and could be highly charged. Some writers blamed the city magistrates for poor policies and insufficient or sluggish responses.[30] Accusations of arson were more complicated but were frequently directed at marginalized groups such as Jews, gypsies, and vagabonds. Even when early moderns maintained that fires were divine punishment,[31] those accused of arson could be seen as agents of divine wrath, though to many minds no less guilty of crimes against the city and their neighbors.

Such concerns were hardly limited to Christian Europe, as examples from Asia and the Ottoman Empire reveal. The great fire of Istanbul in 1660, for example, betrayed latent political and religious tensions and allowed for significant spatial reorganization and theological polemic as parts of the city were reconstructed.[32] In a growing process of Islamization, the deteriorating position of the Jews, especially in comparison to that of Greek Orthodox Christians, allowed for the appropriation of Jewish property and the expulsion of Jews from several areas and their relocation to other districts. In constructing a great mosque—expanded from the foundations that had lain incomplete for many years—local authorities appropriated many surrounding Jewish properties, now cleared of Jewish houses, giving it a position of great visibility and prominence to people entering the city. The deed included the following language:

> By the decree of God the exalted the fire of divine wrath turned all the neighbor-hoods of the Jews upside down. The effect of the flames of the wrath of God made the homes and abodes belonging to the straying community resemble ashes. Every one of the Jewish households was turned into a fire temple full of sparks. Since the residences and dwellings of Jews, who are the enemy of Islam, resembled the deepest part of Hell, the secret of the verse which is incontro-vertible, "those that do evil shall be cast into the fire" (Q 32:20), became clear, and in order to promise and threaten those who deny Islam with frightening things, the verse, "woe to the unbelievers because of a violent punishment" (Q 14:2), also became manifest.[33]

Muslim authorities similarly portrayed the great fire in Galata in 1696 as pun-ishment for the "blasphemy, impiety, superstition, idolatry, and adultery" of the Jews and Christians who had recently settled in the affected quarter, and the fire served as an excuse for the confiscation of burned-down Jewish and Christian houses, as part of a larger project of Islamization.[34]

Responses to fires could be complex, especially as cities and communities grappled with associated financial, social, and political challenges.[35] Even when damage was localized within a city or urban district, the disaster could have significant resonance throughout the broader city and region.[36] Recon-struction had huge financial implications; likewise any decision not to rebuild particular structures or neighborhoods carried other, equally significant impli-cations, as diverse populations were forced to compete for resources and, in the immediate aftermath of the fire, for housing. Even in relatively localized fires, weakened communal infrastructure and compromised food supplies could lead to epidemics and rebellions or armed conflicts.

Fires and Jews

As for other urban residents, fires affected Jews in a variety of ways. Since the Middle Ages numerous fires have had direct impact on German Jewish com-munities. Already with the famous medieval charter for the Jews in Speyer we read:

> At the outset, when we came to establish our residence in Speyer—may its foundations never falter!—it was the result of the fire that broke out in the city of Mainz. The city of Mainz was the city of our origin and the residence of our

ancestors, the ancient and revered community, praised above all communities in the empire. All the Jews' quarter and their street was burned, and we stood in great fear of the burghers. . . . The bishop of Speyer greeted us warmly, sending his ministers and soldiers after us. He gave us a place in the city and expressed his intention to build about us a strong wall to protect us from our enemies, to afford us fortification.[37]

While fires could lead to new settlement and opportunities for Jewish residents, accounts of significant fires more typically reveal extreme danger to the Jewish communities because of loss of property or anti-Jewish animus that could manifest itself in accusations of Jewish conspiracy against or malevolence toward Christians. For the year 1541, for example, David Gans wrote, "There were many and great fires in the entire territory of Bohemia in the year 301, according to the shorter calculation, and it was not known who started them. And it was a libel against the shepherds and against the Jews, saying that they did this evil thing . . . and many were burned in martyrdom." Gans went on to note, "Ferdinand, King of Bohemia, because of the complaints of the people, expelled all the Jews of his kingdom; only in the city of Prague there remained ten [Jewish] men for a short time." (Gans recorded that the Jews were recalled a short time later.)[38]

Other Jewish chroniclers registered occurrences of fires as well. An anonymous chronicle from Prague discussed a fire in 1559. In a traditional approach to theodicy, the author ascribed specific suffering within the community, such as expulsions and fires in the Jewish street, to the sins of the community:

> Due to our iniquities, there was a fire in the Judenstrasse here in Prague, in which seventy-two houses were consumed by the flames, as well as the Hochschul. This occurred on the 17th of Tammuz [a fast day instituted to recall numerous tragedies in Jewish history, especially related to the destruction of the Second Temple]. A woman named Friedel Niches perished in the fire as well, due to our iniquities.[39]

Of course, fires affecting the Jewish communities were not limited to the lands of the Holy Roman Empire. To take one further, eastern European example, we have accounts of other fires that affected early modern Jewish communities. Consider, for example, the memoirs of Ber of Bolochow,[40] in which the author detailed a conflagration in 1729 (5489). That fire consumed five large buildings on the town's main street, and Ber noted the reconstruction and reallocation of housing, as well as the death of one woman.[41] The fire began in the church, when a candle fell onto a covered table and spread to the main street, before eventually dying out due to the gap created between the houses.[42] Ber mentioned other fires that were the result of military encounters.[43] In other cases, Ber noted the amount of damage and the need for Jews (including himself and his brother) to find other, temporary lodging with extended family.[44] Like their

Christian neighbors, Jews understood and responded to fires in ways that were simultaneously theological and practical. As we will see below, early modern fires could also reveal complex and at times positive relations among Jews and between Jews and Christians—neighbors, clergy, and secular authorities.

The Frankfurt Ghetto

The Jews in Frankfurt were sequestered into a special quarter in 1462, constituting one of the earliest formal Jewish ghettos in Europe. The ghetto would remain in existence, despite needing to be rebuilt, until the end of the eighteenth century. Paralleling some of the dramatic economic and demographic growth within the larger city and despite the expulsion of the Jews for a period in the early seventeenth century in the wake of the disruptive Fettmilch Uprising, the Jewish community in Frankfurt was one of the largest and most influential Jewish communities in the Holy Roman Empire. The ghetto initially enclosed some 10 houses and 100 residents. By the second decade of the seventeenth century there were roughly 2,700 Jews from 453 Jewish households (occupying 195 houses) in Frankfurt.[45] The Jewish population rose still further to 3,000 by the end of the seventeenth century, constituting 10 percent of the total city population. Contracting a bit, the Jewish population in Frankfurt was still over 2,400 in the early eighteenth century.

Like other medieval and early modern German Jewish quarters, the Jewish quarter in Frankfurt was devastated by fire at various times in the Middle Ages, and the residents suffered major fires in 1711, 1721, and again in 1774. The great fire of 1711, confined to the Jewish quarter, was cast by some contemporary Christians as the result of Jewish machinations against Christians or, alternately, by later historians (regardless of religious background) as a result of the unhygienic and polluted nature of the ghetto—depending on the perspectives or agendas of the author, the latter could take the form of complaints against the difficult conditions that Jews experienced in forced ghettoization or as the manifestation of traditional anti-Jewish sensibilities that characterized Jews as dirty.[46] Regardless of how the fire was discussed, most contemporary observers would have seen it to some extent as divine punishment for some transgression. Christians could argue that God was angry about Jewish stubbornness in rejecting Christianity, while Jewish writers could assert that the fire demonstrated the need for some form of communal or religious improvements. The fire left a significant imprint on the Jewish community immediately after and for decades to follow. Disputes before the Frankfurt rabbinical court (*bet din*) in the 1770s continued to reference the fire of 1711—noting, for example, remains of walls that dated from the time or the disposition of various property lots.[47]

The fire broke out on Wednesday 14 January, around eight in the evening, apparently in the house of Rabbi Naphtali Cohen.[48] Accused by some Christian writers of kabbalistic intrigues, the rabbi was detained in prison and investigated before being released some four or five months later[49] and moving to Istanbul. The fire spread quickly and soon threatened walls and gates in the Jewish ghetto as well as some adjacent Christian houses.[50] However, on several occasions strong winds turned the flames back in on the Jewish quarter—a development that would be seen by some, Jews as well as Christians, as some sort of divine punishment.[51]

Christians arrived to douse the flames. Fearing looting, however, the Jewish residents kept the doors locked. Finally carpenters with axes smashed the door to the small bridge leading to the ghetto.[52] Realizing the futility of battling the flames, many Christians assisted Jews in moving their possessions with carts and wagons. The Jews' fears were partially realized, however, by looters who plundered some of the burning houses.

Early on 15 January, while the fire continued unabated, the city council met, sounded fire signals, and formed a committee that was sent to the Jewish quarter to assess the situation. The Jews were accommodated in other parts of the city—the poor in the sick house— and supplied with provisions. By the evening of 15 January much of the ghetto and the Jews' possessions had been consumed.[53] A large number of Jews fled to the cemetery. Only four people succumbed to the flames, however.[54]

Responses to the Fire

Various Jewish and Christian writers attributed a range of causes to the fire. Some within the Jewish community criticized the life in the ghetto as too worldly. As a result, the Jewish community council banned all comedies and plays for a period of fourteen years, and it issued stringent sumptuary laws.[55] The day of the fire was marked by the community as one of penance and lamentation, which continued to be observed annually for decades.[56] Some lamentations, like that written by David ben Simon Sougers of Prague and published in Frankfurt, drew parallels to the destruction of the Temple and noted the complete devastation of and panic within the Jewish ghetto.[57] Inveighing standardized language, the author attributed the fire to "our great sins."[58] Still, the author recognized the protection and assistance provided by the authorities and concluded somewhat formulaically, "Day and night we pray for our lords and authorities that God should protect them from all misfortune."[59]

Initial Legal Responses

The Holy Roman Emperor responded quickly, within two months, to the catastrophe with a decree that was widely circulated.[60] In it, he noted the unforeseen and sudden conflagration that devastated the entire Jewish quarter, referring to it as a great misfortune for the Jews. The document mentioned several evil and licentious (Christian) residents of the city who took possessions from the burning houses and others who threatened the Jews that if another fire were to break out they would slay the Jews and cast them in the flames, causing great fear among the Jews. The decree absolved the Jews of any guilt in the kindling of the fire. Any actions against, mishandling of, or threats to the Jews, the emperor asserted, would be severely punished, since the Jews were under imperial protection. Finally, the emperor dictated that arrangements had to be made as soon as possible for the reconstruction of the Jewish quarter, so as not hinder or overburden the Jews.

Other, more localized Christian depictions of the fire could vary, but they revolved around some central themes. An illustrated broadsheet circulating in 1711, for example, summarized the events but also quickly placed the fire in the context of divine punishment against the Jews. The Christian author wrote that "[through] God's anger the fire suddenly came into the Jewish quarter."[61] He concluded more broadly, however, "How this fire actually arose and began—regarding this much has been spoken: It is as He wills, so we must hereby learn of God's fire-burning anger, to distance [ourselves] from all vices, and pray to God that such fires will not destroy the city of Frankfurt."[62]

Discussions about Reconstruction

Negotiations between representatives of the Jewish community and the Frankfurt city council related to the reconstruction of the Jewish quarter began immediately.[63] The Jews pressed the city council for permission to rebuild already a month later (on 12 February). The council was not certain how the ghetto should be reconstructed and gave initial permission only for the synagogue to be rebuilt—its foundations were laid on 23 March, and it was completed by September.[64]

Negotiations for the reconstruction of the remainder of the ghetto proved to be a more protracted affair.[65] Although a construction ordinance was issued by the council on 7 April, it would be challenged and debated over the course of the next two years.[66] What is more, many Jews lacked the funds for reconstruction, and the community was forced to seek financial assistance from other Jewish communities.[67] Still, the Jewish Construction Ordinance of April 1711, which was seen as too favorable to the Jews by some, provided important details for how the Jewish quarter should be reconstructed.[68] The Jews were to pay to have the quarter paved in such a way that water could be channeled to fight future fires. The ordinance stipulated that all the Jews' houses should be the same height, and none more than three stories high—an ordinance from 24 January 1594 had long before, in part over concern about fire, dictated that no Jewish houses could be higher than three stories.[69] The ordinance stipulated the height and construction of each story, and it provided details about the scope and construction of firewalls, as well as the proximity of houses to the walls.

The ordinance further stipulated that "all the walls that surround the Jewish quarter should be visible [and demarcated] with eagles and a [letter] 'F' [for Frankfurt] . . . as a sign that the city alone has jurisdiction," undercutting imperial authority over and protection of the Jews. According to the ordinance, houses were to remain elevated and no sub-cellars were permitted, addressing a particularly volatile issue that would be discussed repeatedly over the next several years. The Jewish stables that had previously stood by the moat were to be relocated within the Jewish quarter, though no more houses were permitted to be added in compensation for the loss of living space. The Jews were to be allowed, at their own expense, to locate and build their own hospital, behind the synagogue and against the innermost quarter where the brew house and communal bake oven had stood previously.

Similar ordinances were enacted after other fires in the city. Consider, for example, the construction ordinance for houses later burned down in the Bock-Gasse in 1719.[70] Aside from the labeling of the Jewish quarter as under Frankfurt jurisdiction, the legislation about the sub-basements, and the requirement for Jews to assume the costs of some construction and improvements, there is little that differentiates this ordinance. The initial response of the authorities to the fire in the Jewish quarter, therefore, was typical of responses to other fires in the city.

The reconstruction of the Jewish quarter, however, induced opposition from other parties. The archbishop of Mainz registered a complaint in 1712 that a western row of houses opposite the monastery, and particularly the windows, were being constructed higher than before and that such construction was offensive to the Christian religion. The windows, the council later decided, should be bricked over.[71] Even more quarrelsome, however, were the objections to the construction of sub-basements and the height of the buildings, which the burghers' deputies articulated.[72] They also raised concerns about the expansion of the Jews' spaces (e.g., cemetery, bake ovens) outside the ghetto, initiating a significant debate over the expansion of Jewish space into the public *Bleichgarten* (bleach-field).[73] The council rejected any initial agreements to expand the height of buildings or the footprint of the ghetto. Imperial authorities intervened, however, in 1714 and overturned the more limited and revised construction ordinance in favor of the original one, which was more favorable to the Jewish community, and allowing construction to continue.[74]

Turning their attack now on the city council, the irate deputies representing the burghers thundered that the burned-down quarter should not be improved and expanded, for that would favor the Jews, who are the ruin of the Christian citizens, and only strengthen them in their obduracy and enmity against the name of Jesus and his adherents.[75] Similarly, in 1714—precisely as the Jews were displaced by the fire from their ghetto—local merchants submitted a petition to an imperial commission. Complaints were also raised about the number of Jews who had settled in Frankfurt—who were required to possess a certain amount of money—and their business practices.[76] Initial patience with and support for the Jewish community by local Christians appears to have given way to opposition in the months after the fire.[77]

In its objection to the expansion of Jewish trade into new commodities, the petitioners asserted that both the number of Jews involved in trade and the range of products with which they dealt had expanded. Jews were accused of being unfair by nature and of using improper trade techniques. Finally, the petition argued that Jews should be kept inferior to Christians, otherwise their hatred of Christians would grow and they would be further discouraged from conversion.[78] The merchants implied that the Jews were forming a "state within a state," and they called for a significant reduction in their numbers, a ban on additional Jewish settlement, and the removal of Jewish commerce into outlying rural areas.[79]

Nonetheless, the bulk of the Jewish quarter had been reconstructed by the middle of 1716.[80] By 1718 the construction outside the Jewish ghetto on the previous public *Bleichgarten*—with five community bake ovens and a hospital—was also completed.[81] While it made sense to relocate these Jewish spaces outside the ghetto because of space limitations and efforts to prevent fire, it is likely that this further facilitated Jewish interaction with non-Jewish neighbors outside the ghetto. Already by January of 1716 the council had ordered Jews to return to the ghetto and Christians no longer to house them.[82] During the period outside the ghetto, the Jews, in a notice to the council, pointed out that "the entire time that we dwelled in the city there were no complaints raised against us."[83] Some Christian writers chided polemically that there were indeed some benefits to the temporary housing arrangements for the Jews, namely that, as the Christian Hebraist Johann Jacob Schudt (1664–1722) asserted, "through their contact with the Christians [they] learned how to maintain their households better and cleaner."[84] Schudt, a native of Frankfurt, had studied theology at the university in Wittenberg and Orientalia in Hamburg with Esdras Edzard, the Protestant theologian noted for his missionary activity among the Jews and his contention that the full-scale conversion of the Jews to Christianity was a necessary precursor to the Second Coming of Christ.

Polemics

The Frankfurt ghetto continued to be the topic of many legal, ethnographic, historical, and literary works.[85] Schudt himself authored a massive work on the Jews in Frankfurt, which, despite its polemical twists, remains a valuable source on Jewish history and society in the eighteenth century. His enormous *Jewish Curiosities* (*Jüdische Merckwürdigkeiten*) included four volumes—the first three published in 1714 and the fourth in 1718. Schudt had devoted earlier work to Jewish history. Given its tone and scope, *Jewish Curiosities* was not a book that would have secured Jewish conversions to Christianity. The work appears to have been inspired, at least in part, by the fire of 1711, which is referenced frequently. Chapter 6 of book 6 is completely dedicated to an extensive treatment of it.[86] Schudt reviewed several general and common explanations of the fire:

> Regarding what caused this fire there are many and diverse, but uncertain, opinions. Several Jews gave the foolish explanation that the fire fell from the heavens. . . . Many truthful people saw ravens flying in the air with glowing coals in their jaws. Others maintain that the rabbi, who was a great kabbalist, had himself set the fire to let his underlings know that he could extinguish the fire and how he could do it. Others maintain that he had guests, and indeed the *Baumeister* was with him, when the fire had ignited from goose fat. Others argue that the fire consumed the books and paper lying near it. And many more similarly ungrounded things are noted.[87]

Schudt noted that within twenty-four hours the entire Jewish quarter was destroyed, and he recounted the vast suffering and crying of the Jews as well as the kindness of the authorities and burghers, who helped save and protect Jewish possessions and who provided housing.[88] Individual Christian citizens took in Jewish families during the cold night and maintained them for several days until they could find food and supplies—for which many Jews expressed their gratitude.[89] Schudt praised the Jews during this time for expressing no harsh words against God and patiently and quietly suffering, while proclaiming their own sins.[90]

Schudt's extended discussion about permission for Jews to reside in or rent Christian houses in the aftermath of the fire reveals both traditional anti-Jewish sensibilities as well as a good deal of Jewish and Christian interaction. The Jews who did not leave the city were given permission to seek housing where they could and to live in Christian houses.[91] According to Schudt, many Christians did not want to take in Jews, however, due to what they characterized as the Jews' stench and scurrilous lifestyle and household conduct—a position that Schudt seemed to share despite some less derogatory comments. Some objected to the Jews' religious sensibilities, in which they allegedly showed themselves to be enemies of and blasphemers against Christ and the saints. In their hostility to Christians, Schudt noted that the rabbis themselves had frequently forbidden Jews to lend houses to any Christian, because they alleged that Christians committed idolatry. According to Schudt, there were, as a result, very few pious people who were willing to open their houses to such blasphemers.[92] Although most Christians believed that Jews would not openly blaspheme in their Christian houses, they were troubled that Jews would conduct prayers with anti-Christian content. By 12 December 1712 the council had indeed forbidden Jews to hold religious services in Christian houses. Since the synagogue had been reopened by then, presumably this restriction was related to smaller prayer services that were sometimes held in private homes or, more likely, to general domestic religious observances. Beyond specific concerns about liturgy, Schudt believed that some Christians also feared that simply hosting Jews would make their houses targets for fires.

Schudt cited previous theologians, such as Martin Luther and Johannes Müller, to the effect that even if Jews could be given shelter, it should be not in a Christian house, rather only in a stable.[93] According to Schudt, the Christians who did take Jews in did so to learn from them evil and usury and to conduct business with them.[94] In bolstering his position, Schudt provided historical episodes, drawn from alleged events in Frankfurt and other locations, in which Jews rented Christian houses and effaced the name of Jesus.[95] Some Christians who accepted Jews in their houses, Schudt concluded, did so only for financial gain—such people were, for Schudt, culpable as sinners against God and their coreligionists. Other Christians consulted religious authorities about whether they could accept Jews in their houses and under their roofs. Regardless of the decisions made by individual Christians, the urging of the authorities to accommodate Jews was not, Schudt stressed, to be interpreted as approval for any kind of Jewish religious service or assistance with the Jews' Sabbath or religious observances. In particular, Schudt asserted that those who allowed Jews to perform circumcisions in their houses had sinned.[96] Not only should Jewish religious rituals be limited or forbidden in Christian houses, Jews who did reside in Christian houses were themselves not to be permitted to transgress the Christian Sabbath or holidays.

In line with much of the rest of *Jewish Curiosities*, Schudt at times presents Judaism and contemporary Jewish society positively but almost invariably returns to some typical anti-Jewish presentation or motif. In his discussion of the fire and his larger explication of Jewish history and customs, Schudt published some Jewish writings related to the fire, in their original Hebrew or Yiddish, along with his German translation. On one hand, these writings are valuable in understanding Jewish responses to the fire and broader Jewish culture in Frankfurt. At the same time, Schudt leverages them for his own polemical purposes. Jewish theological responses to the great fire rehearsed many standard motifs related to catastrophe. One prayer for a day of penance and remembrance was penned by Rabbi Samuel Schotten on the second anniversary of the fire. The prayer contained formulaic requests for God to protect the Jews from their enemies—which Schudt glossed as "several harsh expressions against Christianity."[97] In commenting on the passage referring to "the wicked ones who forsake your law," Schudt asserted that this referred to Jews who had converted to Christianity.[98] What is more, Schudt read the term "wicked" as referring to the "insolent" in the phrase "because the insolent dig pits for us, flouting our teaching," asserting that the author had changed the biblical text (Psalm 119:85) from "your" teaching (God's) to "our" teaching (referring to the Jews' law). Schudt expanded his analysis to suggest that by the term "insolent," the author of the prayer was referencing all Christians. The end of the prayer, he suggested, also spoke of saving the Jews from the Christians and leading them home to Jerusalem.

Internal Jewish Responses

The fire left a lasting imprint on the Jewish community. The title page of the new Frankfurt memory book itself opened with a lengthy discussion of the great fire of 1711, pointing to the fire as a process of purification that wrought extensive damage:

> Suddenly, in the evening of Wednesday, at the eve of Thursday, the tenth of the month of Tevet, in the complete year 1711, God judged with fire. The fire causes purging and smelting of silver and gold (Malachi 3:3: He shall act like a smelter and purger of silver; and he shall purify the descendants of Levi and refine them like gold and silver, so that they shall present offerings in righteousness to eliminate filth) . . . for days we experienced trouble and were pained like a woman in childbed, and our faces were flaming, as many stood against us. . . . It is the Satan, it is the evil inclination, who ascended and accused us and then descended and then burned and destroyed the fences and vineyards [Song of Songs 2:15]. The fire crossed both sides of the public space. . . . Above and below the fire caused great damage, such that one could not save even the commentaries to the Torah, books of the Bible, Midrashim, Tosefta, Aramaic translations of biblical writings, books in press, communal ordinances of the wise, "for gold and silver are in the crucible and furnace" [Proverbs 17:2].

The memory book went on, in more typical style for its genre, to recall the valiant efforts of a leading philanthropist to rebuild the synagogue—"And even when we were amidst the children of the world: God gave us favor in the eyes of Egypt and sent a king who freed and released our people. We built synagogues as in previous days. We established the house so that God would open His eyes toward it day and night" [1 Kings 8:29]. The memory book then recounted in detail the deeds of Eliezer Oppenheim, who supported the new memory book and the reconstruction of the synagogue:

> And behold the Lord has aroused the spirit [Jeremiah 51:11] of the leader, very learned like one of the sages, the head and the judge and the philanthropist, R. Eliezer Lezer Oppenheim, may the Lord avenge his blood, father of the poor and the orphans. He returned the former glory, he built the fence and leveled (prepared) the highway for the house of our God, to pray [there] days and nights. The intention of this holy work was to glorify God and His house and to make it possible to pray there three times a day in every generation. May God remember him well that he performed so many good deeds in his youth and old age. He published the ledger [*pinkas*] of the burial society [*chevra kadisha*] of the upright and pure men, in which all the names of the deceased were registered for more than one hundred years. He commanded that the names of the holy pious men and women in the land be recorded and thereby remembered for all time.

In addition to the prayer penned by Rabbi Samuel Schotten, presented by Schudt and mentioned above, several other theological writings—lamentations and prayers—were also authored in response to the destruction of the fire. Their authors focused on some central themes of loss, punishment, and exile. One lamentation, referenced above, was written by David ben Simon Sougers of Prague. The author reviewed the outline of events—timing, location of the fire, destruction of vessels and other material goods such as clothes, loss of books and Torah scrolls, locking of the quarter, plundering of Jewish possessions when the gates were opened, as well as the burning of houses and study halls and synagogues. He noted that people were running around in a great panic. While he formulaically attributed the great fire to "our great sins," he also noted that such a punishment was unprecedented. In the lament he mentioned that many Jews were scattered and their whereabouts could not be confirmed.[99] David wrote to console his readers, though he nevertheless questioned, "Why should we desire anything better in exile?"[100] Still, even in this catastrophe, he noted that God continued to be merciful to the Jews, as the authorities ordered that the Jews should be taken in and protected in all the areas where they were located.[101] Further, homes were opened up and the poor house was allocated for the common people and their children to spend the winter.[102] David petitioned God to measure His justice with His mercy.[103]

The fire of 1711 was not the last trial to face the Jewish community in the eighteenth century. Ten years after the first conflagration that destroyed the Jewish quarter another struck (1721), destroying more than a hundred houses. That fire broke out in the ghetto on 28 January 1721 (the fast day the tenth of Tevet) around eight in the evening in the home of the *Baumeister* Moses Elkan. This was just two years after another major fire, this time outside the Jewish quarter, had already caused extensive damage in 1719 in the Bock-Gasse.[104] Fears of plundering were indeed realized in 1721, as the Jews complained to the council: "even in the houses that were preserved, the household effects, including oven, windows, and roofs, were stolen; not even victuals, wine, and precious flour were spared." Personal effects and furnishings that could be secured were also wantonly carried off.[105] Jews remained outside the ghetto for another extended period and would be ordered back to the ghetto again only in May of 1727.[106] Early eighteenth-century Frankfurt evinced a certain degree of flexibility in Jewish–Christian relations, and perhaps enough practical experience with responses to fires and other disasters, to allow Jews to disperse through the city and its surroundings for a limited period until the ghetto could be reconstructed. However, a more permanent displacement of Jews from the ghetto was out of the question in the early modern city.

Conclusions

Our review of the fire of 1711 and subsequent responses reveals that there were a range of interactions between Jews and Christians. In some cases, negative religious representation and economic accusations prevailed. Yet, there were many levels of response. The imperial authorities were quick, at least initially, to write in support of the Jews, and the early discussions about reconstruction fit largely into more general civic legal and practical responses to fires. Despite a long and protracted debate over various aspects of reconstruction, which surfaced a variety of tensions and anti-Jewish motifs, Jews did succeed in finding housing in the city and in surrounding areas for an extended period of time. Schudt's lengthy discussion of the merits of renting to Jews or sharing a roof with them needs to be read in this context. There clearly were numerous Christians who opened their houses to Jews, and the interactions, despite the religious objections Schudt raised, seem to have been relatively harmonious, as the Jews themselves pointed out.

Theological responses by Jews and Christians alike drew from a long and established discourse, which we often refer to as the "economy of sin," by which human sin provokes divine punishment. Schudt's presentation was likely affected by his own training, including the missionary orientation of his own teacher, and experiences. Despite Schudt's assertion that Jews were expressing anti-Christian animus, the prayers authored by Jews wove together a range of biblical quotes that praised God for His mercy and requested protection from their enemies (as a general category), even as He punished the Jews themselves. It is hard to maintain Schudt's critical reading, especially as some of the lamentations simultaneously recorded the support of the authorities and Christian burghers.

Jews were separate in many ways from the broader civic community, but also part of it—even when they suffered particular legal and social disabilities. Jews had both the ability to adapt to conditions and to lobby for the reconstruction of their homes and buildings. Jewish writers could emphasize the unique nature of the Jewish people, even as they stressed imperial support and peaceful interactions with Christian neighbors. Jews may have been marginalized in some ways, but as recent theories of marginalization have noted, the marginalized could simultaneously be central to the broader society.[107] As I have noted elsewhere, Jewish and Christian relations in early modern Germany could be multivalent and not always defined by conflict and animus.[108] What is more, Jewish and Christian communities in late medieval and early modern Germany faced some similar challenges and often developed in surprisingly parallel ways. Jews and Christians utilized governing tools, crafted social hierarchies, and employed religion in a sacralization of communal life in ways that suggest deep and even fruitful interactions.[109] At times, even the anti-Jewish animus that was expressed by some Christians served various, and primarily, internal religious purposes. Some Christian responses noted that the fire in the Jewish quarter demonstrated God's punishment, for example, but often they cast such assertions quite broadly as a means to encourage Christians themselves to repent.

As Alexandra Walsham has recently noted, in regard to religious and social tolerance and intolerance in early modern England, "both separation and co-operation remained critical to guaranteeing the durability of the community."[110] Walsham argues that "the conventional opposition of tolerance and intolerance is a false dichotomy" and that "the relationship between them is fundamentally dialectical and symbiotic." "These two impulses," she asserts, "were caught in a kind of vicious circle: persecution could be a side effect and by-product of toleration and vice versa. Separation and assimilation, introversion and integration, were similarly interwoven features of social experience, cross-currents that constantly muddled and muddied the waters of interpersonal and interdenominational relations."[111] Although quite different from interdenominational Christian conflict, simply casting Jewish and Christian interactions in the dialectical hue of toleration and persecution misses the complexity of the period and the range of interactions and concerns reflected in Jewish and Christian relations. Confessional polemics against Jews could be leveraged to address many general political, legal, economic, religious, and social concerns. In some cases these concerns had little or nothing to do with Jews directly. At the same time, the fire of 1711 affected real people—Jews and Christians—who interacted in many different ways. Our limited sources suggest a much more complex picture that can hardly be satisfactorily explained by simple recourse to traditional historical narratives emphasizing theological prejudice, economic competition, or slow-developing toleration. More work needs to be done—particularly through the examination of individual cases where they may be available—to understand early modern Jewish and Christian interaction. In the meantime, the fire of 1711 provides a useful opportunity to consider how early modern German Jews and Christians engaged and utilized history and theology to construct their own religious and communal identities.

Dean Phillip Bell is provost, vice president, and professor of Jewish history at Spertus Institute for Jewish Learning and Leadership in Chicago. He earned his PhD at the University of California, Berkeley and has taught at the University of California, Berkeley, DePaul University, University of Illinois at Urbana-Champaign, and Northwestern University. He is author of *Sacred Communities: Jewish and Christian Identities in Fifteenth-Century Germany* (2001); *Jewish Identity in Early Modern Germany: Memory, Power and Community* (2007); *Jews in the Early Modern World* (2008); editor of *The Bloomsbury Companion to Jewish Studies* (2013); and, with Stephen G. Burnett, coeditor of *Jews, Judaism and the Reformation in Sixteenth-Century Germany* (2006).

Notes

1. See Dean Phillip Bell, "Confessionalization and Social Discipline in Early Modern Germany: A Jewish Perspective," in *Politics and Reformations: Studies in Honor of Thomas A. Brady, Jr.*, ed. Peter Wallace, Peter Starenko, Michael Printy, and Christopher Ocker (Leiden, 2007): 345–72.
2. See, for example, Christopher R. Friedrichs, *The Early Modern City, 1450–1750* (London, 1995), 280.
3. See Mordechai Breuer and Michael Graetz, ed., *German-Jewish History in Modern Times*, vol. 1, *Tradition and Enlightenment, 1600–1780* (New York, 1996), 240.
4. See, for example, Dean Phillip Bell, "Navigating the Flood Waters: Perspectives on Jewish Life in Early Modern Germany," *Leo Baeck Institute Yearbook* 56 (2011): 29–52; and Bell, "The Little Ice Age and the Jews: Environmental History and the Mercurial Nature of Jewish–Christian Encounters in Early Modern Germany," *AJS Review* 32, no. 1 (Spring 2008): 1–27.
5. Stephen J. Pyne, *Vestal Fire: An Environmental History, Told through Fire, of Europe and Europe's Encounter with the World* (Seattle, 1997), 64–66.
6. Pyne, *Vestal Fire*, 66–67.
7. Christopher Friedrichs, as cited in Marie Luisa Allemeyer, "Profane Hazard or Divine Judgement? Coping with Urban Fire in the 17th Century," *Historical Social Research* 32 (2007): 145–68, here 146.
8. Allemeyer, "Profane Hazard," 146.
9. George Bankoff, Uwe Lübken, and Jordan Sand, ed., *Flammable Cities: Urban Conflagration and the Making of the Modern World* (Madison, 2012), 10ff. Consider the case of Rome and specifically the great fire of 64 and the position of Nero as presented by Tacitus and other writers or imperial attempts to manage and respond to disasters; Jerry Toner, *Roman Disasters* (Cambridge, 2013), 19, 52. Or consider

the case of early modern Russia, Cathy A. Frierson, "Imperial Russia's Urban Fire Regimes, 1700–1905," in Bankoff, Lübken, and Sand, *Flammable Cities*, 103–25, here 106–8.

10. Pyne, *Vestal Fire*, 63–64.

11. Allemeyer, "Profane Hazard," 150.

12. David Gans, *Zemah David* (Jerusalem, 1983), 393.

13. Johannes Merclius, *Himlische Fewerzeichen, so im grossem lichten Gesicht des Himmels den 30. tag des Monds Januarii dieses 1560. jars auffgangen und erschienen . . .* (Nuremberg, 1560).

14. He also references a range of illnesses, earthquakes, and general misfortunes. While such fire could be terrifying, it was also a sign that the light of redemption through the Son of God was approaching.

15. Kaspar Goldwurm, *Wunderzeichen* (Frankfurt am Main, 1567), 72b.

16. Goldwurm, *Wunderzeichen*, 73b.

17. Goldwurm, *Wunderzeichen*, 74a–b. The fires in Wiesbaden he attributed to blasphemy, as well as the sins of foreigners.

18. Allemeyer, "Profane Hazard," 145–46. "Nothing on earth can be stronger / Than the sighs of pious Christians / As often a terrible fire's glow / Extinguishes the dear prayer" (146).

19. Allemeyer, "Profane Hazard," 148–49.

20. Allemeyer, "Profane Hazard," 149; Marie Luisa Allemeyer, "'Daß es wohl recht ein Feuer vom Herrn zu nennen gewesen . . .': Zur Wahrnehmung, Deutung und Verarbeitung von Stadtbränden in norddeutschen Schriften des 17. Jahrhunderts," in *Um Himmels Willen: Religion in Katastrophenzeiten*, ed. Manfred Jakubowski-Tiessen and Hartmut Lehmann (Göttingen, 2003), 201–34, here 208–9.

21. For broad categories of "disaster management," see Dirk Schubert, "The Great Fire of Hamburg, 1842: From Catastrophe to Reform," in Bankoff, Lübken, and Sand, *Flammable Cities*, 212–34, here 213.

22. Allemeyer, "Profane Hazard," 146.

23. Allemeyer, "Profane Hazard," 152–53.

24. Allemeyer, "Profane Hazard," 151; Allemeyer, "'Daß es wohl recht ein Feuer ,'" 214ff. See also *Verneute Feuer-Ordnung Eines Erbarn Raths allhie zu Nüremberg . . .* (Nuremberg, 1616), which gives particular detail for a variety of communal positions intended to prevent and fight fires.

25. Allemeyer, "Profane Hazard," 153–54; Allemeyer, "'Daß es wohl recht ein Feuer'" 217–18.

26. Niklaus Bartlome and Erika Flückiger, "Stadtzerstörungen und Wiederaufbau in der mittelalterlichen und frühneuzeitlichen Schweiz," in *Stadtzerstörung und Wiederaufbau: Zerstörungen durch Erdbeben, Feuer und Wasser*, ed. Martin Körner (Bern, 1999), vol. 1, 123–46, here 140. For a general overview, see Reinhold Reith, *Umwelt-Geschichte der Frühen Neuzeit* (Oldenbourg, 2011), 68–69, 89–91.

27. Susanne Pils, "'Vom Umgang der Stadt Wien," in Körner, *Stadtzerstörung und Wiederaufbau*, vol. 1, 173–86, here 176–86.

28. See Bartlome and Flückiger, "Stadtzerstörungen und Wiederaufbau," regarding Chur in 1574, for example, 132–33.

29. Allemeyer, "Profane Hazard," 156 ff.; for an example, see the *Kirchwärder Feuerordnung* (1673), an excerpt of which is provided in Allemeyer, "'Daß es wohl recht ein Feuer," 221.

30. Allemeyer, "Profane Hazard," 159–60.
31. Allemeyer, "Profane Hazard," 160–61, 162; Allemeyer, "'Daß es wohl recht ein Feuer,'" 229. See also Jordan Sand and Steven Wills, "Governance, Arson, and Firefighting in Edo, 1600–1868," in Bankoff, Lübken, and Sand, *Flammable Cities*, 44–62, here 47.
32. Marc David Baer, "The Great Fire of 1660 and the Islamization of Christian and Jewish Space in Istanbul," *International Journal of Middle East Studies* 36 (2004): 159–81, here 159.
33. Cited in Baer, "The Great Fire of 1660," 172.
34. Cornel Zwierlein, "The Burning of a Modern City? Istanbul as Perceived by the Agents of the Sun Fire Office, 1865–1870," in Bankoff, Lübken, and Sand, *Flammable Cities*, 82–102, here 95.
35. Bartlome and Flückiger, "Stadtzerstörungen und Wiederaufbau in der mittelalterlichen und frühneuzeitlichen Schweiz," 136.
36. Bartlome and Flückiger, "Stadtzerstörungen und Wideraufbau," 140–42.
37. Cited in numerous locations, for example, Robert Chazan, *In the Year 1096: The First Crusade and the Jews* (Philadelphia, 1996), 6.
38. Gans, *Zemah David*, 139; he also mentioned this incident in the second book of his chronicle, 393–94.
39. Abraham David, ed., *A Hebrew Chronicle from Prague, c. 1615*, trans. Leon J. Weinberger with Dena Ordan (Tuscaloosa, 1993), 46–47. In part, the purpose of such recounting was to serve as a memory for the future. The Prague chronicler simply explained, "I shall recount the events occurring in the Exile subsequent to the fifth millennium: the expulsions, miracles, and news of other occurrences befalling [the Jews] in Prague and the other lands of our long exile because of our iniquities, to serve as a token of remembrance for us and our descendants forever" (David, ed. *Hebrew Chronicle*, 21). The retelling of specifics, however, might also serve as something of a communal record.
40. Ber of Bolechow, *The Memoirs of Ber of Bolechow (1723–1805)*, trans. M. Vishnitzer (Oxford, 1922).
41. Ber of Bolechow, *The Memoirs of Ber of Bolechow*, 69–70, 71.
42. Ber of Bolechow, *The Memoirs of Ber of Bolechow*, 71.
43. Ber of Bolechow, *The Memoirs of Ber of Bolechow*, for example, 72, 74.
44. Ber of Bolechow, *The Memoirs of Ber of Bolechow*, 107.
45. Cilli Kasper-Holtkotte, *Die jüdische Gemeinde von Frankfurt/Main in der Frühen Neuzeit: Familien, Netzwerke und Konflikte eines jüdischen Zentrums* (Berlin, 2010), 19.
46. Eoin Bourke, "The Frankfurt Judengasse in Eyewitness Accounts from the Seventeenth to the Nineteenth Century," in *Ghetto Writing: Traditional and Eastern Jewry in German-Jewish Literature from Heine to Hilsenrath*, ed. Anne Fuchs and Florian Krobb (Columbia, SC, 1999), 11–24, here 15.
47. See, for example, Edward Fram, *A Window on Their World: The Court Diary of Rabbi Hayyim Gundersheim, Frankfurt am Main, 1773–1794* (Cincinnati, 2012), 162–63, 221ff.
48. Isidor Kracauer, *Die Geschichte der Judengasse in Frankfurt am Main* (Frankfurt am Main, 1906), 334; 337–38, for biographical background.
49. Thomas Carstensen and Wolfgang Henningsen, "'Gaßverbrennner,' Rabbi Cohen: Eine Frankfurter Brandstifter-Legende über die Feuerbrunst vom 14. Januar 1711,"

Tribüne: Zeitschrift zum Verständnis des Judentums 28, no. 109 (1989): 166–71, here 169. See also Kracauer, *Die Geschichte der Judengasse*, 339.

50. Carstensen and Henningsen, "'Gaßverbrennner,' Rabbi Cohen," 166.
51. Carstensen and Henningsen, "'Gaßverbrennner,' Rabbi Cohen," 166. See also Kracauer, *Geschichte der Judengasse*, 336.
52. Kracauer, *Geschichte der Judengasse*, 335; see also 338n3.
53. Kracauer, *Geschichte der Judengasse*, 336.
54. Kracauer, *Geschichte der Judengasse*, 336.
55. Kracauer, *Geschichte der Judengasse*, 337.
56. Carstensen and Henningsen, "'Gaßverbrennner,' Rabbi Cohen," 166.
57. Johann Jacob Schudt, *Jüdische Merckwürdigkeiten* (Frankfurt am Main, 1714), vol. 3, 63ff., here 65.
58. Schudt, *Jüdische Merckwürdigkeiten*, vol. 3, 66.
59. Schudt, *Jüdische Merckwürdigkeiten*, vol. 3, 72.
60. Schudt, *Jüdische Merckwürdigkeiten*, vol. 4, 128–29.
61. *Das unter den Christen vor Zeiten die Juden mit gewohnet haben . . .* (Frankfurt am Main, 1711).
62. *Das unter den Christen.*
63. Kracauer, *Geschichte der Judengasse*, 342.
64. Kracauer, *Geschichte der Judengasse*, 342–43.
65. Kracauer, *Geschichte der Judengasse*, 343.
66. Kracauer, *Geschichte der Judengasse*, 344. A couple of days later, on April 9, the city council issued an ordinance calling for street lanterns. While unrelated to the Jews, the ordinance does point to a broader concern for safety in the various quarters in the city. As the ordinance itself noted, it was in imitation of similar developments in other cities. Johann Conradin Beyerbach, *Sammlung der Verordnungen der Reichsstadt Frankfurt* (Frankfurt am Main, 1798), vol. 5, 1087; see Craig Koslofsky, *Evening's Empire: A History of the Night in Early Modern Europe* (Cambridge, 2011).
67. Kracauer, *Geschichte der Judengasse*, 346.
68. Kracauer, *Geschichte der Judengasse*, 344–46.
69. Beyerbach, *Sammlung*, 1107–8.
70. Beyerbach, *Sammlung*, 1099–1101; for the Jewish ordinance, see 1104–7.
71. Kracauer, *Geschichte der Judengasse*, 347.
72. Kracauer, *Geschichte der Judengasse*, 351.
73. Kracauer, *Geschichte der Judengasse*, 350, 352. Regarding the Bleichgarten, for example, see 356; see also reference in the imperial decree, 72–73.
74. Kracauer, *Geschichte der Judengasse*, 353.
75. Quoted in Kracauer, *Geschichte der Judengasse*, 355.
76. Kracauer, *Geschichte der Judengasse*, 341.
77. Kracauer, *Geschichte der Judengasse*, 340.
78. Robert Liberles, *Jews Welcome Coffee: Tradition and Innovation in Early Modern Germany* (Waltham, MA, 2012), 100–1.
79. Liberles, *Jews Welcome Coffee*, 102–3.
80. Kracauer, *Geschichte der Judengasse*, 358.
81. Kracauer, *Geschichte der Judengasse*, 359.
82. Kracauer, *Geschichte der Judengasse*, 359.
83. Kracauer, *Geschichte der Judengasse*, 359.
84. Kracauer, *Geschichte der Judengasse*, 359.

85. See Christhard Hoffman, "From Heinrich Heine to Isidor Kracauer: The Frankfurt Ghetto in German-Jewish Historical Culture and Historiography," in *The Frankfurt Judengasse: Jewish Life in an Early Modern German City*, ed. Margarete Schlüter, Fritz Backhaus, Gisela Engel, and Robert Liberles (London, 2010), 40–58.
86. Beginning already on page 8, in his preface.
87. Schudt, *Jüdische Merckwürdigkeiten*, vol. 6, 70–71.
88. Schudt, *Jüdische Merckwürdigkeiten*, vol. 6, 84, 85, 68.
89. Schudt, *Jüdische Merckwürdigkeiten*, vol. 6, 84, 85, 68.
90. Schudt, *Jüdische Merckwürdigkeiten*, vol. 6, 87.
91. Schudt, *Jüdische Merckwürdigkeiten*, vol. 6, 90.
92. Schudt, *Jüdische Merckwürdigkeiten*, vol. 6, 91.
93. Schudt, *Jüdische Merckwürdigkeiten*, vol. 6, 93.
94. Schudt, *Jüdische Merckwürdigkeiten*, vol. 6, 94.
95. Schudt, *Jüdische Merckwürdigkeiten*, vol. 6, 104.
96. Schudt, *Jüdische Merckwürdigkeiten*, vol. 6, 95.
97. Schudt, *Jüdische Merckwürdigkeiten*, vol. 3, 74.
98. Schudt, *Jüdische Merckwürdigkeiten*, vol. 3, 80.
99. Schudt, *Jüdische Merckwürdigkeiten*, vol. 3, 64, 69.
100. Schudt, *Jüdische Merckwürdigkeiten*, vol. 3, 70.
101. Schudt, *Jüdische Merckwürdigkeiten*, vol. 3, 71.
102. Schudt, *Jüdische Merckwürdigkeiten*, vol 3, 71.
103. Schudt, *Jüdische Merckwürdigkeiten*, vol. 3, 72.
104. Kracauer, *Geschichte der Judengasse*, 361.
105. Kracauer, *Geschichte der Judengasse*, 363.
106. Kracauer, *Geschichte der Judengasse*, 366.
107. See Dean Phillip Bell, "Marginalization and the Jews in Late Medieval Germany," *Das Mittelalter* 16 (2011): 72–93.
108. See Bell, "The Little Ice Age and the Jews."
109. See Dean Phillip Bell, *Sacred Communities: Jewish and Christian Identities in Fifteenth-Century Germany* (Leiden, 2001).
110. Alexandra Walsham, *Charitable Hatred: Tolerance and Intolerance on England 1500–1700* (Manchester, 2006), 306.
111. Walsham, *Charitable Hatred*, 322.

Bibliography

Allemeyer, Marie Luisa. "'Daß es wohl recht ein Feuer vom Herrn zu nennen gewesen . . .': Zur Wahrnehmung, Deutung und Verarbeitung von Stadtbränden in norddeutschen Schriften des 17. Jahrhunderts." In *Um Himmels Willen: Religion in Katastrophenzeiten*, edited by Manfred Jakubowski-Tiessen and Hartmut Lehmann, 201–34. Göttingen, 2003.

———. "Profane Hazard or Divine Judgement? Coping with Urban Fire in the 17th Century." *Historical Social Research* 32 (2007): 145–68.

Baer, Marc David. "The Great Fire of 1660 and the Islamization of Christian and Jewish Space in Istanbul." *International Journal of Middle East Studies* 36 (2004): 159–81.

Bankoff, George, Uwe Lübken, and Jordan Sand, ed. *Flammable Cities: Urban Conflagration and the Making of the Modern World*. Madison, 2012.

Bartlome, Niklaus, and Erika Flückiger. "Stadtzerstörungen und Wiederaufbau in der mittelalterlichen und frühneuzeitlichen Schweiz." In *Stadtzerstörung und Wiederaufbau: Zerstörungen durch Erdbeben, Feuer und Wasser*, edited by Martin Körner, vol. 1, 123–46. Bern, 1999.

Bell, Dean Phillip. "Confessionalization and Social Discipline in Early Modern Germany: A Jewish Perspective." In *Politics and Reformations: Studies in Honor of Thomas A. Brady, Jr.*, edited by Peter Wallace, Peter Starenko, Michael Printy, and Christopher Ocker, 345–72. Leiden, 2007.

———. "The Little Ice Age and the Jews: Environmental History and the Mercurial Nature of Jewish–Christian Encounters in Early Modern Germany." *AJS Review* 32, no. 1 (Spring 2008): 1–27.

———. "Marginalization and the Jews in Late Medieval Germany." *Das Mittelalter* 16 (2011): 72–93.

———. "Navigating the Flood Waters: Perspectives on Jewish Life in Early Modern Germany." *Leo Baeck Institute Yearbook* 56 (2011): 29–52.

———. *Sacred Communities: Jewish and Christian Identities in Fifteenth-Century Germany*. Leiden, 2001.

Ber of Bolechow. *The Memoirs of Ber of Bolechow (1723–1805)*. Translated by M. Vishnitzer. Oxford, 1922.

Beyerbach, Johann Conradin. *Sammlung der Verordnungen der Reichsstadt Frankfurt*, vol. 5. Frankfurt am Main, 1798.

Bourke, Eoin. "The Frankfurt Judengasse in Eyewitness Accounts from the Seventeenth to the Nineteenth Century." In *Ghetto Writing: Traditional and Eastern Jewry in German-Jewish Literature from Heine to Hilsenrath*, edited by Anne Fuchs and Florian Krobb, 11–24. Columbia, SC, 1999.

Breuer, Mordechai, and Michael Graetz, ed. *German-Jewish History in Modern Times*. Vol. 1, *Tradition and Enlightenment, 1600–1780*. New York, 1996.

Carstensen, Thomas, and Wolfgang Henningsen. "'Gaßverbrennner,' Rabbi Cohen: Eine Frankfurter Brandstifter-Legende über die Feuerbrunst vom 14. Januar 1711." *Tribüne: Zeitschrift zum Verständnis des Judentums* 28, no. 109 (1989): 166–71.

Chazan, Robert. *In the Year 1096: The First Crusade and the Jews*. Philadelphia, 1996.

Das unter den Christen vor Zeiten die Juden mit gewohnet haben . . . Frankfurt am Main, 1711.

David, Abraham, ed. *A Hebrew Chronicle from Prague, c. 1615*. Translated by Leon J. Weinberger with Dena Ordan. Tuscaloosa, 1993.

Fram, Edward. *A Window on Their World: The Court Diary of Rabbi Hayyim Gundersheim, Frankfurt am Main, 1773–1794*. Cincinnati, 2012.

Friedrichs, Christopher R. *The Early Modern City, 1450–1750*. London, 1995.

Gans, David. *Zemah David*. Jerusalem, 1983.

Goldwurm, Kaspar. *Wunderzeichen*. Frankfurt am Main, 1567.

Hoffman, Christhard. "From Heinrich Heine to Isidor Kracauer: The Frankfurt Ghetto in German-Jewish Historical Culture and Historiography." In *The Frankfurt Judengasse: Jewish Life in an Early Modern German City*, edited by Margarete Schlüter, Fritz Backhaus, Gisela Engel, and Robert Liberles, 40–58. London, 2010.

Kasper-Holtkotte, Cilli. *Die jüdische Gemeinde von Frankfurt/Main in der Frühen Neuzeit: Familien, Netzwerke und Konflikte eines jüdischen Zentrums*. Berlin, 2010.

Koslofsky, Craig. *Evening's Empire: A History of the Night in Early Modern Europe*. Cambridge, 2011.

Kracauer, Isidor. *Die Geschichte der Judengasse in Frankfurt am Main*. Frankfurt am Main, 1906.

Liberles, Robert. *Jews Welcome Coffee: Tradition and Innovation in Early Modern Germany*. Waltham, MA, 2012.

Merclius, Johannes. *Himlische Fewerzeichen, so im grossem lichten Gesicht des Himmels den 30. tag des Monds Januarii dieses 1560. jars auffgangen und erschienen . . . .* Nuremberg, 1560.

Pils, Susanne. "'. . . damit nur an wasser khain menngl erscheine . . .' Vom Umgang der Stadt Wien mit dem Feuer der frühen Neuzeit." In *Stadtzerstörung und Wiederaufbau: Zerstörungen durch Erdbeben, Feuer und Wasser*, edited by Martin Körner, vol. 1, 173–86. Bern, 1999.

Pyne, Stephen J. *Vestal Fire: An Environmental History, Told through Fire, of Europe and Europe's Encounter with the World*. Seattle, 1997.

Reith, Reinhold. *Umwelt–Geschichte der Frühen Neuzeit*. Oldenbourg, 2011.

Schudt, Johann Jacob. *Jüdische Merckwürdigkeiten*. 4 vols. Frankfurt am Main, 1714.

Toner, Jerry. *Roman Disasters*. Cambridge, 2013.

Verneute Feuer-Ordnung Eines Erbarn Raths allhie zu Nüremberg . . . Nuremberg, 1616.

Walsham, Alexandra. *Charitable Hatred: Tolerance and Intolerance on England 1500–1700*. Manchester, 2006.

III

Excavating Histories
of Religion

Figure 10.1. *Luther verbrennt die Bannandrohungsbulle* (Paul Thumann, 1872). Eisenach, Wartburg-Stiftung.

CHAPTER TEN

The Early Roots of Confessional Memory
Martin Luther Burns the Papal Bull on 10 December 1520

NATALIE KRENTZ

In the early morning of 10 December 1520, Martin Luther burned the papal bull *Exsurge Domini* ("Arise, O Lord") in front of the Elster gate in Wittenberg. This moment became a pivotal event in the German Reformation, representing for many the final and official separation of Luther and the Wittenberg reformers from the pope and the Roman Church. It also turned out to be decisive for the emergence of a new evangelical group identity. In Reformation histories of the nineteenth century, this scene is always described in a dramatic, colorful manner. Visual depictions of the event were among the most common Reformation motifs in historic paintings at that time.[1]

Within the process of Protestant identity formation, the burning of the papal bull played and still plays an important cultural role in remembering the reformers' initial triumph over the papal church. This specific rendition of the founding myth became part of memory and memorialization for the Protestant community in later centuries, and as such, the narrative demonstrates a good example for the process of "forgetting plurality." Later confessional historians imagined the events of the early Reformation within their own contexts of distinction and identity formation, and the resulting historiography reshaped the initial plurality of perceptions of what happened on 10 December 1520. As the case of the burning of the papal bull shows, the shape and direction of this later confessional historiography, however, were strongly predetermined already by the contemporaries and the protagonists themselves.

Focusing on these early roots of confessional memory, this essay explores the process of forming a confessional master narrative of the Reformation by stressing the importance of early perceptions and forms of communication in the construction of historical memory. Perceptions of and communication about the burning of the papal bull demonstrate that this process started as early as only a few days after the event itself. First, the initial plurality of perceptions and different layers of memory show the Wittenberg reformers' own contributions to later hegemonic interpretations. Second, these initial perceptions were linearized and ordered by contemporary interpretations, setting the course for the memory of subsequent generations. Finally, further shifts of meaning of these early interpretations had a significant impact on the scholarly and popular accounts on Reformation history in the nineteenth century.

The Burning of the Papal Bull *Exsurge Domini* and Its Contemporary Contexts

The history of the papal bull *Exsurge Domini* is well known and needs only to be summarized here briefly. The bull threatened Luther and his adherents with excommunication unless they recanted within a sixty-day period. It condemned forty-one tenets of Luther's doctrine as heretical, erroneous, and disruptive and ordered all of his printed works burned.[2] As a consequence, the proclamation of the bull by papal nuncio Jerome Aleander in the cities of Leuven, Liège, Mainz, Treves, and Cologne had been accompanied by the burning of Luther's books in September and October 1521.[3] In Wittenberg, the bull was delivered on 10 September 1520 along with a cover letter from the papal nuncio in Germany, the Leipzig theologian Johannes Eck.[4] In this accompanying letter, Eck requested that the University of Wittenberg no longer teach Luther's doctrine and that they ban the professors Martin Luther, Andreas Karlstadt, and Johann Dölsch.[5] When Luther and his colleagues still had not recanted by early December, about 150 students left the university and town of Wittenberg, as requested by their own local authorities.[6]

As the subsequent events show, those remaining in Wittenberg developed a growing solidarity with Luther, Karlstadt, and Dölsch. The university as well as the electoral court in Wittenberg had expected the bull and had prepared a strategy to refuse Luther's extradition to the papal authorities. Three Wittenberg law professors had proposed dismissing the bull as forged by the theologian Johannes Eck, who had been a well-known opponent to the Wittenberg professors since the Leipzig Disputation.[7] In a letter to Elector Frederick III of Saxony, Peter Burkhard, the head of the university, mentioned the bull's legally questionable delivery method as well as its missing credentials.[8] Eck had in fact contributed fodder for this effort to discredit the bull by adding a few names of his personal enemies to the bull, including humanists such as Willibald Pirckheimer.[9] Thus, the university and the electoral court decided to treat the bull as a common threat wrongly accusing some of their members.

When Luther's time to recant expired on the morning of 10 December, the Wittenberg students found a posting by Philipp Melanchthon on the parish church doors, inviting them to Holy Cross Chapel.[10] At nine in the morning, a group of students and professors gathered in the named place. The main protagonist in the subsequent events was Master Johann Agricola, who lit a bonfire and burned a few volumes of canon law, Angelo Carletti of Chivasso's *Summa angelica de casibus conscientiae* and several works of the Leipzig theologians Johann Eck and Hieronymus Emser.[11] The planned burning of books of scholastic theology had failed, as no one could spare their copies.[12] Finally, Luther himself stepped forward to the fire and tossed a copy of the papal bull into the flames. In doing so, he quietly said a few words in Latin, of which the sources give different accounts, but approximately they were "Because you have confounded the truth of God [or: the saints] may the Lord confound you in this fire," which was answered by the others with "Amen."[13]

While the professors' participation ended at that time, the students stayed at the fire and began their own spectacle. Around ten in the morning they performed a requiem for the papal books.[14] Afterward, they held a procession around town with a horse cart, decorated with the banner of a papal bull made to resemble a wind-filled sail. The citizens of Wittenberg came out onto the streets or watched the show from their windows. Along their route, the students collected more books meant for the fire. Finally, the procession returned to the fire at the Elster gate, where the students staged an elaborate burning of the collected books: A trumpet sounded the Easter Vigil, while the students carried their banners and sang the triumphal hymn "Te Deum laudamus" and the popular song "Oh du armer Judas" ("Oh poor Judas"), and, alluding to the symbolic funeral for the books, "Requiem aeternam" ("Eternal rest grant unto them").[15] The theological works from Leipzig were read out loud, provoking bursts of laughter, and then were tossed into the fire.

Obviously, these events alongside the burning of the papal bull are a telling example of the Reformation as a "ritual process," since they contain various layers of ritual language.[16] With the fire, the students gave the papal bull the punishment that its contents intended for Luther's works, which alludes to the carnival motif of the world turned upside down.[17] Moreover, this act utilizes the meaning of fire as a punishing as well as purifying element, which played an important role in medieval jurisdiction and in later Reformation iconoclasm.[18] The students' procession in the afternoon certainly contained many elements of carnival plays.[19] Ulinka Rublack has described the horse cart with the sail as an allusion to Sebastian Brant's *Ship of Fools*.[20] R. W. Scribner has interpreted the singing of the hymn "Te Deum laudamus" after the burning as an expression of joy for defeating the wrong and recovering the right order.[21]

As all these aspects show, the events of 10 December were highly symbolic acts. They contributed to the students and townspeople forming a group identity as an "evangelical" community and demonstrated their dissociation from the papal church.[22] While these aspects have been researched quite thoroughly, the different contemporary sources, the further communication of the event, and its historiographical perception have received little attention in the literature to date.[23]

The narrative of the events of 10 December, as they are depicted here, draw first from a number of eyewitness reports. These accounts mention various elements and different contexts of the event and illustrate how its meaning was not yet defined, but open to multiple interpretations. As these reports form the basis for the later historiographical narrative, their particular emphases and chronological sequencing must be established. The earliest eyewitness reports are two letters by Luther dated 10 January and 14 January 1520 and a record by the main protagonist Johann Agricola dated 10 January.[24] Also Luther's own pamphlet on the event, *Why the Books of the Pope and His Disciples Were Burned by Dr. Martin Luther*, can count as an eyewitness report, even though Luther was present only in the morning, not during the students' events in the afternoon.[25] The first copies of this pamphlet were printed in Wittenberg during December 1520. Since the new year began at Christmas, Luther must have written this report very soon after the event, between 10 December and 24 December. Another early eyewitness report is a record, probably written by an unknown Wittenberg student soon after the event.[26] In 1521, this Latin report was published in Leipzig and reprinted in Strasbourg, indicating it was written soon, but not necessarily immediately, after the event. A final early report was written by the Brandenburg bishop Hieronymus Schulz, presumably to the papal nuncio Aleander.[27] Schulz's claims to be an eyewitness seem implausible.[28]

These reports reveal a plurality of contemporary perceptions and different focal points. First, it was not only the papal bull that was burned, but also works of canon law and of critics of Luther and the other Wittenberg theologians, especially of those from Leipzig University. During the students' spectacle, these works were even read out loud and derided. The traditional rivalry between the universities of Leipzig and Wittenberg was obviously an important feature in both book-burning ceremonies. Among these different books discussed, the papal bull was not even the main focus for many of the organizers and participants. Melanchthon's announcement on the door of the parish church mentioned papal decretals and books of scholastic theology (*impii pontificarum constitutionum et theologiae scholasticae libri*), but not the bull.[29] In his letter written on 10 December to George Spalatin, Luther listed the papal bull as only one document among many other books, of which canon laws and the works of his academic opponents seemed much more important.[30]

Even Johann Agricola, one of the main protagonists, names various different "books written by the pope and his adherents" along with the papal bull in his early report.[31] Overall, among the different books burned that day, the works of canon law and of the academic opponents from Leipzig, Emser, and Eck appear to have been the main target of their efforts.

Second, plurality can be observed concerning the protagonists involved. The burning of the papal bull was obviously not only Luther's historic deed. A number of different people were important to the events. Philipp Melanchthon and Johann Agricola planned the burning of the books in the morning: Melanchthon posted the invitation to the parish church door, and Agricola was the main protagonist during the burning ceremony. Finally, the students performed the spectacle in the afternoon. As the early reports of the eyewitnesses show, the meaning of these two ceremonial burnings of books was ambivalent and not yet defined. The various different layers of meaning demonstrated the academic rivalry between Wittenberg and Leipzig, the process of identity formation of citizens and students, juvenile exuberance, the rejection of traditional church ceremonies, and finally, the rejection of the papal authority.

These observations raise the question, how did the burning of the papal bull by Luther—and not for instance the burning of the canon law by Agricola or the much more prominent spectacle of the Wittenberg students—become the decisive historical event for Protestant memory? Luther initially played only a minor role in the whole progression of events. Even if we assume that he tossed the bull into the fire himself, which has been a matter of scholarly debate, since not all reports mention it, this action was little noticed in contrast to the other events of the day.[32] The whole ceremony of the professors in the morning took place outside the walls of town. Thus, the citizens of Wittenberg would have been unable to observe or perhaps even notice these events. It was only the spectacle of the students in the afternoon that drew public attention in town. For these reasons, Luther's burning of the papal bull would probably have quickly disappeared into oblivion were it not for Luther's next action.

Forgetting Plurality—Toward a Hegemonic Interpretation

This plurality of perceptions of the event changed the very next day when Luther took back the reins steering the interpretation. As a first step, he explained the meaning of the previous day's actions to his students in his morning lecture at the university. The report of the anonymous student gives an account of Luther's words and their reception by the students. According to the student, Luther presented the events as having drastic consequences by giving the choice between eternal hell for those who stayed with the Roman Church and temporal martyrdom for those who went with Luther.[33] Luther explained the act of the burning of the papal laws (*papisticis statutis*) as a symbol, a turning point in the history of salvation when the pope was recognized as the Antichrist.[34] As the student reported, Luther's audience adopted this interpretation and was deeply impressed by the lecture. In the work, the student compares Luther to the angel from the book of Revelation, who pastured the sheep of Christ in the true word of God.[35] Only with Luther's subsequent interpretations did the event reach its full potential for impact. The initial book-burning ceremony had been unremarkable: it took place outside town with only a small audience, and Luther played a minor part in it. Moreover, at the outset it seemed as much an ironic attack on the theological faculty in Leipzig as on the pope or the Roman Church. But with his explanation to the students, Luther generated and spread a hegemonic interpretation, which made the burning of the books an act of liberation from the Roman Church and Luther himself its main protagonist.

How did this shift in interpretation occur? This process began during the afternoon of 10 December, when the act of burning the papal books in the morning developed a life of its own, which changed and broadened its initially intended interpretation. First, the students and citizens did not know or care about the plans of the professors to treat the bull as a forgery by Johannes Eck. The spectacle in the afternoon became an attack on the Roman Church as a whole when they ridiculed the Mass and requiems or ironically used hymns. Thus, when the book burning became known in town through the ceremony of the students and townspeople, it was already performed in a different, broader context of meaning. Second, as his lecture indicates, Luther realized, or constructed, the meaning of his own symbolic action at the Elster gate in response to the students' actions in the afternoon. With his lecture the next morning explaining the book burning, Luther not only adopted these new interpretations, he also reclaimed leadership over the movement by stressing his own role in the ceremony. This shift becomes apparent if one compares the short, casual description of his gestures and words during the ceremony itself with his long and powerfully eloquent explanations in the lecture of the next day.

Publications soon spread information about the events of 10 December outside the town of Wittenberg. The unknown student's report, with its record of Luther's 11 December lecture, was printed in 1521 at Leipzig and Strasbourg only in Latin and with a small print run.[36] In contrast, Luther's own pamphlet, *Why the Books*, published in numerous German and two Latin editions, addressed a broader audience.[37] The first print run circulated by late December 1520 in Wittenberg and Leipzig.[38] This pamphlet rendered Luther as the main protagonist and spread the interpretation of the burning ceremony as the final breakup of the Reformation with the papal church.[39] Luther's emphasis still remained on the burning of the canon law and the books of the controversial theologians, not the burning of the papal bull. The work contains a list of thirty articles proving canon law illegitimate, whereas the burning of the papal bull is not even mentioned.[40] The shift of meaning from the different local and academic contexts toward the burning ceremony as a symbol for the breakup with Rome was reinforced and spread by another anonymous pamphlet, *A German Requiem for the Burned Bull and Canon Law*, printed in 1520.[41] Although the burning of the bull appears here in the title, the pamphlet only mentions in its contents on the burning of the canon law, the "limping and lame papal Canon Laws," which Luther burned fearlessly.[42] Here, the interpretation moves even further toward the later German national view, as the burning of the canon law is seen as liberation from "Roman tyranny."[43] Luther's interpretation in the lecture and these early pamphlets thus contained at this stage already many but not all important elements of a specific evangelical narrative.

Just as with the pamphlets of the reformers, the pamphlets of Luther's opponents and critics reinforced and spread Luther's interpretation of the event. The Catholic controversialist theologian Thomas Murner picked up the topic immediately in 1521 by countering Luther's pamphlet and his thirty articles against the canon law.[44] In the same year, Henry VIII of England used the burning of the canon law as an argument against Luther's cause in a letter responding to Luther. This letter was reprinted in a German translation by Murner to demonstrate Henry's rejection of the Lutheran Reformation.[45] Subsequently, various other Catholic controversialists and critics of Luther followed suit and frequently used the subject of Luther's burning of the canon law in pamphlets against Luther.[46] Paul Bachmann questioned Luther's motives for the burning of the canon law, highlighting Luther's negative character as someone who sought revenge for the burning of his own books.[47] Although all of these pamphlets disapproved of the burning ceremony in Wittenberg and presented it as the final proof of Luther's heresy, they reinforced the impression that it was a decisive event and that Luther was its main protagonist.

With his university lecture and the ensuing pamphlet controversy, Luther laid a path for the subsequent memory of the burning of the papal books by placing himself into the spotlight as the protagonist and by interpreting the event as an important turning point within the history of the Reformation and of Christian salvation in general. With the printed pamphlets, this view not only spread among contemporaries, but also was passed on to future generations of historians.

Historiographical Perception in the Sixteenth and Nineteenth Century

The shape and direction of the narrative was set when later confessional historiography processed the subject. This process began during the second half of the sixteenth century immediately after Luther's death, when Protestants felt an urgent need to record their own history.[48] One of the first projects of Protestant history was the compilation and edition of Luther's works. The first edition was printed in Wittenberg in 1546, immediately after Luther's death, a second edition in Jena in 1557.[49] With the publication of these early editions of Luther's works, the initial plurality of accounts, interpretations, and events on 10 December were further reduced to those centering on Luther. It is notable that none of the early editions include the report about the students' actions in the afternoon of 10 December. Even when the unknown student's report of 10 December events is included, the editors shortened its second part describing the students' actions. This applies to the Wittenberg edition of 1546 and the Jena edition of 1557 as well as to further sixteenth-century editions.[50] This was not a conscious act of censorship. Rather, the early editors of Luther's works were not interested in the students' actions because their purpose was to preserve the memory of Luther's theology and his deeds. They sought to create a common memory and identity to keep the group of his followers together during the theological controversies of the late sixteenth century. Although the actions and rituals of the Wittenberg students reveal a plurality of perception of great interest to modern scholars, they might just not have seemed relevant to the editors at this time.

These tendencies toward uniformity of narrative can be observed in sixteenth-century Protestant history writing on the Reformation. The first and most influential example of this genre is the scholarly work of the sixteenth-century historian Johannes Sleidanus.[51] Sleidanus's main historical work on Reformation history, *De statu religionis et reipublicae Carolo Quinto, Caesare, Commentarii* (1555), written for the Protestant Schmalkaldic League, provides a chronological narrative of the reform movement from 1517 to 1555.[52] Recent scholars, such as Donald R. Kelley, writing on sixteenth-century historiography have used Sleidanus as an example of an emerging professionalization of history, arguing that he pursued the ideal of an "objective" history and collected a great number of contemporary sources.[53] Other scholars have pointed out that Sleidanus's selection of sources clearly reveals that he was a Protestant historian.[54] Matthias Pohlig argues that Sleidanus's Protestant bias is evident in how he placed the Reformation within his work as a singular historical event.[55] Alexandra Kess outlined the different political contexts of his work but stressed that Sleidanus's work, unlike typical Protestant historiography of his time, was only indirectly polemical.[56]

These observations are all exemplified in Sleidanus's description of the burning of the papal books on 10 December, which Sleidanus presents as one of the important events of the Reformation. He draws this historical narrative from the above-mentioned pamphlets, paraphrasing Luther's *Why the Books* in detail.[57] In his narrative, based on the interpretation found in Luther's pamphlet, Luther appears as not simply the main actor, but rather as the only protagonist, leading his students and colleagues to the place outside the Elster gate where he burned the canon law and the "most recent papal decree" (i.e., the bull).[58] By contrast, he does not mention the background of the rivalry between the scholars of Leipzig and Wittenberg or the burning and ridiculing of Emser's and Eck's works. The same applies to the spectacle of the students and citizens in the afternoon, which Sleidanus omits. In his narrative, there is only one event: the burning of the papal bull and books performed by Luther alone.

Sleidanus further established and aligned the narrative of the Wittenberg book burning. Typical for Sleidanus's work is the use of contemporary sources, often quoted literally. But his selection of the sources, which was generally influenced by his privileged access to Protestant material, led also in this case to a bias. Based on Luther's printed pamphlets, his description was influenced by Luther's own interpretation, developed immediately after the event. Just as he had singled out the Reformation as a historical event, Sleidanus singled out specific events such as the burning of the papal books and, due to his sources, thereby privileged specific views. Sleidanus's early historical work established these interpretations and passed them on to subsequent generations, and he reinforced the unambiguity of the narrative by eliminating the afternoon spectacle afternoon and strengthening Luther's own role. In this way, his sixteenth-century work already contained the most important elements of the later historiography on the bonfire in Wittenberg.

In the nineteenth century, the subject of the Wittenberg book burning of 10 December became increasingly relevant. In the post-Napoleonic era, German history developed toward a new discipline characterized by both new academic standards of objectivity grounded in a critical interpretation of the sources and a political claim of serving the emerging nation-state.[59] The Reformation became a key subject of historians in Protestant Prussia, and Reformation histories, scholarly as well as popular, began to illustrate the burning of the papal bull extensively and dramatically. One of the most influential scholarly works of this era of "historicism" is Prussian historian Leopold von Ranke's *German History at the Age of the Reformation* (1839–47).[60] The burning of the papal bull appears here as an act of the "hero" (*Held*) Martin Luther and as a crucial scene by instigating a national resistance against Rome for the first time. According to Ranke, this act drew the attention of the whole "nation" to Wittenberg.[61]

The nineteenth-century Catholic historian Johannes Janssen wrote about the scene in a similar way, yet with a different judgment. As many Prussian Catholics did, the ordained priest, theologian, and historian Janssen changed his initial pro-Prussian position in the 1870s in reaction to the Kulturkampf policy against Catholicism in Otto von Bismarck's Prussia.[62] His views on the Reformation contradicted Ranke's; with his positive view on late medieval religion and his anti-national interpretation of the Reformation, his works have been even described as the "Anti-Ranke."[63] The second volume of his work, *History of the German People: State of the German People since the Beginning of the Political-Ecclesiastical Revolution* (1879), describes the Reformation as leading to a social revolution, which culminated in the Peasants' War of 1525.[64] The burning of the papal bull by Luther had an important place within his narrative of the Reformation. Like Ranke, Janssen regarded the burning of the papal bull as an incident of national importance and Luther as its only protagonist.[65] But while Protestant Ranke presented the event as the beginning of national liberation and unity leading to the Prussian-German nation-state, the Catholic Janssen saw it as the beginning of upheaval and antagonism leading to enduring social unrest and wars of religion.

A third example of trends in nineteenth-century scholarship is the account of historian Friedrich von Bezold, *History of the German Reformation* (1886).[66] Born in 1848 and more than fifty years younger than Ranke, Bezold was a national-liberal history professor whose scholarly career postdated the foundation of the German Empire in 1870. While confessional conflicts did not play a major role in his work, he saw the importance of the Reformation in its influence on the growing role of the territorial states, which finally led to the nineteenth-century national state. Depicting the burning of the papal bull, Bezold shared Ranke's and Janssen's interpretation of Luther's central role as the only protagonist, although he abstained from confessional judgments. More than that, he shared their views of the crucial importance of this event within the history of the Reformation, calling the burning of the papal bull a "beacon in a war of life and death."[67] The central meaning of this historical event thus remained, even without strong confessional motives of the author.

As these three different scholarly accounts show, regardless of their confessional or political bias, nineteenth-century interpretations made the burning of the papal bull a question of national identity and reinforced Luther's central role by declaring him a hero. But even with this shift of meaning, the narrative itself essentially remained as prepared by Luther and reinforced in the pamphlet controversy and by the early historian Sleidanus. Just as in the late sixteenth-century accounts, the students' actions are not mentioned by Ranke, Janssen, and Bezold, who describe only the actions of the professors in the morning. More important than the reactions of random students seemed those of Luther's important contemporaries, such as Lazarus Spengler, Ulrich Zasius, or the imperial councilor Hieronymus von Endorf, whose reaction Ranke quotes as proof that the "attention of the whole nation" focused on Luther's deed.[68]

For these nineteenth-century historians focusing on "great men making history," the Wittenberg students' actions would not have been of much interest in any way. But their view on the event was also biased by the available compilations of sources, which focused the historian's view on Luther. By the end of the nineteenth century, the first critical editions rediscovered the description of the students' procession and rituals, which the Weimar edition describes as "a record that gives us a graphic image of the events during and after the burning of the papal bull on 10 December 1520."[69] Heinrich Boehmer's critical early twentieth-century account was thus the first since 1520 to deal again with the students' spectacle, which Boehmer found interesting, though by contrast to modern cultural historians, not essentially relevant to his interpretation of the event.[70]

This narrative received its final version by the alteration of one further detail during the nineteenth century. As shown above, the burning of the papal bull by Luther had played only a minor role within the events of 10 December 1520, and the bull was burned together with the canon law and other books. Luther, as well as his opponents in the pamphlet controversy, mainly referred to the burning of the canon law or the books of the theologians from Leipzig. The burning of the papal bull was mentioned only in passing. The nineteenth-century accounts changed the burning of the canon law and the books of political opponents into the burning of the papal bull. A possible explanation for the shift, which was suggested by Heinrich Boehmer, was that canon law had lost its importance in nineteenth-century Prussia and might have been less known to historians of that era.[71] By contrast, for historians of earlier centuries and for Luther's contemporaries, the burning of the canon laws was a much greater attack on the legal and social order in general than the burning of a single bull would have been. For nineteenth-century scholars, the thunderbolt of the Roman ban added a more adequate and fitting object for colorful allegories in paintings and vivid historical narratives. As the following examples show, the growing national-liberal movement used the image of the burning of the bull in numerous popular and scholarly contexts.

Similar observations to those in scholarly works were made in nineteenth-century popular accounts describing Luther's burning of the papal bull. One of the first works to deal with the burning of the papal bull instead of the canon law was Zacharias Werner's popular stage play *Martin Luther or the Consecration of Power* (1807), often performed in early nineteenth-century Prussia.[72] As in the scholarly works, Luther not only appears here as the main protagonist, but acts as a lone hero, even against the advice of his future wife Katharina and his closest friend Philipp Melanchthon.[73] Writing during the Napoleonic era, Werner depicts Luther as an example for the future of German national identity, combining Germanic and Christian elements as typical for this era.[74] The book-burning ceremony emerged as a declaration of German national independence from the Roman papal slavery, now recast as an analogy for the contemporary wish for liberation from the Napoleonic reign.[75]

A few years later, Werner's play was burned at the Wartburg Festival in 1817, after Werner had converted to Catholicism in 1811. Ironically, the students at the Wartburg Festival used the memory of the Reformation and the burning of the papal bull in the same way as Werner had in his stage play. On the three hundredth anniversary of the Reformation in 1817 and the fourth anniversary of the Battle of Leipzig, about five hundred national-liberal students ascended to Wartburg Castle near Eisenach, where Luther hid after the Diet of Worms in 1521–22 to celebrate the end of the Napoleonic era and demonstrate for liberal reforms and national unity.[76] After the official festival, a number of students staged a book burning of "reactionary" literary works and symbols of Napoleon.[77] During this book-burning ceremony, two of the students, Ludwig Roediger and Hans Ferdinand Massmann, gave a brief address with reference to the burning of the papal bull by their German "fatherland's hero" (*Vaterlandshelden*) Martin Luther.[78]

These nineteenth-century interpretations used the memory of the Reformation event for their own purposes of national identity. The plurality of protagonists, burned works, motives, and contexts was now turned into a linear narrative. The burning of different books was reduced to the burning of one single bull, and Luther became one of the few "great men making history," who, according to the nineteenth-century concept of history, influenced the course of things. However, this narrative was not newly constructed in the nineteenth century in its entirety. Rather, it was strongly influenced by the interpretations of earlier times, such as Luther's own lecture, and those of the pamphlets, which provided the sources for later generations of historians.

The Early Roots of Confessional Memory

While the Wittenberg book burning initially was a rather small and unremarkable event, the history of the shift in its relative importance began by the afternoon of the same day with the students' action that first drew local attention to the book burning. Its significance as a decisive event in the history of salvation emerged the next day in Luther's lecture, an interpretation spread further in pamphlets. Luther's later role as a hero was predisposed by his own lecture given the day after the event and the pamphlet published shortly thereafter. By contrast, the role of Agricola and Melanchthon as organizers and main protagonists, the burning of the books of the academic rivals from Leipzig, and the students' spectacle soon disappeared from the later master narrative. These observations on the importance of early interpretations, which continue to affect current historical accounts, draw the attention back to the contemporary use of memory. The burning of the books in Wittenberg became an identity-forming memory of the early Wittenberg Reformation very soon after the event itself, which was kept carefully and intentionally.

An early perception of this memory from the outside is stated in the report of the traveler Johannes Kessler from Switzerland, who visited Wittenberg in summer 1522, one and a half years after the event.[79] Kessler adopted Luther's interpretation, including quoting long portions of Luther's pamphlet in his report. During his stay in Wittenberg, Kessler visited many memorial sites of the Reformation, such as the castle church and the parish church, but also the site outside the Elster gate, where the canon law had been burned. To give his report more credibility, he added that he had seen the "battlefield" with his own eyes.[80] In the summer of 1522, the site of the book burning was already considered a place of historical memory, which was shown to foreign visitors. This illustrates again that the Wittenberg reformers understood their own symbolic actions—such as the burning of the papal bull or the canon laws—as historically meaningful and started to build their own monuments for their contemporaries early on.

Natalie Krentz is a lecturer in early modern history at Friedrich-Alexander-University Erlangen-Nuremberg. Her research interests include the history of the Reformation, rituals in the early modern community, memory cultures, and gender in early modern Europe. Her dissertation on rituals and power in early Reformation Wittenberg was distinguished with the doctoral award of the German Staedtler Foundation and appeared in print in the series "Studies in the Late Middle Ages, Humanism and the Reformation" as *Ritualwandel und Deutungshoheit. Die frühe Reformation in der Residenzstadt Wittenberg 1500–1533* (Tübingen, 2014).

Notes

1. Isabel Skokan, *Germania und Italia: Nationale Mythen und Heldengestalten in Gemälden des 19. Jahrhunderts* (Berlin, 2009), 193–94; and Werner Hofmann, *Luther und die Folgen für die Kunst* (Munich, 1983), 493–570.
2. On the bull itself and the theological criticism of Luther's doctrine, see Hans J. Hillerbrand, "Martin Luther and the Bull Exsurge Domine," *Theological Studies* 30 (1969): 108–12. For an English translation of the bull, see Beresford J. Kidd, ed., *Documents Illustrative of the Continental Reformation* (Oxford, 1967), 74–79.
3. Gerhard Müller, "Die drei Nuntiaturen Aleanders in Deutschland 1520/21, 1531/32, 1538/39," in *Causa Reformationis: Beiträge zur Reformationsgeschichte und zur Theologie Martin Luthers*, ed. Gerhard Müller (Gütersloh, 1989), 249–303, esp. 255–56.
4. Johannes Eck to the University of Wittenberg, 3 October 1520, in *Urkundenbuch der Universität Wittenberg*, ed. Walter Friedensburg, 2 vols. (Magdeburg, 1926), vol. 1, 160–61; and Martin Brecht, *Martin Luther*, 3 vols. (Stuttgart, 1987), vol. 1, 382. It is unclear why Eck decided to send a messenger instead of delivering the bull himself. Brecht suggests that Eck did not dare to enter the territory of Electoral Saxony.
5. Friedensburg, *Urkundenbuch*, vol. 1, 106–7.

6. Ruth Kastner, ed., *Quellen zur Reformation 1517–1555* (Darmstadt, 1994), 107–9, George Spalatin to the Elector Frederick of Saxony, 3 December 1520.

7. Friedensburg, *Urkundenbuch*, vol. 1, 107, Professors Wolfgang Stählin, Hieronymus Schurff, and Christian Beyer to Duke John of Saxony, 23 October 1520.

8. Peter Fabisch and Erwin Iserloh, ed., *Dokumente zur Causa Lutheri 1517–1521* (Münster, 1991), vol. 2, 335.

9. Euan Cameron, *The European Reformation* (Oxford, 1991), 102; and Lewis W. Spitz, *The Religious Renaissance of the German Humanists* (Cambridge, MA, 1963), 177–78.

10. "Philippi Melanchthonis intimatio Wittenbergae in aede Parochiali affixa," *D. Martin Luthers Werke: Kritische Gesamtausgabe. Schriften* (c. 80 vols., Weimar, 1883–), vol. 7 (1897), 183 (hereafter cited as WA). The original document was not preserved. Although the earliest transcription does not name the author of the posting, the first editor, Ernst Ludwig Emser, reprinted it in the nineteenth century as "Luther's posting." Ernst Ludwig Emser, ed., *Luthers Briefwechsel*, vol. 3 (Stuttgart 1898), 18. This shows again that the nineteenth-century historian's view of the whole event was centered on Luther as the main protagonist. However, the content of the posting makes clear that Luther cannot be the author, since he is mentioned here in the third person: "ut pios ac euangelicos Lutheri libros exusserint." The editors of the WA follow a handwritten inscription that was found on an early print of the pamphlet *Exustionis Antichristianorum Decretalium Acta* (Leipzig, 1521), [VD 16 E4740]; WA, vol. 7, 184–86, n. 14.

11. Jens-Martin Kruse, *Universitätstheologie und Kirchenreform: Die Anfänge der Reformation in Wittenberg 1516–22* (Mainz, 2002), 267. The reports are contradictory about which exact books were burned.

12. "Thomam habere non potuimus, dan nymandtt hatt In wellen lassen fahren, alioque combustus, Scotum nemo dedit." [Johann Agricola], Max Perlach, and Johannes Luther, ed., "Ein neuer Bericht über Luthers Verbrennung der Bannbulle," *Sitzungsberichte der königlich-preußischen Akademie der Wissenschaften* (Berlin, 1907), 95–102, here 100. Presumably the books were used for teaching and composing controversial literature.

13. For the different Latin versions, see "Quia tu contubasti veritatem Dei, conturbet te hodie Dominus in ignem istum," in [Johann Agricola], Perlach, and Luther, "Ein neuer Bericht," 6, and "'Quia,' inquit, 'tu conturbasti sanctum Domini, Ideoque te conturbet ignis aeternus,' Anonymus, *Exustionis Antichristianorum Decretalium Acta*, WA, vol. 7, 184. See also, Kurt Aland, *A History of Christianity*, trans. James L. Schaaf, 2 vols. (Philadelphia, 1985–86), vol. 1, 91.

14. *Exustionis Antichristianorum Decretalium Acta*, WA, vol. 7, 184–86. The following part is drawn from this printed report by the unknown student.

15. Robert W. Scribner, "Ritual and Reformation," in *The German People and the Reformation*, ed. R. Po-Chia Hsia (London, 1990), 122–44, here 119. Scribner argues that song "Oh du armer Judas" became typical for later iconoclastic actions.

16. Edward Muir, "The Reformation as a Ritual Process," in *Ritual in Early Modern Europe*, 3rd ed. (Cambridge, 2000), 185–228. On the burning of the papal bull, see Robert W. Scribner, "Reformation, Carnival, and the World Turned Upside-Down," *Social History* 3 (1978): 303–29, here 304–5; Anselm Schubert, "Das Lachen der Ketzer. Zur Selbstinszenierung der frühen Reformation," *Zeitschrift für Theologie und Kirche* 108 (2011): 405–30; Brecht, *Martin Luther*, 403–6; Kruse, *Universitäts-*

theologie, 267–73; and Julius Boehmer, "Luther und der 10. Dezember 1520," *Luther-Jahrbuch* 2–3 (1920–21): 7–53, esp. 33–34.

17. Scribner, "Reformation, Carnival," 326–29.

18. Jacques LeGoff, *The Birth of Purgatory*, trans. Arthur Goldhammer (Aldershot, 1990). On Reformation iconoclasm, see Margaret Aston, "Iconoclasm in England: Rites of Destruction by Fire," in *Bilder und Bildersturm im Spätmittelalter und in der frühen Neuzeit*, ed. Robert W. Scribner (Wiesbaden, 1990), 175–202.

19. Scribner, "Reformation, Carnival," 304.

20. Ulinka Rublack, *Die Reformation in Europa*, 2nd ed. (Frankfurt am Main, 2006), 26.

21. Scribner, "Reformation, Carnival," 328.

22. For a more detailed interpretation of this aspect, see Natalie Krentz, *Ritualwandel und Deutungshoheit: Die frühe Reformation in der Residenzstadt Wittenberg (1500–1533)* (Tübingen, 2014), 125–39.

23. No scholar has revisited these subjects since Boehmer's first critical article about the sources and their historiographical perception.

24. *Martin Luthers Werke. Kritische Gesamtausgabe (Weimarer Ausgabe). 4. Abteilungen, Briefwechsel* (Weimar: Böhlau, 1883–) (hereafter WA Br.), vol. 2, 234–35, Luther to George Spalatin, 10 December 1520; WA Br., vol. 2, 245–47, Luther to Johann von Staupitz, 14 January 1521; and [Johann Agricola], Perlach, Luther, "Ein neuer Bericht," 6.

25. Martin Luther, *Warumb des Bapsts und seyner Jungernn bucher von Doct. Martino Luther vorbrannt seynn. Lasz auch antzeygen wer do will, warumb sie D. Luthers bucher vorprennet haben* (Wittenberg, 1520); WA, vol. 7, 161–86. The WA follows the Wittenberg print, which is not included in VD 16. A second early print was issued in Leipzig in 1520 (VD16 L 7362), in 1521 in Zürich (VD16 L 7374), Worms (VD16 L 7373 and L 7372); and Schlettstatt (VD16 L 7370 and L 7371). There are also two Latin translations of this pamphlet, printed in Worms and Antwerp (?); see WA, vol. 7, 157. On the different early prints, see WA, vol. 17, 154–55.

26. *Exustionis Antichristianorum decretalium acta* (Leipzig, 1521) [VD16 E 4740]; the Strasbourg print is not included in VD 16, but mentioned in WA, vol. 7, 184.

27. "Die Verbrennung der Bannbulle durch Luther (1520 Dezb. 10). Ein zeitgenössischer Bericht (von Hieronymus Schulz)," ed. Walter Friedensburg, *Quellen und Forschungen aus italienischen Archiven und Bibliotheken* 1 (1898): 320–21. Only a fragment of the original letter is preserved. Friedensburg found it in the documents of the papal nuncio Aleander in the Vatican Archives in Rome.

28. "nempe quod heri sub crepusculum ab Havelburgio domum reversus acceperim." Friedenberg, *Quellen*, 320–21. Schulz writes that he saw Luther burning the book in the dawn on his way back home from Havelberg. By contrast, according to all other reports, Luther's action at the fire took place in the morning, not in the evening. Schultz seems to confuse the events of the morning and the afternoon. Moreover, Wittenberg and Havelberg are in opposite directions to the bishop's residence in Ziesar so that it seems unlikely that he passed by Wittenberg on his way home. For these reasons, we can either assume that the bishop presented himself as an eye-witness to give his report credibility or that these discrepancies result from reading mistakes in the edition of the fragmentary original source.

29. "Philippi Melanchthonis imitatio Wittenbergae in aede Parrochiali affixa," WA, vol. 7, 163.

30. "exusti sunt Wittenbergae, ad orientalem portam, juxta S. Crucem, omnes libri Papae: Decretum, Decretales, Sext[us], Clemen[tinae], Extravargantes et Bulla novissima Leonis X., item Summa Angelica, Chrysopassus Ecii, et alia eiusdem autoris, Emseri, et quaedam alia, quae adiectam per alios sunt." WA Br., vol. 2, 234–35, Luther to Spalatin, 10 December 1520.

31. "seyn alhir zu Wittenberg verbrent worden alle die bucher, die vom Babst zu Rhome, vnnd die Ime anhengigk geschrieben vnnd publiciert als Nemlich Decretum Decretales Sextus Clemenciarum com extrauagantibus dicbolicis." [Johann Agricola], Perlach, and Luther, "Ein neuer Bericht," 6.

32. Hans Beschorner, "Die sogenannte Bannbulle und ihre angebliche Verbrennung durch Luther am 10. Dezember 1520," in *Forschungen aus mitteldeutschen Archiven: Zum 60. Geburtstag von Helmut Kretzschmar*, ed. Staatliche Archivverwaltung im Staatssekretariat für innere Angelegenheiten (Berlin (East), 1953), 315–28.

33. *Exustionis*, WA, vol. 7, 186.

34. *Exustionis*, WA, vol. 7, 186.

35. "Luttherum esse viventis dei angelum, qui palabundas christi oves pascat solo veritatis verbo." *Exustionis*, WA, vol. 7, 186.

36. See n. 26.

37. Luther, *Warumb des Bapsts*, WA, vol. 7, 161–82; see also n. 25.

38. Luther, *Warumb des Bapsts*, WA, vol. 7, vol. 7, 154.

39. "Der Bapst ist eyn gott auff erdenn ubir alle hymmlische, erdisch, geystlich unnd weltlich und ist alles seynn eygen, dem niemandt darff sagenn. Was thustu?" Luther, *Warumb des Bapsts*, WA, vol. 7, 177.

40. Luther, *Warumb des Bapsts*, WA, vol. 7, 165–75.

41. *Das deutsche Requiem der verbrannten Bulle und der päpstlichen Rechte* (Augsburg/Straßbourg, 1520) [VD16 D 676], in *Flugschriften der frühen Reformationsbewegung (1518–1524)*, ed. Adolf Laube, Sigrid Looß, and Annerose Schneider, 2 vols. (Vaduz, 1983), vol. 1, 58–60.

42. "hinckenden vnnd lamen// Bäbpstlich gaystlichen Recht." *Das deutsche Requiem*, 58. The fact that the bull appears in the title, but not the contents of the pamphlet is also mentioned by Boehmer, "Luther und der 10. Dezember," 52.

43. "ir erledigte Teutschen erfrewet euch, ja frolocket, alle christglaubige menschen, dan der hart strick der menschlichen recht und gesetz ist durch goetlichen willen und hilff gleich als mit einem scharpfen beyel zerhawen." *Das deutsche Requiem*, 58.

44. Thomas Murner, *Wie doctor. M.|| Luter vß falsch||en vrsachen bewegt Dz || geistlich recht ver||brennet hat* (Strasbourg, 1521) [VD16 M 7094]. For a general overview on early Reformation Catholic polemical pamphlets, see Adolf Laube, "Einleitung," in *Flugschriften gegen die Reformation (1518–1524)*, ed. Adolf Laube and Ulman Weiss (Berlin, 1997), 21–50.

45. Henry VIII / Thomas Murner, *Ein brieff des Edlen Künigs vß Engelandt/ zů || den Fürsten von Sachßen/ von dem Luther.|| Hertzog J[oe]rgen vß Sachßen antwurt.||(Doctor T.Murner || hats verteutscht.||)* (Strasbourg, 1521) [VD 16, E 1316], in *Flugschriften gegen die Reformation (1525–1530)*, ed. Adolf Laube and Ulman Weiss, 2 vols. (Berlin, 2000), vol. 1, 371–98, here 383.

46. "Paul Bachmann, *Martin[us] lu||ther Wy es eyn man sey Vnnd || was er furt im schylde Das || vindest du in diesem spruch || hy bey Gleych wye in || eynem bylde.|| Omnis caro ad similem sibi cō||iungetur et omnis homo simili || suo sociabitur Ecclesiastici ter||cio*

decimo capitulo || (Leipzig, 1522)," in Laube et al., *Flugschriften gegen die Reformation (1518–1524)*, 362–84, esp. 373.

47. "Luther hat nicht auß liebe der warheyt, sunder auß argelist tzu czornygem neit, wolbedachter rachung ... daß geistliche recht verprent." Bachmann, "Martin Luther," 373.

48. For sixteenth-century historiography on the Reformation, see Markus Völkel, "German Historical Writing from the Reformation to the Enlightenment," in *The Oxford History of Historical Writing*, ed. José Rabasa, Masayuki Sato, Eduardo Tortarolo, and Daniel Woolf, 5 vols. (Oxford, 2011), vol. 3, 325–46, esp. 329–31; Matthias Pohlig, *Zwischen Gelehrsamkeit und konfessioneller Identitätsstiftung. Lutherische Kirchen- und Universalgeschichtsschreibung 1546–1617* (Tübingen, 2007); and Bruce Gordon, "The Changing Face of Protestant History and Identity in the Sixteenth Century," in *Protestant History and Identity in Sixteenth Century Europe*, ed. Bruce Gordon, 2 vols. (Aldershot, 1996), vol. 1, 1–22.

49. Eike Wolgast and Hans Volz, *Geschichte der Lutherausgaben im 16. Jahrhundert*, WA, vol. 60, 429–637.

50. WA, vol. 7, 184. Even the popular eighteenth-century German edition by Walch printed only a translation of the shortened text; Johann Georg Walch, *Dr. Martin Luthers sämtliche Schriften*, 23 vols. (Jena, 1740–53), vol. 15, col. 1915–27.

51. For a discussion of Sleidanus's work as a historian, see Alexandra Kess, *Johannes Sleidanus and the Protestant Vision of History* (Aldershot, 2008), 89–118; Pohlig, *Gelehrsamkeit*, 161–72; Donald R. Kelley, "Johannes Sleidanus and the Origins of History as a Profession," *Journal of Modern History* 52 (1980): 573–98; and Thomas Lau, "Johannes Sleidanus (urspr. Philippi)," in *Hauptwerke der Geschichtsschreibung*, ed. Volker Reinhardt (Stuttgart, 1997), 584–87.

52. Johannes Sleidanus, [*De statu religionis et rei publicae Carolo V. Caesare commentarii* (1555)] *Warhafftige Beschreibung aller fürnemer Händel, so sich in Glaubens und andern Weltlichen Sachen bey Regierung Carls deß Fünfften, biß auff das tausent fünff hundert und sechß und funfftzigste Jar verlauffen und zugetragen, Erstlich in Latein beschriben, und in sechß und zwentzig Bücher abgetheilt)*, trans. Michael Beuther, 2 vols. (Frankfurt am Main, 1572).

53. Kelley, *Sleidanus*, 589.

54. Lau, *Johannes Sleidanus*, 585.

55. Pohlig, *Gelehrsamkeit*, 164. As Pohlig argues, it is not the way Sleidanus interprets the Reformation, but its singularity as a historical event within his work as Sleidanus presents the Reformation without mentioning any late medieval background.

56. Kess, *Johannes Sleidanus*, 117.

57. Sleidanus, *Warhafftige Beschreibung*, 23.

58. "verbrannte er das Bäpstische Recht mit sampt dem new außgegangenem Decret deß Bapstes offentlich." Sleidanus, *Warhafftige Beschreibung*, 22.

59. Benedikt Stuchtey, "German Historical Writing," in *The Oxford History of Historical Writing*, ed. Stuart Macintyre, Juan Maiguashca, Attila Pók, and Daniel Woolf, 5 vols. (Oxford, 2011), vol. 4, 163–83.

60. Leopold von Ranke, *Deutsche Geschichte im Zeitalter der Reformation*, 5 vols. (Berlin, 1839–1843), vol. 1, 441–42.

61. "Notwendig wendete sich nun die Aufmerksamkeit der gesamten Nation auf diesen Widerstand." Ranke, *Deutsche Geschichte*, vol. 1, 442.

62. On Catholic nineteenth-century historiography, see Andreas Holzem, *Weltversu-chung und Heilsgewissheit: Kirchengeschichte im Katholizismus des 19. Jahrhunderts* (Altenberge, 1995), esp. 180–90. On Janssen, see Walter Troxler, "Johannes Janssen (1829–1891)," in *Hauptwerke der Geschichtsschreibung*, ed. Volker Reinhardt (Stuttgart, 1997), 303–6.

63. Troxler, "Johannes Janssen," 305.

64. Johannes Janssen, *Geschichte des deutschen Volkes seit dem Ausgang des Mittelalters*, 7 vols. (Freiburg im Breisgau, 1878–1894), vol. 2, *Zustände des deutschen Volkes seit dem beginn der politischkirchlichen Revolution bis zum Ausgang der socialen Revolution von 1525* (Freiburg im Breisgau, 1878).

65. Janssen, *Zustände*, 116–17.

66. Friedrich von Bezold, *Geschichte der deutschen Reformation: Mit Porträts, Illustrationen und Beilagen* (Berlin, 1886), 304.

67. "Es war das Feuerzeichen eines Krieges auf Leben und Tod." Bezold, *Geschichte*, 304.

68. Ranke, *Deutsche Geschichte*, vol. 1, 442–44.

69. "Schrift, die uns ein plastisches Bild der Vorgänge bei und nach der Verbrennung in Wittenberg der päpstlichen Bulle am 10. Dezember 1520 gibt." A full-length reprint of the student's account was first published in vol. 7 of the Weimar edition 1897; for the earlier Erlangen edition (1868) quoted it in the notes, see WA, vol. 7, 184.

70. Boehmer, "*Luther und der 10. Dezember*," 40–41.

71. Boehmer, *Luther und der Bann*, 24.

72. Zacharias Werner, *Martin Luther oder die Weihe der Kraft: Eine Tragödie* (Berlin, 1807), 70–75.

73. Melanchthon commented on Luther's deed in the scene as follows: "Was so eben das ganze Land mit Schrecken füllt—die That, die ungeheure, unsers allzuraschen, tollkuehnen Freundes! Nie hatte ich's geträumt—des heil'gen Vaters Bulle zu verbrennen!" Werner, *Martin Luther*, 73.

74. Dieter Hensing, "Der Bilder eigner Geist. Das schwierige Verhältnis der Lutherbilder zu ihrem Gegenstand," in *Luther-Bilder im 20. Jahrhundert: Symposion an der Freien Universität Amsterdam*, ed. Ferdinand van Ingen and Gerd Labroisse (Amsterdam, 1984), 1–25, esp. 6–7.

75. Manfred Kranick, "Martin Luther als Bühnenfigur: Historische Wertung und Dramaturgie," in *Martin Luther*, ed. Ernst Ludwig Arnold (Munich, 1983), 178–204.

76. Etienne François, "Die Wartburg," in *Deutsche Erinnerungsorte*, ed. Etienne François and Hagen Schulze, 3 vols. (Munich, 2001), vol. 2, 154–70; and Wichmann von Meding, "Das Wartburgfest im Rahmen des Reformationsjubiläums 1817," *Zeitschrift für Kirchengeschichte* 96 (1986): 203–36.

77. Steven Michael Press, "False Fire: The Wartburg Book-Burning of 1817," *Central European History* 42 (2009): 621–46. Press argues that the connection between the book burning and the Wartburg Festival was not as strong as previously assumed, but rather was retrospectively constructed.

78. Ludwig Roediger, "Rede am Feuer gehalten auf dem Wartenberge," in *Das Warburgfest am 18. October 1817: In seiner Entstehung, Ausführung und Folgen. Nach Actenstücken und Augenzeugnissen*, ed. Georg Kieser (Jena, 1818), 114–27, here 115.

79. Johannes Kessler, *Sabbata: Mit kleineren Schriften und Briefen*, ed. Emil Egli and Rudolf Schoch (St. Gallen, 1902), 72.

80. "Die walstat hab ich gesechen." Kessler, *Sabbata*, 72.

Bibliography

Aland, Kurt. *A History of Christianity*. Translated by James L. Schaaf. Vol. 1. Philadelphia, 1985.

Aston, Margaret. "Iconoclasm in England: Rites of Destruction by Fire." In *Bilder und Bildersturm im Spätmittelalter und in der frühen Neuzeit*, edited by Robert W. Scribner, 175–202. Wiesbaden, 1990.

Beschorner, Hans. "Die sogenannte Bannbulle und ihre angebliche Verbrennung durch Luther am 10. Dezember 1520." In *Forschungen aus mitteldeutschen Archiven: Zum 60. Geburtstag von Helmut Kretzschmar*, edited by the Staatliche Archivverwaltung im Staatssekretariat für innere Angelegenheiten, 315–28. Berlin (East), 1953.

Bezold, Friedrich von. *Geschichte der deutschen Reformation: Mit Porträts, Illustrationen und Beilagen*. Berlin, 1886.

Boehmer, Julius. "Luther und der 10. Dezember 1520." *Luther-Jahrbuch* 2–3 (1920–21): 7–53.

Brecht. Martin. *Martin Luther*. 3 vols. Stuttgart, 1987.

Cameron, Euan. *The European Reformation*. Oxford, 1991.

Emser, Ernst Ludwig, ed. *Luthers Briefwechsel*. Vol. 3. Stuttgart 1898.

Fabisch, Peter, and Erwin Iserloh, ed. *Dokumente zur Causa Lutheri 1517–1521*. Vol. 2. Münster, 1991.

François, Etienne. "Die Wartburg." In *Deutsche Erinnerungsorte*, edited by Etienne François and Hagen Schulze, vol. 2, 154–70. Munich, 2001–2.

Friedensburg, Walter, ed. *Urkundenbuch der Universität Wittenberg*. Vol. 1. Magdeburg, 1926.

Gordon, Bruce. "The Changing Face of Protestant History and Identity in the Sixteenth Century." In *Protestant History and Identity in Sixteenth Century Europe*, edited by Bruce Gordon, vol. 1, 1–22. Aldershot, 1996.

Hensing, Dieter. "Der Bilder eigner Geist. Das schwierige Verhältnis der Lutherbilder zu ihrem Gegenstand." In *Luther-Bilder im 20. Jahrhundert: Symposion an der Freien Universität Amsterdam*, edited by Ferdinand Van Ingen and Gerd Labroisse, 1–25. Amsterdam, 1984.

Hillerbrand, Hans J. "Martin Luther and the Bull Exsurge Domine." *Theological Studies* 30 (1969): 108–12.

Hofmann, Werner. *Luther und die Folgen für die Kunst*. Munich, 1983.

Holzem, Andreas. *Weltversuchung und Heilsgewissheit: Kirchengeschichte im Katholizismus des 19. Jahrhunderts*. Altenberge, 1995.

Janssen, Johannes. *Geschichte des deutschen Volkes seit dem Ausgang des Mittelalters*. 7 vols. Freiburg im Breisgau, 1878–94.

Kastner, Ruth, ed. *Quellen zur Reformation 1517–1555*. Darmstadt, 1994.

Kelley, Donald R. "Johann Sleidan and the Origins of History as a Profession." *Journal of Modern History* 52 (1980): 573–98.

Kess, Alexandra. *Johann Sleidan and the Protestant Vision of History*. Aldershot, 2008.

Kessler, Johannes. *Sabbata: Mit kleineren Schriften und Briefen.* Edited by Emil Egli and Rudolf Schoch. St. Gallen, 1902.

Kidd, Beresford J., ed. *Documents Illustrative of the Continental Reformation.* Oxford, 1967.

Kranick, Manfred. "Martin Luther als Bühnenfigur: Historische Wertung und Dramaturgie." In *Martin Luther*, edited by Ernst Ludwig Arnold, 178–204. Munich, 1983.

Krentz, Natalie. *Ritualwandel und Deutungshoheit: Die frühe Reformation in der Residenzstadt Wittenberg (1500–1533).* Tübingen, 2014.

Kruse, Jens-Martin. *Universitätstheologie und Kirchenreform: Die Anfänge der Reformation in Wittenberg 1516–22.* Mainz, 2002.

Lau, Thomas. "Johannes Sleidanus (urspr. Philippi)." In *Hauptwerke der Geschichtsschreibung*, edited by Volker Reinhardt, 584–87. Stuttgart, 1997.

Laube, Adolf, Sigrid Looß, and Annerose Schneider, ed. *Flugschriften der frühen Reformationsbewegung (1518–1524).* 2 vols. Vaduz, 1983.

———, and Ulman Weiss, ed. *Flugschriften gegen die Reformation (1518–1524).* Berlin, 1997.

LeGoff, Jacques. *The Birth of Purgatory.* Translated by Arthur Goldhammer. Aldershot, 1990.

Luther, Martin. *D. Martin Luthers Werke: Kritische Gesamtausgabe.* Weimar, 1883–2009.

Meding, Wichmann von. "Das Wartburgfest im Rahmen des Reformationsjubiläums 1817." *Zeitschrift für Kirchengeschichte* 96 (1986): 203–36.

Muir, Edward. *Ritual in Early Modern Europe.* 3rd ed. Cambridge, 2000.

Müller, Gerhard. "Die drei Nuntiaturen Aleanders in Deutschland 1520/21, 1531/32, 1538/39." In *Causa Reformationis: Beiträge zur Reformationsgeschichte und zur Theologie Martin Luthers*, edited by Gerhard Müller, 249–303. Gütersloh, 1989.

Murner, Thomas. *Wie doctor. M. Luter vß falschen vrsachen bewegt Dz geistlich recht verbrennet hat.* Strasbourg, 1521.

Perlach, Max, and Johannes Luther, ed. "Ein neuer Bericht über Luthers Verbrennung der Bannbulle." *Sitzungsberichte der königlich-preußischen Akademie der Wissenschaften zu Berlin* (1907), 95–102.

Pohlig, Matthias. *Zwischen Gelehrsamkeit und konfessioneller Identitätsstiftung: Lutherische Kirchen- und Universalgeschichtsschreibung 1546–1617.* Tübingen, 2007.

Press, Steven Michael. "False Fire: The Wartburg Book-Burning of 1817." *Central European History* 42 (2009): 621–46.

Ranke, Leopold von. *Deutsche Geschichte im Zeitalter der Reformation.* 5 vols. Berlin, 1839–1843.

Roediger, Ludwig. "Rede am Feuer gehalten auf dem Wartenberge." In *Das Warburgfest am 18. October 1817: In seiner Entstehung, Ausführung und Folgen. Nach Actenstücken und Augenzeugnissen*, edited by Georg Kieser, 114–27. Jena, 1818.

Rublack, Ulinka. *Die Reformation in Europa.* 2nd ed. Frankfurt am Main, 2006.

Schubert, Anselm. "Das Lachen der Ketzer. Zur Selbstinszenierung der frühen Reformation." *Zeitschrift für Theologie und Kirche* 108 (2011): 405–30.

Scribner, Robert W. "Reformation, Carnival, and the World Turned Upside-Down." *Social History* 3 (1978): 303–29.

———. "Ritual and Reformation." In *The German People and the Reformation*, edited by R. Po-Chia Hsia, 122–44. London, 1990.

Skokan, Isabel. *Germania und Italia: Nationale Mythen und Heldengestalten in Gemälden des 19. Jahrhunderts*. Berlin, 2009.

Sleidanus, Johannes. *Johannis Sleidani Warhaftige Beschreibung aller Händel, . . . under dem Großmächtigsten Keyser Carln dem Fünfften zugetragen und verlauffen haben.* Frankfurt am Main, 1558.

———. *Warhafftige Beschreibung aller fürnemer Händel, so sich in Glaubens und andern Weltlichen Sachen bey Regierung Carls deß Fünfften, biß auff das tausent fünff hundert und sechß und funfftzigste Jar verlauffen und zugetragen, Erstlich in Latein beschriben, und in sechß und zwentzig Bücher abgetheilt.* 2 vols. Frankfurt am Main, 1572.

———. *Warhafftige beschreibung geystlicher und weltlicher sachen/ under Keyser Carolo dem Fünfften verloffen.* Basel, [1555] 1556.

Stuchtey, Benedikt. "German Historical Writing." In *The Oxford History of Historical Writing* edited by Stuart Macintyre, Juan Maiguashca, Attila Pók, and Daniel Woolf, vol. 4, 163–83. Oxford, 2011.

Troxler, Walter. "Johannes Janssen (1829–1891)." In *Hauptwerke der Geschichtsschreibung*, edited by Volker Reinhardt, 303–6. Stuttgart, 1997.

Völkel, Markus. *Geschichtsschreibung: Eine Einführung in globaler Perspektive*. Cologne, 2006.

Walch, Johann Georg, ed. *Dr. Martin Luthers sämtliche Schriften*. 20 vols. Jena, 1740–53.

Werner, Zacharias. *Martin Luther oder die Weihe der Kraft: Eine Tragödie*. Berlin, 1807.

CHAPTER ELEVEN

Early Modern German Historians Confront the Reformation's First Executions

ROBERT CHRISTMAN

On 1 July 1523, before a crowd of stunned spectators, two young friars, Hendrik Voes and Johann van den Esschen, were burned alive on the Grand Plaza of Brussels. Members of the Augustinian cloister in nearby Antwerp, the friars had been convicted of holding heretical Lutheran ideas. The man responsible for the deaths, Frans van der Hulst, played the double role of imperial and papal inquisitor, reflecting the fact that both pope and emperor were involved in the proceedings. In Wittenberg, Martin Luther and his circle were keeping close tabs on the events in Brabant via contacts with members of the Antwerp Augustinian cloister.[1] Thus the event engaged the direct interest of important participants on both sides in the early Reformation.

What is more, news of the Reformation's first executions spread quickly, sending a shock wave across Europe. Particularly in the German-speaking lands, their story elicited impassioned responses across the social and theological spectrum. *Flugschriften* recounting the event quickly went through twenty-three editions, thereby becoming some of the most published texts of the period.[2] In response, Luther composed his first song, "A New Song Here Shall Be Begun," a twelve-stanza ballad recounting the trial, degradation, and burning of the friars.[3] Printed first as a broadsheet, the song was regularly included in German hymnals for the remainder of the sixteenth century, editions of which number well over one thousand.[4] The impact did not end there. For centuries afterward polemicists and historians of various confessions continued to point to these executions to support their own interpretations of the Reformation's history and meaning or used the friars as exemplars for proper behavior in the face of persecution. In short, few events in the early

Reformation were more widely publicized or had a broader impact than the deaths of these two men.

Curiously, however, in more recent times these executions have received little attention. Granted, in some specific contexts, aspects of the event have been investigated by modern historians.[5] But the story of how the executions came to occur and an understanding of their deep significance in the early Reformation has faded. In German historiography, this is undoubtedly in part because the executions occurred outside the German lands; in the Belgian and Dutch historiography, more recent scholarship has focused on the second half of the sixteenth century, leaving events such as this underemphasized.

But part of the reason that the importance of these executions has been forgotten can be traced back to interpretations of the event in the century after it occurred—the subject of this essay. Early modern reactions to the deaths of Voes and van den Esschen appeared in three distinct chronological waves and genres: eyewitness accounts; responses to the eyewitness accounts by literate individuals in the event's immediate aftermath; and, beginning in the mid-1550s and continuing through the early modern period, treatment by confessional historians.[6] This third wave may be further divided into two distinct genres: martyrologies, which were compilations of the stories of the suffering and/or death of individuals for the sake of their beliefs; and more traditional histories in which the authors attempted to place the executions into a broader historical framework.

This essay identifies the central themes found in the eyewitness accounts and explores the interpretations of the event articulated in its early aftermath (the first two waves), texts that would provide the raw material for martyrologists and historians in the early modern period. It then turns to their historical accounts, asking to what extent early modern historians employ, reject, or reinterpret the views of their predecessors, what this might tell us about changing historical circumstances and the impact of confessionalization, and more broadly, how this might help account for the fact that the importance of the event has been largely missed by modern historians.[7] As will become clear, although the earliest interpreters and the early modern historians both considered this event enormously important, the significance assigned to it changed over the course of the sixteenth century as the miraculous and shocking elements found in early accounts were increasingly replaced by an understanding of the event within the confines of earthly and human experience.[8] In some cases the interpretations of the earliest commentators were forgotten altogether. In others they were recast to support new claims more pertinent to the struggles of this later period. In the end, the changing needs of an increasingly confessionalized Europe muffled the initial shock of the event, reduced the variety of interpretations of it, and helped provide the conditions for the current tendency to assign so little significance to it in the broader early

Reformation. A plurality of interpretations, not to mention a comprehension of the event's broader impact, was forgotten.

Historical Background

Upon his return from the Diet of Worms to the Low Countries in autumn of 1521, the Holy Roman Emperor Charles V established a new, state-run inquisition, naming the Leuven jurist Frans van der Hulst as its director. Having witnessed widespread support for Martin Luther among the German princes and laity in Worms, Charles was keen to confront this heresy in his ancestral homelands. Van der Hulst, a layman, enlisted the help of ecclesiastics who had already been working to stem the tide of the reform movement, among them the papal nuncio Jerome Aleander, the Leuven professors of theology Nicholas of Egmond and Jacob Latomus, and the well-known Dominican inquisitor Jacob Hochstraten of Cologne. Under van der Hulst's direction, this group immediately began pursuing the church's most outspoken critics in the Low Countries, in particular Erasmus of Rotterdam and Jacob Probst, prior of the Antwerp Augustinians and close personal friend and outspoken supporter of Martin Luther.[9]

Prior to the events of 1 July 1523, members of this inquisitorial body had celebrated a string of successes in the Low Countries. Aleander had published the Edict of Worms and completed a dozen or so book burnings in major cities. By candidly labeling him a heretic, the group had been able to pressure Erasmus to leave the Low Countries in autumn of 1521, never to return. Spectacular public recantations soon followed. In April 1522, Cornelius Grapheus, the humanist city secretary of Antwerp, was forced to openly revoke his views in the city square in Brussels and again a few days later in Antwerp. Most stunning of all was the fate of Jacob Probst, the prior of the Antwerp Augustinians. Jailed for months under constant threat of the stake, he finally recanted from the pulpit of a packed St. Gudula's Church in Brussels, condemning the teachings of his friend Luther and embracing the authority of the Roman Church.[10]

But van der Hulst's successes against their prior did not deter the remaining Augustinians of Antwerp from preaching Lutheran doctrines and criticizing the church. So vocal were they that the emperor's queen-regent in Brabant (Charles had left the Low Countries for Spain in May of 1522), Margaret of Austria, decided to dissolve the Augustinian cloister altogether. On 6 October 1522, she arrested the remaining friars, although their new prior, Henry of Zutphen, another close friend of Luther's, was able to escape. On the following day, Margaret led a procession of the Eucharist out of the cloister church, symbolically demonstrating the heterodoxy of the Augustinians. She would eventually have the cloister destroyed and its church made into a parish church.

Between 6 October 1522 and 1 July 1523, van der Hulst, who, in addition to his imperial title was also named papal inquisitor on 1 June 1523, took charge of the interrogations of the captive Augustinians, all but three of whom eventually recanted.[11] On 1 July 1523 one of the three, Lambert Thorn, requested time to reconsider his views and received a permanent stay of execution. The other two, Voes and van den Esschen, were burned.

The Eyewitness Accounts

The first media by which news of the event spread, sources that would become important material for later historians writing in the early modern period, were three eyewitness accounts of the executions, all from the pens of pro-Reformation authors. The works of the anonymous authors are characterized by four themes.[12] First, they emphasized the corrupt and immoral behavior of the churchmen and inquisitors in charge of the trial. The inquisitors, we are told, were covert in their actions so that no one would know what they were doing until it was too late.[13] They avoided the tradition in Brussels of publicly reading the charges against the condemned "out of shame for the great injustice that was perpetrated."[14] Most telling, remarks one author, was the fact that one inquisitor viciously slandered the men by claiming that at the last moment they recanted, were converted by a miracle of the Virgin Mary, and died in the arms of the church. But, writes this author, all those standing near the fire deny this.[15]

The second common feature of these eyewitness accounts is their emphasis on similarities between the situation of the Augustinians and that of Christ. One author writes that "some say that [the younger Augustinian] insisted he would be obedient unto death," echoing the words of Saint Paul in Philippians 2:6–8, who described Christ as "obedient unto death, even the death of the cross."[16] Two of the accounts claim that when the father confessors began to weep as they led the men to the stake, the condemned friars responded that they should not cry on their account, but on account of their own sins, an echo of Christ's words on the way to the cross, "Daughters of Jerusalem, don't weep for me, but weep for yourselves and for your children" (Luke 23:28).[17] Another author explicitly ties the event to the trial of Jesus, noting that the Augustinians were handed over to the temporal authorities for execution, "as Christ was given over to the heathen by the Jews."[18] And when one of the inquisitors told the condemned friars that he had the power to execute them, they answered, "These are the words of Pilate, and you would have no power over men unless it were given you from above," which is the precise response that Jesus gave Pontius Pilate in John 10:10–11.[19]

The extraordinary demeanor of the two men, exemplified by repeated claims of their willingness and even happiness to die, is a third theme in the firsthand accounts. The friars, we are told, "praised God that he had given them the grace to die for his word," and "went to the fire joyfully smiling."[20] Furthermore, "they thanked God that they could die for his word. And they suffered such innocent martyrdom and death willingly, eagerly, happily, and steadfastly."[21] In the fire, writes the author, they never became cowardly, rather the longer it went on, the more steadfast and courageous they became, "so that many even thought that they were smiling."[22]

The fourth theme that runs through these accounts is the Augustinians' defiance of the church, particularly their criticism of ecclesiastical authority demonstrated most clearly in the sixty-two articles for which they were executed.[23] Although heavily influenced by Luther's ideas, these articles have little to do with his notions of salvation. Rather, they censure the papacy for prohibiting Luther's books, limit the power of bishops and the pope to the ministry of the word, and insist that all men are priests before God and that all men and even women with an understanding of the Gospel may remit sins. They eliminate the priests' exceptional status in the consecration of the Eucharistic elements and limit the number of sacraments to three, while championing the right of the laity to receive communion in both kinds. The central critique in each of these assertions is that the church has overstepped its authority. Moreover, when the confessors attending them asked them if they remained hardened in their denial of true faith they replied, "We believe in God and in a Christian church, but we do not believe in your church."[24]

Brad Gregory has argued that the authors of the pamphlets "strove to make their interpretations, however highly charged, however shaped by literary conventions, fit the best available information about the executions. Facts, not fabrications, best served propaganda."[25] For the purposes of this essay, the point is not to question the truth or falsity of these accounts, but to assume that events described by partisan individuals, using certain literary conventions, will necessarily be presented through the lens of those authors' experiences, from their point of view, and in a way that supported their objectives. Because these authors needed to justify the beliefs and actions of two men officially executed for heresy by a legally authorized inquisition, it is not surprising that they framed the men's refusal to recant as faithfulness to a higher power. Underscoring the dishonesty of the inquisitors and questioning the authority of the church they represented further damaged the integrity of the prosecuting authorities. Stressing that the men were absolutely steadfast and unwavering, as Christ had been when faced with persecution and death, bolstered the justice of their cause and their connection to Christ. These men were not common heretics; they were "knights of Christ," as one of the eye-witnesses labeled them in the title of his pamphlet.[26] Thus authors' depictions of this event are in keeping with their outlook and the objectives.

Early Interpretations

Like the eyewitness accounts, the initial reactions to news of the deaths of Voes and van den Esschen also provided later historians with potential source material for their own interpretations. The first reaction comes from Frans van der Hulst himself. In a letter to another inquisitor, Jan Pascha, dated the day of the executions, van der Hulst related his joy at having been told by the confessors that with their last breaths, the friars had recanted their heresies, returned to the church, and professed among other things "that our lord, the pope, is the true successor to Peter."[27] This retraction was done with such fervor and conviction, wrote van der Hulst, that to the bystanders, it appeared miraculous. He also urged Pascha to publicize this information.[28]

The confessors appear to have passed this story to others as well, as one of the eyewitness accounts relates how, on the day after the executions, the festi-val of the Visitation of Mary, a second cleric who had been among the inquisi-tors preached a sermon in which he, too, claimed that at the last moment the men had recanted, attributing their change of heart to the miraculous interces-sion of the Virgin Mary.[29] And yet another inquisitor, Nicholas Egmond, said in a sermon on the day after the executions that he, too, had received a letter describing the last-minute recantation.[30] Between van der Hulst's letter and these other references we are left with two significant pieces of information regarding this Catholic portrayal of this event: the men died as faithful sons of the church, and the Virgin Mary miraculously inspired their last-second recantation—an assertion connected to the fact that the executions took place on the eve of the festival of her visitation.

This description, so dramatically different from the eyewitness accounts, may be explained by the specific circumstances and broader goals of the inquisitors. For van der Hulst, the execution of Voes and van den Esschen was a failure. Where he had succeeded in "convincing" high-profile men such as Grapheus and Probst to recant, he had been unable to do likewise with these otherwise unexceptional friars, one of whom, it seems, was barely out of his teens.[31] That his goal was to avoid burning them is apparent, as no effort was spared to convince them to recant, and when the third Augustinian asked for time to reconsider, his request was immediately granted.[32] Success for van der Hulst would have been a recantation with full acceptance of papal author-ity. Thus in this letter, van der Hulst snatches victory from the jaws of defeat, accepting and then publicizing the claims about a last-second recantation.

A very different, but still Catholic interpretation comes from a sermon preached later in the summer of 1523 in the south German city of Ingolstadt, where Georg Hauer raised the event in order to dispute the reformers' critique of Marian piety. A jurist at the University of Ingolstadt and priest at that city's Church of Our Lady, Hauer took exception to the way Mary was being treated by followers of Luther, but insisted that she would defend herself.

> Thus there are already some who have attacked Mary in a most dishonorable manner [and who] have been punished, namely with the loss of their minds, swift death, and other such plagues. And this summer the executioner rewarded some on the eve of Mary's Visitation, for they were not worthy of the day itself. For in Brussels, two Augustinian monks were burned to ashes. They did not go to the fire willingly and of their own accord, as the Lutherans say. Rather they were dragged there by the executioner.[33]

Thus Hauer rejected the claim that the men died willingly but maintained the link between the Virgin Mary and the execution of the two Augustinians. But instead of employing the earlier interpretation that her miraculous intervention caused the men to recant, he insinuated that she did not save them, but abandoned them to death and damnation. The point here is that these Augustinians were punished precisely for their disrespect for the Virgin, not only with death, but with eternal damnation as signified by the fact that they refused to accept their fate, demonstrating fear rather than peaceful resignation. Clearly their consciences were troubled. Hauer frames the Marian connection to suit his purposes—namely to argue against a Lutheran understanding of the Virgin Mary.

Another commentator in the aftermath of the executions was Erasmus of Rotterdam, who offered his thoughts in a series of letters that would prove highly influential among early modern historians. In accordance with his classical-humanist background, Erasmus took a more earthly approach to the event, omitting any allusions to supernatural involvement. Already prior to the executions he had been a fierce critic of the inquisitors and their methods due to his own experiences in the Low Countries.[34] At the end of August 1523, he wrote to Ulrich Zwingli noting the steadfastness of the Augustinians, but questioning the beliefs for which they died, which he referred to as "Luther's paradoxes" (*paradoxa Lutheri*).[35] But eighteen months later, Erasmus raised the event in order to condemn the actions of hard-line churchmen, writing to Duke George of Saxony, a vocal critic of Luther, "What worries me now is that these common remedies, that is, recantations, imprisonment, and the stake, will simply make the evil worse. Two men were burned at Brussels, and it was precisely at that moment that the city began to support Luther."[36] The following year Erasmus again suggested that such tactics produced the opposite effect of that which was intended: "The infection spread with every blow and took strength and courage from our cruelty."[37] And, he claimed, the hard-line approach had so invigorated the Protestants that the spread of the Reformation looked like the work of heaven. By 1529, he added a further critique, recounting how the inquisitor at the time of the executions had spread the "ridiculous lie" (*ridiculam fabulam*) that the condemned friars had recanted at the last moment and made supplications to the Virgin Mary.[38]

For Erasmus, as the event receded into the past it increasingly became a cautionary tale about how the church should proceed against the Lutheran heresy and a means by which to focus his ire on the inquisition. Among the early interpreters, he alone saw the event as a primarily human affair in which individual character flaws and poor institutional policies resulted in an unwanted outcome. Desirous of remaining in the good graces of the church and emperor, but at the same time a victim of the very inquisitors who had executed Voes and van den Esschen, Erasmus chose a middle path. But his assessment was influenced by his own preconceptions, demonstrated most dramatically by his statement that Brussels first embraced Reformation ideas as a result of the executions, a claim with little basis in reality. Living in the Low Countries until autumn of 1521, Erasmus was well aware of the massive popularity of Luther and the broad availability of his works there prior to the events of 1 July 1523.[39] Like other interpreters, he employed the executions in the service of his own argument.

Deeply moved by the deaths of the friars, Martin Luther did the same. For years Luther had been following the events surrounding his fellow Augustinians in Antwerp, and he must have thought that if van der Hulst could break a man like Probst, a pillar among the Augustinians, an ardent supporter of the Reformation, and a personal confidant, the remaining Antwerp Augustinians, now leaderless, had little chance. But their steadfastness surprised him, and he immediately penned a letter of consolation to the Christians in the Netherlands, then composed his first song.[40] In twelve verses, Luther recounted the capture, interrogation, degradation, execution, and fallout from the case. But it was his framing of the event that was most remarkable. It was not a political act by the temporal or ecclesiastical authorities, nor an act of defiance against church authority, nor even an attempt at reform by the Augustinians. Rather the entire event was one sharp salvo in the continuing cosmic war between God and his servants, on the one hand, and the devil and his minions, on the other.[41] The extraordinary steadfastness and joy of the Augustinians was, for Luther, a clear demonstration that God was directly at work; indeed Luther asserted in the first verse of his song that the entire event was a miracle (*Wunder*), accomplished by God with his own hand.[42] The brazenness and impudence of the inquisitors indicated that the devil was also active, as it was he who "called them to the showdown."[43] They do his will. To underscore this point, Luther directly addressed the chief inquisitor's assertion that the two men had recanted, calling it outright slander.[44] Ultimately the event convinced Luther that the Reformation was the work of God, a point he made in a letter to his friend Georg Spalatin, where he reported the event and then concluded, "thanks be to Christ, who has finally begun to let my, nay rather His, prophecy bear fruit."[45]

This survey of the early interpretations of the executions in Brussels makes clear that just as with the eyewitness accounts, each author responded in light of his own experiences, interpreting the event in a way favorable to his own viewpoint and objectives. As a result, future historians had open to them a variety of directions in which they might take their own interpretations. Depending upon what they read, who they believed, and their own training and outlook, it might demonstrate the authenticity and power of heavenly intercessors to save or punish; it might act as a case study by which to criticize the tactics of the church against the Reformation and demonstrate the corruption of ecclesiastical officials; or it might prove that the hand of God was directly at work promoting the success of the Reformation. Taken together, however, this smattering of responses to the deaths provides some insight into their deep importance in the early Reformation.

The Historians

But as will become clear, the early modern historians employed, rejected, or reinterpreted the early sources in light of the requirements of their increasingly confessional period and, in doing so, significantly reduced the event's overall impact. The four major Protestant martyrologists, each of whom included the story of Voes and van den Esschen in some detail, took a straightforward approach.[46] Writing in the second half of the sixteenth century, they use as sources exclusively the eyewitness accounts, which they paraphrase, synthesize, or even translate word for word.[47] None incorporate any of the early interpretations, nor do they raise the specter of supernatural elements. We might explain their treatment in a few ways. First, it is well known that these authors borrowed from one another, thereby improving the likelihood that their entries on this event would be similar. But second, and more importantly, the goals of the martyrologists coincided with those of the early eyewitness accounts so well that they simply allowed the pamphlets to speak for themselves. Much has been written on the role of martyrologies in the construction of group identities.[48] By their very nature they were meant to tell the story of a confession's heroes to inspire the faithful, provide legitimacy for the group, and delegitimize the authority of those who persecuted them, goals very similar to those of the authors of the eyewitness accounts. Emphasizing the steadfastness of the victims in the face of persecution by treacherous churchmen fit their objectives; allowing the eyewitnesses to speak for themselves gave the martyrologies a further air of objectivity. But what is new with the martyrologists is context. The deaths of Voes and van den Esschen are placed among a host of martyrdoms. As a result, the exceptionality of the event and the broader impact of their deaths are muted.

Other historians also addressed the event. Appearing in the German-speaking lands first in the mid-1550s (about the same time as the martyrologies), most include neither excerpts nor the full text of the eyewitness accounts, marking them as something different from the martyrologies.[49] Like the martyrologies, many ignore the early interpretations altogether; unlike the martyrologies, some authors offer their own evaluation of the event. Their various treatments of the executions of Voes and van den Esschen reflect three key aspects of confessional identity building.

First, there are those Protestant authors who describe the event briefly and without any commentary, indicating that it is significant, but providing no explanation as to why. For example, publishing in 1555, Johannes Sleidanus includes the episode in his history of the Reformation, placing it between one of the emperor's edicts and responses to that edict.[50] In other words, it almost comes as an aside. Likewise Lucas Osiander briefly includes it as one of a number of unrelated, but important, events of the year 1523.[51] Writing a history of the popes, Georg Nigrinus seems to have thought in similar terms. Having recounted the deeds of a particular pope, he ends each chapter with a list of "other important events" that occurred during that pontificate. Among those for Adrian VI's pontificate are various battles and natural disasters and "in Brussels two Augustinians, Johann and Henry, were burned for the sake of the gospel."[52] Perhaps the intent here is simple memorialization, which also seems to be the thrust in Paul Eber's *Calendarium Historicum cum Conscriptum*, published in 1556. This daily calendar of important events, a sort of on-this-day-in-history book, includes for 1 July entries on events from ancient Roman history and notes more contemporary royal births, then concludes with the following remark: "In 1523, two monks, Heinrich and Johannes, were burned in Brussels on account of their pious, steadfast confession of the true doctrines of the Gospel of Christ."[53] Remembrance of key events in the life a group could provide that group with a clear identity, but it did little to capture the overall impact of the event.

A second way in which the historians used the event to enhance confessional identity was by critiquing its interpretations by individuals outside the group. In 1574, the Carthusian monk Larentius Surius published a history of the world up to his own day, in which he acknowledged that the event occurred but provided the following assessment:

> Lutherans consider them martyrs, just like Huss and others—but the devil has his martyrs. Surely people outside of the church cannot imagine themselves united with Christ. Profound and inexcusable guilt for discord is not expunged by suffering, and one cannot be a martyr outside of the church. Let them be burned and surrender their souls.[54]

Surius admits that the executions happened and that the men suffered, but for him the significance lay not in the event itself, but rather in its misinterpretation by the Protestants. Veit Ludwig von Seckendorf, writing his history of Lutheranism in the late seventeenth century, also used the event to critique his confessional adversary. Included in his extensive entry on the executions is a subheading that reads as follows: "Maimburg's silence concerning this martyrdom" (*Maimburgii silentium de illo martyrio*).[55] Louis Maimburg, a Jesuit historian of the Reformation whose account inspired Seckendorf to write his own history, did not refer to the event at all. For Seckendorf, this was an intentional omission to "defraud the nascent Reformation the glory of martyrs."[56] Seckendorf's argument has nothing to do with the event itself and everything to do with the Catholic failure to acknowledge it.[57] But in the larger picture, by making it into a tool to critique an opponent's historiography, the event's original importance is diminished.

A third group of historians did interpret the event as having an important impact on the early Reformation. As Protestant confessional historians, we might have expected these individuals to follow the lead of Luther. But when mentioned at all, the reformer is merely the authority who designated the friars as the first martyrs of the Reformation, or the authors simply note that he wrote a song about the executions, as demonstrated by Osiander's succinct formulation, "Luther composed a song celebrating their martyrdom."[58] None adopt his interpretation that the event was somehow a miracle proving the hand of God in the early Reformation, although most of the historians refer to the exceptional steadfastness of the Augustinians as they faced the fire. The friars are adherents of the truth, perhaps even exceptionally committed adherents, but only in a standard, human sense.[59] In short, the entire event takes place within the confines of human endeavor. Nor do these Protestant historians include any commentary on alleged deceptive actions of the inquisitors who claimed the men recanted. They could have used the executions to rebuke the Roman Church as corrupt, its officials as liars, but they did not.

When assessing the significance of the event for the Reformation, more than a few Protestant historians follow the lead of Erasmus, claiming that it led Reformation ideas to multiply in Brussels, in other words, an argument of historical causality. Three of the authors quote directly from Erasmus's letters in which he argues that the burnings had the opposite of their intended effect, multiplying the numbers of adherents to Lutheranism there rather than ending the heresy.[60] And whereas Erasmus had made this point to critique the aggressive policies of the church, now his interpretation was being used to demonstrate a positive historical impact. For such authors, the burning of Voes and van den Esschen becomes an important catalyst in the spread of the Reformation in the Low Countries, but no mention is made of its impact on the broader early Reformation.

Conclusions

Interpretations of the events surrounding the burning of Heinrich Voes and Johann van den Esschen were highly malleable. From the eyewitness accounts on, authors on all sides of the confessional divide shaped the story to respond to their own experiences and the particular confessional requirements of the moment. This is not (necessarily) to assign duplicitous motives, but rather to acknowledge that authorial objectives, context, and audience each played a significant role in how the event was understood and then framed, a fact that should come as no surprise to historians. In this case, looking at how various authors addressed the events of 1 July 1523 provides a window into the changing confessional contexts of the early modern period, but it also demonstrates how the overall impact and importance of an event can be lost.

In the immediate aftermath of the event, the sympathetic eyewitnesses shaped their narratives in ways that underscored their critique of the church: the inquisitors were cruel and arrogant, and the church as represented by them had lost its legitimacy. At the same time these authors were forced to demonstrate that the friars were not heretics but martyrs, an effort already under way in the most popular eyewitness account, which labeled them "Christian knights." Their overwhelming steadfastness and their willingness to suffer as Christ had accentuated their credibility. These were the key issues of the moment, and the eyewitness accounts responded to each of them in their construction of the narrative.

Early interpreters likewise understood the event in light of their own experiences and from their own partisan point of view. Most important to Frans van der Hulst was acceptance of the authority of the Roman Church and papacy, so it is not surprising that his letter responded to the needs of his objectives and his party. For Georg Hauer, also staunchly Catholic, such heretics deserved their fate, and the fact that they had blasphemed the Blessed Virgin Mary caused her to respond with anger. For Erasmus, who was pushing for an irenic church reform and whose views were informed in part by a humanist worldview, the event was the overzealous work of hard-liners in the church, whose actions were so extreme as to have the opposite of their intended effect. For Martin Luther, the steadfastness of the men, particularly when compared with the irresoluteness of Probst, looked like the hand of God, offering confirmation of the entire Reformation.

By the time that the martyrologists and historians began writing, the situation had changed drastically. The Peace of Augsburg had made Protestantism legal, and the Council of Trent was in the process of defining Roman Catholic orthodoxy. In other words, the lines between the confessions as well as their own internal definitions were becoming clearer. The specifics of the original context were largely forgotten, and at the same time, the burning of individuals who went steadfastly to their fate, convinced in their beliefs, had become increasingly common on all sides of the confessional divide. Such actions were no longer startling.

Not surprisingly the martyrologists and historians of the later sixteenth and seventeenth centuries used the early accounts and interpretations to craft narratives that spoke to their own experiences and the confessional needs of their audiences. For the martyrologists, suggesting that the event was a miracle of God, as Luther had done, did not support their message that those executed should be models for proper behavior in the face of persecution; nor were the martyrologists as interested in the larger picture of how the executions impacted the course of the Reformation. Their objective was to demonstrate that their confessional tradition was legitimate, while providing inspirational models for the faithful, goals that fit well with those of the original eyewitnesses and pamphleteers. As such, they incorporated wholesale those sources, and Voes and van den Esschen take their place among a crowd of others like them.

Others found different reasons to include the event in their histories. For some Protestant historians, the burning of Voes and van den Esschen was simply an important event in the early Reformation, worthy of being remembered, especially since Luther had made so much of it, even if Luther's immediate context and the interpretation it elicited no longer seemed applicable. Other historians on all sides of the confessional divides demonstrated the event's usefulness as a means to critique their opponents' interpretation of history. And finally, some Protestant historians, attempting to understand the event's impact on the early Reformation, were drawn to the insights of Erasmus because they reinforced their confessional understanding of development of the Reformation, particularly in the Low Countries. But gone were Erasmus's original context and personal experiences; remaining was his (mis) interpretation of the event's impact on the spread of Luther's ideas. In the end, the specific context surrounding the executions of Voes and van den Esschen, the authority of the early commentators, and the plurality of early interpretations all gave way to the confessional demands of the moment. And along with the silencing of these early voices, the tendency to diminish the broad importance of the event in the early Reformation found its genesis; modern historians, partly for their own reasons, have simply continued the practice.

Robert J. Christman is an associate professor in the Department of History at Luther College in Decorah, Iowa. He earned his PhD in late medieval and early modern European history from the University of Arizona. His first book, published in 2012 by Brill Publishers and entitled *Doctrinal Controversy and Lay Religiosity in Late Reformation Germany: The Case of Mansfeld*, was a social history of Flacian controversy over original sin. Dr. Christman has received numerous scholarships and awards including, most recently, a grant from the Alexander von Humboldt Foundation.

Notes

1. Jos Vercruysse, "'Was Haben die Sachsen und die Flamen gemeinsam?': Wittenberg von außen gesehen," in *Wittenberg als Bildungszentrum, 1502–2002* (Wittenberg, 2002), 9–32, here 11–17.
2. Hildegard Hebenstreit-Wilfert, "Märtyrerflugschiften der Reformationszeit," in *Flugschriften als Massenmedium der Reformationszeit: Beiträge zum Tübinger Symposion 1980*, ed. Hans-Joachim Köhler (Stuttgart, 1981), 397–446.
3. Martin Luther, "Eynn hubsch Lyed von denn zcweyen Marterern Christi, zu Brussel von den Sophisten zcu Louen verbrandt," *D. Martin Luthers Werke: Kritische Gesamtausgabe, Abteilung Werke*, vols 1- (Weimar, 1883 -), vol. 35, 411–15 (hereafter cited as WA).
4. Christopher Brown, *Singing the Gospel: Lutheran Hymns and the Success of the Reformation* (Cambridge, MA, 2005), 8.
5. For their influence on the Reformation's early pamphlet literature, see Hebenstreit-Wilfert, "Märtyrerflugschiften der Reformationszeit"; and Bernd Moeller, "Inquisition und Martyrium in Flugschriften der frühen Reformation in Deutschland," in *Ketzerverfolgung im 16. und frühen 17. Jahrhundert*, ed. Silvana Seidel Menchi (Wiesbaden, 1992), 21–48. For their impact on notions of martyrdom, see Brad S. Gregory, *Salvation at Stake: Christian Martyrdom in Early Modern Europe* (Cambridge, MA, 1999); and Robert Kolb, "God's Gift of Martyrdom: The Early Reformation Understanding of Dying for the Faith," *Church History* 64 (1995): 399–41. For their impact on Martin Luther's thought and use of media, see Dick Akerboom and Marcel Gielis, "'A New Song Shall Begin Here . . .': The Martyrdom of Luther's Followers among Antwerp's Augustinians on July 1, 1523 and Luther's Response," in *More Than a Memory: The Discourse of Martyrdom and the Construction of Christian Identity in the History of Christianity*, ed. Johan Leemans (Leuven, 2005), 243–70; Rebecca Oettinger, *Music as Propaganda in the German Reformation* (Aldershot, 2001), 61–69; Paul Casey, "'Start Spreading the News': Martin Luther's First Published Song," in *In Laudem Caroli: Renaissance and Reformation Studies for Charles G. Nauert*, ed. James V. Mehl (Kirksville, 1998), 75–94; and Martin Rössler, "Ein neues Lied wir heben an: Ein Protestsong Martin Luthers," in *Reformation und Praktische Theologie: Festschrift für Werner Jetter zum siebzigsten Geburtstag*, ed. Hans Martin Müller and Dietrich Rössler (Göttingen, 1983), 216–32. For their influence on local history, see Otto Clemen, "Die Ersten Märtyrer des evangelischen Glaubens," *Beiträge zur Reformationsgeschichte* 1 (1900): 40–52; and Paul Kalkoff, *Die Anfänge der Gegenreformation in den Niederlanden*, 2 vols. (Halle, 1903–4), esp. vol. 2, 57–81.

6. Included in this study are histories written through 1700, after which time Enlightenment impulses change the nature of historical writing.

7. Confessionalization may be broadly defined as the process by which various states and territories incorporated confession building and state formation in the second half of the sixteenth and the beginning of the seventeenth centuries. See Heinz Schilling, "Confessionalization and the Empire," in *Religion, Political Culture and the Emergence of Early Modern Society: Essays in German and Dutch History*, ed. Heinz Schilling (Leiden, 1992), 208. That aspect of confessionalization most important for this discussion is the formation of confessional identity, or, as Ute Lotz-Heumann has put it, "the development of cultural and political—often national—identities in which the confessional factor played a key role." Ute Lotz-Heumann, "Confessionalization," in *Reformation and Early Modern Europe: A Guide to Research*, ed. David Whitford (Kirksville, 2008), 136–57, here 138.

8. For more on the reformers' notions and understanding of history, see Robin Barnes, *Prophecy and Gnosis: Apocalypticism in the Wake of the Lutheran Reformation* (Stanford, 1988), esp. 100–103.

9. Aleander claimed that Erasmus and Probst were the most dangerous enemies of the church in the Low Countries. Kalkoff, *Die Anfänge der Gegenreformation*, vol. 2, 39. On Luther's friendship with Probst, see Ortwin Rudloff, "Bonae Literae et Lutherus: Texte und Untersuchungen zu den Anfängen der Theologie des Bremer Reformators Jakob Probst," *Hospitium Ecclesiae: Forschungen zur Bremischen Kirchengeschichte* 14 (1985): 11–239, esp. 198–204.

10. Jacques Proost, *Anathematizatio ac revocatio fratris Jacobi Praepositi, olim prioris fratrum heremitarum Sancti Augustini, opidi Antverpiensis* (Antwerp, 1522), 4.

11. Paul Fredericq, ed., *Corpus Documentorum Inquisitionis Haereticae Pravitatis Neerlandicae*, 5 vols. (The Hague, 1889–1902), vol. 4, 86–189.

12. My analysis of the key emphases of these texts differs from that of Brad Gregory's. See Gregory, *Salvation at Stake*, 145–53.

13. *Historia de Duobus Augustinensibus, ob Evangelij doctrinam exustis Bruxellae, die trigesima Iunij. Anno domini M.D.XXIII. Articuli LXII. per eosdem asserti* (n.p., 1523), 1. This pamphlet was translated into German and published with slight additions and emendations: Martin Reckenhofer, *Dye histori so zwen Augustiner Ordens gemartert seyn tzu Bruxel in Probant von wegen des Evangelj. Dye Artickel darumb sie verbrent seyn mit yrer asßlegung und verklerung, etc.* (Erfurt, 1523).

14. WA, vol. 12, 79–80, here 80. This firsthand account is a fragment of a letter purportedly sent to Luther by an eyewitness to parts of the trial. Some printers appended it to the reformer's open letter, *Ein brief an die Christen ym Nidder land* (Wittenberg, 1523), WA, vol. 12, 77–79, under the title "Die Artickel warumb die zwen Christliche Augustiner münch zu Brussel verprandt sindt."

15. *Historia de Duobus Augustinensibus*, 4.

16. *Historia de Duobus Augustinensibus*, 3.

17. "Als sie nun zum fewr komen sein haben die vier Beichtvetter geweynet, da haben diße zwen gesagt sie dürffen nitt umb sy weynen / sonder uber ire sund, Sagten weiter weynnet uber das groß unrecht so ir die Gottliche gerechtigkeyt also vervolgt." Anonymous, *Der Actus und handlung der degradation und verprennung der Christlichen dreyer Ritter und Merterer, Augustiner ordens geschehen zu Brüssel* (1523), 3. So important did Reckenhofer find this element of the story that although it is not included in

the *Historia de Duobus Augustinensibus*, he inserts it in his translation *Dye histori/ so zwen Augustiner Ordens gemartert*, 3.

18. "Die Artickel," WA, vol. 12, 80.
19. "Die Artickel," WA, vol. 12, 80.
20. *Actus und Handlung*, 3.
21. "Die Artickel," WA, vol. 12, 80.
22. *Historia de duobus Augustinensibus*, 3.
23. *Historia de duobus Augustinensibus*, 6–12. These sixty-two articles were included under the title "Articuli Asserti per fratrem Henricum, etc."
24. *Actus und Handlung*, 3.
25. Gregory, *Salvation at Stake*, 21.
26. See note 18.
27. "Letter of Francis Van der Hulst to Jan Pascha, 1 July 1523," in Fredericq, *Corpus Documentorum*, vol. 4, 204.
28. *Corpus Documentorum*, vol. 4, 204.
29. *Historia de Duobus Augustinensibus*, 4.
30. *Historia de Duobus Augustinensibus*, 4.
31. *Historia de Duobus Augustinensibus*, 2; and John Foxe, *Actes and monuments of these latter and perillous dayes, etc.* (London, 1570), 1044. He is described as being without facial hair in *Historia* and twenty-four years old in *Actes and monuments*.
32. Kalkoff, *Die Anfänge der Gegenreformation*, vol. 2, 80–81. This is the essence of Kalkoff's argument.
33. "Also sein schon etlich/ die mit sondern unern Maria angriffen haben/ gestraft worden/ nemlich mit unsinnigkait/ Jähem todt und der gleichen plag. Es hat auch disen sumer der hencker etlich belonet/ als am abent der haimsuechung Marie (sye wurden des tags nit wirdig) zu brussel zwen Augustiner munch zu pulver verbrent/ die nit willig/ und von in selbs/ wie die Lutherischen außgeben/ in das fewr gangen/ sonder von im dem hencker darein gezogen worden." Georg Hauer, *Drey christlich Predig vom Salue regina, dem Evangeli unnd heyligen schrift gemeß* (Ingolstadt, 1523), 4.
34. Kalkoff, *Die Anfänge der Gegenreformation*, vol. 1, 75. Kalkoff claims that hardly a letter written by Erasmus in 1521 did not include complaints about the inquisitors, and in particular about the "fanatical monk" Egmond.
35. "Erasmus to Huldrych Zwingli, 31 August 1523," in Desiderius Erasmus, *Opus epistolarum Des. Erasmi Roterodami denuo recognitum et auctum*, 12 vols., ed. P. S. Allen and H. M. Allen (Oxford, 1903–55), vol. 5, 327. For an insightful analysis of this statement, see Gregory, *Salvation at Stake*, 321.
36. "Erasmus to Duke George of Saxony, 12 December 1524," in Erasmus, *Opus epistolarum*, vol. 5, 606.
37. "Erasmus to Johann Henckel, 7 March 1526," in Erasmus, *Opus epistolarum*, vol. 6, 275.
38. "Erasmus to Charles Utenhove, 1 July 1529," in Erasmus, *Opus epistolarum*, vol. 8, 211–12.
39. J. G. de Hoop-Scheffler, *Geschichte der Reformation in den Niederlanden von ihrem Beginn bis zum Jahre 1531* (Leipzig, 1886), 69. Already in May of 1518 Erasmus wrote that he could hardly stick his hand out the window without one of Luther's works landing in it. What is more, Kalkoff has argued precisely the opposite of Erasmus's assessment, namely that the work of the inquisitors, culminating in the burning of Voes and van den Esschen, was very successful in reducing the spread of heresy, particularly in the southern Low Countries. Kalkoff, *Die Anfänge der Gegenreformation*, vol. 2, 80–81.

40. Luther, *Ein brief*; WA, vol. 12, 77–80; Luther, "Eynn hubsch Lyed," WA, vol. 35, 411–15. The song was distributed first as a broadsheet then included in Lutheran hymn collections produced during the remainder of the sixteenth century.

41. Heiko A. Oberman, *Luther: Man between God and the Devil*, trans. Eileen Walliser-Schwarzbart (New Haven, 1989) 265–67.

42. "Zu singen was Gott hat gethan // zu seynem lob und ehre. // Zu Brüssel in dem niederlandt // woll durch zwen iunge knaben // Hat er seyn wunder macht bekandt." WA, vol. 35, 411.

43. "Vonn Löuen der Sophisten viel // mit yrer kunst verloren // Versamlet er [Der alte Feynd] zu diesem spyell." WA, vol. 35, 412.

44. "noch laßen sie yr lugen nicht, // den grossen mordt zu schmucken. // Sie geben fur eyn falsch getycht, // yr gwissen thut sie drucken; // die Heylgen Gots auch nach dem todt // von yn gelestert werden. // Sie sagen, in der letzten nott // die Knaben noch auff erden // sich sollen han umbkeret." WA, vol. 35, 414.

45. Luther to Spalatin, 23 or 24 July 1523, *D. Martin Luthers Werke: Kritische Gesamtausgabe, Briefwechsel*, vols. 1–18 (Weimar, 1930–85), vol. 3, 114–16.

46. For this study I have analyzed a smattering of early editions of the martyrologies. A thorough investigation of the myriad editions awaits scholarly attention however. First editions of the martyrologies are as follows: Jean Crespin, *Histoire des Martyrs: persecutes et mis a mort pour la verité de l'Evangile, etc.* (Geneva, 1554); Ludwig Rabus, *Historien der auserwählten heiligen Gottszeugen, Bekenner, und Martyrer* (Strasbourg, 1555–56); Adriaen Cornelis van Haemstede, *De Gheschiedenisse ende den doodt der vromer Martelaren die om het ghetuyghenisse des Euangeliums haer bloedt ghestort hebben, etc.* (Antwerp, 1559); and Foxe, *Actes and monuments* (London, 1563).

47. Crespin, Haemstaede, and Foxe paraphrase and synthesize the eyewitness accounts, while Rabus's entry is a word-for-word translation of *Historia de Duobus Augustinensibus*; with regard to the similarities between the original accounts of executions during this period and what is found in the martyrologies, Gregory asserts, "The most important themes of the famous Protestant martyrologies . . . were already in place by the 1520s or early 1530s." Gregory, *Salvation at Stake*, 139.

48. Gregory, *Salvation at Stake*, 139–96.

49. The exceptions are Abraham Scultetus, *Abrahami Sculteti Annalium Evangelii passim per Europam Saeculo XV Renovat. Decades I et II* (Heidelberg, 1618), 179–82; and Veit Ludwig Seckendorf, who includes *Commentarius historicus et apologeticus de Lutheranismo: Sive de reformatione religionis ductu D. Martini Lutheri in magna Germaniae parte alliisque regionibus* (Frankfurt am Main, 1692), 279–82. Scultetus includes Reckenhofer's translation, *Dye histori/ so zwen Augustiner Ordens gemartert* in its entirety, and Seckendorf includes multiple pamphlets and Luther's ballad.

50. Johannes Sleidanus, *Warhafftige beschreibung geystlicher und weltlicher sachen/ under Keyser Carolo dem Fünfften verloffen* (Basel, [1555] 1556), vol. 4, 76. Sleidanus is well-known among historians for his "objectivity" and rejection of confessional polemics. See Alexandra Kess, *Johannes Sleidanus and the Protestant Vision of History* (Aldershot, 2008); and A.G. Dickens, "Johannes Sleidanus and Reformation History," in *Reformation Studies* (London, 1982), 537–63.

51. Lucas Osiander, *Epitomes Historiae Ecclesiasticae Centuriae Decimae sextae pars prima, continens Annos Quinquaginta* (Tubingen, 1602), 98.

52. "Zu Brüssel worden zwen Augustinerern, Johannes und Henricus verbrandt deß
Evangelii halben." Georg Nigrinus, *Papistische Inquisition und gulden Flüs der
Römischen Kirchen . . .* (Strasbourg, 1582), 522.

53. Paul Eber, *Calendarium Historicum cum Conscriptum* (Wittenberg, 1556), 242.

54. Laurentius Surius, *Commentarius brevis rerum in orbe gestarum, ab anno salutis M.D.
usque in annum M.D.LXXIIII* (Cologne, 1574), 145–46.

55. Seckendorf, *Commentarius historicus*, 280.

56. Seckendorf, *Commentarius historicus*, 280.

57. Future historians would continue to critique one another's interpretation of the event.
In an effort to respond to Seckendorf, the Belgian Catholic historian Jean Dierxsens
first published van der Hulst's letter to Pascha as part of a larger argument that the
friars were executed on legitimate grounds by legitimate authorities. Jean Diercxsens, *Antverpia Christo Nascens et crescens seu Acta Ecclessiam Antverpiensem ejusque
Apostolos ac Viros pietate conspicuous concernentia usque ad speculum XVIII*, vol. 4,
1523–1566 (Antwerp, 1773), 5.

58. Osiander, *Epitomes Historiae Ecclesiasticae Centuriae*, 91; Scultetus, *Abrahami Sculteti
Annalium Evangelii*, 183; and Gottfried Arnold, *Unparteyische Kirchen und Ketzer
Historie von Anfang des Neuen Testaments bis auff das Jahr Christi 1688* (Frankfurt
am Main, 1700), vol. 1, 81.

59. Sleidanus suggests that all looked on with amazement "von wegen ihrer standhaff-
tigkeit"; *Warhafftige beschreibung*, vol. 4, 76. Eber says they were burned "ob piam &
constantem confeßionem"; *Calendarium Historicum*, 242. Buchholzer suggests only
that Luther celebrated their constancy, "Lutherus ob confessionis constantiam Can-
tico, quod in multorum est ore, celebravit"; Abraham Bucholzer, *Index Chronologicus*,
(Görlitz, 1599), 550.

60. Bucholzer, *Index Chronologicus*, 550; Scultetus, *Abrahami Sculteti Annalium Evangelii*,
183; and Seckendorf, *Commentarius historicus*, 281.

Bibliography

Akerboom, Dick, and Marcel Gielis. "'A New Song Shall Begin Here . . .': The Martyrdom of Luther's Followers among Antwerp's Augustinians on July 1, 1523 and
Luther's Response." In *More Than a Memory: The Discourse of Martyrdom and
the Construction of Christian Identity in the History of Christianity*, edited by Johan
Leemans, 243–70. Leuven, 2005.

Arnold, Gottfried. *Unparteyische Kirchen- und Ketzer-Historie: Vom Anfang des Neuen
Testaments bis auff das Jahr Christi 1688*. Frankfurt am Main, 1700.

Barnes, Robin. *Prophecy and Gnosis: Apocalypticism in the Wake of the Lutheran Reformation*. Stanford, 1988.

Buchholzer, Abraham. *Index Chronologicus*. Görlitz, 1599.

Brown, Christopher. *Singing the Gospel: Lutheran Hymns and the Success of the Reformation*. Cambridge, MA, 2005.

Casey, Paul. "'Start Spreading the News': Martin Luther's First Published Song." In
In Laudem Caroli: Renaissance and Reformation Studies for Charles G. Nauert,
edited by James V. Mehl, 75–94. Kirksville, 1998.

Clemen, Otto. "Die Ersten Märtyrer des evangelischen Glaubens." *Beiträge zur Reformationsgeschichte* 1 (1900): 40–52.

Crespin, Jean. *Histoire des Martyrs: persecutes et mis a mort pour la verité de l'Evangile, etc.* Geneva, 1554.

Der Actus und handlung der degradation und verprennung der Christlichen dreyer Ritter und Merterer, Augustiner ordens geschehen zu Brüssel. N.p., 1523.

Dickens, A. G. "Johannes Sleidanus and Reformation History." In *Reformation Studies*, 537–63. London, 1982.

Diercxsens, Jean. *Antverpia Christo Nascens et crescens seu Acta Ecclessiam Antverpiensem ejusque Apostolos ac Viros pietate conspicuous concernentia usque ad speculum XVIII, Vol. 4 1523–1566.* Antwerp, 1773.

Eber, Paul. *Calendarium Historicum cum Conscriptum.* Wittenberg, 1556.

Erasmus, Desiderius. *Opus epistolarum Des. Erasmi Roterodami denuo recognitum et auctum.* Edited by P. S. Allen and H. M. Allen. 12 vols. Oxford, 1903–55.

Foxe, John. *Actes and monuments of these latter and perillous dayes, etc.* London, 1563.

Fredericq, Paul, ed. *Corpus Documentorum Inquisitionis Haereticae Pravitatis Neerlandicae.* 5 vols. The Hague, 1889–1902.

Gregory, Brad S. *Salvation at Stake: Christian Martyrdom in Early Modern Europe.* Cambridge, MA, 1999.

Haemstede, Adriaen Cornelis van. *De Gheschiedenisse ende den doodt der vromer Martelaren die om het ghetuyghenisse des Euangeliums haer bloedt ghestort hebben, etc.* Antwerp, 1559.

Hauer, Georg. *Drey christlich Predig vom Salue regina, dem Evangeli unnd heyligen schrift gemeß.* Ingolstadt, 1523.

Hebenstreit-Wilfert, Hildegard. "Märtyrerflugschiften der Reformationszeit." In *Flugschriften als Massenmedium der Reformationszeit: Beiträge zum Tübinger Symposion 1980,* edited by Hans-Joachim Köhler, 397–446. Stuttgart, 1981.

Historia de Duobus Augustinensibus, ob Evangelij doctrinam exustis Bruxellae, die trigesima Iunij. Anno domini M.D.XXIII. Articuli LXII. per eosdem asserti. N.p., 1523.

Hoop-Scheffler, J. G. de. *Geschichte der Reformation in den Niederlanden von ihrem Beginn bis zum Jahre 1531.* Leipzig, 1886.

Kalkoff, Paul. *Die Anfänge der Gegenreformation in den Niederlanden.* 2 vols. Halle, 1903–4.

Kess, Alexandra. *Johann Sleidan and the Protestant Vision of History.* Aldershot, 2008.

Kolb, Robert. "God's Gift of Martyrdom: The Early Reformation Understanding of Dying for the Faith." *Church History* 64 (1995): 399–441.

Lotz-Heumann, Ute. "Confessionalization." In *Reformation and Early Modern Europe: A Guide to Research,* edited by David M. Whitford, 136–57. Kirksville, 2008.

Luther, Martin. *D. Martin Luthers Werke: Kritische Gesamtausgabe.* Weimar, 1883–2009.

Moeller, Bernd. "Inquisition und Martyrium in Flugschriften der frühen Reformation in Deutschland." In *Ketzerverfolgung im 16. und frühen 17. Jahrhundert,* edited by Silvana Seidel Menchi, 21–48. Wiesbaden, 1992.

Nigrinus, Georg. *Papistische Inquisition und gulden Flüs der Römischen Kirchen. . . .* Strasbourg, 1582.

Oberman, Heiko A. *Luther: Man between God and the Devil.* Translated by Eileen Walliser-Schwarzbart. New Haven, 1989.

Oettinger, Rebecca. *Music as Propaganda in the German Reformation.* Aldershot, 2001.

Osiander, Lucas. *Epitomes Historiae Ecclesiasticae Centuriae Decimae sextae pars prima, continens Annos Quinquaginta.* Tübingen, 1602.

Proost, Jacques. *Anathematizatio ac revocatio fratris Jacobi Praepositi, olim prioris fratrum heremitarum Sancti Augustini, opidi Antverpiensis.* Antwerp, 1522.

Rabus, Ludwig. *Historien. Der Heyligen Außerwoelten Gottes Zeügen, Bekennern, vnd Martyrern . . . worden seind.* 8 vols. Strasbourg, 1554.

———. *Historien der auserwählten heiligen Gottszeugen, Bekenner, und Martyrer.* Strasbourg, 1555–56.

Reckenhofer, Martin. *Dye histori so zwen Augustiner Ordens gemartert seyn tzu Bruxel in Probant von wegen des Evangelj. Dye Artickel darumb sie verbrent seyn mit yrer asßlegung und verklerung, etc.* Erfurt, 1523.

Rössler, Martin. "Ein neues Lied wir heben an: Ein Protestsong Martin Luthers." In *Reformation und Praktische Theologie: Festschrift für Werner Jetter zum siebzigsten Geburtstag,* edited by Hans Martin Müller and Dietrich Rössler, 216–32. Göttingen, 1983.

Rudloff, Ortwin. "Bonae Literae et Lutherus: Texte und Untersuchungen zu den Anfängen der Theologie des Bremer Reformators Jakob Probst." *Hospitium Ecclesiae: Forschungen zur Bremischen Kirchengeschichte* 14 (1985): 11–239.

Schilling, Heinz. "Confessionalization and the Empire." In *Religion, Political Culture and the Emergence of Early Modern Society: Essays in German and Dutch History,* 205–45. Leiden, 1992.

Scultetus, Abraham. *Abrahami Sculteti Annalium Evangelii passim per Europam Saeculo XV Renovat. Decades I et II.* Heidelberg, 1618.

Seckendorf, Veit Ludwig. *Commentarius historicus et apologeticus de Lutheranismo: Sive de reformatione religionis ductu D. Martini Lutheri in magna Germaniae parte alliisque regionibus.* Frankfurt am Main, 1692.

Sleidanus, Johannes. *Warhafftige beschreibung geystlicher und weltlicher sachen/ under Keyser Carolo dem Fünfften verloffen.* Basel, 1556.

Surius, Laurentius. *Commentarius brevis rerum in orbe gestarum, ab anno salutis M.D. usque in annum M.D.LXXIIII.* Cologne, 1574.

Vercruysse, Jos. "'Was Haben die Sachsen und die Flamen gemeinsam?': Wittenberg von außen gesehen." In *Wittenberg als Bildungszentrum, 1502–2002,* 9–32. Wittenberg, 2002.

CHAPTER TWELVE

Prison Tales
The Miraculous Escape of Stephan Agricola and the Creation of Lutheran Heroes during the Sixteenth Century

MARJORIE ELIZABETH PLUMMER

In his *Life of Stephan Agricola the Elder*, a short work within his *Against the Seven in the Devil's Game of Knaves* (1562), Lutheran theologian Cyriacus Spangenberg described how Stephan Castenbauer (later Agricola the Elder) languished in jail because he "would not allow himself . . . to recant any part of what he taught."[1] Spangenberg described Castenbauer's patient suffering during his "three years" in prison in Salzburg, his "cheerful" teaching of God's word to comfort his fellow prisoners, his consistent refusal to recant his beliefs even when threatened, and most importantly, the devious plot hatched by his archiepiscopal captors to murder him. Fearing executing Castenbauer outright lest they provoke the peasants' wrath during the Peasants' War, the "priests of Baal and servants of the devil" planned to bring Castenbauer to Salzburg, place him in an "old tower in the [city] walls" filled with powder, and rig it to explode so the peasants would believe that God had struck the tower with lightning to punish the "evil heretic." According to Spangenberg, as Castenbauer approached the city, God sent a fire from the sky that destroyed the tower and shocked his confused captors into releasing him.[2]

Although not as well known as other early Lutheran reformers, Castenbauer has been the subject of biographies stretching from the sixteenth to the twenty-first century.[3] Spangenberg and historians using his work present Castenbauer as the model true Christian, whose dramatic escape from martyrdom at the hand of ecclesiastical officials could "strengthen belief." Yet, as Willibald Hauthaler, a nineteenth-century monk, teacher, and local historian of Salzburg, wryly remarked, Spangenberg's description is "much too adventurous to be taken seriously." His contemporary Theodor von

Kolde, a professor of Protestant church history at Erlangen, agreed that the story was "just as legendary as the story of his supposed three-year imprisonment," citing Castenbauer's 1523 involvement in the Augsburg reform movement.[4] As the essays in this volume have demonstrated, understanding how eighteenth-, nineteenth-, and twentieth-century historians constructed their confessional histories and discovering traces of earlier remnants of memory serve as a useful word of caution for current historians. This knowledge leaves the historian of the sixteenth century with a methodological problem. Should we take a written account, even an eyewitness account, at face value? As shown in this essay, the personal, confessional, or national agendas exhibited by sixteenth-century, nineteenth-century, and even contemporary historians discussing Castenbauer's prison escape often obscure the spectrum of beliefs in the early Reformation behind a stark depiction of a hero resisting temptation. By revisiting diverse archival and printed sources from differing viewpoints, the contradictory voices show that the process of reform was far from straightforward or defined for the first followers of Luther. Such diversity of opinions and experiences left considerable room for negotiation and recantation for clergy and conciliation and concession for ecclesiastical and territorial authorities still unwilling to give up on the idea of reform within a single church.

At least three distinct phases of historical remembrance and forgetting exist for Castenbauer's imprisonment. The first-person historical accounts published by Castenbauer and other imprisoned clergy in the 1520s highlighted doctrinal debate with ecclesiastical leaders. These works often left out significant details of pastors' imprisonment, including any recantation of doctrine. The second stage began in the mid-sixteenth century, when confessional-minded historians like Spangenberg published narratives in which doctrinal debate and compromise were removed from confessional memory because the participants remained committed to truth even when threatened.[5] The third phase began during the nineteenth century, when authors utilized the confessional histories to reinforce their confessional and national identity even as they sought archival documents to verify the earlier historical accounts. Castenbauer's reform activity in the Tyrol and Augsburg made him a popular subject for regional historians of Bavaria and Austria, while his involvement with Archbishop Matthias Lang of Salzburg, Johann Staupitz, and Lutheran reformers in Augsburg and Mansfeld gained the interest of nineteenth-century and early twentieth-century professional and nonprofessional church historians such as Hauthaler, Kolde, Friedrich Roth, a teacher in Munich and Augsburg, and Gustav Bossert, a Lutheran pastor.[6] Such accounts continue to dominate current discussions of Castenbauer and other first-generation reformers and to obscure the plurality and diverse focal points of the early reform movement.

Discrepancies concerning Castenbauer's imprisonment between 1522 and 1525 in all three of these phases make this episode an opportunity to observe the construction of historical memory, although this essay will concentrate on only the sixteenth-century phases. Uncovering the variations in retellings of prison tales demonstrates how the clerical experience of episcopal prisons shaped confessional identity in sixteenth-century Germany. At the same time, excavating the multiple layers of the events and interpretations of Castenbauer's imprisonment reveals how much historians have forgotten about the uncertainty and plurality of the early reform movement.

Escape through God's Providence: Creating a Model Lutheran Prisoner

In *Against the Seven in the Devil's Game of Knaves*, Spangenberg accused Stephan Agricola the Younger, a former Lutheran pastor, of abandoning his reason when he converted to Catholicism, which he called, following the rules of the sixteenth-century card game Karnöffel, the devil's card.[7] Spangenberg criticized this decision, reminding Agricola how the archbishop of Salzburg imprisoned his father, Stephan Castenbauer, for preaching Lutheran ideas in 1522. Spangenberg described the pressure episcopal authorities exerted on Castenbauer to accept four doctrines concerning papal supremacy and the theological authority of church councils. In Spangenberg's account, Castenbauer refused, stating that he would rather "rot in a tower than deny God and God's word."[8] He accepted his fate, did not recant, and did not flee voluntarily. Rather, his escape was an act of divine providence, just as his death would have been due to human evilness. In this account, Castenbauer exemplifies the stylized true Christian martyr that Spangenberg's readers would recognize. Spangenberg concluded by returning to the crucial moment of escape, asserting that Agricola's "pious Christian father would rather have rotted in a tower than to have allowed such an abomination" as his son's conversion to Catholicism. In other words, Castenbauer would have suffered martyrdom rather than allow subsequent generations to recant or slip into apostasy.

Spangenberg published his biography of Castenbauer in the midst of a controversy with Jaspar Gennep, a Catholic Cologne printer. In 1559, Gennep wrote a history of the Holy Roman Empire under Charles V in response to Johannes Sleidanus's history of the same events.[9] Gennep complained that Sleidanus had "planted lies for truth in the common man" without shame when he praised clergy "who had been judged by God." He promised to write a history to show "how grossly Sleidanus had forgotten the truth."[10] Both Sleidanus and Gennep mentioned that in 1522 Archduke Ferdinand had severely punished "those in his territories who did not want to be obedient," a likely reference to Castenbauer. The Lutheran Sleidanus attributed Ferdinand's actions "to papal law," while Catholic Gennep says Ferdinand bent "to the Christian church."[11] This disagreement about the source of Ferdinand's motivation inspired a controversy between Spangenberg and Gennep about what was truth in history. Spangenberg argued, "The study of history especially requires a high intellect, the gift of reason, attention to detail . . . proper discernment, and good memory," all of which he argued Gennep's work lacked because his Catholic bias distorted his historical method: "I have learned how often lies and half-truths are produced under the name of true history."[12] Spangenberg made Gennep the seventh devil's card, immediately after Agricola, since he considered him another force distorting the truth.[13] Gennep subsequently accused Spangenberg of writing history only from a confessional stance, because he called the younger Agricola "a godless man."[14] For both men, historical truth was tied closely to confessional identity; trustworthy historical narratives could only be produced by moral men of one's own confession.

His concern for historical method and preservation of "truth" is evident in Spangenberg's biography of Castenbauer. Spangenberg states that his evidence comes from works published in the 1520s, research in Castenbauer's library and personal papers, and his discussions with Castenbauer's friends. His careful references to earlier published works make it possible to understand how Spangenberg constructed his biography.[15] Spangenberg also draws on the presentation style and focus of Lutheran martyr books, such as Ludwig Rabus's *History of the Holy God-Chosen Witnesses, Confessors, and Martyrs* (1552/1558) and the *Magdeburg Centuries* (1559–74). Expanding on the definition of martyrdom as only ending in death, Rabus's work encompassed biographical sketches of all those who suffered for their belief, including clergy recanting their beliefs to gain release from prison. In addition to the eight executed German evangelical clergy also mentioned in John Foxe's Latin *Book of Martyrs* (1554), Rabus recounted the lives, among others, of Paul Speratus, Martin Luther, and Stephan Castenbauer, using substantial direct quotes from pamphlets published in the 1520s. Rabus subtly depicted their suffering as a continuation of that experienced by biblical and early Christian martyrs. The *Magdeburg Centuries* took a similar long-range historical approach reaching back into biblical and early Christianity but focused on the true Christian's unwillingness to waiver.[16] Thus recanting becomes impossible for a potential Lutheran martyr or true Christian exemple.

In his work, Spangenberg consciously shaped Castenbauer's life in line with the Lutheran ideal of consistent faith. After outlining Castenbauer's illustrious early career, Spangenberg described how, after reading Luther's writings, "the Doctor . . . had his eyes opened by the holy ghost and his heart enlightened so he recognized the difference between the pure and false teachings." Castenbauer felt compelled to "preach the truth," leading the archbishop of Salzburg to imprison him in Mühldorf.[17] Like Rabus, Spangenberg used long passages of quotes from earlier texts. Citing Urbanus Rhegius, Spangenberg described how the archbishop sent Nicholas Ribeisen to pressure Castenbauer to accept Roman teachings.[18] He cited Wolfgang Russ to establish how Castenbauer accepted his imprisonment and refused to recant. After an extensive description of Castenbauer's escape, Spangenberg provided an outline of Castenbauer's consistent work in his later career supporting orthodoxy in Augsburg, Marburg, Brandenburg-Ansbach, and finally Mansfeld, where he and the other theologians harmoniously struggled to bring about the "true evangelical religion." He concluded with Castenbauer's death during Easter week in 1547 after choosing his own epitaph as having "lived in the belief of the son of God, who loved me and gave himself for me."[19]

The murder plot and the escape of Castenbauer are the dramatic focus of the chapter. Spangenberg provided no written source for his description of the murder plot and escape, stating only that he heard it directly from Castenbauer and Johann Spangenberg, his father. In their *Funeral Oration* (1550), published after Castenbauer's death, Johann Spangenberg and Hieronymus Mencel praised his steadfastness of faith and compared his suffering for his belief to those of Christ.[20] Mencel's biographical sketch included a description of Castenbauer's miraculous escape from a tower rigged with gunpowder. He commented that Castenbauer's survival occurred "lest those who preach God's true word be killed by blasphemers and frauds."[21] Mencel did not give any dates for the events or name the "tyrant" involved in plotting the murder, although he hinted that it was the archduke. Cyriacus Spangenberg left no doubt in his 1562 account that the archbishop plotted the explosion and that Castenbauer was freed without recanting in 1524. He specifically called the fire in the tower a demonstration of "God's providential care" for Castenbauer's survival, thereby affirming his place as a true Christian and dismissing any role of mercy on the archbishop's part.[22] Spangenberg's biography of Castenbauer shared Rabus's focus on spiritual development and steadfast belief, creating what Markus Lommer called "an almost martyr."[23] Indeed elements of Spangenberg's story of Castenbauer's suffering—imprisonment, refusal to recant, the tower, and lightning—are reminiscent of the martyrdom of Saint Barbara, lacking only the execution. In doing so, even the non-martyr becomes a Christian hero.

Why did Spangenberg tell this story of Castenbauer's imprisonment and escape? Spangenberg described his wish to save the "pious" father's name from association with the "deceptive" writings of the son. Spangenberg also distanced the Mansfeld reformers from any association with the younger Agricola and showed how correct their position was in their ongoing theological dispute with Wittenberg.[24] Castenbauer's miraculous escape from the archbishop served a central function as a model of faith and suffering for the true religion. In contrast, he called the younger Agricola an "apostate slave" and a voluntary prisoner of deception and false teachings.[25] Spangenberg's cutting remark to the younger Agricola that his father would have rather suffered death, accepting his martyrdom, in the tower than have allowed his son's conversion is a central moment in the work. By showing how the son's willingness to convert contrasted with his father's consistent refusal to recant to the bishop, this episode illustrates the stakes in contemporary doctrinal controversies. In doing so, Spangenberg's work represents a shift in how previous authors had represented similar moments in early sixteenth-century polemic and mirrors his own debates over doctrine, not only with Catholic historians, but also with Lutherans deviating from orthodoxy, even to the point of conversion.

A Prisoner's Tale: Prison and the Art of Not Dying

Tales of clergy imprisoned by bishops related in late sixteenth-century chronicles and histories, and repeated in subsequent Reformation histories, have created a sense that these were common experiences for the first clerical supporters of the Lutheran reform movement. They also show that evangelical clergy were resolute in their resistance and confident in their theological positions. Yet, imprisonment by bishops, whether of short or long duration, remained rare for Lutheran clergy in German-speaking territories.[26] Following late medieval episcopal synodal and canon law, bishops sought recantations from clergy accused of evangelical activity.[27] Most of the early evangelical clergy complied, which contradicts the heroic ideal of the early reformers presented by Spangenberg and later confessional historians. The evangelical clergy in the 1520s initially sought to convince bishops to reform doctrine by engaging in debate and were more ready to discuss compromise than later narratives often portray. Even during the early 1520s, however, these authors also simultaneously sought to maintain a narrative for their supporters to believe that such recantations did not mean that they had abandoned their teachings. This twofold approach produced material that allowed for later historians to ignore the first act and focus on the second.

Early reformers certainly anticipated and even expected possible risks when engaging with ecclesiastical authorities. In one of the earliest examples (1518), Luther described how his initial discussions with Cardinal Thomas Cajetan in Augsburg led to a conversation in which Luther tentatively agreed to "silence" on doctrinal points. When the tone of the conversation changed, Luther justified his secret departure as motivated by his fear that Cajetan would demand a formal recantation of doctrine and his concern about being executed should he refuse.[28] After 1521, Johannes Schwalb and subsequent authors compared Luther's encounter at Worms to Jan Hus's execution at Constance and warned evangelical clergy that martyrdom could await them as well.[29] Published reports from the clergy and their supporters emphasized such expectations of death and their preparations for that event.[30] Throughout the 1520s, this fear that evangelical activity would lead to execution and martyrdom was never far from the minds of Luther's supporters, even though imprisonment remained rare and executions even rarer.

Those few evangelical clergy who were imprisoned did produce numerous prison and inquisition narratives in the early 1520s designed to publicize their detention for having taught specific doctrines. During his imprisonment in the city hall in Mühldorf, for instance, Castenbauer published *Articles Presented against Stephan Castenbauer* (1523), with the help of a visiting local priest, Wolfgang Russ. The work, signed "from his miserable prison," stated his beliefs in response to the questions asked by an episcopal official.[31] These works recounted theological debates between prisoner and inquisitor over doctrines, usually in the form of a dialogue or trial transcript, and challenged bishops' authority by discussing how they were questioned.[32] Authors focused on doctrinal debate rather than the conditions of their imprisonment or physical suffering. Such works served a dual purpose: defending specific doctrinal positions by showing the theological errors of ecclesiastical authorities and illustrating the undue pressure placed on clergy to recant.

The expectation that interactions with bishops and ecclesiastical authorities could lead to execution contributed to circulating rumors about the treatment of evangelical clergy throughout the Holy Roman Empire. Rumors exaggerated the dangers of imprisonment to elicit greater sympathy from political leaders. In 1523, Hans van Planitz reported to Elector Frederick that he had heard how Archduke Ferdinand had arrested "a monk [Castenbauer] at Rattenberg on the Inn" and had him "inhumanly tortured" because of his Lutheran teachings until he "begged death."[33] Such rumors made their way into publications as well. In his *Apology* (1523), Russ justified his refusal to "place himself freely into the ill-intended hands" of Archbishop Lang when he was cited to appear in Salzburg as prompted by the archbishop leaving Castenbauer "to rot in a tower."[34] Growing apprehension eroded episcopal effectiveness in subsequent attempts to question imprisoned clergy and made it difficult for bishops to act forcefully.[35]

Unable to get relapsed evangelical clergy to appear in courts after release from prison, bishops and their representatives confronted retractions of recantations by publishing the trial transcripts and recantation of clergy.[36] Prominent early examples include the interrogation of Arsacius Seehofer for heretical writings by the faculty of University of Ingolstadt.[37] In defending Seehofer (1524), Argula von Grumbach argued that such men and women served as an example to teach God's word against the "Pharisees" through their "constancy, suffering, agony, and death." She pointed out that young Seehofer in Ingolstadt was forced "through prison and threat of fire" to deny God's word in a "prescribed and forced oath" against his free conscience. Luther echoed Grumbach's condemnation by describing Seehofer's recantations as resulting from "deadly sacrilege and force" of the university officials.[38] Evangelical leaders and supporters subsequently denounced bishops' misuse of spiritual authority in forcing clergy to deny true teachings and presented such recantations as torture.

Many clergy who had formally renounced their belief after an extended prison stay subsequently publicly defended their commitment to the evangelical cause. They described efforts to resist any doubts emerging during the significant physical and spiritual suffering at the hands of a misguided bishop and using coercion or scriptural misrepresentation to extract forced recantations. After his release, Castenbauer published *Considerations of Agricola Boius on the True Service to God Commanded by God Himself* (1524), which outlined his position on everything from communion in both kinds and the Mass to his opinion about monastic life. He reminded bishops that God commanded them to teach God's word "with fatherly kindness," not to misuse their position "with violence or prison and fire."[39] His use of the pseudonym Agricola Boius signaled his transition to his new identity as Stephan Agricola, a preacher firmly supporting the Lutheran reform movement, and distanced himself from his recantation.

Were there other ways imprisoned clergy escaped imprisonment other than recanting? Not many. Bishops released some evangelical clergy after imposing fines, banishment, or excommunication, although that does not preclude the possibility that the pastor had already recanted. Another explanation for release from prison that emerges in at least five cases was that of "escape" from custody of a bishop or secular authority. None of the clergy who supposedly escaped between 1522 and 1525 produced a pamphlet about their miraculous escape, nor do they appear in any of the later discussions of Lutheran martyrs or heroes. Many imprisoned clerics managed to avoid a heresy trial and potential execution by renouncing their previous actions and signing an oath of peace (*Urphede*) promising to refrain from evangelical activity. Many, if not most, resumed evangelical activity soon after their release.[40]

Only in the mid-1520s did German bishops briefly use execution as a disciplinary measure, as demonstrated in the Constance consistory court's 1527 interrogation of Johann Hüglin, a primissary from Lindau. Lutheran authors publicized Hüglin's excommunication and execution after he steadfastly refused to recant his beliefs.[41] The publicity surrounding subsequent executions led clergy to flee when cited to meet with bishops, leading the bishops to concede the failure of their disciplinary efforts. By the late 1520s, clergy, including those imprisoned and questioned, their colleagues, and reformer leaders avoided or downplayed mention of prison experience in their pamphlets and letters. In 1528, Georg, margrave of Brandenburg-Ansbach, wrote Rhegius asking whether he could recommend Castenbauer for a position as pastor, inquiring whether he was "a learned, capable, and serious" man and asking for assurance that he was not inclined to "fanaticism."[42] In response, Rhegius described calling Castenbauer to Augsburg precisely because he was a "pious, learned man" and said that the local leaders had begged Castenbauer to remain "to preach the gospels in the churches of Augsburg," which he had promised "modestly . . . in the honor of God" rather than answer this call. Rhegius did not mention Castenbauer's previous preaching activity or long imprisonment.[43] Despite early examples of defending forsworn evangelical clergy, reform leaders viewed recantations by evangelical clergy, even when imprisoned, with concern, and silence on the matter became crucial.

With that, any further evangelical discussion of recanting or prison during the sixteenth century only occurred when the story could demonstrate the complete conviction of the prisoner. Thus, the polemic shifted to those clergy executed while in prison or whose experiences were recast to include such conviction as seen in the later case of Castenbauer. The plurality of opinions and experiences gave way to uniform narratives highlighting unwavering confessional conviction.

Excavating the Archives: A Tale of Five Prisons

Scholarly and popular presentations of Castenbauer's experiences between his imprisonment and his arrival in Augsburg have demonstrated how historical interpretation and memory molded the complicated life of an early reformer into a straightforward narrative of heroicism and conviction. Even recent scholars returning to the archives to explore Castenbauer's early involvement in the Tyrolean and Bavarian reform movement continue to emphasize specific aspects of this narrative. Many authors have sought to reconcile the gap between the story told by Spangenberg and the skepticism expressed by nineteenth- and twentieth-century authors about how Castenbauer left prison and when he arrived in Augsburg.[44] Because these biographical studies mostly deal with Castenbauer within a specific geographic or thematic context, they inadvertently replicate some of the same tendencies of the sixteenth-century accounts to present Castenbauer as heroic. Tracing Castenbauer through his travels between 1522 and 1525 in recent scholarship and to the archives where those travels left trails has allowed me to reconstruct a complex and multifaceted narrative, largely missing from either Castenbauer's or Spangenberg's histories.

After the imperial council called for halting the spread of Lutheran ideas by improving disciplinary efforts, bishops in Saxony undertook visitations in 1522 but failed to stop evangelical preaching.[45] Ferdinand feared similar episcopal ineffectuality in the Tyrolean territories, despite Archbishop Lang's Mühldorf mandate (1522) that threatened imprisonment for Lutheran preachers in the archdiocese of Salzburg.[46] Ferdinand praised the mandate but pushed Lang for assurances that evangelical clergy would be removed. After Lang interrogated and released Burghausen preacher Hans Lindmair due to his uncertainty about whether the questionable doctrines in Lindmair's sermons resulted from "carelessness" or "evil opinion," Ferdinand resolved to act without the cooperation of bishops in the Habsburg Tyrolean territories.[47] As a result, when the provocative sermons of Stephan Castenbauer came to his attention in November 1522, Ferdinand turned to the Rattenberg city council, not the archbishop, to arrest and try Castenbauer, then active as a preacher in the city.[48]

This stage of Castenbauer's imprisonment is the one most often overlooked by subsequent authors, with almost all authors through the nineteenth century claiming that he was taken immediately to Mühldorf. At the same time, this part of the story was the most public because of the involvement of so many constituencies.[49] Tensions in Rattenberg escalated as the volatile negotiations to protect the rights of the miners' union within the city limits combined with local support of the popular "Doctor Steffan," as he was identified. In late 1522, representatives from Rattenberg met with imperial officials to advocate sending Castenbauer to the archbishop of Salzburg to stabilize the deteriorating situation with the miners. While meeting in Innsbruck, Rattenberg's delegates described how the situation had worsened after Castenbauer broke his leg after falling from a window of the city hall while calming a large crowd protesting his imprisonment. When Castenbauer voluntarily returned to the city hall, the city council brought in a doctor to care for him, but the peasants and miners remained apprehensive.[50] Stuck between his desire to squelch the Lutheran movement in his territory and his need to protect critical financial agreements with the Fuggers involving the mining industry in the area, Ferdinand remained firm: the Rattenberg city council was to try Castenbauer and inform the miners that he was reconsidering their rights.[51] While still pushing for a trial in Rattenberg, Ferdinand did allow Castenbauer to be moved from confinement in the city hall to the castle under the oversight of his local official, Christoph Philipp von Liechtenstein.[52]

After the situation deteriorated in early 1523, Ferdinand finally conceded to the city council's request to turn Castenbauer over to the archbishop of Salzburg and kept all negotiations a secret from the miners to prevent rioting.[53] Charles V issued a public proclamation after the successful transfer of Castenbauer by ship to the archbishop's closest territory in Mühldorf, an exclave in Bavaria on the Inn River. The emperor explained that he sought to prevent any "future danger" from Castenbauer's preaching "the condemned teachings of Martin Luther" to the laity and promised that the archbishop would deal with the "preacher of Rattenberg" according to canon law. Christoph Philipp read this mandate to the miners in the public square, with reassurances that this was best for Castenbauer and that the city would continue to help him.[54] The miners accepted this, but Duke William of Bavaria did not. William demanded payment from Lang for violating his jurisdictional rights by secretly crossing Bavarian territory during the transfer and claimed that Castenbauer now fell under his authority. Lang refused to pay the fine because to do so would amount to recognition of William's authority, which prevented him from moving Castenbauer to Salzburg.[55]

Aside from the hints in the work of Russ and Spangenberg, Castenbauer's imprisonment in Mühldorf has been told through the perspective of the records sent to the archbishop of Salzburg and the duke of Bavaria. As in Rattenberg, records located in the city archive of Mühldorf have been overlooked because Castenbauer was identified as "the monk" rather than by name. After his arrival in Mühldorf before the March regional diet in Salzburg, Castenbauer was held in the Altöttingen tower closest to the river, where he was given candles to read by, until moved in late June into the city hall, where he remained until early January 1524.[56] Over the next seven months, Castenbauer was joined briefly by other prisoners but was later housed separately and allowed visitors. The city council paid to make improvements to his room, including repairing the windows, a sign that he was held in one of the upper rooms, and providing Castenbauer with more candles and two quills, which he used to write those works published during 1523 and 1524.[57] During this time, the episcopal council sent officials, including Johann Staupitz, to assess Castenbauer's orthodoxy and then worked to get a recantation once it was decided he was not as much heretical as misguided.[58] In December 1523, Nikolaus Ribeisin presented Castenbauer with a choice of remaining indefinitely in prison or being released if he agreed to avoid the hereditary Habsburg lands and any further preaching, which Castenbauer refused.[59] This refusal is the one described by Russ, Castenbauer, and Spangenberg. It was not, however, the last time Castenbauer was asked to recant.

Castenbauer's publication of two pamphlets from prison and growing public attention about the case prompted action from the archbishop's council in Salzburg. As documents held in Salzburg and Mühldorf show, the archbishop's council requested that Castenbauer be moved from the city hall into the archbishop's administrative center in Mühldorf on 2 January 1524, and the city council watchman was given his final payment. The episcopal jailer restricted Castenbauer's visitors and placed him in solitary confinement in chains.[60] After a few months of further imprisonment, Ruprecht Hirschauer, a judge from Mühldorf, reported that Castenbauer admitted to having preached two "fervid" sermons in Rattenberg. He pushed Castenbauer to ask for forgiveness and presented him a document that repeated that admission and included a promise never to enter the Habsburg hereditary territories or the archdiocese of Salzburg, disobey the Holy Christian Church, or preach again. While it remains uncertain whether Castenbauer signed the document, the letter written by Hirschauer indicates that Castenbauer was involved in editing the document, and all evidence points to his release from the Mühldorf prison shortly after that meeting.[61]

What Castenbauer did between that and his arrival in Augsburg in mid-1525 remains uncertain, although the publication of his *Consideration* (1524) near Leipzig has led at least one scholar to suggest that Castenbauer followed the path of his fellow evangelical clergy questioned or imprisoned by bishops and headed to Ernestine Saxony.[62] As to Spangenberg's account of Castenbauer's escape, no archival evidence has turned up of a tower being blown up in Rattenberg, Mühldorf, or Salzburg between 1523 and 1524. Reports do survive of an incident in Mühldorf in which the watch accidently damaged a tower during a traditional shooting match held in celebration of Saint Michael's Day in 1524.[63] Rattenberg and Salzburg were attacked during the Peasants' War between 1525 and 1526, with miners and peasants damaging the Hohensalzburg Castle during a siege that began in May 1525. By this point, however, Castenbauer had already published his 1524 pamphlet condemning his imprisonment and arrived in Augsburg mid-July 1525, and so could not have been involved in these incidents.[64]

Although not fully answering the question of what happened to Castenbauer and how he left prison, the archival documents do show how each of the constituencies had their own concerns during the imprisonment of Castenbauer. Although the direct voices of the miners or burghers of Mühldorf are lacking, their participation and reactions guided the course of events. Each of the groups holding Castenbauer—the Rattenberg city council, the imperial official Christoph Philipp, the city of Mühldorf, and archiepiscopal officials in Mühldorf—sought to resolve the case without trying or executing Castenbauer lest this cause local problems. During the complex negotiations about what to do with Castenbauer between 1522 and 1524, the involved parties presented evidence of the jurisdictional questions and assessed the potential harm they feared Castenbauer represented and shaped their correspondence and records to reflect that. From the evidence in these archival sources, Castenbauer's prison experience followed the pattern experienced by many evangelical preachers arrested in the first decade of the reform movement.

Conclusion

Variations in historical interpretations over time should force historians to reconsider even oft-repeated stories like that of Castenbauer's miraculous escape and dig deeper into published and archival sources. Such a reassessment reveals an unexpected complication in Castenbauer's prison experience. He was held in not one, but rather five separate prisons in two different locations by four separate authorities between 1522 and 1524, and none were in Salzburg. That discovery necessitates reexamining how Castenbauer, Spangenberg, and other sixteenth-century authors engaged in constructions of historical memory designed for specific contexts. Overlooking either the contexts for those works or the variety of Castenbauer's prison experiences makes difficult either understanding the building of confessional identity in the mid-sixteenth century or the reform movement of the early sixteenth century. Spangenberg's presentation in the mid-sixteenth century and later historians' acceptance of his version of events in Salzburg ignored this complexity, consciously or unconsciously, to tell a contemporary specific story of confessional identity.

Historical accounts of Castenbauer's life have served specific, often confessional, agendas. First, early Lutheran clergy released from episcopal prisons exploited their experience as an opportunity to further their reform movement. Second, beginning in the mid-sixteenth century, Lutheran authors transformed these episodes by establishing stylized, normative models of clerical prison experiences during the early reform movement. Finally, later historians retold Castenbauer's imprisonment to fit into regional, confessional, and historiographical concerns of the nineteenth and twentieth centuries. These authors either accepted Spangenberg's version of spiritual constancy and episcopal deceit or rejected it by selectively using historical evidence. Modern historians continue to rewrite Castenbauer's biography using new evidence from the historical records and archives, a task that often stumbles on the misinformation contained in previous histories, the vagaries of record-keeping, and the splintering of archival holdings during later centuries.

Many elements of Spangenberg's biography of Castenbauer, notably the description of the dramatic escape from prison, are not found in the archival records held in Rattenberg and Mühldorf, where he was imprisoned. Other parts that are in the archival records, such as Ferdinand's command for his arrest and his time in captivity in Rattenberg, are missing from Castenbauer's and Spangenberg's biographies and most subsequent works. This silence is due first to Castenbauer's desire to keep the support of political leaders in Rattenberg and Mühldorf who were assisting him. Continued silence is largely the product of a forgetting of the political aspect of the early reform movement and the concentration on theology and confessional concerns established in the histories of the mid-sixteenth century. Although Castenbauer did expect martyrdom, as his publication on dying indicates, he, like many of Luther's early followers, was not executed. Perhaps most surprising, given Spangenberg's tale or even Castenbauer's pamphlets, he even held extended negotiations with episcopal representatives in 1524 on an acceptable recantation document he could, and probably did, sign, something he had to forget.

The retelling of his prison tale by later historians served a different purpose than Castenbauer's own work. To borrow from his own use of the metaphor of the card game, Spangenberg made a conscious choice to reshuffle the deck to play a knave to win the trick against the seven, or the devil's card, as the rules of Karnöffel establish.[65] Spangenberg invoked divine intervention on behalf of the father to contrast with the younger Agricola as the devil's agent. This intentional juxtaposition suggests that Spangenberg expected the younger Agricola to be brought to his senses by the reminder of this story, and thus trump the devil. The story served as a reminder to Castenbauer's son, or any other potential convert, of what they give up through conversion: the true religion. Nineteenth-century historians like Hauthaler or Kolde rejected Spangenberg's account as "fantastic" and "legendary" but did so motivated by their particular confessional and national perspectives. Although based on archival sources, these works contributed complicated biases that need closer examination: Hauthaler, a Catholic Salzburg historian, demonstrated that the archbishop of Salzburg had not perpetrated such a calculated act, and Kolde, the Lutheran theologian at Erlangen trained in Rankean methodology, focused on Castenbauer's rational leadership in the Augsburg Lutheran reform he perhaps sought in the ongoing theological and political debates in Erlangen and Bavaria.[66] Castenbauer crossed many borders and themes, and so his story is often told in fragments determined by modern boundaries and regional interests of his biographers.

What happened to Stephan Castenbauer between his arrest in late 1522 and his arrival in Augsburg in 1525 may never be known with complete certainty and probably does not matter. That authors remembered, created, or forgot parts of his story, and their readers expected certain elements, does. Whether he was imprisoned in one prison or five, escaped from a tower in Salzburg filled with gunpowder or was released after having signed a recantation, Stephan Castenbauer has become a fictionalized version of himself used by historians for specific purposes, many of them confessional. Understanding the plurality of retellings has become a vital part of his story. To forget this and to read the story without a nuanced understanding of the multiple purposes of the production of his biography misses the point. Castenbauer, like numerous other early evangelical clergy, had his own constructions of his prison experiences turned into exempla of faith by the next generation of Lutheran pastors and historians as attention shifted from activism to church-building to unified confessional identity. Uncovering those involved in the events surrounding

Castenbauer's imprisonment and remembering the ambiguity of their reactions underscore how uncertain participants were of the new reform movement or of its ultimate outcome. As these earlier sources demonstrate, even leaders of the reform movement such as Castenbauer may not always have shown the consistency of belief later authors attributed to them. Even when such individuals did remain consistent in desiring reform, the choice to die did not always meet with an equal choice to execute, and thus martyrdom was not their fate.

Marjorie Elizabeth Plummer is Susan C. Karant-Nunn Chair for Reformation and Early Modern European History at the University of Arizona. She specializes in the history of the impact of the early reform movement on family and gender roles and on the changing legal definitions of social norms and religious identity in early modern Germany. Her publications include *From Priest's Whore to Pastor's Wife: Clerical Marriage and the Process of Reform in the Early German Reformation* (Farnham, 2012) and a number of articles, including "'Partner in His Calamities': Pastors' Wives, Married Nuns and the Experience of Clerical Marriage in the Early German Reformation," *Gender & History* 20 (2008): 207–27. She is also coeditor of *Ideas and Cultural Margins in Early Modern Germany: Essays in Honor of H. C. Erik Midelfort* (Farnham, 2009).

Notes

I would like to thank the Western Kentucky University's Office of Research and History Department for generous financial and institutional support to complete the research for this essay.

1. Name variations include Castenbauer, Agricola Boius, "Doctor Steffan," and "Mönche von Rattenberg." Castenbauer adopted Agricola first as a pseudonym to publish and then permanently after his return to evangelical activity after 1525. This essay uses Castenbauer, as the elder Stephan Agricola was known in the early 1520s, to distinguish him from his son.
2. Cyriacus Spangenberg, *Wider die böse Sieben ins Teufels Karnöffelspiel* (Eisleben, 1562), piiir–siiir.
3. For example, Christian August Salig, *Vollständige Historie Der Augspurgischen Confeßion und derselben zugethanen Kirchen, Dritter Theil* (Halle, 1735), 159; Christian Adam Dann, "Stephan Castenbauer (Juli 15)," in *Anekdoten für Christen zur stärkung des Glaubens, der Hoffnung und der Liebe* (Basel, 1833), 199–200; and Karl Friedrich Dobel, *Kurze Geschichte der Auswanderung der evangelischen Salzburger* (Kempten, 1832), 6–8.
4. Willibald Hauthaler, *Cardinal Matthäus Lang und die religiös-sociale Bewegung seiner Zeit (1517–1540)* (Salzburg, 1896), 87; Theodor von Kolde, "Agricola, Stephen," in *Realenzyklopädie für protestantische Theologie und Kirche*, 24 vols. (Leipzig, 1896), vol. 1, 253–54; and Theodor von Kolde, "Zur Bibliographie," *Beiträge zur bayerischen Kirchengeschichte* 3 (1897): 293.

5. C. Scott Dixon, "The Sense of the Past in the Reformation: Part II," *German History* 30 (2012): 180.
6. Friedrich Roth, *Augsburgs Reformationsgeschichte*, 4 vols. (Munich, 1881), vol. 1, 125–26; Gustav Bossert, "Beiträge zur Geschichte Tirols in der Reformationszeit," *Jahrbuch der Gesellschaft für die Geschichte Protestantismus in Oesterreich* 6 (1885): 147–50; Franz Paul Datterer, *Des Cardinals und Erzbischofs von Salzburg Matthäus Lang* (Erlangen, 1890), 29–32; and Josef Schmid, "Das Cardinals und Erzbischofs von Salzburg Mätthaus Lang Verhalten zur Reformation (Capital IV)," *Jahrbuch der Gesellschaft für die Geschichte Protestantismus in Oesterreich* 20 (1899): 154–84, here 167–68.
7. For the rules of Karnöffel, see David Sidney Parlett, *The Oxford Guide to Card Games* (Oxford, 1990), 165–67; and Martin Luther, *Ein Frage des gantzen Heiligen Ordens der Kartenspieler von Karnöffel an das Concilium zu Mantua gebessert* (1537).
8. Spangenberg, *Karnöffelspiel*, qir–v.
9. Johannes Sleidanus, *Johannis Sleidanusi Warhaftige Beschreibung aller Händel, . . . under dem Großmächtigsten Keyser Carln dem Fünfften zugetragen und verlauffen haben* (Frankfurt am Main, 1558); and Jaspar Gennep, *Epitome. Warhaftiger Beschreibung der Vornembsten Händel- so sich in Geistlichen unnd Weltlichen sachen, von Jahr unsers Herren M.D. biss in das jar der mynderen zal LIX zuggeragen und verlauffen haben* (Cologne, 1559).
10. Gennep, *Epitome*, Aiiir–v.
11. Sleidanus, *Beschreibung*, Giiir; Gennep, *Epitome*, Fivr.
12. Cyriacus Spangenberg, *Antwort und bereicht auff das uch, welchs Jaspar Gennep . . . wider des Sleidanusi Commentarios . . . , mit anzeigung worinnen sich gedachter Genep anders dan einem rechten Historienschriber gebüret* (Eisleben, 1560), Aiiiv–Aivr, Aviir.
13. Jaspar Gennep, *Eyn Ernsthafftigs Gesprech, zwischen Jaspar Gennep, . . . und Cyriaco Spangenberg, über die Geschicht Beschreibung, Johannis Sleidanusi* (Cologne, 1561); and Jaspar Gennep, *Catholischer Spangenbergischer Catechismus* (Cologne, 1561).
14. Jaspar Gennep, *Red und Antwort jetziger Zweyspalt in Glaubenssachen . . . mit Christlicher Widerlagung des ünuerschampten schreiben so Cyriac Spangenberg im jar M.D. Lxii widet . . . herren Stephanum Agricolam, und Jaspar Gennep, Ausgeben hat* (Cologne, 1563), 116.
15. Spangenberg, *Karnöffelspiel*, pivv. This is clearest in his use of Urbanus Rhegius's collected works (1550) and the introduction Wolfgang Russ, a local priest visiting Castenbauer in prison, added to *Articles Presented against Stephen Castenbauer* (1523).
16. Ludwig Rabus, *Historien. Der Heyligen Außerwoelten Gottes Zeügen, Bekennern, vnd Martyrern . . . worden seind*, 8 vols. (Strasbourg, 1554), vol. 3, lijr–lviiir, vol. 8, 1r; Robert Kolb, *For All the Saints: Changing Perceptions of Martyrdom and Sainthood in the Lutheran Reformation* (Macon, GA, 1987), 63–65; Brad S. Gregory, *Salvation at Stake: Christian Martyrdom in Early Modern Europe* (Cambridge, MA, 2001); and Matthias Pohlig, *Zwischen Gelehrsamkeit und konfessioneller Identitätsstiftung: Lutherische Kirchen- und Universalgeschichtsschreibung 1546–1617* (Tübingen 2007).
17. Spangenberg, *Karnöffelspiel*, piiv–qiir; and Johann Georg Schelhorn, *Historische Nachricht vom Ursprunge, Fortgang und Schicksale der Evangelischen Religion in den Salzburgischen Landen* (Leipzig, 1732), 88–92.
18. Urbanus Rhegius, *Loci Theologici, e Patribus et Scholastici Neotericisque collecti* (Frankfurt am Main, 1550), 222.
19. Spangenberg, *Karnöffelspiel*, qiir–qiiiv.

20. Johann Spangenberg and Hieronymus Mencel, *Epitaphia Reverendi Viri, D. Stephani Agricolae* (Erfurt, 1550).
21. Spangenberg and Mencel, *Epitaphia*, Biiv.
22. Spangenberg, *Karnöffelspiel*, qir.
23. Markus Lommer, "Der altbayerische Frühlutheraner Dr. Stephan Kastenbauer/ Agricola (um 1491/1547): Ein Biogramm auf erneuertem Forschungsstand," *Zeitschrift für bayerische Kirchengeschichte* 69 (2000): 229.
24. Robert Christman, *Doctrinal Controversy and Lay Religiosity in Late Reformation Germany: The Case of Mansfeld* (Leiden, 2012), 44.
25. Spangenberg, *Karnöffelspiel*, piv–piiir.
26. Marjorie Elizabeth Plummer, *From Priest's Whore to Pastor's Wife: Clerical Marriage and the Process of Reform in the Early German Reformation* (Farnham, 2012), 6–7. Between 1521 and 1533, bishops imprisoned forty-eight and questioned two hundred of twenty-seven hundred identified Lutheran clergy active in Mainz and Magdeburg about evangelical activity.
27. Anton Joseph Binterim, *Pragmatische Geschichte der Deutschen National=, Provinzial= und vorzüglichsten Diöcesanconcilien*, 7 vols. (Mainz, 1831–1848), vol. 5, 196–97, 258, 263; vol. 6, 67, 229, 471.
28. Martin Luther, *Acta F. Luther August. Apud D. Legatum Apostolicum Augustae* (Leipzig, 1518); and Bernhard Löhse, *Luthers Theologie in ihrer historischen Entwicklung und in ihrem systematischen Zusammenhang* (Göttingen, 1995), 127–34.
29. Johannes Schwalb, *Beclagung aines leyens genant Hanns schwalb* über *vil mißbreüch Christliches lebens, vnd dariñ begriffen kürtzlich von Johannes Hußen* (Augsburg, 1521); and Nikolaus von Amsdorf, *Grund vnd vrsach ausz der Cronicke, Warumb Johannes Husz vnd Jeronimus von Prag verbrant seyn* (Magdeburg, 1525).
30. Stephen Agricola, *Ain köstlicher gutter notwendiger Sermon von Sterben . . . Außgangen Von Doctor Steffan Castenbaur Augustiner ordens in seiner gefäncknuß umb gottes worts willen, zu Müldorff* (Augsburg, 1523); and Bernd Moeller, "Sterbekunst in der Reformation: Der 'köstliche, gute, notwendige Sermon vom Sterben' des Augustiner-Eremiten Stefan Kastenbauer," in *Vita Religiosa im Mittelalter*, ed. Franz Felten and Nikolas Jespert (Berlin, 1999), 739–65.
31. Stephan Agricola, *Artickel wider Doctor Steffan Castenpawr Eingelegt, auch was er darauf geantwort hat, auß seine gefencknus, Newlich von jm außgangen* (Augsburg, 1523); and Tiroler Landesarchiv [TLA], Stadtarchiv Rattenberg [StadtARatt], Schuber, 168, 17v (18 April 1523); 23r–v (22 May 1523).
32. Plummer, *Priest's Whore*, 101–2.
33. Hans von der Planitz, *Bericht aus dem Reichsregiment in Nürnberg, 1521–1523*, ed. Ernst Wülcker and Hans Virck (Leipzig, 1899), 478 (4 July 1523), 493 (22 July 1523).
34. Wolfgang Ruess, *Ayn entschuldigung aines Priesters, Wolfgang Ruß, Gesellpaff zu Oting in Bayern gewest, welcher von wegen des Gotßworts den Gemaynen man fürgehalten, nach der Ordnung seines Apts, gen Saltzpurg Citiert worden ist, oder nit erschinen* (Nuremberg, 1523), Aiir, Bir–v, Biiir.
35. Thüringisches Hauptstaatsarchiv Weimar [ThHStAW], Ernestinisches Gesamtarchiv [EGA], Reg. N25, 37 (2 April 1522).
36. *Sententia contra Joannē Vásel . . . Widerruff herr Hans Vásel briester von der Newenstat, mit vrtail vnd recht auffgelegt vnd erkant zû Wien in Osterreich* (Vienna, 1524); and *Sententia contra Jacobū Peregrinum . . . Widerrueff herr Jacob Peregrinus briester Passawer bistumbs, mit vrtail vñrecht auffgelegt vnd erkant zû Wienn in Osterreich* (Vienna, 1524).

37. *Sybentzehen Artickel so die Doctorn, der Wolberuembtē Vniuersitet Jngolstatt, für ketzer-isch verdammet, vnd Mayster Arsacij Seehofer von München offenntlich an vnnser frawen gepurdt abendt widerruefft hat* (Munich, 1523).

38. Argula von Grumbach, *Wye ein Christliche fraw des adels, in Beyern durch iren, in Gotlicher schrifft, wolgegrundtenn Sendbrieffe, die hohenschul zu Jngolstat, vmb das sie eynen Euangelischen Jungling, zu widersprechung des wort Gottes, betrangt haben, straffet* (Erfurt, 1523), Aiv–Aiiv, Aivv; and Martin Luther, *Wider das blindt vnnd Toll ver-damnuß der Sybenzehen Artickel, von der Ellenden Schendtlichen Vniuersitet zů Jngolstat außgangen* (Augsburg, 1524).

39. Stephen Agricola, *Ein bedencken des agricola Boius wie der warhafftig Gottes dienst von Gott selbst geboten und außgesetzt* möcht mit *besserung gemeyner Christenheyt widerumb auffgericht werden* (Eilenburg, 1524), Ciir–v.

40. Plummer, *Priest's Whore*, 101, 251–52. I have found signed *Urphede* in archives and confirmed recantations for at least half the imprisoned clergy.

41. Plummer, *Priest's Whore*, 249–53.

42. Staatsarchiv Nürnberg [StAN], Rep. 111 Ansbacher Religionsakten, Tom. 11, 26r–v.

43. StAN, Rep. 111, Tom. 11, 34 (11 October 1528).

44. Matthias Simon, "Zur Lebensgeschichte des Stephan Agricola und zur Person des Agricola Boius," *Zeitschrift für bayerische Kirchengeschichte* 30 (1961): 168–74; Hans Roser, *Altbayern und Luther: Portraits* (Munich, 1996), 148–54; Stephen B. Boyd, *Pilgram Marpeck: His Life and Social Theology* (Durham, 1992), 15–18; Johann Sallaberger, *Kardinal Matthäus Lang von Wellenburg (1468–1540)* (Salzburg, 1997), 269–78; and Lothar Graf zu Dohna, "Consultatio super confessione fratris Stephani Agricolae," in *Johann von Staupitz, Sämtliche Schriften: Abhandlungen, Predigen, Zeug-nisse*, vol. 5, *Gutachten und Satzugen*, ed. Lothar Graf zu Dohna and Richard Wetzel (Berlin, 2001), 63–91.

45. TLA, OÖ Regierung Kopialbuch An und von den fürstlichen Durchlaucht [AVFD], Bd. 1, 1521–22, 56r (7 November 1522); ThHStAW, EGA, Reg. N25, 2 (7 February 1522); and Plummer, *Priest's Whore*, 58–59, 71–74.

46. Archiv der Erzdiözese Salzburg [AES] Altbestände/19/48/RA II, 3 (March 1522), 4 (31 May 1522); and Hauthaler, *Cardinal*, 29–30.

47. AES/Altbestände/19/48/RA II, 5 (September 1522); Bayerisches Hauptstaatsarchiv Munich [BayHStAMü], Kurbayern Äußeres Archiv [KÄA] 1680, 47r–v (10 November 1522); and Sallaberger, *Kardinal*, 269.

48. TLA, AVFD, Bd. 1, 56v (17 November 1522), 455r–v (1 December 1522).

49. Bossert, *Beiträge*, 149; Schmid, "Cardinals," 167–68; and Boyd, *Marpeck*, 16.

50. TLA, StadtARatt, Schuber, 251 [SR 1522], 20r–21r (mid-November, 24–29 December [Nuremberg], 27 November 1522 [Innsbruck]), 22r; TLA, AVFD, Bd 1, 338v–339r; Bossert, *Beiträge*, 149; and Boyd, *Marpeck*, 16.

51. TLA, AVFD, Bd. 1, 74v (13 December 1522), 76v (22 December 1522); 77r–v (24 December 1522); TLA Kaiserliche Kanzlei Wien (Hofregistratur A) Akteneinlauf, Karton 27, XII, Nr. 11 (4 August 1524); TLA, OÖ Regierung Kopialbuch Von der fürstlichen Durchlaucht, Bd 2, 1523–26, 129r–131v (27 July 1524); and Karl-Heinz Ludwig, "Miners, Pastors, and the Peasant War in Upper Austria, 1524–26," in *Religion and Rural Revolt*, ed. János M. Bak and Gerhard Benecke (Manchester, 1984), 156–57. Negotiations with the Rattenberg miners erupted into rebellion in mid-1524.

52. TLA, AVFD, Bd. 1, 74v (13 December 1522), 77v (27 December 1522).

53. TLA, StadtARatt, Schuber, 168, Ratsprotokolle 1523–32, 4v (27 February 1523), 6r–v (1 March 1523), 8v–9v (7 March 1523).
54. BayHStAMü, KÄA 1680, 55r–v (7 March 1523); TLA, StadtARatt, Schuber, 168, 12v (13 March 1523).
55. TLA, StadtARatt, Schuber, 168, 14v (21 March 1523); AES/Altbestände/19/48/RA II, 9; BayHStAMü, KÄA 1680, 58 (21 March 1523), 61r–64v (20 April 1523); and Sallaberger, *Kardinal*, 271–74.
56. Stadtarchiv Mühldorf [StadtAMühl], R1, Nr. 40, 52r.
57. StadtAMühl, R1, Nr. 40, 54r, 56v.
58. AES/Altbestände/19/48/RA II, 10 (March/April 1523); BayHStAMü, KÄA 1680, 62r–v (19 April 1523), 63r–v (20 April 1523); AES/Altbestände/19/48/RA II, 14a (23 April 1523); AES/Altbestände/19/48/RA II, 19 (16 August 1523); TLA, StadtARatt, Schuber, 168, 25r–v (5 June 1523), 34r (11 August 1523); and Franz Posset, *The Front-Runner of the Catholic Reformation: The Life and Works of Johann von Staupitz* (Aldershot, 2003), 314–17.
59. AES/Altbestände/19/48/RA IV, 5 (31 December 1523); and TLA, StadtARatt, Schuber, 168, 51v (22 January 1524).
60. StadtAMühl, R1, Nr. 41, 89r; AES/Altbestände/19/48/RA IV, 5 (2 January 1524); AES/Altbestände/19/48/RA IV, 5 (2 January 1524); and Dohna, "Consultatio," 73.
61. TLA, StadtARatt, Schuber, 168, 55r (5 April 1524), 55v (15 April 1524); AES/Altbestände/19/48/RA IV, 7, 35–37 (6 May 1524), 9–12 (22 May 1524), 47–50; and Dohna, "Consultatio," 72–74.
62. Simon, "Lebensgeschichte," 171–73.
63. StadtAMühl, R1, Nr. 41, 95r–v; and Ann Tlusty, ed., *Augsburg during the Reformation Era: An Anthology of Sources* (Indianapolis, 2013), 164–66.
64. Peter Blickle, *From the Communal Reformation to the Revolution of the Common Man* (Leiden, 1998), 117–18; and Simon, "Lebensgeschichte," 168–70.
65. See note 2.
66. Gottfried Seebass, "Kolde, Theodore Ritter v," in *Neue Deutsche Biographie* (Berlin, 1990), vol. 12, 457–58.

Bibliography

Agricola, Stephan. *Ain köstlicher gutter notwendiger Sermon von Sterben . . . Außgangen Von Doctor Steffan Castenbaur Augustiner ordens in seiner gefäncknuß umb gottes worts willen, zu Müldorff.* Augsburg, 1523.

———. *Artickel wider Doctor Steffan Castenpawr Eingelegt, auch was er darauf geantwort hat, auß seine gefencknus, Newlich von jm außgangen.* Augsburg, 1523.

———. *Ein bedencken des agricola Boius wie der warhafftig Gottes dienst von Gott selbst geboten und außgesetzt möcht mit besserung gemeyner Christenheyt widerumb auffgericht werden.* Eilenburg, 1524.

Amsdorf, Nikolaus von. *Grund vnd vrsach ausz der Cronicke, Warumb Johannes Husz vnd Jeronimus von Prag verbrant seyn.* Magdeburg, 1525.

Binterim, Anton Joseph. *Pragmatische Geschichte der Deutschen National=, Provinzial= und vorzüglichsten Diöcesanconcilien.* 7 vols. Mainz, 1831–48.

Blickle, Peter. *From the Communal Reformation to the Revolution of the Common Man.* Leiden, 1998.

Bossert, Gustav. "Beiträge zur Geschichte Tirols in der Reformationszeit." *Jahrbuch der Gesellschaft für die Geschichte Protestantismus in Oesterreich* 6 (1885): 147–50.

Boyd, Stephen B. *Pilgram Marpeck: His Life and Social Theology.* Durham, 1992.

Christman, Robert. *Doctrinal Controversy and Lay Religiosity in Late Reformation Germany: The Case of Mansfeld.* Leiden, 2012.

Dann, Christian Adam. "Stephan Castenbauer (Juli 15)." In *Anekdoten für Christen zur stärkung des Glaubens, der Hoffnung und der Liebe,* 199–200. Basel, 1833.

Datterer, Franz Paul. *Des Cardinals und Erzbischofs von Salzburg Matthäus Lang.* Erlangen, 1890.

Dixon, C. Scott. "The Sense of the Past in the Reformation: Part II." *German History* 30 (2012): 175–98.

Dobel, Karl Friedrich. *Kurze Geschichte der Auswanderung der evangelischen Salzburger.* Kempten, 1832.

Dohna, Lothar Graf zu. "Consultatio super confessione fratris Stephani Agricolae." In *Johann von Staupitz, Sämtliche Schriften: Abhandlungen, Predigen, Zeugnisse.* Vol. 5, *Gutachten und Satzugen,* edited by Lothar Graf zu Dohna and Richard Wetzel, 63–91. Berlin, 2001.

Gennep, Jaspar. *Catholischer Spangenbergischer Catechismus.* Cologne, 1561.

———. *Epitome. Warhaftiger Beschreibung der Vornembsten Händel- so sich in Geistlichen unnd Weltlichen sachen, von Jahr unsers Herren M.D. biss in das jar der mynderen zal LIX zugegragen und verlauffen haben.* Cologne, 1559.

———. *Eyn Ernsthafftigs Gesprech, zwischen Jaspar Gennep, . . . und Cyriaco Spangenberg, über die Geschicht Beschreibung, Johannis Sleidani.* Cologne, 1561.

———. *Red und Antwort jetziger Zweyspalt in Glaubenssachen . . . mit Christlicher Widerlagung des* ünuerschampten *schreiben so Cyriac Spangenberg im jar M.D. Lxii widet . . . herren Stephanum Agricolam, und Jaspar Gennep, Ausgeben hat.* Cologne, 1563.

Gregory, Brad S. *Salvation at Stake: Christian Martyrdom in Early Modern Europe.* Cambridge, MA, 1999.

Grumbach, Argula von. *Wye ein Christliche fraw des adels, in Beyern durch iren, in Gotlicher schrifft, wolgegrundtenn Sendbrieffe, die hohenschul zu Jngolstat, vmb das sie eynen Euangelischen Jungling, zu widersprechung des wort Gottes, betrangt haben, straffet.* Erfurt, 1523.

Hauthaler, Willibald. *Cardinal Matthäus Lang und die religiös-sociale Bewegung seiner Zeit (1517–1540).* Salzburg, 1896.

Kolb, Robert. *For All the Saints: Changing Perceptions of Martyrdom and Sainthood in the Lutheran Reformation.* Macon, GA, 1987.

Kolde, Theodor von. "Agricola, Stephen." In *Realenzyklopädie für protestantische Theologie und Kirche,* 3rd ed., 24 vols., vol. 1, 253–54. Leipzig, 1896–1913.

———. "Zur Bibliographie." *Beiträge zur bayerischen Kirchengeschichte* 3 (1897): 292–94.

Löhse, Bernhard. *Luthers Theologie in ihrer historischen Entwicklung und in ihrem systematischen Zusammenhang.* Göttingen, 1995.

Lommer, Markus. "Der altbayerische Frühlutheraner Dr. Stephan Kastenbauer/Agricola (um 1491/1547): Ein Biogramm auf erneuertem Forschungsstand." *Zeitschrift für bayerische Kirchengeschichte* 69 (2000): 227–30.

Ludwig, Karl-Heinz. "Miners, Pastors, and the Peasant War in Upper Austria, 1524–26." In *Religion and Rural Revolt*, edited by János M. Bak and Gerhard Benecke, 154–60. Manchester, 1984.

Luther, Martin. *Acta F. Luther August. Apud D. Legatum Apostolicum Augustae.* Leipzig, 1518.

———. *Ein Frage des gantzen Heiligen Ordens der Kartenspieler von Karnöffel an das Concilium zu Mantua gebessert* ([Wittenberg], 1537).

———. *Wider das blindt vnnd Toll verdamnuß der Sybenzehen Artickel, von der Ellenden Schendtlichen Vniuersitet zů Jngolstat außgangen.* Augsburg, 1524.

Moeller, Bernd. "Sterbekunst in der Reformation: Der 'köstliche, gute, notwendige Sermon vom Sterben' des Augustiner-Eremiten Stefan Kastenbauer." In *Vita Religiosa im Mittelalter*, edited by Franz Felten and Nikolas Jespert, 739–65. Berlin, 1999.

Parlett, David Sidney. *The Oxford Guide to Card Games.* Oxford, 1990.

Planitz, Hans von der. *Bericht aus dem Reichsregiment in Nürnberg, 1521–1523.* Edited by Ernst Wülcker and Hans Virck. Leipzig, 1899.

Plummer, Marjorie Elizabeth. *From Priest's Whore to Pastor's Wife: Clerical Marriage and the Process of Reform in the Early German Reformation.* Farnham, 2012.

Pohlig, Matthias. *Zwischen Gelehrsamkeit und konfessioneller Identitätsstiftung: Lutherische Kirchen- und Universalgeschichtsschreibung 1546–1617.* Tübingen, 2007.

Posset, Franz. *The Front-Runner of the Catholic Reformation: The Life and Works of Johann von Staupitz.* Aldershot, 2003.

Rabus, Ludwig. *Historien. Der Heyligen Außerwoelten Gottes Zeügen, Bekennern, vnd Martyrern . . . worden seind.* 8 vols. Strasbourg, 1554.

Rhegius, Urbanus. *Loci Theologici, e Patribus et Scholastici Neotericisque collecti.* Frankfurt am Main, 1550.

Roser, Hans. *Altbayern und Luther: Portraits.* Munich, 1996.

Roth, Friedrich. *Augsburgs Reformationsgeschichte.* 4 vols. Munich, 1881.

Ruess, Wolfgang. *Ayn entschuldigung aines Priesters, Wolfgang Ruß, Gesellpaff zu Oting in Bayern gewest, welcher von wegen des Gotßworts den Gemaynen man fürgehalten, nach der Ordnung seines Apts, gen Saltzpurg Citiert worden ist, oder nit erschinen.* Nuremberg, 1523.

Salig, Christian August. *Vollständige Historie Der Augspurgischen Confeßion und derselben zugethanen Kirchen, Dritter Theil.* Halle, 1735.

Sallaberger, Johann. *Kardinal Matthäus Lang von Wellenburg (1468–1540).* Salzburg, 1997.

Schelhorn, Johann Georg. *Historische Nachricht vom Ursprunge, Fortgang und Schicksale der Evangelischen Religion in den Salzburgischen Landen.* Leipzig, 1732.

Schmid, Josef. "Das Cardinals und Erzbischofs von Salzburg Mätthaus Lang Verhalten zur Reformation (Capital IV)." *Jahrbuch der Gesellschaft für die Geschichte Protestantismus in Oesterreich* 20 (1899): 154–84.

Schwalb, Johannes. *Beclagung aines leyens genant Hanns schwalb über vil mißbreüch Christliches lebens, vnd dariñ begriffen kürtzlich von Johannes Hußsen.* Augsburg, 1521.

Seebass, Gottfried. "Kolde, Theodore Ritter v." In *Neue Deutsche Biographie*, vol. 12, 457–58. Berlin, 1990.

Sententia contra Jacobū Peregrinum . . . Widerrueff herr Jacob Peregrinus briester Passawer bistumbs, mit vrtail vñrecht auffgelegt vnd erkant zů Wienn in Osterreich. Vienna, 1524.

Sententia contra Joannē Vásel . . . Widerruff herr Hans Vásel briester von der Newenstat, mit vrtail vnd recht auffgelegt vnd erkant zů Wien in Osterreich. Vienna, 1524.

Simon, Matthias. "Zur Lebensgeschichte des Stephan Agricola und zur Person des Agricola Boius." *Zeitschrift für bayerische Kirchengeschichte* 30 (1961): 168–74.

Sleidanus, Johannes. *Johannis Sleidani Warhaftige Beschreibung aller Händel, . . . under dem Großmächtigsten Keyser Carln dem Fünfften zugetragen und verlauffen haben.* Frankfurt am Main, 1558.

Spangenberg, Cyriacus. *Antwort und bereicht auff das uch, welchs Jaspar Gennep . . . wider des Sleidani Commentarios . . . , mit anzeigung worinnen sich gedachter Genep anders dan einem rechten Historienschriber gebüret.* Eisleben, 1560.

———. *Wider die böse Sieben ins Teufels Karnöffelspiel.* Eisleben, 1562.

Spangenberg, Johann, and Hieronymus Mencel. *Epitaphia Reverendi Viri, D. Stephani Agricolae.* Erfurt, 1550.

Sybentzehen Artickel so die Doctorn, der Wolberuembtē Vniuersitet Jngolstatt, für ketzerisch verdammet, vnd Mayster Arsacij Seehofer von München offenntlich an vnnser frawen gepurdt abendt widerruefft hat. Munich, 1523.

Tlusty, Ann, ed. *Augsburg during the Reformation Era: An Anthology of Sources.* Indianapolis, 2013.

CHAPTER THIRTEEN

Invented Memories
The Convent of Wesel and the Origins of German and Dutch Calvinism

JESSE SPOHNHOLZ

In the first days of November 1568, over fifty Calvinist leaders from the Habsburg Netherlands stealthily made their way from underground locations and foreign refuges to Wesel, the largest city in the German duchy of Kleve. These religious dissenters were enemies of the state, forced to live in secrecy, hoping that one day they might achieve victory for what they believed was the true church of God. The ducal court and city officials looked the other way as the delegates drafted a set of articles that laid out the structure and rituals for a new church. In 1572, a military campaign led by Protestant rebels liberated large swaths of the Netherlands from Habsburg rule. Calvinists could draw on the principles agreed upon at Wesel, and those approved at a subsequent meeting in Emden in 1571, as a guide for the formation of the new Reformed public church in the new Dutch Republic. In the coming years, Calvinists in northwestern Germany also used the articles drawn up at Wesel as a model for German Reformed churches in the Lower Rhine and Westphalia.

The narrative above summarizes the most frequently articulated summary of an event now most often called the Convent of Wesel, regarded as one of the foundational moments in the formation of the Reformed, or Calvinist, churches in the Netherlands and northwest Germany. By the mid-sixteenth century, as Lutherans and Catholics were constructing standards of doctrine, ritual, and church structures in the post-Reformation world, the Convent of Wesel marked an early step in this process for Calvinists in this region of Europe. My research has uncovered, however, that the idea of a "Convent of Wesel" was invented by historians generations later. The only evidence upon which it rests is a twenty-five-page Latin manuscript now resting in a Dutch state archive in Utrecht.[1] The document offers a list of over a hundred recommendations for the ecclesiology and liturgy of the Reformed churches in the Netherlands. The central focus of this essay is not the content or nature of the document itself, though a few points are worth noting.[2] In brief, the manuscript was produced by an eager Dutch minister who awaited news of a rebel victory in the autumn of 1568. In subsequent weeks, he and a friend collected signatures on the document in exile communities in Germany and England. Two months after they began, however, rebel troops were in retreat; the manuscript was quietly set aside in the archive at Austin Friars, home to the Dutch church in London, where the last signatures had been added. By the time that rebel troops had more success, in 1572, the articles had either been forgotten or deemed irrelevant; no one made any mention of them for the next fifty years, as Reformed Protestants were building their new church. This essay explains how this failed effort was transformed within historical memory and academic writing into the records of a foundational meeting for Calvinism in the Netherlands, the German Rhineland and, later, Westphalia. In doing so, it highlights how seventeenth-century confessional conflicts shaped the meaning of surviving evidence from the sixteenth century. Further, it argues that when historians today treat that evidence primarily within the interpretative framework of the construction of confessional churches or of confessionalization, they can inadvertently align themselves with protagonists in those confessional battles.

The National Synod of Wesel in the Confessional and Enlightenment Eras

The idea that the manuscript constituted evidence of a major meeting of religious leaders was only introduced in 1618, when the document was rediscovered. At the time, the Netherlands was experiencing the climax of a major clash between the so-called Remonstrants and Calvinists, also called Counter-Remonstrants. The debate began over the doctrine of predestination, but it soon escalated into a political and social conflict that nearly thrust the young republic into civil war. A critical difference between the parties was whether the public church, the Dutch Reformed Church, would be a voluntary, self-governing church with well-defined doctrinal standards or a broadly defined church under magisterial supervision. By 1618, Calvinists had secured victory; they organized the National Synod of Dordt, which condemned the Remonstrant heresies and adopted Calvinist standards for the public church. In the run-up to this assembly, Simeon Ruytinck, a Dutch Counter-Remonstrant minister in London, discovered the 1568 manuscript, which he used to write a book titled *Harmony of the Netherlandish Synods* [*Harmonia synodorum belgicarum*].[3] The book offered fifteen chapters briefly summarizing the complete agreement of all previous national synods on matters of church structure, the duties of church offices, the celebration of the sacraments, and the operation of church discipline. Ruytinck called the first of these meetings the National Synod of Wesel of 1568. That is, for reasons he never recorded, he treated the articles as the resolutions of a large, formal assembly that established the foundations for the new church. By doing so, he also implied that the origins of the Dutch Reformed Church dated to three years before the establishment of the republic, and thus that it had been founded independent of any governmental oversight.

Ruytinck's enthusiasm for the victory of Calvinists, though, caused him to reach beyond the evidence in his claims about the manuscript's significance. It is impossible to know whether Ruytinck's errors were the result of his confusion, his deliberate suppression of evidence, or whether they simply reflect the strength of his preconceived assumptions.[4] In any case, he did not address why no one had mentioned any such event before. He also did not identify discrepancies between the 1568 articles and later synods, nor did he list the signatories, many of whom were unidentified and some of whom were neither Dutch nor Calvinist.[5] But his readers could not have known about these problems; Ruytinck did not print the articles or the signatures or comment on either. He merely placed the National Synod of Wesel first in a list of all the ecclesiastical councils of his church before 1618.

The idea of a national synod in Wesel spread as individuals read Ruytinck's book or the original document, which was moved to a church archive at the Kloosterkerk in The Hague in 1639, or examined transcriptions that were made for archives in Dordrecht, Breda, and Wesel.[6] The meeting most often appeared in seventeenth-century Dutch Calvinist writings, such as Gisbertus Voetius's *Ecclesiastical Politics* [*Politica Ecclesiastica*, 1664–76]. Voetius frequently cited the National Synod of Wesel to support his orthodox Calvinist vision for the public church, as, for instance, his argument that national synods could be called without the consent of political authorities.[7] By the late seventeenth century, German Reformed in the Rhineland too began to cite the Synod of Wesel in describing the birth of Reformed churches in the region, though they removed the word "national" to avoid the impression that the meeting was primarily a Dutch event.[8] The context of seventeenth-century Wesel explains what these men found appealing about the idea. According to the Treaty of Xanten (1614) and the Peace of Westphalia (1648), three confessions had legal permission in the duchy of Kleve: Lutheran, Reformed, and Catholic. These agreements expanded religious toleration, but they also forced supraconfessional and accomodationalist churches like the one in sixteenth-century Wesel to pick a side. Wesel's magistrates chose the Reformed confession, which aligned them with their prince, the elector of

Brandenburg. Seventeenth-century historians legitimized this choice by identifying the origins of Wesel's Reformed Church in the early Reformation.[9]

Into the eighteenth century, changes associated with the Enlightenment simultaneously reinforced and weakened the idea that the 1568 articles documented a foundational meeting for the Reformed Church.[10] First, the new efforts to systematize archival collections entrenched the idea into the very organization of historical knowledge.[11] In response to the critiques of religious orthodoxy offered by rationalists and ecumenicists, church historians and archivists took on heightened importance as documenters of the historical traditions of their church, demonstrating continuity over centuries as a way of defending the status quo.[12] The key moment for the entrenchment of the 1568 articles into a specific archival narrative of Calvinist church building was 1736–37, when Dutch Reformed leaders assigned deputies to catalogue the haphazardly organized collections held at the Kloosterkerk.[13] The minister Quintinus Noortbergh took responsibility for authenticating and ordering documents recording the foundational meetings of the Dutch church. If Noortbergh's marginal notations on the document are a good indication, he focused less time on the content of the articles than on trying to identify the signers. Many were surely unknown to Noortbergh, as they remain to historians today. Some, he may have realized, were not Calvinists at all. We may never know what he thought about these mysteries. But if he pondered these questions, they did not keep him from verifying the articles as the original records of a national synod and binding them in a collection he called "The Acts of the National Synods." Within the archive, the National Synod of Wesel now literally stood as page one in the institutional history of the Dutch Reformed Church. Noortbergh's actions ensured that when using the Kloosterkerk archive or any archive that later housed the articles, historians would be introduced to Ruytinck's claim that the articles represented an early foundational moment in Reformed Church building.[14]

Meanwhile, the Enlightenment-era demands that historians comply with standards of rational argumentation and verifiable evidence were pushing in the opposite direction. The most remarkable contribution came in a 1769 book by Adrianus 's-Gravenzande, titled *The Two Hundred Year Commemoration of the First Synod of the Dutch Churches.* His book compiled virtually all that was then known about the event, informed by relevant historical context and traceable citations in footnotes that sometimes took up over 90 percent of the page. If Ruytinck had invented the idea of the National Synod of Wesel, 's-Gravenzande was the first to recognize (openly at least) a mystery about it. Why, he asked, was there no mention of the assembly until 1618? Indeed, he admitted, one might reasonably wonder whether it ever happened at all![15] This rhetorical flourish, though, served as a starting point for a lengthy argument that the synod did indeed happen, as Ruytinck had claimed. His case rested on three main points. First, participants successfully avoided leaving any trace of their activities, which would have brought attention to Wesel's magistrates' role in harboring criminals. Second, the silence also gave the duke of Kleve plausible deniability about his willingness to tolerate Calvinists. Finally, the Netherlands government was distracted by a military campaign in Brabant in 1568, making Wesel a perfect place to hold such a meeting. All three arguments were specious. No evidence supported them even as they ignored conflicting evidence that people were leaving records of similar church-building efforts and that the city and the ducal governments did not sanction the activities of Calvinists.[16] 's-Gravenzande had even seen the original document and knew that it was not titled "National Synod of Wesel." Still, he continued to use the more august title. 's-Gravenzande had begun by accepting Ruytinck's claim that the articles recorded what would have been the largest Reformed synod of the sixteenth century and then developed an explanation for why the behaviors of everyone involved pointed to the exact opposite conclusion: that no synod had ever happened in Wesel and that the surviving articles that were written had no long-term impact on the Reformation. And so, even in the face of the Enlightenment's heightened standards for argumentation, the idea of the National Synod of Wesel remained essentially in place.

Celebrating the Past: The Politics of Romanticism in the Netherlands and Germany

The dramatic cultural, political, and intellectual changes of the early and mid-nineteenth century helped spread the myth of the Synod of Wesel into popular culture as well. In the context of increased disenchantment with sterile Enlightenment-era rationality, many in the Romantic era idealized an earlier bucolic time in which people were guided by deeply held piety. In the Netherlands, the most prominent articulation of these sentiments came in a movement called the Réveil, which blended a commitment to defining Dutch national identity with a devotion to Reformed orthodoxy, both of which had their origins in a romanticized vision of the Reformation.[17] Far more than earlier Dutch Reformed, supporters of the Réveil insisted that a separation of church and state served as a bulwark against government intervention into internal church affairs (even as they also called for public financial support for their church). These orthodox Reformed were particularly concerned about the new constitution in 1815 and church order of the following year (*Algemeen Reglement*), which gave the new king extensive regulatory power over the Dutch church and loosened requirements that ministers conform to the principles of the National Synod of Dordt.[18]

By the 1840s, one of the most prominent figures in the Réveil was Guil-laume Groen van Prinsterer, who had gained a national reputation promoting anti-Enlightenment, anti-rationalist, and anti-liberal views. He saw the roots of liberty and freedom not in the Enlightenment and the French Revolution (which he argued only promoted atheism), but in the religious struggles of the Dutch Revolt and, more generally, in the orthodox Reformed tradition. In his political writings, Groen advocated for a return to the standards of the National Synod of Dordt, the expulsion of liberals from the church, and the removal of state interference in church affairs.[19] While the National Synod of Wesel did not receive significant attention in his two-volume church history, its rhetorical place was important. As for Ruytinck before him, it helped estab-lish that the Dutch Reformed Church had been founded *before* the creation of the Dutch Republic, and thus remained from its onset independent from state meddling.[20]

In his scholarship as well as his increasing political activity, Groen gained a formidable ally in Abraham Kuyper, a famed preacher who shared Groen's romanticized historical vision of the Dutch Reformation. Kuyper would gradually develop the theological views of those like Groen into a distinct theological movement known as Neo-Calvinism.[21] The two men teamed up in the mid-1860s, when Kuyper was organizing a historical association, called the Marnix Society, which published primary sources from the refugee churches of the sixteenth century, as a way of demonstrating the Calvinist foundations of the Dutch church.[22] His goal was, as he wrote in a pamphlet advertising the organization, "to seek weapons in history itself to fend off what seemed to be counter to the spirit of the Reformation and threatens the survival of its great achievements."[23] Kuyper's society transcribed and published thousands of pages of archival sources, including the 1568 Wesel articles, in its 1889 volume.[24] In an 1869 essay on the history of the Dutch Reformation, Kuyper too cited the meeting as an example of the voluntary and Calvinist origins of the Reformed Church. Kuyper must have read 's-Gravenzande's book, though, because he conceded that its articles were probably only "provisional." Still, he confirmed that they had indeed first established key institutions and rituals for the church.[25] He later wrote that the "puritanical type of our national culture came into self-consciousness in 1568."[26]

The high point of the idea of the Synod of Wesel in popular culture came in 1868, when Reformed Protestants from the German Rhineland and West-phalia took the initiative in organizing a three-day festival that took place in Wesel on the tercentenary of the supposed synod.[27] Leaders of the Rhineland churches invited hundreds of theologians and ministers from the two coun-tries as delegates. Thousands of laypeople from the region flocked to Wesel.[28] Flags, streamers, flowers, and other adornments hung all over the churches, the train station, and through the streets. A banner over the entrance to the city proclaimed Wesel "*Vesalia hospitales.*" Festival-goers lined the central street on the morning of 3 November 1868 to see about two hundred delegates, mostly clergy, march in a procession through the city. The bulk of the events were speeches, interspersed with communal meals and worship services, each celebrating the deep spiritual bonds of the Reformed churches in the Netherlands, Rhineland, and Westphalia and recounting both the persecution in the sixteenth-century Netherlands and the warm welcome that refugees received in Wesel. In St. Willibrord's Church hung flags with the names of all the signers of "the first synod" as well as other heroes of sixteenth-century Netherlands and northwest Germany "who had spilled their blood for the Reformation and liberty." A minister from Wesel, Maximilian Hasbach, noted that their ancestors had shared communion together in that same room three hundred years before. That was true, though he knew well enough that the shared ritual was forced on both sides by magistrates, who refused to allow Reformed exiles to worship according to their own rites, despite some complaints from Lutherans and Reformed alike.[29] Hasbach also told his audience that the Synod of Wesel took place in St. Willibrord's Church. He just made that part up, probably because he was also collecting money from his guests to refurbish the aging church.[30]

Besides these evidentiary problems, from the perspective of the Germans two further complications loomed over the celebration. First, the merger of the Lutheran and Reformed Churches in Prussia starting in 1817 made the recognition of brotherhood between German Reformed with their Dutch coreligionists a potential sore spot. The king had been working to convince Lutheran and Reformed ministers to set aside their differences and form a national, ecumenical, and Prussian church. In the German northwest, some subtle resistance came from those eager to celebrate what they saw as the region's distinctive form of Protestantism, which identified more closely with the Dutch church.[31] The locally organized presbyterial-synodal ecclesiastical system recommended by the 1568 articles, and later adopted by Reformed churches in northwest Germany, provided an excellent example not only of the early roots of the region's Reformed confession, but also of a church system that operated independent from state directives.

The European military context of 1868 presented an additional complication; following the Austro-Prussian War of 1866, during which Prussia conquered much of northern Germany, many in the Netherlands feared that Prussia would invade. There was some reason for this concern. After all, because Limburg and Luxembourg had joined the German Confederation in 1839, their status as Dutch, Belgian, Prussian, or independent remained uncertain. Many suspected that King Wilhelm I aimed to bring these regions into the newly formed North German Confederation. In 1867 the Dutch king, Willem III, who simultaneously held titles to both smaller territories, even offered to sell the duchy of Luxembourg to the king of France in order to fore-stall a Prussian invasion. The Dutch public sphere was abuzz with rumors that this would only provoke such an invasion. The resulting diplomatic crisis nearly pushed Prussia into war with France.[32] Aware of the political and religious tensions surrounding the three-hundred-year anniversary, Wilhelm made sure that Berlin retained a conspicuous presence at the event; he dispatched his court minister, Johannes Theodor Rudolf Kögel, who offered a toast to the Prussian king as "protector of the evangelical church." The king also sent a Prussian military commander to attend and a military orchestra to perform. Wilhelm even sent a telegram offering his "Christian greeting" to attendees. The gathering in Wesel was hardly at the top of the king's agenda, and he had no incentive to celebrate the Synod of Wesel—indeed, he had good reason to let the anniversary pass in obscurity. Yet rather than repressing the event, his more prudent strategy was to co-opt it as far as possible. Competing dis-courses thus shaped the tercentenary celebration: Rhenish and Westphalian regionalism, Prussian Protestant nationalism, Protestant ecumenicism, and Dutch Neo-Calvinism. In this context, it is not surprising that the adjective "national" was never applied to the Synod of Wesel at the event. Still, attendees could at least all agree on a shared commitment to Protestantism.

The nineteenth-century resurgence of Catholicism in the Netherlands and the German Rhineland also played a role at the festival. Wesel's head minis-ter, Gerhard Sardemann, declared that this Protestant festival was especially important given recent events in Rome. He did not indicate what he meant exactly, though many Protestants were increasingly anxious about the rapid Catholic revival in both countries. In the Netherlands, Dutch Protestants were aghast when Pope Pius IX reestablished the Dutch Catholic episco-pal system in 1853, which had not functioned since the sixteenth century.[33] Successful Jesuit missions in the Rhineland fueled similar anxieties among German Protestants.[34] Most recently, the previous June, Pius had called for the First Vatican Council, a central goal of which was to endorse the doctrine of papal infallibility. The pastor from Wesel, Maximilian Hasbach, described the recent Catholic assault, "such as we have not seen since the days of the Council of Trent," with the result that Protestants were now the minority even in Wesel.[35] The bonds of evangelical unity expressed at the festival were thus both positive—attendees were bound together in Christ—and negative—they had a mutual enemy in the Roman Catholic Church.

The festival at Wesel was accompanied by new histories of the Reformation that emphasized the importance of the Synod of Wesel. In the Netherlands, the Neo-Calvinist Simon van Velzen published *Wittenberg-Wesel-Dordrecht*, which traced the lineage of Protestantism from Martin Luther to the Synod of Wesel, culminating in the National Synod of Dordt.[36] For German audi-ences, the minister from Bonn, Albrecht Wolters, published *The Reformation*

History of the City of Wesel up to the Establishment of Its Reformed Confession by the Wesel Synod, which included the first German translation of the articles. For Wolters, the Synod of Wesel marked the city's formal adoption of the Reformed Church. It also marked the founding of that tradition in the Netherlands, as well as in the German Rhineland and Westphalia.[37] This remained the standard version of events for another generation.

The "Convent of Wesel": A Twentieth-Century Mystery

While the nineteenth century saw the high point of celebrations of this event, the simultaneous emergence of a new style of academic history pioneered by Leopold von Ranke demanded a level of attention to source criticism that made claims about the Synod of Wesel difficult to maintain. In its place, historians began adopting a new title for the event—the "Convent of Wesel"—a neologism that distanced itself from the discredited term yet preserved its place in the chronology of Reformed Church building proposed by Ruytinck over two centuries before. The first usages of the term came from German historicists, who were increasingly sensitive from the 1830s and '40s to what conclusions regarding church history could be verifiably made using available evidence. The first reference I have found to the term comes from 1851, in a book summarizing the history of German Protestant church law by Ämilius Ludwig Richter (1808–86). The author was a professor of church law at the University of Berlin and a member of the governing body of the Evangelical Church in Prussia. He was also among those reformers who had been pushing for the complete separation of church and state. Like other historicists, he argued that the institutional forms of churches varied according to historical context, rather than being theologically determined. Like other German authors before him, Richter turned to the 1568 articles to point to the distinct presbyterial and synodal ecclesiastical systems that had developed in the Reformed churches of the German Rhineland.[38] Surely it was the absence of evidence for treating the articles as the records of a "synod" that convinced him to abandon the older term. What persuaded him to adopt the new phrasing, however, is unclear. The word "convent" derived from the Latin word *conventus* (meeting or assembly) and had no specialized meaning in the Reformed tradition the way that "synod" did. The new term, *Der Weseler Konvent*, implicitly suggested that it was a hitherto unknown ecclesiastical body—a formal preparatory assembly that laid the groundwork for future assemblies.

For the next fifty years, however, a variety of terms were used by authors, including the "Synod of Wesel," "the synodal Convent of Wesel," "pre-Synod in Wesel," "the Cross-Synod of Wesel," and "the particular meeting" at Wesel.[39] By about 1900, agreement formed around "the Convent of Wesel."

The diminution of the meeting's name and the stabilization of terminology led, for the first time, to a general scholarly consensus among orthodox Reformed, liberal ecumenicists, and secular historians alike on both sides of the border: the Convent of Wesel was a foundational meeting for the Reformed tradition in northwest Germany and the Netherlands, but its decisions were only provisional.[40] Of course, the new name did nothing to solve the mystery about the absence of evidence regarding the event.[41]

If the idea that the 1568 articles recorded an important foundational meeting remained remarkably durable, the lack of evidence has also allowed for a degree of malleability on a range of specific facts relating to the supposed event. Some authors have claimed that it probably took place openly in the city's Augustinian church, while others suggested that the city council colluded in a conspiracy with the exiles to make sure that the meeting would remain secret.[42] There has been all sorts of speculation about the central figures organizing the event.[43] In the late twentieth century, two historians even suggested that the solution to the mystery was to reimagine when and where the meeting took place (one suggested Antwerp in late December 1566 or early January 1567, and the other, Wesel in July 1571).[44] The central problem both authors sought to solve was the inability of evidence to demonstrate that all the signers could have ever been in Wesel on 3 November 1568. Their solution was to find an alternative time and place where the meeting could have happened. That is, like others before them, they began by assuming Ruytinck's assertion in 1618 that the 1568 articles were the product of a large-scale assembly of church leaders and built an explanation for why there was no evidence that such an event ever happened. Unfortunately, each raised more questions than it answered, and neither solution produced any new evidence.

As a result of the widespread speculation about the Convent of Wesel, by the turn of the twenty-first century two features were most striking. First, no one knew when the meeting happened, where it happened, what it impacted, or who attended. Second, the idea that the articles recorded a foundational meeting of Reformed leaders, an idea that had its origins in the seventeenth-century polemical battles of the Dutch Remonstrant controversy, has been surprisingly stable for over four centuries. Today, even the most sensitive and responsible historians cite the Convent of Wesel as a window into the construction of Calvinist churches in the sixteenth century. Many authors explicitly or implicitly acknowledge the mystery surrounding the alleged meeting but use wiggle words, scare quotes, or ambiguous phrasing in their treatment of it.[45] Most commonly, they cite a 1980 reprint of the 1889 edition produced by the Marnix Society.[46]

Confessional Histories after the Reformation

The example of the Convent of Wesel is more than a cautionary tale about how historians in the twenty-first century both use evidence and evaluate evidence used by others; it is also a story about how much the motivations of confessional actors in the past continue to shape our interpretive frameworks for that evidence today. The actual history of this document, only briefly alluded to here, is not the story of the establishment of confessional churches after the Reformation. Rather it is a tale of intrigue, the machinations of war, confessional boundary crossing, dead-end reform efforts, personal animosities, and European-wide political and religious dynamics, all made more complicated by poor communications and misunderstandings. For my purposes here, though, an explanation of the nature and meaning of the articles is less important than the story of how those articles got turned into something quite different.

Simeon Ruytinck played the most critical role. His decision to treat the articles as the National Synod of Wesel in 1618 was a political act (intentional or not) within a specific context that affected German and Dutch historiography alike for centuries. Further, when Quintinus Noortbergh organized the archival collections at the Kloosterkerk around Ruytinck's narrative, the archive itself became an agent in organizing knowledge about the past in ways that treated an aspirational prescriptive document with little long-term significance as descriptive of a coherent movement. When modern historians today use these articles as a window into church building or the process of confessionalization, we inadvertently re-create a narrative of the past that privileges one group in the confessional struggles of the past over others. In many cases, we do this because we approach the evidence from the sixteenth century with confessional categories that were handed down to us from protagonists in a series of struggles from the sixteenth to the nineteenth centuries. This is not just a problem with this one document. It points to methodological challenges facing the historiography of the Reformation itself: when historians treat prescriptive documents as descriptive, they can often imagine confessionalization as far more successful much earlier than it was. The solution to this problem, of course, is not to abandon our use of prescriptive sources altogether. Rather, it is imperative for historians to recognize the power relations embedded in the survival of documents, the organization of those documents, and the categories that we use to describe those documents, lest we misrepresent the complexities of the past in ways that serve the interests of others.

Jesse Spohnholz is a professor of history at Washington State University. His research focuses on confessional coexistence, religious exile, and gender in the early modern Netherlands and northwest Germany. His books include *The Tactics of Toleration: A Refugee Community in the Age of Religious Wars* (Newark, 2011); *The Convent of Wesel: The Event That Never Happened and the Invention of Tradition* (Cambridge, 2017); and (coedited) *Exile and Religious Identity, 1500–1800* (London, 2014). His research has been awarded the Fritz Stern Prize in Germany history, the Gerald Strauss Book Prize in German Reformation history, and the Harold Grimm Prize in Reformation Studies.

Notes

1. Het Utrechts Archief, Oude Synodaal Archief (henceforth as UA OAS), inventaris nummer 1401.1.
2. I am currently completing *The Convent of Wesel* that explains the meaning of these articles within their immediate sixteenth-century context and explores how meaning was changed by historians and archivists in the seventeenth, eighteenth, nineteenth, and twentieth centuries.
3. Simeon Ruytinck, *Harmonia synodorum belgicarum, sive Canones regiminis ecclesiastici in synodis nationalibus: à reformatione in Belgio celebratis* (Leiden, 1618).
4. In his 1620 history, however, Ruytinck omitted the National Synod of Wesel and emphasized only the synod held at Emden in 1571. Simeon Ruytinck, *Gheschiedenissen ende handelingen die voornemelick aengaen de Nederduytsche natie ende gemeynten: wonende in Engelant ende int bysonder tot Londen*, ed. J. J. van Toorenenbergen (Utrecht, 1873), 85.
5. Ruytinck also treated the provincial synod held at Dordrecht in 1574 as if it were a national synod. The most obvious discrepancies between the 1568 articles and decisions of later synods center on the nature and number of church offices. For instance, the 1568 document approves of women deacons and "the order of the prophets," which were never adopted by later synods. The 1568 document also gave political authorities a role in appointing clergy, a point that most later Reformed commenters ignored. Among those signers who were neither Calvinist nor Dutch were Philip Raesfeld and Gerhardt Venraid.
6. In 1639, the Streefkerk minister Johannes Gysius made copies of the original manuscript and sent them to coreligionists in these three cities. Afterward, he put aside the original in the archive at the Kloosterkerk, in The Hague. I have not been able to locate the Breda copy. The copy sent to Dordrecht is currently at the Koninklijk Bibliotheek (The Hague) in a volume with the signature KW 131 G 45. The copy sent to Wesel remains at the Evangelisches Kirchenarchiv Wesel, in a collection catalogued as Gefach 12,3, which also includes a letter written by Gysius explaining his searching and transcribing. In the late seventeenth century, an additional copy was made by ministers in the German Reformed county of Lippe and is currently at the Landesarchiv Nordrhein-Westfalen Abteilung Ostwestfalen-Lippe Staatsarchiv Detmold L 65 Nr. 20.

7. E.g., Gisbertus Voetius, *Politicae Ecclesiasticae, Partis Primae, Libro duo Priores* (Amsterdam, 1663), 184, 879, 886. Voetius had not consulted the articles themselves, however, but only Ruytinck's book, whose errors he repeated. Other authors who cited the articles as evidence of a foundational meeting include Johannes Hoornbeek, *Tractaat van catechisatie: Haare oorsprong, gebruick, ende nuttigheit in de Christen-Kercke* (Leiden, 1654), 56–57; and Jacobus Trigland, *Kerckelycke Geschiedenissen begrypende de swaere en Bekommerlijke Geschillen in de Vereenigde Nederlanden voorgevallen* (Leiden, 1650), 161. Trigland consulted the copy at Dordrecht, though he did not use Ruytinck's term "National Synod of Wesel," but still described the articles as a church order produced by a large gathering of Calvinist leaders.

8. When Wesel's minister Anton von Dort in the 1680s revised an earlier regional history, he inserted the "Synod of Wesel" into the history of church building efforts in this region. Werner Teschenmacher, *Annales Ecclesiastici* (Düsseldorf, 1962), 292.

9. For a more complicated history of Wesel's Reformation, see Jesse Spohnholz, *The Tactics of Toleration: A Refugee Community in the Age of Religious Wars* (Newark, 2011).

10. For an example of eighteenth-century uses of the Synod of Wesel, see Isaac Le Long, *Kort historisch verhaal van den eersten oorsprong der Nederlandschen Gereformeerden Kerken onder't kruys* (Amsterdam, 1751), 53, 85, 135. A Dutch translation of the articles was first published in 1738 in the *Kerkelijk Handboekje*, a liturgical guide for the Dutch Reformed Church.

11. For studies of the politics of archival organization, see for instance Randolph Head, "Knowing like a State: The Transformation of Political Knowledge in Swiss Archives, 1450–1770," *Journal of Modern History* 75 (2003): 745–82; Eric Ketelaar, "Tacit Narratives: The Meanings of Archives," *Archival Science* 1 (2001): 131–41; and Carolyn Steedman, *Dust: The Archive and Cultural History* (New Brunswick, NJ, 2001).

12. John Stroup, "Protestant Church Historians in the German Enlightenment," in *Aufklärung und Geschichte: Studien zur deutschen Geschichtswissenschaft im 18. Jahrhundert*, ed. Hans Erich Bödeker et al. (Göttingen, 1992), 169–92.

13. For reports of the delegates' activities, see UA OAS, inventarisnummer 1401.318, 406–7, 425, 465–69, 475, 494.

14. In 1737, these documents were a part of the archive of the South Holland Synod in The Hague. In the early nineteenth century, they became part of the national archive for the newly centralized Dutch Reformed Church, also in The Hague. In 1987, they were incorporated into the state collections of the Algemeen Rijksarchief (and since 2002 called the Nationaal Archief). In 2006, they were again relocated to Het Utrechts Archief, in the same city as the central offices for the Protestantse Kerk in Nederland, which was formed in the 2004 ecclesiastical merger of leading Dutch Protestant churches.

15. Adrianus 's-Gravenzande, *Twee honderd jarige gedachtenis van het eerste synode der Nederlandsche kerken* (Middelburg, 1769), 107–12.

16. For ducal proclamations against Calvinists and warnings to territorial officials and urban magistrates, see Stadtarchiv Wesel A1/275,1, fols. 10r–11v, 16r–v, 49r–62r; A3/56 fols. 4r, 7r, 8r, 72v, 118r. See also Spohnholz, *Tactics of Toleration*; and Christian Schulte, *Versuchte konfessionelle Neutralität im Reformationszeitalter: Die Herzogtümer Jülich-Kleve-Berg unter Johann III. und Wilhelm V. und das Fürstbistum Münster unter Wilhelm von Ketteler* (Münster, 1995). Other efforts to coordinate churches were well documented, such as the meetings held at Bedburg (Jülich) and

Emden (East Friesland) in 1571. For correspondence, see Johannes Henricus Hessels, ed., *Epistulae et Tractatus cum Reformationis tum Ecclesiae Londino-Batavae Historiam illustrantes, 1544–1622*, 3 vols. (Cambridge, 1889), vol. 2, 365–69, 378–87, 391–96.

17. M. E. Kluit, *Het Réveil in Nederland, 1817–1854* (Amsterdam, 1936).

18. On these developments in general, see E. H. Kossmann, *The Low Countries, 1780–1940* (Oxford, 1978), 67–100. In 1834, discontent led some Calvinists to break from the Dutch Reformed Church. For references to the Synod of Wesel by leaders in this schism, known as the *Afscheiding*, see *Handelingen van de opzieners der gemeente Jesu Christi vergaderd te Amsterdam den 2den maart en volgenden dagen Ao 1836* (Amsterdam, 1836), 24–25; and *Handelingen van de opzieners der gemeente Jesus Christi vergaderd te Utrecht den 28sten september en volgende dagen Ao 1837* (Amsterdam, 1838), 77–78, 83.

19. Guillaume Groen van Prinsterer, *Ongeloof en Revolutie: Eene reeks van historische voorlezingen* (Leiden, 1847). The resurgence of orthodox Calvinism in the Netherlands was part of a broader shift taking place elsewhere in late nineteenth-century Europe. Some people were adopting heightened commitments to confessionalism in response to the rise of secularism, liberalism, and industrialization. For German history, Olaf Blaschke has called this the "second confessional age." Olaf Blaschke, "Das 19. Jahrhundert: Ein Zweites Konfessionelles Zeitalter?," *Geschichte und Gesellschaft* 26 (2000): 38–75.

20. Guillaume Groen van Prinsterer, *Handboek der geschiedenis van het vaderland*, 2 vols. (Leiden, 1841), vol. 1, 119, 153.

21. Justus M. van der Kroef, "Abraham Kuyper and the Rise of Neo-Calvinism in the Netherlands," *Church History* 17 (1948): 316–34.

22. The society named for the sixteenth-century Calvinist politician Philip Marnix, who had been commissioned to write a history of the Dutch Reformation in 1571 but never completed this task. Not all of the Marnix Society's early supporters were Calvinists. Those who were not, however, gradually became disappointed with the results. J. Vree, "The Marnix-Vereeniging: Abraham Kuyper's First National Organisation (1868–89)," *Dutch Review of Church History* 84 (2004): 388–475.

23. "Programma der Marnix Vereeniging," Nationaal Archief 2.19.001, inventaris-nummer 5.

24. F. L. Rutgers, ed., *Acta van de Nederlandsche synoden der zestiende eeuw* (Utrecht, 1889), 1–41.

25. Kuyper wrote the chapter titled "De eerst Kerkvergadering of de vesting onzer Hervormde kerk, en de strijd aan haar zelfstandig bestaan," printed in Bendt ter Haar and Willem Moll, ed., *Geschiedenis der christelijke kerk in Nederland, in tafeleeren* (Amsterdam, 1869), vol. 2, 71–86. Discussion of the meeting at Wesel is on 75–79.

26. Abraham Kuyper, *Ons program* (Amsterdam, 1879), 25.

27. The nineteenth century was filled with tercentenary celebrations commemorating the events of the Reformation in Germany and the Netherlands. For this broader trend, see Roland Quinault, "The Cult of the Centenary, c. 1784–1914," *Historical Research* 98, no. 71 (1998): 303–23.

28. The following discussion draws on two published reports of the event. One was written by the Amsterdam church elder Henricus Höveker and printed in an 1869 edition of *De Vereeniging: Christelijke Stemmen*, a Dutch Calvinist journal. H. Höveker, "Festviering te Wezel den 3en en 4en november 1868," *De Vereeniging: Christelijke Stemmen* 23 (1869): 385–424. The other was produced by Wesel's city ministers.

Fest-Bericht über das am 3. November 1868 in Wesel gefeierte 300-jährige Jubelfest der ersten Synode von Wesel (Wesel, 1868).

29. He had already read Albrecht Wolters's history of these events, discussed below.

30. The next day, one Netherlander, apparently moved by his appeals to brotherly love, presented Hasbach with one hundred *Reichsthaler*. Höveker, "Festviering te Wezel," 401, 409. The fund-raising efforts were largely unsuccessful; four years later the church went bankrupt.

31. Klaus Fitschen, "The Protestant Churches in Germany and Ecclesiastical Reform," in *The Dynamics of Religious Reform in Northern Europe, 1780–1920: The Churches*, ed. Joris van Eijnatten and Paula Yates (Leuven, 2010), 185–214. For some examples of Lutheran resistance to unification as well as examples of support for it, see chapter 2 in this volume.

32. For the Luxembourg Crisis in Dutch and Prussian perspective, respectively, see Kossmann, *The Low Countries*, 212–13, 227; and Hajo Holborn, *A History of Modern Germany, 1840–1945*, 3 vols. (Princeton, 1969), vol. 3, 209–10.

33. L. J. Rogier, *In vrijheid herboren: Katholiek Nederland, 1853–1953* (The Hague, 1953), 101–19.

34. See Michael B. Gross, *The War against Catholicism: Liberalism and the Anti-Catholic Imagination in Nineteenth-Century Germany* (Ann Arbor, 2004), 74–96.

35. *Fest-Bericht*, 19–20.

36. Simon van Velzen, *Wittenberg-Wesel-Dordrecht: Leerrede ter gedachtenis aan de kerkhervorming, de Synode van Wesel, en de Synode van Dordrecht van 1618 en 1619* (Kampen, 1868).

37. Albrecht Wolters, *Reformationsgeschichte der Stadt Wesel bis zur Befestigung ihres reformirten Bekenntnisses durch des Weseler Synode* (Bonn, 1868), 314–32. Wolters was not the first German author to identify the importance of the Synod of Wesel for local Wesel and regional German history, but his book became the most widely cited. See also, for instance, Johann Arnold von Recklinghausen, *Reformations-Geschichte der Länder Jülich, Berg, Cleve, Meurs, Mark, Westfalen, und der Städte Aachen, Cöln, und Dortmund*, 2 vols. (Elberfeld, 1818), vol. 1, 55–56, 593. For alternative ways that Lutheran historians of the era dealt with related issues in the neighboring county of Mark, see chapter 5 in this volume.

38. Ämilius Ludwig Richter, *Geschichte der evangelischen Kirchenverfassung in Deutschland* (Leipzig, 1851), 178–81.

39. E.g., Abraham Kuyper, *Revisie der revisie-legende* (Amsterdam, 1879); Albrecht Wolters, *Der Heidelberger Catechismus in seiner ursprünglichen Gestalt* (Bonn, 1864), 98, 133n16; *Fest-Bericht*, 3, 30. F. L. Rutgers, *De geldigheid van de oude kerkenordening der Nederlandsche gereformeerde kerken* (Amsterdam, 1890), 9–14; and Johannes Reitsma, *Geschiedenis der Hervorming en de Hervormde Kerk der Nederlanden* (Groningen, 1893), 55, 111–12.

40. For Dutch examples, see for instance H. H. Kuyper, *De opleiding tot den dienst des woords bij de gereformeerden* (The Hague, 1891); Bernadus van Meer, *De synode te Emden: 1571* (The Hague, 1892); A. A. van Schelven, *De Nederduitsche vluchtelingenkerken der XVIe eeuw in Engeland en Duitschland* (The Hague, 1909), 297; and J. T. de Visser, *Kerk en staat* (Leiden, 1926), vol. 2, 142–43. In 1897, Eduard Simons, theology professor at the University of Bonn (and later Berlin), referred to the document as the "magna carta" of Lower Rhine Protestantism. Eduard Simons, *Niederrheinisches Synodal- und Gemeindeleben "unter dem Kreuz"* (Freiburg im Breisgau and Leipzig,

1897), 1–3. For other German examples, see Ernst Christian Achelis, *Praktische The-ologie* (Freiburg im Breisgau, 1891), 283; Heinrich Kessel, "Reformation und Gegen-reformation im Herzogtum Cleve (1517–1609)," *Düsseldorfer Jahrbuch* 30 (1920): 38–40; H. Forsthoff, *Rheinische Kirchengeschichte* (Essen, 1929), 443–56; and Otto R. Redlich, *Staat und Kirche am Niederrhein zur Reformationzeit* (Leipzig, 1938), 119–20.

41. A few authors around the turn of the twentieth century did attempt to solve the mystery. The first were rather speculative. E.g., Robert Fruin, "De voorbereiding in de ballingschap van de Gereformeerde Kerk van Holland," *Archief voor Nederlandsche Kerkgeschiedenis* 5 (1895): 27–28. A more far-reaching effort came in a 1911 dis-sertation at the Vrije Universiteit Amsterdam written by Jan de Jong. The author, reflecting the general consensus now in place, concluded that it was not a synod, but a "Convent," but affirmed its role as a foundational event. Jan de Jong, *De voorbere-iding en constitueering van het kerkverband der Nederlandsche Gereformeerde kerken in de zestiende eeuw: Historische studiën over het Convent te Wezel (1568) en de Synode te Emden (1571)* (Groningen, 1911). A. A. van Schelven, another church historian trained at the Vrije Universiteit Amsterdam, applied detailed source criticism to the 1568 articles but still concluded that Convent of Wesel was a "*conventus praepara-torius.*" A. A. van Schelven, "Het autographon van het Convent te Wesel," *Nederlands Archief voor Kerkgeschiedenis* 9 (1912): 165–83.

42. E.g., Herbert Frost, "Der Konvent von Wesel im Jahre 1568 und sein Einfluß auf das Entstehen eines deutschen evangelische Kirchenverfassungsrechts," in *Ausgewälte Schriften zum Staats- und Kirchenrecht*, ed. Manfred Baldus, Martin Heckel, and Stefan Muckel (Tübingen, 2001), 87; and Jutte Prieur, "Wesels große Zeit—Das Jahrhundert in den Vereinigten Herzogtümern," in *Geschichte der Stadt Wesel*, ed. Jutte Prieur, 2 vols. (Düsseldorf, 1991), vol. 1, 180.

43. Frans Lukas Bos, "De structuur van de artikelen van Wesel (1568)," *Gereformeerde Theologisch Tijdschrift* 33 (1932): 353–88; Willem Dankbaar, "Marnix van St. Alde-gonde en zijn betekenis voor de vestiging van de Nederlanse Gereformeerde Kerk," in *Hoogtepunten uit het Nederlandsche Calvinisme in de zestiende eeuw* (Haarlem, 1946), 56–57; J. F. Gerhard Goeters, "Der Weseler Konvent niederländischer Flüchtinge vom 3. November 1568," in *Weseler Konvent 1568–1968* (Düsseldorf, 1968), 92; and Hermann Hames, "Der Weseler Konvent von 1568 und das Brüsseler Compromis des Nobles von 1565," *Monatshefte für evangelische Kirchengeschichte des Rheinlandes* 20–21 (1971–72): 1–32.

44. Jan Pieter van Dooren, "Der Weseler Konvent 1568: Neue Forschungsergebnisse," *Monatshefte für evangelische Kirchengeschichte des Rheinlandes* 31 (1982): 41–55; and Owe Boersma, *Vluchtig voorbeeld: De Nederlandse, Franse en Italiaanse vluchtelingen-kerken in Londen, 1568–1585* (Nieuwerkerk, 1994), 197–205. More precisely, Boersma argues that some men signed earlier that year at Bedburg, others at Wesel, and others later at Emden. He does not explain why Wesel took priority in the text of the manuscript.

45. I did this myself in 2007. Jesse Spohnholz, "Olympias and Chrysostom: The Debate over Wesel's Reformed Deaconesses, 1568–1609," *Archiv für Reformationsgeschichte* 98 (2007): 92–93. For a few examples by scholars whose work I greatly admire, see Charles H. Parker, *The Reformation of Community: Social Welfare and Calvinist Char-ity in Holland, 1572–1620* (Cambridge, 1998), 112; J. J. Woltjer, "De plaats van de calvinisten in de Nederlandse samenleving," *De zeventiende eeuw* 10 (1994): 14; Philip Benedict, *Christ's Churches Purely Reformed: A Social History of Calvinism* (New

Haven, 2002), 74, 89, 178, 210, 242, 300, 453, 453, 455; Stefan Ehrenpreis, "Die Vereinigten Herzogtümer Jülich-Kleve-Berg und der Augsburger Religionsfrieden," in *Der Augsburger Religionsfrieden 1555*, ed. Heinz Schilling and Heribert Smolinsky (Münster, 2007), 264–65; Harm Klueting, "Reformierte Konfessionalisierung in West- und Ostmitteleuropa," in *Konfessionalisierung: Geistes- und Kulturgeschichte des 16. Jahrhundert in Siebenbürgen*, ed. Volker Leppin and Ulrich Wien (Göttingen, 2005), 25–55; and H. J. Selderhuis and P. H. A. M. Abels, ed., *Handboek Nederlandse kerkgeschiedenis* (Kampen, 2006), 316–17.

46. F. L. Rutgers, ed., *Acta van de Nederlandsche synoden der zestiende eeuw* (Dordrecht, 1980).

Bibliography

Achelis, Ernst Christian. *Praktische Theologie*. Freiburg, 1891.

Benedict, Philip. *Christ's Churches Purely Reformed: A Social History of Calvinism*. New Haven, 2002.

Blaschke, Olaf. "Das 19. Jahrhundert: Ein Zweites Konfessionelles Zeitalter?" *Geschichte und Gesellschaft* 26 (2000): 38–75.

Boersma, Owe. *Vluchtig voorbeeld: De Nederlandse, Franse en Italiaanse vluchtelingen-kerken in Londen, 1568–1585*. Nieuwerkerk, 1994.

Bos, Frans Lukas. "De structuur van de artikelen van Wesel (1568)." *Gereformeerde Theologisch Tijdschrift* 33 (1932): 353–88.

Dankbaar, Willem. *Hoogtepunten uit het Nederlandsche Calvinisme in de zestiende eeuw*. Haarlem, 1946.

Dooren, Jan Pieter van. "Der Weseler Konvent 1568: Neue Forschungsergebnisse." *Monatshefte für evangelische Kirchengeschichte des Rheinlandes* 31 (1982): 41–55.

Ehrenpreis, Stefan. "Die Vereinigten Herzogtümer Jülich-Kleve-Berg und der Augsburger Religionsfrieden." In *Der Augsburger Religionsfrieden 1555*, edited by Heinz Schilling and Heribert Smolinsky, 239–67. Münster, 2007.

Fest-Bericht über das am 3. November 1868 in Wesel gefeierte 300-jährige Jubelfest der ersten Synode von Wesel. Wesel, 1868.

Fitschen, Klaus. "The Protestant Churches in Germany and Ecclesiastical Reform." In *The Dynamics of Religious Reform in Northern Europe, 1780–1920: The Churches*, edited by Joris van Eijnatten and Paula Yates, 185–214. Leuven, 2010.

Frost, Herbert. "Der Konvent von Wesel im Jahre 1568 und sein Einfluß auf das Entstehen eines deutschen evangelische Kirchenverfassungsrechts." In *Ausgewälte Schriften zum Staats- und Kirchenrecht*, edited by Manfred Baldus, Martin Heckel, and Stefan Muckel, 63–115. Tübingen, 2001.

Fruin, Robert. "De voorbereiding in de ballingschap van de Gereformeerde Kerk van Holland." *Archief voor Nederlandsche Kerkgeschiedenis* 5 (1895): 1–46.

Goeters, J. F. Gerhard. "Der Weseler Konvent niederländischer Flüchtinge vom 3. November 1568." In *Weseler Konvent 1568–1968*, 88–114. Düsseldorf, 1968.

's-Gravenzande, Adrianus. *Twee honderd jarige gedachtenis van het eerste synode der Nederlandsche kerken*. Middelburg, 1769.

Groen van Prinsterer, Guillaume. *Handboek der geschiedenis van het vaderland*. Vol. 1. Leiden, 1841.

Gross, Michael B. *The War against Catholicism: Liberalism and the Anti-Catholic Imagination in Nineteenth-Century Germany*. Ann Arbor, 2004.

Haar, Bendt ter, and Willem Moll, eds. *Geschiedenis der christelijke kerk in Nederland, in tafeleeren*. Vol. 2. Amsterdam, 1869.

Hames, Hermann. "Der Weseler Konvent von 1568 und das Brüsseler Compromis des Nobles von 1565." *Monatshefte für evangelische Kirchengeschichte des Rheinlandes* 20–21 (1971–72): 1–32.

Handelingen van de opzieners der gemeente Jesu Christi vergaderd te Amsterdam den 2den maart en volgende dagen Ao 1836. Amsterdam, 1836.

Handelingen van de opzieners der gemeente Jesu Christi vergaderd te Utrecht den 28sten september en volgende dagen Ao 1837. Amsterdam, 1838.

Head, Randolph. "Knowing Like a State: The Transformation of Political Knowledge in Swiss Archives, 1450–1770." *Journal of Modern History* 75 (2003): 745–82.

Hessels, Johannes Henricus, ed. *Epistulae et Tractatus cum Reformationis tum Ecclesiae Londino-Batavae Historiam illustrantes, 1544–1622*. Vol. 2. Cambridge, 1889.

Holborn, Hajo. *A History of Modern Germany, 1840–1945*. 3 vols. Princeton, 1969.

Hoornbeek, Johannes, *Tractaat van catechisatie: Haare oorsprong, gebruick, ende nuttigheit in de Christen-Kercke*. Leiden, 1654.

Höveker, H. "Festviering te Wezel den 3en en 4en november 1868." *De Vereeniging: Christelijke Stemmen* 23 (1869): 385–424.

Jong, Jan de. *De voorbereiding en constitueering van het kerkverband der Nederlandsche Gereformeerde kerken in de zestiende eeuw: Historische studiën over het Convent te Wezel (1568) en de Synode te Emden (1571)*. Groningen, 1911.

Kessel, Heinrich. "Reformation und Gegenreformation im Herzogtum Cleve (1517–1609)." *Düsseldorfer Jahrbuch* 30 (1920): 1–113.

Ketelaar, Eric. "Tacit Narratives: The Meanings of Archives." *Archival Science* 1 (2001): 131–41.

Klueting, Harm. "Reformierte Konfessionalisierung in West- und Ostmitteleuropa." In *Konfessionalisierung: Geistes- und Kulturgeschichte des 16. Jahrhundert in Siebenbürgen*, edited by Volker Leppin and Ulrich Wien, 25–55. Göttingen, 2005.

Kluit, M. E. *Het Réveil in Nederland, 1817–1854*. Amsterdam, 1936.

Kossmann, E. H. *The Low Countries, 1780–1940*. Oxford, 1978.

Kroef, Justus M. van der. "Abraham Kuyper and the Rise of Neo-Calvinism in the Netherlands." *Church History* 17 (1948): 316–34.

Kuyper, Abraham. *Ons program*. Amsterdam, 1879.

———. *Revisie der revisie-legende*. Amsterdam, 1879.

Kuyper, H. H. *De opleiding tot den dienst des woords bij de gereformeerden*. The Hague, 1891.

Long, Isaac Le. *Kort historisch verhaal van den eersten oorsprong der Nederlandschen Gereformeerden Kerken onder't kruys*. Amsterdam, 1751.

Meer, Bernadus van. *De synode te Emden: 1571*. The Hague, 1892.

Parker, Charles H. *The Reformation of Community: Social Welfare and Calvinist Charity in Holland, 1572–1620.* Cambridge, 1998.

Prieur, Jutte. "Wesels große Zeit—Das Jahrhundert in den Vereinigten Herzogtümern" In *Geschichte der Stadt Wesel,* edited by Jutte Prieur. Vol. 1. Düsseldorf, 1991.

Quinault, Roland. "The Cult of the Centenary, c. 1784–1914." *Historical Research* 98, no. 71 (1998): 303–23.

Recklinghausen, Johann Arnold von. *Reformations-Geschichte der Länder Jülich, Berg, Cleve, Meurs, Mark, Westfalen, und der Städte Aachen, Cöln, und Dortmund.* Vol. 1. Elberfeld, 1818.

Redlich, Otto R. *Staat und Kirche am Niederrhein zur Reformationzeit.* Leipzig, 1938.

Reitsma, Johannes. *Geschiedenis der Hervorming en de Hervormde Kerk der Nederlanden.* Groningen, 1893.

Richter, Ämilius Ludwig. *Geschichte der evangelischen Kirchenverfassung in Deutschland.* Leipzig, 1851.

Rogier, L. J. *In vrijheid herboren: Katholiek Nederland, 1853–1953.* The Hague, 1953.

Rutgers, F. L. *De geldigheid van de oude kerkenordening der Nederlandsche gereformeerde kerken.* Amsterdam, 1890.

———, ed. *Acta van de Nederlandsche synoden der zestiende eeuw.* Utrecht, 1889.

———, ed. *Acta van de Nederlandsche synoden der zestiende eeuw.* Dordrecht, 1980.

Ruytinck, Simeon. *Gheschiedenissen ende handelingen die voornemelick aengaen de Nederduytsche natie ende gemeynten: wonende in Engelant ende int bysonder tot Londen,* edited by J. J. van Toorenenbergen. Utrecht, 1873.

———. *Harmonia synodorum belgicarum, sive Canones regiminis ecclesiastici in synodis nationalibus: à reformatione in Belgio celebratis.* Leiden, 1618.

Schelven, A. A. van. *De Nederduitsche vluchtelingenkerken der XVIe eeuw in Engeland en Duitschland.* The Hague, 1909.

———. "Het autographon van het Convent te Wesel." *Nederlands Archief voor Kerkgeschiedenis* 9 (1912): 165–83.

Schulte, Christian. *Versuchte konfessionelle Neutralität im Reformationszeitalter: Die Herzogtümer Jülich-Kleve-Berg unter Johann III. und Wilhelm V. und das Fürstbistum Münster unter Wilhelm von Ketteler.* Münster, 1995.

Selderhuis, H. J., and P. H. A. M. Abels, ed. *Handboek Nederlandse kerkgeschiedenis.* Kampen, 2006.

Simons, Eduard. *Niederrheinisches Synodal- und Gemeindeleben "unter dem Kreuz."* Freiburg im Breisgau and Leipzig, 1897.

Spohnholz, Jesse. "Multiconfessional Celebration of the Eucharist in Sixteenth-Century Wesel." *Sixteenth Century Journal* 39 (2008): 705–29.

———. "Olympias and Chrysostem: The Debate over Wesel's Reformed Deaconesses, 1568–1609." *Archiv für Reformationsgeschichte* 98 (2007): 84–106.

———. *The Tactics of Toleration: A Refugee Community in the Age of Religious Wars.* Newark, DE, 2011.

Steedman, Carolyn. *Dust: The Archive and Cultural History.* New Brunswick, NJ, 2001.

Stroup, John. "Protestant Church Historians in the German Enlightenment." In *Aufklärung und Geschichte: Studien zur deutschen Geschichtswissenschaft im 18. Jahrhundert*, edited by Hans Erich Bödeker, Georg G. Iggers, Peter Hanns Reill, and Jonathan B. Knudsen, 169–92. Göttingen, 1992.

Teschenmacher, Werner. *Annales Ecclesiastici*. Düsseldorf, 1962.

Trigland, Jacobus. *Kerckelycke Geschiedenissen begrypende de swaere en Bekommerlijke Geschillen in de Vereenigde Nederlanden voor-gevallen*. Leiden, 1650.

Velzen, Simon van. *Wittenberg-Wesel-Dordrecht: Leerrede ter gedachtenis aan de kerkhervorming, de Synode van Wesel, en de Synode van Dordrecht van 1618 en 1619*. Kampen, 1868.

Visser, J. T. de. *Kerk en staat*. Leiden, 1926.

Voetius, Gisbertus. *Politicae Ecclesiasticae, Partis Primae, Libro duo Priores*. Amsterdam, 1663.

Vree, J. "The Marnix-Vereeniging: Abraham Kuyper's First National Organisation (1868–89)." *Dutch Review of Church History* 84 (2004): 388–475.

Wolters, Albrecht. *Der Heidelberger Catechismus in seiner ursprünglichen Gestalt*. Bonn, 1864.

———. *Reformationsgeschichte der Stadt Wesel bis zur Befestigung ihres reformirten Bekenntnisses durch des Weseler Synode*. Bonn, 1868.

Woltjer J. J. "De plaats van de calvinisten in de Nederlandse samenleving." *De zeventiende eeuw* 10 (1994): 3–23.

IV

Remembering
and Forgetting

CHAPTER FOURTEEN

~:~

"Our Misfortune"
National Unity versus Religious Plurality in the Making of Modern Germany

THOMAS A. BRADY, JR.

Once upon a time not many years ago, Professor X, a prominent American historian of modern Germany, was dining in the home of Professor Y, a leading German scholar of the same subject. Well after dinner the host, his tongue doubtless loosened by a few glasses, burst forth in these words: "The Catholics are our misfortune." The American immediately recognized the parody of the historian Heinrich von Treitschke's notorious words, "The Jews are our misfortune."[1] Professor X almost certainly was not proposing that Germany's huge Roman Catholic minority—one-third of the modern German nation—should share the fate of its Jews. Yet his words expressed a lament for history's failure to force the Catholics to become part of "us" by accepting the majority Protestant religion. Although undeniably German in descent, language, citizenship, and residence, by their stubborn loyalty to Rome, the Catholics had frustrated the dream of Germany as one nation in one state and of one religion. He lamented, in other words, the failure of the Kulturkampf, the nineteenth-century Protestant struggle to achieve a truly national Christianity and thereby to end the nation's most durable heritage from the age of the Holy Roman Empire—the plurality of (Christian) religions.[2]

This chapter examines modern Germany's persistent religious plurality against the background of its roots in the Holy Roman Empire. The German heritage of religious plurality, it argues, posed a stubborn barrier to the national dream that arose in the post-Napoleonic era. The first part reviews the post-Reformation legacy of interconfessional relations down to the end of the old empire. The second part follows the rise of the national, anti-Catholic dream from the Napoleonic era through the Luther jubilee of 1883 to its ultimate frustration by the Great War of 1914–18. The last part is an afterword that looks briefly at the post-1945 achievement in the two Germanys—East and West—of a world of confessions largely free of confessionalist hostilities and competition. The chapter's thesis holds that the German culture of biconfessionalism, a product of the Holy Roman Empire, frustrated desires and restrained the dream of replacing the empire's confessional plurality with a Protestant national state.

Legacy of Elder Days:
The Holy Roman Empire and Religious Plurality

The modern state of Germany is a creation of the nineteenth century. In earlier times, the largely German-speaking lands of Central Europe belonged to a loose-jointed monarchy, the Holy Roman Empire. Largely shaped as a mature institution between 1400 and 1650, the polity endured until its dissolution in 1806.[3] Following the public debut of Martin Luther (1483–1546) in 1521, the Catholic revival that began around 1570, and the Thirty Years' War (1618–48), the empire lived another 150 years under its hellishly complex, astonishingly flexible constitution. Then came the Napoleonic destruction, the aborted political revolution of 1848, the defeat of France in 1870, and the creation of a German kingdom in the following year. This formation of a German great power in Central Europe confirmed the hopes of those who dreamed of a united, national Germany. As if driven by divine providence, history itself was transforming the former empire's pluralities into a single, modern state centered not in the old imperial heartlands of the Rhine and Danube basins but in the new northern kingdom of Prussia. The new creation's guardian spirit, its godfather, was the sixteenth-century reformer Martin Luther. His four hundredth birthday in 1883, a mere thirteen years after the crushing defeat of France, seemed to validate the dream of national unity. History, alas, visited two great failures on this dream: the new Germany failed to integrate its huge Catholic minority; it failed to halt the rise of a revolution-minded social democracy. Then erupted the Great War of 1914–18, for which the new state bore a heavy responsibility. It shattered the century-old dream of a German nation united in a single state by a single religion.

The new Germany's journey from triumph to defeat progressed at a dizzying pace. During the relatively peaceful decades that followed the Seven Years' War (1756–63), the Germans had possessed few reasons to expect major changes in the empire's constitution and its complex legalities for assuring peace between the two great religious communities called "confessions," which the Protestant and Catholic Reformations had created. The empire was Europe's supreme example of dispersed sovereignty, in which a weak and relatively pacific monarchy reigned through a government in which a myriad of middling, smaller, and very small polities collaborated. By western European standards, it was a great, ramshackle gathering of pluralities upon pluralities, each county, city, or town having its own dialect, manners, customs, and, in many cases, a strong degree of self-governance. "Empire" was this polity's name, but its hallmark was plurality—social, political, and cultural—to which the Reformations had added religion. Nowhere else, wrote the widely traveled Baron Adolf von Knigge (1752–96), "can one find such a great multiplicity of conversational tones, educational methods, opinions on religion and other matters, and such a great diversity of conditions which claim the attention of various social groups in the different provinces."[4]

Meanwhile, since the sixteenth century the chief German princely states— Bavaria, Prussia, Saxony, Hanover, Württemberg, Baden, Bohemia, and huge Austria—had slowly discarded the smash-and-grab political culture of earlier centuries in favor of borrowed "western"—that is, French and British—policies of conquest, administration, regulation, and extraction. They equipped themselves with more elaborate bureaucratic administrations and courts of law, more regular taxation, more modern military organizations, and more purposeful encouragement of education and other means of social improvement, all aimed at the enhancement of wealth and welfare for rulers and their subjects. By the second half of the eighteenth century, James J. Sheehan writes, "many thoughtful observers recognized that population growth, state efforts at social reform, and increases in the value and productivity of the land had begun to transform rural society and to reorder the relationship between agriculture and manufacturing, between city and countryside."[5] Sheehan's picture describes a familiar image of eighteenth-century Europe.

By European standards of its age, the Holy Roman Empire nonetheless displayed two anomalies. One was the "monstrous" weakness of its central authority. The German jurist Samuel Pufendorf (1632–94) deployed this term, "monstrous," in the sense of an "irregular body," unclassifiable by the political thinking of that age, when sovereignty was conceptually singular, not plural.[6] The empire, he wrote later and in softer terms, is "a system of sovereign political units which at the same time form a single body. . . . The whole is a construction which fluctuates between a monarchy and a confederation."[7] Another jurist went further to formulate a special character of the Germans' situation: "In German history the public law plays the role that reason plays in other legal systems."[8] Nicely put, but theoretically incomprehensible in terms of European doctrines of the state.

Once it was safely defunct, the imperial polity's mysteriously hermaphroditic nature became an easy target of mockery. In 1808 Johann Wolfgang von Goethe (1749–1832) put the puzzle into the mouth of Frosch, a Leipzig student who sings of the waning wonder to his drinking brothers, "The Holy Roman Empire, lads, / How can it possibly hold together?"[9] Heinrich Heine

(1797–1856) heaped scorn on the defunct empire as the "moldiest load of junk with all its trumpery," while somewhat later the novelist Gustav Freytag (1816–95) sarcastically called it a "miraculous creation of a soul without a body."[10] The calmer mind of Belfast-born James Bryce (1838–1922) acknowledged that the empire was "above all description or explanation; not that it is impossible to discover the beliefs which created and sustained it, but that the power of those beliefs cannot be adequately apprehended by men whose minds have been differently trained, and whose imaginations are fired by different ideals."[11] But the mystery lingered on, and in some quarters, it lingers still.[12]

The empire's second peculiarity was its post-Reformation structure of legally established confessions, the religious bodies that guarded and managed engagements and encounters among representatives of the Lutheran, Reformed (Calvinist), and Roman Catholic churches in the empire. Current scholarship fully appreciates, as the past scarcely did, how the empire's peace depended on the process called "confessionalization," which "entailed the enhancement of state control over the local administration of church and poor relief and, most importantly, the imposition of . . . congregational and communal moral discipline."[13] The development of such procedures, rules, and understandings began around 1560 in the Protestant states, a decade or so later in the Catholic ones.

Close study of confessionalization has revised, often radically, the old picture of the confessions as fighting formations in what used to be misnamed "wars of religion."[14] Their main operations lay less in the vagaries of imperial politics than in their clergies' labors of instruction, surveillance, and conduct of worship, sometimes with surprising consequences. The once common notion that the laity, especially the common people, had little or no part in this process, has turned out to be quite misleading. Indeed, stricter regulation of religious life often strengthened rather than weakened or suppressed the local forces that tolerated, often for utterly local reasons, religious diversity. Historians have uncovered a grand showcase of such diversities in the empire's weakly governed regions, most notably in the religious no-man's-land of the northwestern German lands. It was not unknown, for example, that local magistrates would order the members of different confessions to worship together, perhaps separating only for the Lord's Supper.[15] The will to harness the lurking threat of strife that arose from religious competition could express itself as strongly within and between local communities as in alliances between states. The practical formation of local *convivencias*—a lovely and useful Hispanism—arrangements to regulate potential violence between or among plural religious communities, proliferated remarkably in the German lands of Central Europe during the Reformation and post-Reformation eras, but it was by no means confined to them.[16] In the sprawl of the empire there arose, alongside local witch panics and a continuation of anti-Jewish actions, a growing tendency of local rulers to regulate rather than to repress dissenting Christian minorities.[17]

By the mid-eighteenth century, successes in regulating the empire's pluralities began to fuel confidence in a workable political culture that straddled the religious boundaries. Diversity could even be looked upon as an asset, beneficial in the past and promising for the future. When Gotthold Ephraim Lessing (1729–81), a Saxon poet-dramatist and anti-orthodox Lutheran, looked over the German politico-religious landscape, he saw a peaceful land, the stability of which was nourished by a peaceful competition between the two major confessions. They interacted, he mused, like two wines cellared together, sharing their agents of fermentation to the benefit of the entire nation. "Each of the mighty steps pioneered by the Protestant Church through the Reformation," Lessing wrote, "the Catholics soon followed. The papal influence on the State is no less benevolent than that of the Protestant Church."[18] Lessing, of course, was no conservative defender of the old order in church and state but an advocate, in Sheehan's words, of a blend of pietism and rationalism, "each of which undermined the smooth certainties of the established church."[19] His ideas sprang from a historicized concept of Christianity as "an important, but not final, stage in the inevitably progressive education of the race," and he dreamed of a new, enlightened, and free order of things. "It will come, it will surely come," he sighed, "this time of a new eternal gospel."[20] Such a gospel would presumably supersede Roman Catholicism, which many Protestants believed it already had done in principle, but it would also replace "orthodoxy," that is, the Protestant faith as it had established itself since Reformation times. Would such changes enervate the competition between the two confessions and deprive the empire of the beneficial action of their co-fermentation? Lessing did not say.

The eighteenth century's final decades produced in fact not a "new eternal gospel" but a broad outpouring of speculations about the empire's governance, virtues, and need of reforms. This huge literary genre (*Reichspublizistik*) tells much about current thinking on the empire's two great peculiarities, the political duality of monarchy and aristocracy and the religious plurality of the Christian confessions.[21] The literature not only reflects the political ideas that were swarming across the German lands in pre-Napoleonic times, it also offers insights, notions, and a few clear ideas about the possibility of a future different from and, perhaps, better than the present.

A central theme of the German reform literature was the need to guard and enhance the public virtues of a common German fatherland divided rather than united by religion. A program of unity and reform must appeal, therefore, not to the idea of sovereignty in the classically rationalized, absolutist sense, but to history—the empire as shaped by its history into a stupendous panoply of polities. History, after all, offered no comparable situations. Instead, a

German writer had to draw inspiration from religion in the sense not of plural churches or confessions but of a shared devotion to a common good. Such a theme was advanced by Friedrich Carl von Moser (1723–98), a Swabian jurist, son of a more famous jurist, and Lessing's contemporary. His ideas struck contemporaries sometimes as progressive and sometimes as reactionary, but always as the work of "a man who above all thought with his heart, a passionately engaged patriot and an imperial publicist of courage."[22] Gerhard Kaiser sums up Moser's image as that of an "enthusiastic apostle of a political church."[23] That church, the German fatherland of the Holy Roman Empire, lay in terrible danger. For centuries," he wrote in a widely-read, anonymously published (in 1765) essay,

> we have been a political mystery, the booty of neighbors and an object of their jibes, disunited among ourselves, exhausted by our division, strong enough to injure but powerless to save ourselves, heedless of the honor of our name, indifferent to the dignity of the laws, envious of our monarch, mistrustful toward one another, disjointed concerning principles and violent in their enforcement, a great and at the same time despised people possessing the possibility of happiness but in fact most pitiful people.[24]

The roots of this condition, Moser believed, lay in the general ignorance of public law, the shortsighted egoism of the imperial estates, the particularism of the German princes, and the senseless, ruinous militarism that had stunted the bourgeois virtues of law and freedom. How could the empire be reformed without discarding its traditional constitution? How might the Germans be united without suffering a constricting political centralization à la française?

In the empire's weakened condition, Moser mused, religion in the form of the confessional division perpetuated partisanship, envy, and mistrust to the detriment of community spirit and imperial patriotism. "No love and no hate is stronger than where religion lies at its basis or is mixed into it."[25] The Catholics he found no worse in this respect than his own Protestants, who had originally opposed the Catholic enemy in the name of liberty. Indeed, he despised the "men of religion" of whatever confession as "apes," "imposters," and "buffoons."[26] Unlike Lessing, who found the two Christian confessions to be quite compatible, if not intentional, partners in promoting the general welfare of Germans, Moser condemned "the perverse and harmful concept of a double fatherland, of a Catholic and a Protestant Germany."[27]

Friedrich Carl von Moser died in 1789, the birth year of the revolution that would catapult his beloved empire into the grinding maw of historical change. No one could then feel confident that the ancient polity might give birth to a new German state. This question, a matter for all responsible Germans, lay not in their hands but in those of a short, chubby military genius from the Mediterranean island of Corsica.

A Dream of Unity—The German Christian Nation

The decisiveness with which the French emperor's aggressions shaped Germans' futures inspired the late Thomas Nipperdey (1927–92) to open his history of nineteenth-century Germany with an oft-quoted, marvelously Johannine sentence: "In the beginning was Napoleon."[28] During two years of campaigning east of the Rhine, the new emperor's armies crushed those of the two major German powers, Austria in 1805 and Prussia in 1806. With their gates flung wide open to foreign influence, Germans now began to debate their future as a nation. In 1808, two years before Berlin's new Frederick William University opened its doors, the rambunctious Saxon philosopher Johann Gottlieb Fichte (1762–1814) announced that the Germans had already undertaken "an achievement of world-wide importance—the Reformation of the Church"—and presumably would soon be inspired to embark on another.[29] In the following year, his colleague-to-be, the Silesian theologian Friedrich Daniel Ernst Schleiermacher (1768–1834), drew what increasingly seemed a reasonable consequence of the Reformation: the melding of the German nation with Protestant Christianity. "The continued existence of Catholicism for the Latin peoples," he declared, could be tolerated, so long as Protestants strove "with good conscience to spread the reformation among the Germanic peoples as the form of Christianity most properly suited to them."[30]

These two concepts—the Reformation as an inspiring beacon in the past, a Protestant nation as the future's goal—became guideposts of a new vision, the dream of a German state, a Protestant successor to the defunct Holy Roman Empire. In their own minds, the dream's creators were witnessing history's fashioning of a German nation founded on Luther's Christianity, the German idea of freedom, and—not incidentally—Prussian military power. It seemed a winning combination. In 1817, with Napoleon safely interned on the remote isle of Saint Helena, Prussia celebrated its victory and the three hundredth anniversary of Luther's debut as a reformer. Against hefty opposition, King Frederick William III (b. 1770, r. 1797–1840) merged the kingdom's two Protestant confessions, Lutheran and Reformed (Calvinist), into a single ecclesiastical system. In the following year, Berlin called to a professorial chair the intellectual godfather of the coming German national state. The Swabian Georg Wilhelm Friedrich Hegel (1770–1831), the revolutionary age's most influential philosopher, had already declared the idea of the state to be the revolutionary engine of modern history. But not yet for the Germans, whose constitution continued to embody the old territorial fragmentation. This situation, Hegel judged, "involves no thought, no conception of the proper aim of a state."[31] But who or what would define "the proper aim of the State," now that Germany had come into such flux? In 1830 Hegel answered this question in his jubilee address for the three hundredth anniversary of the Lutheran Confession of Augsburg. "It has been our fortune," he announced to Berlin's academic community, "that the commands of religion agree with the State's idea of law."[32] "Our religion" meant, of course, the Protestant faith that entrusted authority not to the church—that age was long past—but to the state, guardian of the nation and its welfare.

During the decade that followed Hegel's death in 1831, his ideas were taken up, discussed, and debated, read and radicalized, denounced and defended in the circles of the "Young Hegelians," the most revolutionary movement of German intellectuals. One of them was Karl Marx (1818–83), who at Hegel's death had been a twelve-year-old Lutheran schoolboy in the ancient archiepiscopal city of Trier. Grandson of the local Jewish rabbi, Marx was a Protestant Christian by virtue of his father's adoption of the Lutheran confession. When he arrived to study at Berlin in 1836, the young Rhinelander was caught up into the Young Hegelian intellectual swirl, at the center of which reigned an ideal trinity of materialism, atheism, and political liberalism.

Radical critics of the Prussian regime and the Christian religion were preparing themselves, at least mentally, for a general revolution in Germany and, by extension, Europe. Religion, Marx wrote in 1836, is "an *inverted consciousness* . . . the *fantastic realization* of the human essence since the *human essence* has not [yet] acquired any true reality."[33] The world, present and future, must be freed of its past dependence on religion, "the criticism of Heaven" must be brought down to "the criticism of Earth."[34] The time approached for the supersession of "Germany's revolutionary past," which "is precisely theoretical, it is the Reformation. As at that time it was a monk, so now it is the philosopher in whose brain the revolution begins."[35] The transformation will be general, Marx wrote, for just as Protestantism had transformed German laymen into priests, "the philosophical transformation of priestly Germans into men will emancipate the *people*."

In these passages the young Marx formulated a new act in the dramatic dream of radical-liberal Protestant thought. The series had begun with the idea that Luther's theology had superseded a backward, superstitious, and tyrannical Catholicism, from which it blossomed into a search for a national, Christian faith for the Germans. Marx, however, raced mentally forward toward the coming sublation of Christianity into a gospel of universal human emancipation and described Luther's role in this grand evolution.

> Luther . . . overcame servitude through [religious] devotion but only by [replacing] servitude by conviction. He demolished faith in authority by restoring the authority of faith. He transformed the priests into laymen by turning the laymen into priests. He liberated mankind from external religiosity by making religiosity the innermost essence of man. He liberated the body from its chains because he fettered the heart with chains.[36]

For Marx, Luther the liberator remained ever as backward as Germany was backward, a fact the reformer demonstrated by his condemnation of the great popular insurrection of 1525, the German Peasants' War. At that moment, the young Marx declared, "the most radical event in German history came to grief because of theology." In the future, when theology itself "comes to grief... the emancipation of Germany will be an emancipation of man."[37] Luther and his Reformation thus embodied one necessary stage in the passage from the dark ages of feudal Europe toward the coming age of universal enlightenment and universal freedom. At this point Marx stood firmly with the more radical elements of the German liberalism that gained public voice in the 1840s.

In 1848 the greatly anticipated moment arrived when the gateway to the future was to open. Or so an American diplomat had reported in the previous year. "All well-informed people express the belief," he wrote, "that the existing crisis is so deeply interwoven in the events of the present that 'it' is but the commencement of that great revolution, which they consider sooner or later is to dissolve the constitution of things."[38] Later rather than sooner, as it turned out, for the Frankfurt Parliament of 1848–50 debated much and decided little. The assembly was the coming-out drama of German political liberalism, a performance that Friedrich Engels (1820–95) found disgusting. "Political liberalism," he exclaimed, "is forever impossible in Germany."[39] Yet Frankfurt proved at least a table setting for the struggles to come. Among many other issues, it stimulated new hostilities between German liberalism and the Roman Catholic Church, and on this account alone it ought to be considered as an opening skirmish in the great German struggle over religion (Kulturkampf) of the 1870s and 1880s.[40]

The dramatic explosion of German anti-Catholicism in the early 1870s drew from older traditions, of course, notably from the solid Protestant belief in the German nation as a covenanted people chosen either by God—the pious-patriotic communities—or by history—the middle-class liberals.[41] The eruption was triggered, however, by two stupendous events in the summer and autumn of 1870: the Vatican Council at Rome and the defeat of France, Rome's closest ally.

In mid-July the Vatican Council approved the dogmatic constitution *Pastor aeternus*, which granted the pope "full and supreme power of jurisdiction over the whole Church" (chapter 3:9). The outrage of German Protestants may be appreciated from a judgment expressed in an Augsburg newspaper:

> The monstrosity has taken place. The paramount party in the church [i.e., the Roman Catholic Church] has committed the crime of declaring to be a heresy the oldest principle of the Catholic faith that revealed truth is made known only by the continuous consent of all churches, and, on the other hand, has declared as a dogma by the mouth of the unhappy Pius IX the crazy opinion of mere human origin that the pope by himself is infallible.[42]

More dramatic and stirring, surely, was France's military defeat at Prusso-German hands. Together with the Vatican Council, the war turned even staunchly conservative Protestant minds toward the prospect of a new Germany. One who turned was the greatly honored Berlin historian Leopold von Ranke (1795–1886). At Rome in the 1820s, Ranke had discovered that "the position of the papacy is tremendous, also in modern times,"[43] and he had returned to Berlin in the belief that the Roman Catholics now were "turning away from the bonds of ecclesiastical formulae to the eternal principles of genuine, interior religiosity."[44] A more complete comprehension of the spiritual among the Catholics, he thought, "must in the end reconcile all enmities. Above all the conflicts arises the unity of a pure, and for this reason confident, consciousness of God."[45] The events of 1870 changed Ranke's mind. Pope Pius IX's *Pastor aeternus* seemed to make German unification under Prussia a necessity; France's defeat at Sedan made it possible. "A convinced Protestant might say," Ranke wrote with sly detachment, "this result was the divine decision against the claim of the pope to be the only interpreter on earth of faith and the divine mysteries."[46]

Other Protestants simply rejoiced. The Saxon pastor Adolf Stoecker (1835–1909), who served at the front in 1870 and later as the emperor's own chaplain, announced his joy at God's decree against Rome and Paris: "The Holy Protestant Empire of the German Nation is now achieved. We recognize in it the workings of God from 1517 to 1871."[47] The eminent liberal theologian Karl Schwarz (1812–85) agreed. In the year of France's defeat, he declared, the First Vatican Council had "raised the bishop of Rome to be a God on earth, a preacher of infallible truth," and now "the most powerful, gifted, and brave people among all who today stand under the lordship of the Roman Church has revealed to all eyes its deep inner decay."[48]

The ensuing decade witnessed the central phase of the new German state's campaign to subdue the Roman Church and thereby end Germany's heritage of plural religions. To call the Kulturkampf a "culture war" hardly does justice to the enmities, humiliations, and political bitterness the struggle inspired and mobilized. In the early 1880s, as the struggle's main phase neared its end, the Catholic journalist and parliamentarian Eduard Hüsgen (1848–1912) summed up the consequences. "That which has been designated as the *Kulturkampf*," he said, "was the mobilization of confessional opposition to Catholicism, the mustering of state power at higher and lower levels, and the use of all instruments of power that education and property could afford against anything labeled Catholic or even remotely associated with the Catholic Church." The struggle's consequence, he concluded, was "that a gaping rift ran through society, carrying division and discord all the way into the bosom of the family."[49]

When Hüsgen spoke these bitter words, the chief damages to German Catholicism were done: the arrest of Catholic prelates, exile for Jesuits and members of other religious orders, vilification in the press, discrimination in public employment, purges of civil service and schools, and obligatory civil marriages. Great injuries, indeed, often mean-spirited and brutal, but not the apocalyptic catastrophe some Catholics had expected following Prussia's defeat of Austria in 1866. At that moment, the papal secretary Giacomo Cardinal Antonelli (1806–76) had declared that the "world is collapsing!"[50] But it did not collapse, and the struggle's most puzzling outcome was surely the refusal of the great majority of Catholics to abandon the faith of Rome and accept a new life as good Germans and anti-papal, national Catholics.

The Kulturkampf exposed to a striking degree the enduring strength of the old pluralities, the webs of religious discipline that descended from the days of the Holy Roman Empire. These webs were deeply embedded in local culture, and nowhere more deeply than in regions of widespread religious pluralism, especially where, in Margaret Lavinia Anderson's words, interconfessional relations were "not always mutually hostile, sometimes even cooperative."[51] The nadir came in the Luther jubilee year of 1883, which stirred old emotions and produced many a tit for a tat. A tale from the north Württemberg village of Affaltrach tells of how the local Lutheran pastor decided to plant a linden tree in the village to Luther's honor.[52] The act became provocative, relates Christopher Clark, only when the pastor and members of his flock decided to plant their "Luther linden" next to the little church that Catholic and Protestant congregations shared, whereupon the pastor salted the moment with polemical denunciations of the Catholic Church. One evening after dark, a person or persons unknown sawed down the tree, leaving only a stump. In June, as the great Catholic feast of Corpus Christi neared, one morning the priest found "a sturdy wooden fence" around the tree's stump. When the Catholics tried to get it removed, relations between the two communities grew worse. The pastor described the events in his annual parish report for 1884: "The Luther anniversary of last year awoke us to a keener awareness of the treasure of our Protestant faith, but it also sharpened our opposition to the Roman Church. This is an undeniable improvement."

In the end, a half millennium of social, political, economic, linguistic, and cultural pluralities made its weight felt. The new German nation was not built on the bones of the Catholic Church. The Catholics remained, on the whole, loyal to their bishops and clergy and supportive of the Center Party, which, founded in 1869, grew into Germany's best organized political party.[53] This strength, plus the rise of social democracy—a second challenge to the bourgeois Protestant hegemony—and the intensification of imperial rivalries among European states gradually sapped anti-Catholic energies. Then came the Great War, which destroyed the Kulturkampf, all but the memories and the bitterness, and with it the dream of the new Germany as a full-grown child of Luther's Reformation.

"The Eternal German"—The Luther Cult and the Great War

Long before the modern German state took form, Martin Luther had appeared in many roles: theologian, churchman, pamphleteer, prophet, and holy man. The great events of 1870–71 added to these a new role as godfather of the modern German nation, chosen not by God or the Protestant clergy but by professors, theologians, and historians or, as they preferred to believe, by history. Their nationalist chorus swelled to its peak in 1883, Luther's four hundredth birthday, when its song shifted beyond the old melody—Luther the anti-Roman prophet—to a mighty new one—Luther the spiritual champion of German civilization. In this change Luther's Reformation completed its evolution from a programmatic restoration of biblical Christianity to a world-historical embodiment of the German people. Out of this evolution came a new Luther: "the eternal German."[54]

During the last quarter of the old century, the new national Protestantism flourished under the spiritual leadership of not a clergyman but a historian. Heinrich von Treitschke (1834–96), son of an ennobled Saxon officer, held professorial chairs successively in the Catholic nest of Freiburg im Breisgau and, since 1874, in Berlin, the new Germany's citadel. As a young man he had lent lip service to the older German notion of the religious dualism as a safeguard of political freedom—Moser's position. Later on, Treitschke joined those who held Catholicism to be un-German and a threat to "the German national faith" and "the independent nation-state."[55] At heart he was through and through a liberal who believed that "the last and real purpose of Christ's efforts was and is, not a Christian Church, but a Christian world,"[56] that is to say, a Protestant Christian world. While Germans could and did differ about the normative authority of Jesus's teachings for modern society, they could agree on Luther's liberating role as the icon of German freedom and cultural superiority.[57] The agency of this ideal lay not with church, and certainly not with pope, but with the new German state. He shared, therefore, the view of Chancellor Otto von Bismarck (1815–98), who in 1875 declared to the Prussian upper house, "Our state is now a Protestant state."[58]

Heinrich von Treitschke was thus a modern through and through. His most celebrated work, *German History in the Nineteenth Century*, defined the man and his age, as across seven huge volumes he marked the German passage since 1750 from plurality and cultural backwardness to unity and cultural innovation. German art and science had sprouted "barely four generations after this hopeless barbarism of the Thirty Years' War ... [as] from the vigorous roots of religious freedom sprouted a new secular culture, just as hostile to the ossified forms of German society as was the Prussian State to the Holy Roman Empire." Then "dawned the finest days of German art and science" that served to open Germany's way to a purer civilization."[59] The new way of thinking "gave rise to a new moral view of the world-order, to a new doctrine of humanism which, though free from all dogmatic rigidity, was yet rooted in the soil of Protestantism." Ultimately, this new doctrine "became a common heritage of all thinking Germans, Catholic and Protestant alike. One to whom this new humanism was unknown was no longer living in the new Germany."[60]

For Treitschke, therefore, history's driving force was neither the sword nor the plow, but the mind. As his religion descended from Schleiermacher, his politics sprang from the legacy of Hegel. And the most terrible enemy of both was Rome. When Ludwig Pastor (1854–1928), a young Rhenish Catholic and future historian of the papacy, came to Berlin to study history in 1876, he discovered that while some of his professors were relatively tolerant, "almost all of the modern [history] professors are filled with an infernal hatred of everything Catholic. . . . Here is taught the science of hatred for Catholics."[61] At the head of the professorial pack stood Professor von Treitschke.

With November 1883 arrived the moment to announce the imminent fall of Rome to the spirit of Luther's Reformation united with the power of the new Germany. On November 7 at Darmstadt in Hesse, Treitschke delivered his contribution to the tsunami of speeches and sermons that marked the reformer's four hundredth birthday. His theme, "Luther and the German Nation," voiced his lament for the absent millions of Germans "who don't want to or can't grasp that our church's reformer blazed the path to a freer way of civilized living, in which we trace everywhere the breath of his spirit in state and society, at home and in school."[62] On the initial wave of enthusiasm for this teaching, alas, had followed "those tired decades of political cowardice and theological quarreling," when "a small tribe construed the reformer after their own image as a mere preacher of the Bible and an honorable family man," who had "to found merely a separate church."[63] But that was not Luther's goal, for "out of the eyes of this primitive German peasant's son flashes the old heroic valor of the [ancient] Germans, who did not flee the world but sought to conquer it through the power of moral will."[64]

Not Luther's Reformation, Treitschke proclaimed, but its defeat had produced the religious division of the nation, and not until the present century "did the heart appear once more to understand the whole Luther, the central figure, in whose soul nearly all of the new ideas of a rich century sounded mightily once again." Only now could be seen "all the cells of a new civilization that he set down, as geniuses will do, into German soil." Now can be seen how truly he fulfilled his promise: "I was born for my Germans, whom I will serve."[65] And serve them Luther did with seven great gifts: learning, the relationship of church and state, the Holy Roman Empire, the language, the middle class, an elevated position of women, and civilization. But the greatest treasure Luther gave to his Germans was himself and "the living power of his soul," for no other of Europe's young nations had witnessed a man "who in both positive ways and negative so embodied his people's inmost nature."[66]

The time had arrived, therefore, for a victory over the past, as today "no good Protestant should lose hope that yet better days lie ahead, in which our entire people will come to honor Martin Luther as its hero and teacher," for "the day when the division among the churches was a blessing, approaches its end."[67] The Papal State, "last and worst of the ecclesiastical states, . . . has sunk into its grave; the freedom of thought and belief is assured to all peoples of the developed world, and in the Protestant churches the unbroken power of a strong life is still at work."[68] Since the Roman Church's declaration on infallibility, "we feel more painfully than ever the gulf that separates the parts of our nation. To close this gulf, and thus to revitalize Protestant Christianity again, so that it will become capable of dominating our whole nation—this is a task we acknowledge, and which later generations will fulfill."[69] In fact, only two generations had passed since Schleiermacher had offered to a Berlin audience his idea of national Christianity.

Even as Treitschke proclaimed the (Protestant) Christian nation as the supreme form of human civilization, other liberal Protestants were mulling over their doubts. One such was the Rhinelander Wilhelm Dilthey (1833–1911), a student of Schleiermacher's disciples and now holder of Hegel's chair of philosophy at Berlin. His great project was to establish the history of culture as a distinct and sovereign discipline. Dilthey warned his fellow Protestants that their own "spiritual poverty" had placed them "between two fires." "It is not only elemental feelings but also their integrated intellectual systems," he wrote in the early 1890s, "that give the social democracy and ultramontanism their predominance over all other political forces of our time."[70] Yet the dream of a Protestant Christian nation maintained its vigor through the era's debates about Germany's destiny as an imperial nation-state and drew new conviction from the doctrines of power, violence, and race that were swarming through Europe.[71]

In post-Treitschkean Berlin flourished two distinct positions about the German future, the racialist Borussianism of Max Lenz (1850–1932) and the liberal Europeanism of Erich Marcks (1861–1938).[72] Lenz, son of a devoutly Lutheran lawyer, grew up at Greifswald in Pomerania. Wounded at the front in 1871, he completed his studies at Berlin in 1874, and later was called to Marburg and then to Berlin in 1890. Lenz's unswerving loyalty to Treitschke's legacy explains his glorification of the state as bearer and guarantor of ethical and cultural values in history. In religion he was a staunch Lutheran of a modern sort, for whom the nation was his church universal and the state his *ecclesia visibilis*. Nothing made his blood boil more fiercely than did debates about the Reformation and Martin Luther. His signature idea united Luther as a religious personality with the traditions of the Protestant churches, the welfare of the German nation, and the authority of the German state.

These themes dominated Lenz's popular lecture commissioned by the city of Berlin for the Luther jubilee of 1883. Its central point was the imminent fulfillment of Luther's revolution. "If we examine the events that accompanied or resulted from Luther's teaching," he said, "we must indeed admit that, since it arose on the ruins of the Roman Empire, the world of the Romance- and German-speaking peoples has never experienced a comparable upheaval."[73] The greatest revolutions, he went on to say, "have ever been those that strove for and carried out a transformation of the worldview. Such a transformation of the world was the one connected with Luther's name and teaching."[74] Citing the words of Jesus, which Luther had appropriated at Worms in 1521—"I come not to bring peace, but to bring a sword" (Matthew 10:34)—Lenz found the parallel so exact that "only the Gospel itself can be compared with the Reformation in its destructive consequences." Whether the world Luther shattered would ever become whole again, whether Germany would become a fully Protestant nation in appearance as it was already in principle and destiny, only time would tell. As for the great religious division, whether and how the Reformation's rift would be repaired, Lenz believed, "lies today, as it did four hundred years ago, in the murky future. Only faith, the convincing power of the conscience, may one day bring again, as it did then, a firm sense of the correct path and, with it, victory."

At the opening of the Great War in 1914, Lenz added an important new element—race—to his earlier fusion of Martin Luther, Protestantism, Germany, and modernity. To the Treitschkean narrative he added a "first German revolution," the ancient Germans' struggle against ancient Rome. "The German God," he trumpeted,

> is the God Who makes iron grow and Who tolerates no lackeys. When the emperor called, we stepped forward praying to Him, the righteous God. To Him, the Almighty, our cry, "Father, I call on You," sounds among the growling cannon. We have given Him ourselves in life and in death. And joyfully, as if to a festival, our young men submit to the divine judgment of battles. Wondrous, sanctifying might of war![75]

Lenz called on his German god of battles against the Russian czar's "god of the Russian earth" and Lloyd George's "English god." His own God, Luther's God, is become once again the god of battles, not Hebrew, Christian, Greek, or Roman but purely Germanic. And Luther? Why, he is become a German Christ—with us but not entirely of us, very God and very man.

A second, radically different diagnosis of the old German religious division appeared from the pen and voice of the Berlin historian Erich Marcks, son of an architect from Magdeburg and descended from Huguenot refugees.[76] This heritage and his studies at Strasbourg encouraged a liberal, Europeanist sensibility that inspired his important studies of England under Elizabeth, the Religious Wars in France, and King Philip II of Spain, plus a long, path-breaking piece on "the Counter-Reformation in Western Europe." Marcks located the German story at the intersection between the European Reformation and the system of European Great Powers that formed between 1550 and 1650. From this vantage point he could identify differences among the various national forms of Catholicism and of Protestantism that seemed as significant in some respects as those between the two confessions. Characteristic of Marcks's writings were political realism and an appreciation for the positive aspects of European religious plurality, whether in Germany or in other important European states.

Marcks's contribution to the Luther jubilee of 1917 still impresses by its political realism and its avoidance of triumphalist anti-Catholicism à la 1883.[77] Today, he said, "a world war surrounds us. We are united and must and will be united, standing and striving together." He hoped that with the return of peace, the German confessions, "these two old, great, and perhaps greatest" spiritual parties, would not resume hostilities, for they live "within the same body, which today is united in a tremendous and authoritative way. People and fatherland have ever been forces of conflict, but also forces of life. So let them be in our future: against, alongside, and with one another! The Protestants approve of this new departure, and we expect the same of the others."

Erich Marcks urged on his hearers and readers the idea of an intra-national alliance between Protestants and Catholics. The Protestants would remain Protestants, of course, but Martin Luther now belonged not to the Protestants solely but to all Germans, "to [our] history, to [our] spiritual prehistory, to the inner being of the entire German world. The German Catholic, too, if he wants to see and does see this fact, can neither get free of it nor ignore it."[78] Without doubting Lutheran spiritual superiority, Marcks in fact rejected Schleiermacher's dream, Treitschke's demands, and Lenz's race worship. His Luther stood godfather to all Germans.

Perhaps the most striking feature of Marcks's lecture is his positive diagnosis of the Germans' confessional division. "Lutheranism could not take the whole country. This is the division that we have a thousand times lamented, the curse of our history."[79] Still, the division had also brought benefits, for if it divided the Germans it also united them in a new way via the forming of confessional solidarities across the north-south divide. Württemberg and Saxony stood together, but so did Bavaria and Cologne, coming together but retaining their own historical characters. Out of this streaming together—Catholic (Italo-French) statecraft with Protestant spirituality—a new Germany was born. It arose not in the old imperial heartlands nor in Prussia, but in the Protestant lands of Saxony, Thuringia, Hesse, and Swabia, the Protestant cultures of which were "a secularized development of Luther's personality traits but still tied to his religiosity."[80] Having come to maturity on Protestant soil, this culture then penetrated the Catholic lands via the Prussian-dominated Catholic lands of the Rhineland. The effect was "a doubling of German life," which the recent political unification made "universally German." The new state and new national culture, created by Protestants, were being received by the Catholics as well.[81]

And so, in the depths of the ever more terrible war, Erich Marcks revived Gotthold Ephraim Lessing's concept of beneficial biconfessionalism, though he did not see the confessions as cross-fermenting each other to the benefit of the entire vintage. In fact, Marcks proposed not a revival of but a supersession to Lessing's idea. The latter's "eternal gospel" was metahistorical; Marcks's was fully historical, not a goal but a process that produced a unity without destroying pluralities. For Marcks, Protestantism and Catholicism were not irreconcilable religious enemies but "two types of religious and ecclesiastical formation. . . . Today they still possess their particular manners and paths of development, their special virtues and perils. . . . Long since Germany has become indivisible, also in confessional matters."[82] In Marcks's mind, therefore, the two confessions had become, like Mary and Martha, two sisters, each with her particular gifts, who are together spiritually stronger than either is separately. Ironically, it is the younger, Protestant sister who has helped her elder, Catholic sibling to make her passage into the modern age. The two will remain separate and in some things even opposed, but a united German nation needs them both.

Erich Marcks's jubilee address of 1917 presented a German version of what in America is called a "civil religion": a common set of religious values and symbols, beyond and beneath which the citizens may, even should, hold to their particular religious heritages. The fixing and regulation of the public zone can transform religious division into strength and advantage, each confession's strengths supplementing the other's weaknesses. In other words, very much what Lessing thought he had seen, except that with Marcks, Martin Luther stands over the whole, no longer just a Protestant but also a Christian German.

In the immediate postwar era, Erich Marcks's idea of beneficial biconfessionalism lived on with a kind of desperation among some German Protestants, believing or unbelieving. And soon, when the war's catastrophic outcome was being intensified by a spectacular revolutionary movement, the situation confronted the seriously Christian members of the German Protestant confession with a specter of irreparable breach with their past. For them spoke the young historian Gerhard Ritter (1888–1967), a Hessian pastor's son, veteran of the front, and serious Protestant. In January 1919 he wrote to his mentor, the Heidelberg historian Hermann Oncken (1869–1945), "I no longer believe that politics can save us."[83] In the following June he wrote to his parents, "Beyond thought, action, writing, work, yes, beyond our very existence constantly stands, as heavy and dull as a leaden atmosphere, one idea: the end of our people in history has arrived."[84] Turning in existential and intellectual anguish to Luther, in 1925 Ritter portrayed Luther as historical *Gestalt* and contemporary *Symbol*. "He is us," Ritter concluded his book of 1925, "the eternal German."[85]

Many, perhaps most, German Protestants did not envisage their Luther as standing both in and beyond history. "Luther was a man of the people," wrote the Swabian pastor Georg Wünsch (1887–1964) in 1921, "but he is so no longer, and no effort, however strenuous, can make him one again."[86] Still, hopes continued to spring, and both Ritter's historical/metahistorical Luther and Erich Marcks's pan-confessional godfather lived on into the interwar era. In the wonder year of 1933 the Protestant church historian Heinrich Bornkamm (1901–77) announced that "in the history of the German spirit," Luther "stands never behind but ever before us. He rises again among us and meets the German people on their way with terrifying directness. Only when we see as one his form and his stern charge do we correctly understand what Gerhard Ritter has said: 'He is us, the eternal German.'"[87] At the same time sounded from the other side a Catholic voice for solidarity and collaboration between the Christian confessions. The Luxembourgeois Joseph Lortz (1887–1975), later widely regarded as the premier Catholic interpreter of the Protestant Reformation, wrote of "an insistent, absolute demand for an inmost oneness of the nation, so that National Socialism, if it is not untrue to itself, must overcome the antagonisms between the confessions."[88] That is very much the policy, if not the agency, that Erich Marcks had urged on his fellow Germans during the most terrible days of the Great War.

Afterword

World War I derailed the Christian nationalist dream of nineteenth-century Protestant Germany; World War II destroyed its moral foundations. To appreciate the dream's significance requires us to recognize that while the dream masqueraded as a culmination of the Reformation of the sixteenth century, it was in fact a fruit of Napoleon's suppression of the Holy Roman Empire and the subsequent consolidation of Prussia as the core of a new Germany. The Kulturkampf was not a correction of German history but the overthrow of the Holy Roman Empire's hard-won ways of dealing with religious plurality. Its overriding goal was to correct history's failure to transform the Germans into a Protestant Christian nation.

History is, as Hegel said, cunning. The end of the old German biconfessionalism began as an unintended consequence of the old Germany among its victorious foes. It appeared in the short-lived state of East Germany (GDR), created in 1949 from the Soviet Zone of Occupation, which for all practical purposes possessed but one Christian confession. Approximately 95 percent of its citizens professed either Protestantism or no religion at all. A mere decade later, in 1960, the ruling Party of Socialist Unity (SED) decided—against nearly the entire tradition of German-speaking Marxism—to integrate Martin Luther and his Reformation into its program for progressive and national civic education. It was an odd fate for a tradition that had for a century followed Friedrich Engels's judgment of 1850 on Luther as the princes' lackey, whose "theology" was little more than an anti-popular ideology in the service of those feudal tyrants. With the abandonment of this line, Marxist historians in the GDR began to explore seriously the Peasants' War of 1525 and the Reformation as twin strands of an "early bourgeois" revolution. The new approach gained strength from party sponsorship in the 1970s and again in 1983, when yet another Luther jubilee (his five hundredth birthday) brought the International Luther Congress to Erfurt. One thing was made clear to every attendee of the Erfurt gathering: a progressive-civic-humanist rehabilitation of Luther was under way in the GDR.

A remarkable feature of the East German rehabilitation of Luther and his theology was that although its intent was political and civic rather than religious, it produced very little in the way of anti-Catholic polemics. Luther's rehabilitation as a progressive German theologian did not reawaken the old anti-Catholicism. Indeed, the GDR's Roman Catholic minority (approximately 5 percent of the population) had no broader cultural presence, and their church continued quietly in the shadow existence to which Marxist literature and GDR policy had relegated it. One eyewitness tells how after a lecture, a Catholic prelate came forward to admonish him for speaking of "the Catholic Church *of* the GDR," whereas he should have said "the Catholic Church *in* the GDR."[89] As for the rehabilitated Luther, he enjoyed the political light of day for a paltry six years until 1989, when the state and the ruling party of the GDR collapsed and faded into history.

Meanwhile, the other Germany, West Germany, now a full partner in the European Union, enjoyed a religious peace based on a new kind of civil religion. Except for a few on either side, the memory of pre-1933 events was fading away, as gradually both Catholics and Protestants looked toward the future. Except to those whose memories were long, the Catholics were no longer "our misfortune."

The story of the German confessions, the Reformation's unruly children, has reached its end. As suggested by the comment of Professor Y, with which this essay opened, some old bitterness lives on. Organizers of the latest Luther jubilee, however, called "Reformation Decade, 2007–2017," have laid on a very different course.[90] Their programs center on secularization and its effects on the place of religion in contemporary public life. Though not devoid of controversy, the jubilee literature is scholarly in character and pacific in tone. A foreign observer is impressed by the highly disciplined obedience to the strict taboo against celebrating the Reformation as an exclusively Protestant, anti-Catholic, and *national* event. The contrast between 1883 and 2013 could hardly be greater.

Thomas A. Brady, Jr. taught for twenty-three years at the University of Oregon and eighteen years at the University of California, Berkeley, where he held the Peder Sather Chair of History. He has also been guest professor at the University of Arizona and the National University of Ireland at Galway. His writings include *Ruling Class, Regime, and Reformation in Strasbourg 1520–1555*; *Turning Swiss: Cities and Empire, 1450–1550*; *Protestant Politics: Jacob Sturm (1489–1553) and the German Reformation*; and *German Histories in the Age of Reformations, 1400–1650*. In addition to his PhD from the University of Chicago, he holds the PhD *honoris causa* from the University of Bern, Switzerland.

Notes

This study is dedicated to Margaret Lavinia Anderson and James J. Sheehan, good colleagues and good friends.

1. Ulrich Langer, *Heinrich von Treitschke. Politische Biographie eines deutschen Nationalisten* (Düsseldorf, 1998), 306; and German History in Documents and Images, "Social Antagonism between Protestant and Catholics (1870s–1880s)," http://germanhistorydocs.ghi-dc.org/sub_document.cfm?document_id=1794.

2. For the present state of scholarship and an excellently commented bibliography, see Gangolf Hübinger, "Confessionalism," in *Imperial Germany: A Historiographical Companion*, ed. Roger Chickering (Westport, CT, 1996), 156–184. An indispensable overview is Margaret Lavinia Anderson, "Afterword: Living Apart and Together in Germany," in *Protestants, Catholics, and Jews in Germany, 1800–1914*, ed. Helmut Walser Smith (Oxford, 2001), 319–32.

3. For the era from the empire's rise through the Thirty Years' War (1618–48), see Thomas A. Brady Jr., *German Histories in the Age of Reformations, 1400–1650* (Cambridge, 2009).

4. Adolf Freiherr von Knigge, *Über den Umgang mit Menschen*, 5th ed. (Hanover, 1796), 23–24, quoted by James J. Sheehan, *German History 1770–1866* (Oxford, 1989), 72.

5. Sheehan, *German History*, 105.

6. See Peter H. Wilson, "Still a Monstrosity? Some Reflections on Early Modern German Statehood," *Historical Journal* 49 (2006): 565–76. On the symbolic and realistic characteristics of the empire, see especially Barbara Stollberg-Rilinger, *Des Kaisers alte Kleider: Verfassungsgeschichte und Symbolsprache des Alten Reiches* (Munich, 2008).

7. Michael Stolleis, *Geschichte des öffentlichen Rechts in Deutschland*, vol. 1, *Reichspublizistik und Policeywissenschaft 1600–1800* (Munich, 1988), 234.

8. Heinrich von Cocceji (1695), quoted in Michael Stolleis, "Die Historische Schule und das öffentliche Recht," in *Konstitution und Intervention: Studien zur Geschichte des öffentlichen Rechts im 19. Jahrhundert* (Frankfurt am Main, 2001), 33–46, here 35.
9. Johann Wolfgang von Goethe, "Faust I," in *Sämtliche Werke: Briefe, Tagebücher und Gespräche*, ed. Albrecht Schöne (Frankfurt am Main, 1994), vol. 7, 90, lines 2090–91.
10. Heinrich Heine, *Deutschland: Ein Wintermärchen*, in *Historisch-kritische Gesamtausgabe der Werke*, vol. 4 (Hamburg, 1985), 130. The Freytag text is quoted by Sheehan, *German History*, 145.
11. James Bryce, *The Holy Roman Empire*, rev. ed. (New York, n.d. [1864]), 388.
12. The late Charles Tilly (1929–2008) asked why "the fragmented Holy Roman Empire lasted so long in the midst of consolidating, bellicose monarchies. Why didn't it disappear into the maws of large, powerful states?" Charles Tilly, *Coercion, Capital, and European States, AD 990–1990* (Cambridge, MA, 1990), 65. For a starkly contrasting but ultimately misleading emphasis on the modern myth of "the Reich" as "the earthly reflection of the Eternal, and as such . . . the ultimate ground of a particular German mission" of leadership of Europe as German "universal calling," see Heinrich August Winkler, *Germany: The Long Road West*, vol. 1, *1789–1933*, trans. Alexander J. Sager (Oxford, 2006), 493.
13. Kaspar von Greyerz, "Confession as a Social and Economic Factor," in *Germany: A New Social and Economic History*, vol. 2, *1630–1800*, ed. Sheilagh Ogilvie (London, 1996), 312.
14. Thomas A. Brady, Jr., "Limits of Religious Violence in Early Modern Europe," in *Religion und Gewalt. Konflikte, Rituale, Deutungen (1500–1800)*, ed. Kaspar von Greyer and Kim Siebenhüner (Göttingen, 2006), 125–51; Thomas A. Brady, Jr., "The Entropy of Coercion in the Holy Roman Empire: Jews, Heretics, Witches," in *Diversity and Dissent: Negotiating Religious Difference in Central Europe, 1500–1800*, ed. Howard Louthan, Gary B. Cohen, and Franz A. Szabo, Austrian and Habsburg Studies, vol. 11 (New York, 2011), 94–113; and Helmut Walser Smith, "On Catastrophic Religious Violence and National Belonging: The Thirty Years War and the Massacre of Jews in Social Memory," in *The Continuities of German History: Nation, Religion, and Race across the Long Nineteenth Century* (Cambridge, 2008), 74–114. Smith unfortunately adopts (75) the archaic view of the vast devastations and great suffering in the Thirty Years' War as consequences of "a religious conflict."
15. Stefan Ehrenpreis and Bernhard Ruthmann, "Jus reformandi—jus emigrandi: Reichsrecht, Konfession und Ehre in Religionsstreitigkeiten des späten 16. Jahrhunderts," in *Individualisierung, Rationalisierung, Säkularisierung: Neue Wege der Religionsgeschichte*, ed. Michael Weinzierl (Vienna, 1997), 67–95; and David M. Luebke, "A Multiconfessional Empire," in *A Companion to Multiconfessionalism in Early Modern Europe*, ed. Thomas Max Safley (Leiden, 2011), 129–54. Recent scholarship has revised a still commonly held belief that the Catholic Reformation/Counter-Reformation forcefully reimposed Catholicism on a large scale. See Marc R. Forster, "The Thirty Years' War and the Failure of Catholicization," in *The Counter-Reformation in the Villages: Religion and Reform in the Bishopric of Speyer, 1560–1720* (Ithaca, 1992), 144–77. The traditional view is argued with vigor by Arno Herzig, *Der Zwang zum wahren Glauben: Rekatholisierung vom 16. bis zum 18. Jahrhundert* (Göttingen, 2000).
16. The capacity for local peacekeeping among plural religious communities appears in other large, weakly governed monarchies. An astonishing example is seventeenth-

century Vilnius, home to six different religious traditions: Roman Catholic, Greek Catholic, Orthodox, Lutheran, Calvinist, and Muslim. See David Frick, *Kith, Kin, and Neighbors: Communities and Confessions in Seventeenth-Century Wilno* (Ithaca, 2013).

17. On the larger questions of treatment of religious minorities, see especially David Nirenberg, *Communities of Violence: Persecution of Minorities in the Middle Ages* (Princeton, 1996). Nirenberg quite directly confronts the prickly aspects of this topic.

18. Gotthold Ephraim Lessing, *Werke*, ed. Herbert G. Göpfert, 8 vols. (Munich, 1970– 79), vol. 8, 713–15. My thanks to Michael O. Printy for this text.

19. Sheehan, *German History*, 178.

20. Sheehan, *German History*, 178, quoting Peter Gay, *Enlightenment: An Interpretation*, 2 vols. (New York, 1966–69), vol. 1, 333.

21. See Stolleis, *Geschichte des öffentlichen Rechts in Deutschland*, vol. 1; and Wolfgang Burgdorf, *Reichskonstitution und Nation: Verfassungsreformprojekte für das Heilige Römische Reich Deutscher Nation im politischen Schrifttum von 1648 bis 1806* (Mainz, 1998).

22. Notker Hammerstein, "Das Politische Denken Friedrich Carl von Mosers," *Historische Zeitschrift* 212 (1971): 316–38, here 318.

23. Gerhard Kaiser, *Pietism und Patriotismus im literarischen Deutschland: ein Beitrag zum Problem der Säkularisation*, 2nd ed. (Frankfurt am Main, 1973), 42.

24. Anonymous [Friedrich Carl von Moser], *Von dem deutschen Nationalgeist* (1765; repr., Selb, 1976), 5–6.

25. Moser, *Von dem deutschen Nationalgeist*, 17.

26. Hammerstein, "Das Politische Denken," 323.

27. Moser, *Von dem deutschen Nationalgeist*, 17–18.

28. Thomas Nipperdey, *Deutsche Geschichte 1800–1860. Bürgerwelt und starker Staat* (Munich, 1983), 11.

29. Johann Gottlieb Fichte, *Addresses to the German Nation*, trans. R. F. Jones and G. H. Turnbull (Chicago, 1922), 91.

30. Werner Schuffenhauer and Klaus Steiner, ed., *Martin Luther in der deutschen bürgerlichen Philosophie 1517–1845* (Berlin, 1983), 364.

31. G. W. F. Hegel, *The Philosophy of History*, sec. 3, chap. 2, trans. John Sibree (Buffalo, NY, 1991), 436.

32. Schuffenhauer and Steiner, *Martin Luther*, 346.

33. Karl Marx, *Critique of Hegel's Philosophy of Right*, ed. and trans. Joseph O'Malley, trans. Annette Jolin (Cambridge, 1970), 132.

34. Marx, *Critique of Hegel's Philosophy of Right*, 132.

35. Marx, *Critique of Hegel's Philosophy of Right*, 137–38, for this and the following quote.

36. Robert C. Tucker, ed., *The Marx-Engels Reader*, trans. T. B. Bottomore (New York, 1972), 18 with slight adaptations.

37. Tucker, *Marx-Engels Reader*, 19.

38. James J. Sheehan, *German Liberalism in the Nineteenth Century* (Chicago, 1978), 49.

39. Sheehan, *German Liberalism*, 77.

40. For orientation to the debates, see Margaret Lavinia Anderson, "Reply to Volker Berghahn," *Central European History* 35 (2002): 83–90; and Roger Chickering, "The Quest for a Usable German Empire," in Chickering, *Imperial Germany*, 1–12.

41. Hartmut Lehmann, "The Germans as a Chosen People: Old Testament Themes in German Nationalism," *German Studies Review* 14 (1991): 261–73.

42. Karl August von Hase, *Handbook to the Controversy with Rome*, ed. A. W. Streane (London, 1906), vol. 1, 311–12; translated from von Hase's *Handbuch der protestantischen Polemik gegen die römisch-katholische Kirche*, 7th ed.

43. Leopold von Ranke to Karl August Varnhagen von Ense, Rome, 9 June 1829, in Leopold von Ranke, *Das Briefwerk*, ed. Walther Peter Fuchs (Hamburg, 1949), 189.

44. Leopold von Ranke, *Die römischen Päpste, ihre Kirche und ihr Staat im sechzehnten und siebzehnten Jahrhundert*, 2nd ed., 3 vols. (Berlin, 1839), vol. 3, 235. For the context, see Thomas A. Brady Jr., "Ranke, Rom und die Reformation: Leopold von Rankes Entdeckung des Katholizismus," *Jahrbuch des Historischen Kollegs* (1999): 43–60.

45. Ranke, *Die römischen Päpste*, vol. 3, 235; and see Brady, "Ranke, Rom und die Reformation," 48–50.

46. Leopold von Ranke, *The History of the Popes during the Last Four Centuries*, trans. E. Ward Fowler and Mrs. Foster, 3 vols. (London, 1913), vol. 3, 570. This edition contains two chapters that Ranke added in the 6th ed. of 1874.

47. Karl Kupisch, *Adolf Stoecker, Hofprediger und Volkstribun: Ein historisches Porträt*, (Berlin, 1970), 18.

48. Karl Schwarz, "1870—Ein Sieg der Reformation," in *Geist und Gesellschaft der Bismarckzeit (1870–1890)*, ed. Karl Heinrich Höfele (Göttingen, 1967), 371–72.

49. German History in Documents and Images, "Proceedings of the Reichstag 5th Legislative Period. First Session 1881," http://germanhistorydocs.ghi-dc.org/pdf/eng/428_Wilhelm%20I_Social%20Policy_129_JNR.pdf.

50. Hübinger, "Confessionalism," 161.

51. Anderson, "Afterword," 320.

52. Christopher Clark, "Religion and Confessional Conflict," in *Imperial Germany 1871–1918*, ed. James Retallack (Oxford, 2008), 83–105, here 83–84. The remaining quotes in this paragraph are from the same source.

53. Margaret Lavinia Anderson, *Practicing Democracy: Elections and Political Culture in Imperial Germany* (Princeton, 2000).

54. Hartmut Lehmann, "Er ist wir selber: der ewige Deutsche. Zur langanhaltenden Wirkung der Lutherdeutung von Heinrich von Treitschke," in *Luthergedächtnis 1817 bis 2017* (Göttingen, 2012), 126–37.

55. Andreas Dorpalen, *Heinrich von Treitschke* (New Haven, 1957), 86.

56. Dorpalen, *Heinrich von Treitschke*, 86.

57. Bernd Faulenbach, *Ideologie des deutschen Weges: die deutsche Geschichte in der Historiographie zwischen Kaiserreich und Nationalsozialismus* (Munich, 1980), 125–31; and Karl Kupisch, *"Von Luther zu Bismarck": Zur Kritik einer historischen Idee: Heinrich von Treitschke* (Berlin-Bielefeld, 1949), 49–94.

58. Replying to Herr von Kleist, 14 April 1875: "Unser Staat ist nun doch einmal evangelisch." Quoted by Hans Rost, *Fehlwege der deutschen Geschichte* (Nuremberg, 1963), 129.

59. Heinrich von Treitschke, *History of Germany in the Nineteenth Century*, trans. Eden Paul and Cedar Paul, 7 vols. (New York, 1915–19), vol. 1, 99. For the purpose of clarity I have slightly altered the quotes from the English translation of this work.

60. Treitschke, *History of Germany*, vol. 1, 102.

61. Ludwig Freiherr von Pastor, *Tagebücher—Briefe—Erinnerungen*, ed. Wilhelm Wühr, (Heidelberg, 1950), 95–96.

62. Heinrich von Treitschke, "Luther und die deutsche Nation," in *Historische und politische Aufsätze*, 2nd ed., 4 vols. (Leipzig, 1897), vol. 4, 4.

63. Treitschke, "Luther und die deutsche Nation," 6.
64. Treitschke, "Luther und die deutsche Nation," 19.
65. Treitschke, "Luther und die deutsche Nation," 6.
66. Treitschke, "Luther und die deutsche Nation," 19.
67. Treitschke, "Luther und die deutsche Nation," 21.
68. Treitschke, "Luther und die deutsche Nation," 20–21.
69. Treitschke, "Luther und die deutsche Nation," 21.
70. Wilhelm Dilthey, *Gesammelte Schriften* (Leipzig, 1914), vol. 2, 91, quoted by Georg Lukács, *Die Zerstörung der Vernunft* (Neuwied, 1962), 362. There is no space here to do more than mention that some historians opposed and criticized the ideas and arguments of the Berlin-centered mainstream commonly called "neo-Rankeans" or "Borussians" or both. Their most tenacious opponent was Karl Lamprecht (1856–1915), on whom consult Roger Chickering's splendid *Karl Lamprecht: A German Academic Life (1856–1915)* (Atlantic Highlands, NJ, 1993).
71. See, for Germany, Roger Chickering, *We Men Who Feel Most German: A Cultural Study of the Pan-German League, 1886–1914* (Boston, 1984); and Woodruff D. Smith, "Colonialism and Colonial Empire," in Chickering, *Imperial Germany*, 430–53.
72. Hans Heinz Krill, *Die Rankerenaissance: Max Lenz und Erich Marcks: Ein Beitrag zum historisch-politischen Denken in Deutschland, 1880–1935* (Berlin, 1962), 139–96 on the neo-Rankean background to Lenz and Marcks, and 197–225 on the development of their ideas during the Great War.
73. Max Lenz, "Martin Luther," in *Kleine historische Schriften*, vol. 2, *Von Luther zu Bismark* (Munich, 1910), 122–31, here 122.
74. Lenz, "Martin Luther," 131; and there, too, the following quotes in this paragraph.
75. Max Lenz, "Der deutsche Gott (August 1914)," in *Kleine Historische Schriften*, vol. 3, *Wille, Macht und Schicksal* (Munich and Berlin, 1922), 115.
76. See Christoph Weiß, *Geschichtsauffassung und politisches Denken Münchner Historiker der Weimar Zeit: Konrad Beyerle, Max Buchner, Michael Doeberl, Erich Marcks, Karl Alexander von Müller, Hermann Oncken* (Berlin, 1970); and Jens Nordalm, *Historismus und moderne Welt: Erich Marcks (1861–1938) in der deutschen Geschichtswissenschaft* (Berlin, 2003).
77. Erich Marcks, *Luther und Deutschland: Eine Reformationsrede im Kriegsjahr 1917* (Leipzig, 1917), 1; and there, too, the following quotes in this paragraph.
78. Marcks, *Luther und Deutschland*, 2; and there, too, the following quote in this paragraph.
79. Marcks, *Luther und Deutschland*, 21.
80. Marcks, *Luther und Deutschland*, 28. The following quotes in this paragraph are from the same source at 29–32.
81. Marcks, *Luther und Deutschland*, 31.
82. Marcks, *Luther und Deutschland*, 32.
83. Gerhard Ritter to Hermann Oncken, Naugard, 18 January 1919, in Klaus Schwabe and Rolf Reichardt, ed., *Gerhard Ritter: Ein politischer Historiker in seinen Briefen* (Boppard am Rhein, 1984), 209, no. 15.
84. Gerhard Ritter to his parents, Heidelberg, 21 June 1919, in Schwabe and Reichardt, *Gerhard Ritter*, 211, no. 18.
85. Gerhard Ritter, *Luther: Gestalt und Symbol* (Munich, 1925), 151: "Er ist wir selber: der ewige Deutsche."

86. See the resigned comment of Georg Wünsch, *Der Zusammenbruch des Luthertums als Sozialgestaltung* (Tübingen, 1921), 6. In 2003, when the Second Channel (ZDF) of German television polled its watchers about "the greatest German of all time," Martin Luther took second place behind Konrad Adenauer and just ahead of Karl Marx.
87. Heinrich Bornkamm, *Luther und der deutsche Geist* (Tübingen, 1934), 20.
88. Gabrielle Lautenschläger, "Neue Forschungsergebnisse zum Thema: Joseph Lortz," in *Zum Gedenken an Joseph Lortz (1887–1975): Beiträge zur Reformationsgeschichte und Ökumene*, ed. Rolf Decot and Rainer Vinke (Stuttgart, 1989), 293–313, here 299.
89. Josef Pilvousek, "Katholische Kirche in der DDR. Kirche für die Gesellschaft?," in *Kolloquien des Max-Weber-Kollegs VI–XIV (1999/2000)*, ed. Wolfgang Schluchter (Erfurt, 2000), 93–116, here 93. The author is professor of church history in the Catholic Theological Faculty at Erfurt.
90. The official theme for 2013, for example, was "Reformation und Toleranz," and for 2016 was "Reformation und die Eine Welt." See http://www.geistreich.de/articles/292; also http://www.kirche-im-aufbruch.ekd.de/themen_projekte/Themen%20_und_Projekte_Reformationsdekade.html.

Bibliography

Anderson, Margaret Lavinia. *Practicing Democracy: Elections and Political Culture in Imperial Germany*. Princeton, 2000.

———. "Afterword: Living Apart and Together in Germany." In *Protestants, Catholics, and Jews in Germany, 1800–1914*, edited by Helmut Walser Smith, 319–32. Oxford, 2001.

———. "Reply to Volker Berghahn." *Central European History* 35 (2002): 83–90.

Bornkamm, Heinrich. *Luther und der deutsche Geist*. Tübingen, 1934.

Brady, Thomas A., Jr. "The Entropy of Coercion in the Holy Roman Empire: Jews, Heretics, Witches." In *Diversity and Dissent: Negotiating Religious Difference in Central Europe, 1500–1800*, edited by Howard Louthan, Gary B. Cohen, and Franz A. Szabo, 94–113. New York, 2011.

———. *German Histories in the Age of Reformations (1400–1650)*. New York, 2009.

———. "Limits of Religious Violence in Early Modern Europe." In *Religion und Gewalt. Konflikte, Rituale, Deutungen (1500–1800)*, edited by Kaspar von Greyer and Kim Siebenhüner, 125–51. Göttingen, 2006.

———. "Ranke, Rom und die Reformation: Leopold von Rankes Entdeckung des Katholizismus." *Jahrbuch des Historischen Kollegs* (1999): 43–60.

Bryce, James. *The Holy Roman Empire*. Rev. ed. New York, n.d. [1864].

Burgdorf, Wolfgang. *Reichskonstitution und Nation: Verfassungsreformprojekte für das Heilige Römische Reich Deutscher Nation im politischen Schrifttum von 1648 bis 1806*. Mainz, 1998.

Chickering, Roger. *Imperial Germany and the Great War, 1914–1918*. Cambridge, 2004.

———. *Karl Lamprecht: A German Academic life (1856–1915)*. Atlantic Highlands, NJ, 1993. 72.

Chickering, Roger. *We Men Who Feel Most German: A Cultural Study of the Pan-German League, 1886–1914*. Boston, 1984.

Clark, Christopher. "Religion and Confessional Conflict." In *Imperial Germany 1871–1918*, edited by James Retallack, 83–105. Oxford, 2008.

Dorpalen, Andreas. *Heinrich von Treitschke*. New Haven, 1957.

Ehrenpreis, Stefan, and Bernhard Ruthmann. "Jus reformandi—jus emigrandi: Reichsrecht, Konfession und Ehre in Religionsstreitigkeiten des späten 16. Jahrhunderts." In *Individualisierung, Rationalisierung, Säkularisierung: Neue Wege der Religionsgeschichte*, edited by Michael Weinzierl, 67–95. Vienna, 1997.

Faulenbach, Bernd. *Ideologie des deutschen Weges: die deutsche Geschichte in der Historiographie zwischen Kaiserreich und Nationalsozialismus*. Munich, 1980.

Fichte, Johann Gottlieb. *Addresses to the German Nation*. Translated by R. F. Jones and G. H. Turnbull. Chicago, 1922.

Forster, Marc R. *The Counter-Reformation in the Villages: Religion and Reform in the Bishopric of Speyer, 1560–1720*. Ithaca, 1992.

Frick, David. *Kith, Kin, and Neighbors: Communities and Confessions in Seventeenth-Century Wilno*. Ithaca, 2013.

Gay, Peter. *Enlightenment: An Interpretation*. 2 vols. New York, 1966–69.

Goethe, Johann Wolfgang von. *Sämtliche Werke: Briefe, Tagebücher und Gespräche*. Edited by Albrecht Schöne. Vol. 7. Frankfurt am Main, 1994.

Greyerz, Kaspar von. "Confession as a Social and Economic Factor." In *Germany: A New Social and Economic History*. Vol. 2, *1630–1800*, edited by Sheilagh Ogilvie, 309–49. London, 1996.

Hammerstein, Notker. "Das Politische Denken Friedrich Carl von Mosers." *Historische Zeitschrift* 212 (1971): 316–38.

Hase, Karl August von. *Handbook to the Controversy with Rome*. Edited by A. W. Streane. Vol. 1. London, 1906.

Hegel, G. W. F. *The Philosophy of History*. Translated by John Sibree. Buffalo, NY, 1991.

Heine, Heinrich. *Historisch-kritische Gesamtausgabe der Werke*. Edited by Manfred Windfuhr. 16 vols. Hamburg, 1973–97.

Herzig, Arno. *Der Zwang zum wahren Glauben: Rekatholisierung vom 16. bis zum 18. Jahrhundert*. Göttingen, 2000.

Hübinger, Gangolf. "Confessionalism." In *Imperial Germany: A Historiographical Companion*, edited by Roger Chickering, 156–84. Westport, CT, 1996.

Kaiser, Gerhard. *Pietism und Patriotismus im literarischen Deutschland: ein Beitrag zum Problem der Säkularisation*. 2nd ed., Frankfurt am Main, 1973.

Krill, Hans Heinz. *Die Rankerenaissance: Max Lenz und Erich Marcks: Ein Beitrag zum historisch-politischen Denken in Deutschland, 1880–1935*. Berlin, 1962.

Kupisch, Karl. *Adolf Stoecker, Hofprediger und Volkstribun: Ein historisches Porträt*. Berlin, 1970.

———. *"Von Luther zu Bismarck": Zur Kritik einer historischen Idee: Heinrich von Treitschke*. Berlin-Bielefeld, 1949.

Langer, Ulrich. *Heinrich von Treitschke. Politische Biographie eines deutschen Nationalisten*. Düsseldorf, 1998.

Lautenschläger, Gabrielle. "Neue Forschungsergebnisse zum Thema: Joseph Lortz." In *Zum Gedenken an Joseph Lortz (1887–1975): Beiträge zur Reformationsgeschichte und Ökumene*, edited by Rolf Decot and Rainer Vinke, 293–313. Stuttgart, 1989.

Lehmann, Hartmut. "Er ist wir selber: der ewige Deutsche. Zur langanhaltenden Wirkung der Lutherdeutung von Heinrich von Treitschke." In *Luthergedächtnis 1817 bis 2017*, 126–37. Göttingen, 2012.

———. "The Germans as a Chosen People: Old Testament Themes in German Nationalism." *German Studies Review* 14 (1991): 261–73.

Lessing, Gotthold Ephraim. *Werke*. Edited by Herbert G. Göpfert. Vol. 8. Munich, 1979.

Lenz, Max. *Kleine Historische Schriften*. 3 vols. Munich and Berlin, 1922.

Luebke, David M. "A Multiconfessional Empire." In *A Companion to Multiconfessionalism in the Early Modern World*, edited by Thomas Max Safley, 129–54. Leiden, 2011.

Lukács, Georg. *Die Zerstörung der Vernunft*. Neuwied, 1962.

Marcks, Erich. *Luther und Deutschland: Eine Reformationsrede im Kriegsjahr 1917*. Leipzig, 1917.

Marx, Karl. *Critique of Hegel's Philosophy of Right*. Edited by Joseph O'Malley and translated by Joseph O'Malley and Annette Jolin. Cambridge, 1970.

[Moser, Friedrich Carl von]. *Von dem deutschen Nationalgeist*. 1765; repr., Selb, 1976.

Nipperdey, Thomas. *Deutsche Geschichte 1800–1860. Bürgerwelt und starker Staat*. Munich, 1983.

Nirenberg, David. *Communities of Violence: Persecution of Minorities in the Middle Ages*. Princeton, 1996.

Nordalm, Jens. *Historismus und moderne Welt: Erich Marcks (1861–1938) in der deutschen Geschichtswissenschaft*. Berlin, 2003.

Pastor, Ludwig Freiherr von. *Tagebücher—Briefe—Erinnerungen*. Edited by Wilhelm Wühr. Heidelberg, 1950.

Pilvousek, Josef. "Katholische Kirche in der DDR. Kirche für die Gesellschaft?" In *Kolloquien des Max-Weber-Kollegs VI–XIV (1999/2000)*, edited by Wolfgang Schluchter, 93–116. Erfurt, 2000.

Ranke, Leopold von. *Das Briefwerk*. Edited by Walther Peter Fuchs. Hamburg, 1949.

———. *The History of the Popes during the Last Four Centuries*. Translated by E. Ward Fowler and Mrs. Foster. Vol. 3. London, 1913.

———. *Die römischen Päpste, ihre Kirche und ihr Staat im sechzehnten und siebzehnten Jahrhundert*. 2nd ed. Vol. 3. Berlin, 1839.

Ritter, Gerhard. *Luther: Gestalt und Symbol*. Munich, 1925.

Rost, Hans. *Fehlwege der deutschen Geschichte*. Nuremberg, 1963.

Schuffenhauer, Werner, and Klaus Steiner, ed. *Martin Luther in der deutschen bürgerlichen Philosophie 1517–1845*. Berlin, 1983.

Schwabe, Klaus, and Rolf Reichardt, ed. *Gerhard Ritter: Ein politischer Historiker in seinen Briefen*. Boppard am Rhein, 1984.

Schwarz, Karl. "1870—Ein Sieg der Reformation." In *Geist und Gesellschaft der Bismarckzeit (1870–1890)*, edited by Karl Heinrich Höfele, 371–72. Göttingen, 1967.

Sheehan, James J. *German History 1770–1866.* Oxford, 1989.

———. *German Liberalism in the Nineteenth Century.* Chicago, 1978.

Smith, Helmut Walser. *The Continuities of German History: Nation, Religion, and Race across the Long Nineteenth Century.* Cambridge, 2008.

Stollberg-Rilinger, Barbara. *Des Kaisers alte Kleider: Verfassungsgeschichte und Symbolsprache des Alten Reiches.* Munich, 2008.

Stolleis, Michael. *Geschichte des öffentlichen Rechts in Deutschland.* Vol. 1, *Reichspublizistik und Policeywissenschaft 1600–1800.* Munich, 1988.

———. *Konstitution und Intervention: Studien zur Geschichte des öffentlichen Rechts im 19. Jahrhundert.* Frankfurt am Main, 2001.

Tilly, Charles. *Coercion, Capital, and European States, AD 990–1990.* Cambridge, MA, 1990.

Treitschke Heinrich von. *Historische und politische Aufsätze.* 2nd ed. Vol. 4. Leipzig, 1897.

———. *History of Germany in the Nineteenth Century.* Translated by Eden Paul and Cedar Paul. 7 vols. New York, 1915–19.

Tucker, Robert C., ed. *The Marx-Engels Reader.* Translated by T. B. Bottomor. New York, 1972.

Weiß, Christoph. *Geschichtsauffassung und politisches Denken Münchner Historiker der Weimar Zeit: Konrad Beyerle, Max Buchner, Michael Doeberl, Erich Marcks, Karl Alexander von Müller, Hermann Oncken.* Berlin, 1970.

Wilson, Peter H. "Still a Monstrosity? Some Reflections on Early Modern German Statehood." *Historical Journal* 49 (2006): 565–76.

Winkler, Heinrich August. *Germany: The Long Road West.* Vol. 1, *1789–1933.* Translated by Alexander J. Sager. Oxford, 2006.

Wünsch, Georg. *Der Zusammenbruch des Luthertums als Sozialgestaltung.* Tübingen, 1921.

❧ INDEX ❧

Lightning Source UK Ltd.
Milton Keynes UK
UKHW021512170619
344551UK00007B/572/P